STUDIES IN OLD PRUSSIAN

STUDIES IN
OLD PRUSSIAN

A Critical Review
of the Relevant Literature
in the Field since 1945

William R. Schmalstieg

To Eric,
Best wishes!
Bill Schmalstieg
State College, Pa,
Apr. 26, 1994

The Pennsylvania State University Press
University Park and London

Library of Congress Cataloging in Publication Data

Schmalstieg, William R.
    Studies in Old Prussian.

    Includes bibliographical references and index.
    1. Prussian Language   I. Title.
PG8202.S3   491'.91   76-19017
ISBN 0-271-01231-5

TABLE OF CONTENTS

Foreword

The purpose of this book is to examine
critically the literature published about the Old
Prussian language since the end of World War II in
1945. This examination has, of course, required
some selectivity and I have omitted for the most
part the discussion of Baltic onomastics, since
this in itself would be the subject of a life-time
study.

For help with the preparation of this book I
am especially grateful to Prof. Vytautas Mažiulis
(Vilnius), undoubtedly the world's foremost
authority on the Old Prussian language. During
the time of the Third All-Union Conference on
Baltic linguistics (September, 1975) Prof. Mažiulis
devoted a great deal of time and energy to personal
conversations with me in spite of the fact that
he was extremely busy with the day-to-day problems
of the conference. I should also like to single
out Algirdas Sabaliauskas (Vilnius) for his
personal help during the time of the conference.
Others to whom I am extremely grateful for help with
various aspects of this book are: Ernst Ebbinghaus
(The Pennsylvania State University), A. Girdenis
(Vilnius), B. Jēgers (Northern Illinois), Antanas
Klimas (Rochester), Jules Levin (Riverside,
California), David Robinson (The Ohio State
University), Wolfgang P. Schmid (Göttingen),
Christian S. Stang (Oslo), V. N. Toporov (Moscow).
Although I have mentioned it briefly in the
Addenda and Corrigenda (11.100-11.108) I have not
been able to take into account in a thoroughgoing
way V. N. Toporov's new book, Prusskij jazyk,
Moscow, Nauka (1975), the first volume of which I
received only recently.

For aid with travel expenses to work in
libraries and consult with colleagues in the Soviet
Union and Norway I am especially grateful to the
American Philosophical Society and the Pennsylvania
State University Central Fund for Research.

William R. Schmalstieg

The Old Prussian People

1.000.   It is possible that the Old Prussians
appear for the first time in history as the Aestians
mentioned in Tacitus' Germania (written at the end
of the first century), according to Mažiulis, 1966,
11.   The Greek scholar Claudius Ptolemaeus(Ptolemy)
in the fifth chapter of the third book of his
Geographia apparently mentioned two Old Prussian
(OP) tribes, the Galindai kai Soudinoi, presumably
the Galindians and the Sudovians.   In what appears
to me to be a highly fanciful hypothesis,
Schmittlein, 1948, 60, wrote that the Galindai
must have participated in the barbarian invasions
of southern Europe, since, he says, we encounter
their name even in Spain.   Schmittlein reports that
an eighth century count of Aragon had the name
Galindo.   Likewise two Spanish bishops, one from
the ninth century and one from the tenth century
had that name.

1.001.   Powierski, 1965a, 175-179, writes that
the Osioi of Ptolemy are located exactly in that
territory where we find the Old Prussians.   We
note, however, that the Osioi are not mentioned in
other sources, whereas the Aistians are not mentioned in Ptolemy.   In the Anglo-Saxon translation
of the world history of Orosius we find the name
Aistians in a different form, i.e., with an initial
o-.   This form would be quite similar to the Osioi
of Ptolemy and if we would accept a slight correction of the Greek iota to tau we may reconstruct a
form *Ostoi.   Powierski, 1965a, 177, suggests that
perhaps this name can also be connected with that
of the Ostiatoi in the story of the travels of
Pytheas of Massilia quoted by Strabo.   Pytheas of
Massilia was a Greek merchant who made a trip to
northern Europe in the second half of the 3rd
century B.C. and brought back the name of an
island Abalus rich in amber.

1.002. The name <u>Aestians</u> (Latin dat. sg. <u>Hestis</u>)
is mentioned again in a letter of thanks for some
amber written by the Roman senator Cassiodorus for
the Ostrogothic king Theodoricus (who ruled Rome
493-526 A.D.). The Gothic historian Jordanes
(chapters 5 and 13) basing himself on a now lost
history by the same Cassiodorus says that the
Aestians lived on the Baltic sea somewhere not
far from the mouth of the Vistula.

1.003. Mažiulis, 1966, 12-13, also notes the
mention of the name Aestians in Einhard's (ca.
770-840) biography of Charlemagne (probably
written after 830 A.D.) and in King Alfred's Anglo-
Saxon translation of Paulus Orosius' history of
the world. In the introduction to this translation
we find references from the traveler Wulfstan to
Êst-<u>um</u>, <u>East-land</u>, <u>East-lande</u>. From other historical and geographical references (e.g., <u>Est-mere</u>,
<u>Ilfing</u> 'Elbing,' <u>Wislemuda</u> 'mouth of the Vistula')
we can identify Wulfstan's Aestians with the Old
Prussians.

1.004. Kuzavinis, 1966, 177, writes that the
name <u>aisčiai</u> 'Aestians' should no longer be connected with Latv. <u>istnieki</u> 'true relatives' and
OCS <u>istъ</u> 'true' nor should it be derived from
Middle Low German <u>este</u> thrashing floor' or Gothic
<u>aistan</u> 'to respect.' Rather it is to be connected
with other Baltic hydronyms such as <u>Aistà</u>
'tributary of the Širvinta,' <u>Aisetà</u> 'tributary of
lake Kiaunas,' <u>Aĩsetas</u>, <u>Aisetà</u>, <u>Aisetaĩ</u> lake near
Labanoras', <u>Jiesià</u> (< *Eisi̯ā) 'tributary of the

Nemunas.' They are all to be derived from an
Indo-European root with the determative <u>s</u>: *<u>eis</u>-/
*<u>ais</u>- (< *<u>ois</u>-) / *<u>is</u>- and have the meaning 'to
go, to move fast, to flow.' Thus from the hydronym
*<u>Aista</u> the name of the country <u>Aista</u>, <u>Aistija</u> was
formed. [1]

1.005.   From the 9th century the name <u>Prussian</u>
replaces the name <u>Aestians</u> last mentioned by
Wulfstan (and perhaps transferred to the Estonians).
The name <u>Bruzi</u> 'Prussians' is mentioned by the
Bavarian geographer for the first time in the middle
of the ninth century. Later, in 965 the Spanish
traveler Ibrahim-ibn-Jakub writes: "The Prussians'
(B^{u}rus) settlements are near the ocean (Baltic Sea).
They have their own language and do not know the
languages of their neighbors."

Other mediaeval forms of the name quoted
by Mažiulis, 1966, 14 are: <u>Pruzze</u>, <u>Pruze</u>, <u>Pruzzorum</u>,
<u>Pruzziae</u>, <u>Pruzis</u>, <u>Pruzorum</u>, <u>Pruzos</u>, <u>Prucorum</u>,
<u>Pruciam</u> etc. That the Prussians themselves used
this form of the name is attested by its existence
in the adjective form <u>prus-isk-an</u> 'Prussian' and the
adverbial form <u>prus-isk-ai</u> found in the Enchiridion.
From this apparently come the names in other
European languages: Lith. <u>prus-ai</u>, Latv. <u>pruš-i</u>,
Germ. <u>Prûzzen</u> > <u>Preuss-en</u>, Pol. <u>prus-y</u>, Russ. <u>prussi</u> >
<u>prussy</u>, etc., including various distorted forms such
as <u>pruzzi</u>, <u>pruteni</u>, <u>prutheni</u>, <u>Pruschia</u>, <u>Borussi</u>,
<u>Borussia</u>.

1.006.   Otrębski, 1955, 76-77, suggests that the
name <u>Prussian</u> is to be connected with Skt. púruṣa-ḥ,
puruṣá-ḥ 'man, human.' The sequence <u>ru</u> in the name
<u>prúṣas</u> is a contraction of the <u>uru</u> in púruṣa-ḥ and
the acute intonation in <u>ru</u> is to be explained by
the initial stress in the Sanskrit cognate. Such
variations occur elsewhere in the Indo-European
languages, cf., e.g., Lat. <u>grus</u> beside OCS <u>žeravlĭ</u>
'crane.'

1.007.   Rudnicki, 1957/58, 23-24, connects the OP
root <u>prūs-</u> 'Prussian' (as in OP <u>Prusiskan</u> [acc.
sg.], <u>prūsiskai</u> [adv.]) with Lith. <u>praũsti</u> 'to
wash,' <u>prusnà</u> 'snout' and Polish <u>prychać</u>, <u>pryskać</u>,

bryzgać 'to splatter, to sprinkle, etc.' and suggests
the name Prūsas meant something like 'sprinkled (with
blood) or something similar.' Rudnicki says that the
parallel forms brych-:prych- ≤ brus : *prus appear
in the name of the Old Prussians. He notes, e.g.,
Pruzi (Life of Saint Wojciech), Bruzi (Bavarian
geographer), Brus (Ibn Jakub, 963 A.D.), Burus
(Al-Bekri). I would comment, however, that the
initial B- of the Arabic forms is not probative at
all, since in principle Arabic has no contrast
between /b/ and /p/ and both would have to be
rendered by the letter b in Arabic.[2] Brus merely re-
resents the unvocalized and Burus the vocalized transcripti
1.008.   Trubačev, 1965, 17, rejects both the etymology of the word Prussian which connects it with
Lith. prusti (sic!) 'to wash' and the etymology which connects it with Skt. purusa- 'man' and suggests rather
that the word is borrowed from Germanic. The basis
for this is the assumption that Balts moved westward to
the Baltic sea and the West Balts, viz., the
Prussians frequently moved into territories formerly occupied by Germanic peoples. For example,
the strip of land which now forms the gulf of the
Vistula was formerly called by a West Germanic name,
Wit-land. (Trubačev, 1965, 18.) Taking this into
consideration as a hypothesis one might suggest a
possible connection of the word *Prusa- and the name
of the West Germanic peoples, the Frisians, which
might be etymologized in the following manner:
*Frusja- > Frysan > Fresan, i.e., with the loss of
the labialization of the umlauted u, well known in
Germanic as a clear common Frisian-Kentish development. One could then suggest the Proto-Germanic
by-forms *Frusa/Frūsja, the first of which was
adapted as Baltic *Prūsa. In this connection it is
useful to call to mind one of the old German names
of the Gulf of the Vistula, viz., Frisches Haff.
Even if the name of the river Frisching (which
empties into the Gulf of the Vistula, known now
as Proxladnaja 'fresh, cool') and the name Frische
Nehrung (the old Witland) are secondary derivative
forms, just the single form Frisches Haff is
sufficiently ancient. (Trubačev, 1965, 19) In

4

the documents of the German Order we find <u>Frische hab</u>
(1351), <u>Vrische Mer</u> (1374), <u>Frysche mehr Hap</u> (1433).
Trubačev 1965, 19, suggests, however that the connection between the ethnonym and the adjective <u>frisch</u>
(< *<u>freska</u>) is a purely secondary phenomenon which
is the result of a folk etymology. Trubačev,
quotes with approval the thought of Brückner, 1900,
238, who said that the mere repetition of a name in
one place or another has little to do with tribal
movements. Trubačev also cites an idea (which he
attributes to Illič-Svityč) to the effect that the
Latvian term for the Estonians, igauņi may be a reflection of the Germanic name <u>Ing(u)aevones</u>.
Trubačev, 1965, 19, also quotes Būga, 1924, LXXI,
(= 1961, 121) to the effect that the name <u>prussy</u>
cannot go back beyond the 9th or 10th centuries,
because if the Poles had learned the name in the
7th or 8th centuries it would be in modern Polish
*<u>prysy</u> rather than <u>prusy</u>.

1.009.   Antoniewicz, 1965, 17, gives a map of the
Baltic area on which he has marked place names
which contain the element <u>Prus-</u> 'Prussian.' Such
names are found to the west of the Vistula, just
to the north of the Bug, as far east as the Sož'
and in the areas of Prussia, Mazovia, Podlasie,
Lithuania, Belorussia and interestingly enough
there are five occurrences in the Novgorod area
along with the name <u>Prussian street</u> (now Zeljabova
street) in Novgorod itself. In any case, however,
Antoniewicz, 1965, 25, concludes that the "name
of the <u>Prussian street</u> in Novgorod was not due to
its south-western direction or to its general
situation in the lay-out of Novgorod...The date
and the purpose of the coming of the <u>first
Prussian group</u> to Novgorod are not clear. It seems
that it might have taken place at the end of the
12th or at the beginning of the 13th century, in
the period of political and economic strength of
Prussia and later Lithuania on the Baltic shore
and of their expansion on the Slavonic states

which were at that time divided into small feudal
principalities...The place-names 'Prusy' and their
derivatives on the territories...of Novgorod, Polock,
and Smolensk, as well [as] in Poland, are evidence
of the Prussian emigration in the 12th-13th centuries as in later periods which was due both to
economic and political reasons."

1.100.   As a basis for his comments on the various
Old Prussian tribes Mažiulis, 1966, 15-22, quotes
directly from Petrus de Dusburg's Cronicon terre
Prussie according to which the Prussian land is
divided up into eleven parts:

1.110.   Colmensis and Lubovia were 'almost
destroyed before the arrival of the Teutonic order.'
Mažiulis, 1966, 16 says that in the time of Petrus
de Dusburg (Peter of Du[i]sburg) the area was
inhabited by Poles up to the river Osa, although
in the region of Lubovia there still were some
Prussians, as is shown by the place name
Sassenpile (attested from 1303) which was translated into German as Hasenberg and into Polish
as Zajączkowo. (The word sasins 'hare' is word
659 in the Elbing vocabulary.)[3]

1.111.   There are several views concerning the
original inhabitants of Colmensis (German
Kulmerland, Polish Ziemia Chełmińska). Ślaski,
1969, 213, says that the German historians for
the most part believed that the territory was
originally inhabited by Prussians and only in
the 11th, 12th or even 13th century, the Polish
administration took it over and attempted to
colonize it. Old Prussian attacks in the first
quarter of the 13th century led to the almost complete destruction of the Polish immigrants here.

1.112.   Polish scholars, however, have assumed
that this region formed a part of Polish territory
from the time of the first Piasts and was

6

inhabited by Poles whom the Old Prussian attacks never succeeded in destroying. Powierski, 1965b, says that the Polish element occupied not only Colmensis, but also the area along the Vistula from which only gradually the Old Prussians pushed out the Poles. Slaski, 1969, 215, says that the great majority of place names of Colmensis in the beginning of the 13th century were clearly Polish. Old Prussian place names are extremely rare and appear chiefly in the northern and eastern border territories. Slaski, 1970, 30, wrote that in the first third of the 13th century Prussians began to invade repeatedly. The Prussian troop commanders then held this territory until the invasion of the Teutonic knights.

1.120. Pomesania is an area bounded by the Osa, Vistula and Nogatas rivers, near Poland. The name comes down to us in a Latinized form apparently from a Pol. *po-miedzanie which latter word (with the addition of the Slavic suffix -anie) is to be derived from OP *Pa-median (pa- 'along, on the edge of,' median 'forest,' cf. Lith. dialect mẽdžias Latv. mežs 'forest').

1.121. Jan Powierski, 1965b, suggests, however, that the original Pomeranian Old Prussian border did not run along the Vistula, but was farther to the east and that Pomesania was connected with the Polish colonization. The Old Prussian expansion took place primarily in the 12th and 13th centuries crossing even the Vistula. Powierski thinks that the Gdansk-Pomeranian princes were protectors of the Cistercian mission in the region of Zantyr and perhaps of Kwidzyn as well as the Dominican mission, the Pasłęka and northern Pomesania where the Premonstratensians were governing the apostolic parish. The Teutonic order conquered northern Pomesania establishing a border on the Vistula and the war between Sviętopełk the Second and the Order in the years 1242-1253 did not change this situation. In the years 1282-1283 the Teutonic knights gained their first domains on the left bank of the Vistula.

1.122.   Criticizing this view, Ślaski, 1967, 359,
writes that it is particularly risky to suggest that
up to the tenth century Baltic peoples had not
passed the territory of Pogesania, since the
account of Wulfstan from the second half of the
ninth century mentions exclusively the Old Prussians.
Wulfstan even says that the Vistula divided the
Aistians from the Slavs. Ślaski, 1967, 359, also
says that Pomesanian place names from the first half
of the 13th century attest only to the Pomeranian
colonization of this area and say nothing about
their age in connection with the Old Prussians.
Some of these names, as even Powierski admits, can
also be explained on the basis of the Old Prussian
language.

1.130.   Pogesania is an area northeast of
Pomesania almost to the river Serija. The Latin
name of the tribe Pogesani is probably to be
derived from Pol. *po-gedzanie < *po-gъdzane
<*pogudiane again with the Slavic suffix *-ane.
The reconstructed OP form is *Pa-gudian, the
second element of which is, in the opinion of
K. Buga, 1961, 114-115, to be compared with OP
gudde 'bush.'

1.140.   Varmia is an area to the north of
Pogesania near Aismarės next to Nattangia and
Barthia. The name is probably derived from the
OP word worm-yan 'red.'

1.150.   Nattangia is an area near Aismarės to the
south of Prėglius to the river Alna (Alle). The
word is probably derived from the name of a river.

1.160.   Sambia or Samland is an area extending
from Aismarės and the Curonian gulf to the Baltic
sea. Mažiulis, 1966, 17, says that the origin of

the name is not clear since it cannot be established whether the initial consonant was the (voiceless) s- or the (voiced) z-.

1.170. Nadrovia is an area to the east of the Curonian gulf to Guldapė in the south and Gilija and Osa in the north. A number of etymologies had been suggested. Būga, 1961, 115, 116, had suggested that na-druvis or nadruvias might mean 'a trusting individual,' cf. OP nadruwīsnan 'hope' from OP na 'on' and druwit 'to believe' or that Nadravō might be derived from na 'on' and *dravis 'hive of wild bees.'

1.171 Kuzavinis, 1966, 178, suggests a connection with the Indo-European root *dreu̯- 'to flow,' cf. Skt. drávati 'runs, flows,' dravā́h 'flowing, running; liquid.' A Lithuanian lake name Nẽdravas can be reconstructed on the basis of various historical sources and one can assume that this meant 'not flowing,' i.e., ne-'not' plus a form of the aforementioned root *dreu̯-. Thus the name of the lake would be conceived as denoting the reverse of the name of its source, the river Drujà 'flowing.' The parallel is clear, but Mažiulis, 1966, 20, mentions that the form ne is not known as a negative elsewhere in Old Prussian. Kuzavinis, 1966, 179, suggests that the initial element na means 'on' (as it does in Old Prussian). In the old Nadrovian territory one finds the Lithuanian river name Drúoja which is a remodeling of the earlier Drava just as Knitúoja was remodeled from Knituvà (Knitavà), etc. Thus the name originally referred to the tribe which was located on or near the river Drava (Drúoja).

1.180. Scalovia is an area on the lower Nemunas between Nadrovia and Samogitia (= Low Lithuania). That there had been a river name Skalvà in this region is shown by the place names between Tilžė

and Ragainė such as Skaĩvė, Paskaĩviai, Skalvkalnis.
The river name Skalvỹs, Skaĩvė (a tributary of
Kruoja [Šiauliai]) is an old u-stem formation con-
nected with the verb skaláuti 'to wash, to rinse.'
See Kuzavinis, 1966, 179.[4]

1.181.   Sudovia is discussed below in the section
on Jatvingians, see 2.000 ff.

1.190   Galindia is an area to the south of Barthia
to the west of the Great Masurian lakes. Otrębski,
1958b, 43, wrote that the Galindians are supposed to be
Baltic tribe but that the name is unclear since it
might be interpreted as a Slavic name. In addition,
according to the testimony of the Hypatian chronicle
for the year 1147 a tribe with the name Golędʜ was
settled on the upper Protva near Možajsk, not far
from Moscow. Otrebski, 1958a, 40, writes that the
Galindians could have indeed been a Baltic tribe
which spoke a language which was closest of all to
Jatvingian, but probably nearer to Slavic than the
latter. They did not, strictly speaking, form
part of the union of Old Prussian tribes and did
not enjoy the advantage of their help in the case
of external danger. Otrębski, 41, believes that
the name Galindian is connected with the element
(Baltic) -gala, (Slavic) -gola found in the
Russian chronicles: Let'-gola 'Latvia,
Latgalia,' Loty-gola 'Latvia,' Zimi-gola
'Zemgalia.' In the collective meaning the name
of the Galindians had two forms, one a-stem form
and one i-stem form, viz. *Galinda from which we
have the form Galindo in various sources and
*Galindis from which the Russ. Goljad'. The
first of the two forms is Baltic and the second
is Slavic. The suffix -ind- may have been a
collective suffix, but we know such a suffix as
a collective only from Slavic, e.g., *govędo

'cattle' > Russ, govjado. The root is the same
as that observed in Old Pol. z-golemo 'multum'
and the Slavic expression can be connected with

the root represented in Lith. galéti 'to be able.'
Etymologically the meaning of the name *Galinda is
then 'strength, troop, crew' from which we have
then 'family' as well as 'tribe.' Otrębski says
that the name of the Galindians would seem to be
the Slavic correspondent of a Baltic name *Gala.
There is also the possibility that the language
of the Galindians was closer to Slavic than to
Lithuanian and therefore could have a collective
suffix in d.

1.191. Rudnicki, 1961, 248, traces the forms
*Golędь, *Go-led-inъ back to an Indo-European root
*lendh- which denoted poorly cultivated land, or
even a steppe, or sands, or swamps which are
drying out and are covered here and there by
bushes. The root is common to those Indo-European
people who were found in the basin of the Baltic
area, more or less to the north of the middle
course of the Bug (which is a tributary of the
Vistula) and extending to the French Atlantic
coast, cf. Celtic-French Landes. In the Baltic
languages the root is known in OP lindan 'valley,'
Lith. léndrè 'reed (phragmistres communis)'; in
the Germanic languages the root is found in
Swedish linda 'fallow field,' Gothic, Old English,
Old Saxon, Old High German land; in the Celtic
languages it is found in Old Irish land, lann
'free space,' Middle Welsh llan 'area,' Breton
lann 'heath.' In the Slavic languages the root
is richly represented: Old Russ. ljadina 'weed,
bush,' modern Russ. ljada 'newly forested field,'
Beloruss. l'ado, l'adzina 'area cleared of trees,'
Bulg. léda, lédina 'meadow, mountain meadow,'
S.-Cr. lèdina 'mountain meadow, meadow cleared
for cattle,' Czech lada, lado 'fallow land,'
pl. 'steppe.' The root is lacking in those Indo-
European languages which did not lie on the
Polish-German-French lowlands and thus it is not
found in Italic, Greek, Albanian, Hittite,
Armenian, Tokharian or the Indo-Iranian languages.

On the course of the middle Warta there
established themselves with a center in Lenda or
Landa, today Ląd, a proto-Polish tribe which called
itself *Lęd-, and from this form the singulative
*Lęd-inъ = Lądzin = written Londzin was created
(Rudnicki, 1961, 249). When the tribe grew larger
it crossed to the right bank of the Vistula where
the new name *Go-lędь appeared. The prefix Go-
has an augmentative meaning as we can see from
Kujawian pĺo 'pool, puddle' vs. the name Go-pĺo,
the largest lake in Kujawy Borowy. Rudnicki
1961, 251, claims that the root *Lęchъ 'Pole'
derives from *Lęd-chъ, so it would appear that he
considers the Galindians Slavs rather than Balts.

1.192.   Savukynas, 1963, 322, says, however,
that the Old Prussian name Galìndas corresponds
semantically and partially morphologically with
Lith. galìnis 'last, extreme, ultimate.'
Savukynas says that this lexeme is widely represented in Lithuanian toponymy and gives the names
Galìnis, Galin-upė, Galìniai, etc. This is a
popular Lithuanian last name even today and is
usually applied to people living at the boundaries.
We also note the Old Prussian place names Galynde,
Galinden and Galindien. We find the suffix -ind-
in other place names: Old Prussian Karw-inden,
Stab-ynden; in Lith. Gel-ind-énai, Ner-ind-aičiai,
etc. Thus Otrębski's attempt to derive
Galindžius < Galinčius is unfounded. We find the
suffix in appelatives also, cf. Lith. klib-indà
'shaky thing, lame person,' lask-ìnda 'ragamuffin.'
The Lithuanian name Galindžius is a derivative of
Galindis or Galindas and this latter is a derivative with the suffix -d- from Galìnis. Thus the
tribal name galìndas is surely a derivative from
galìnis with the suffix -d-. And semantically
galìndas is, perhaps, exactly galìnis 'living at
the extremities, boundaries.' The territorial name
Galìnda bears the same relationship to the ethnonym
galìndas as does Lietuvà 'Lithuania' to lietùvis
'Lithuanian' or Kuršas 'Curonia' to kuršis 'Curonian.'

12

1.193.   Nalepa, 1971a, discusses a variety of
earlier etymologies which have connected the name
Galindai with Lith. gãlas 'end,' OP gallintwey
'to kill' or Lith. galià 'power, might.' Nalepa
himself, nevertheless, 95, believes that the OP
name is derived from a hydronym as are many tribal
names in eastern Europe, e.g., Wisła : Wiślanie;
Ślęża: Ślężanie, etc.   Thus the name Galind- is
derived from that of Gielądzkie Jezioro (Gieląd,
German Gehland-See), a few kilometers to the west
of Mrągowo in the province of Olsztyn, i.e., in
the very center of the ancient Prussian Galindia.
The contemporary form of the lake name differs
from the original. Nalepa quotes from the year
1379 the forms Galent and Galanten and later the
forms Gellant, Gelland, Gellanten, etc. He finds
that the root *gal- was originally a different
ablaut grade of the same root we find in Lith.
gilùs 'deep,' gelmẽ 'depth.' The original meaning of the word then referred to the depth of the
lake in question, a lake which, although it was
not the deepest lake of the Old Prussians, was at
least one of the deepest (24 meters), Nalepa,
1971a, 102. [5]

1.194.   Barthia is an area southeast of Nattangia
more or less in the right tributaries of the river
Alna (Alle).

1.200.   Antoniewicz, 1966, 20-21, divides all
Prussian territories into three zones which are all
entirely different in regard to dialects and
hydronymy. Antoniewicz writes: "The first zone
covers the territories bordering upon the area of
the Slavs, namely upon the following 'partes'
according to Dusburg: Pomezania, Pogezania, the
Sasin Region (Lubovia), Galindia and Sudovia."
He notes that all of the rivers of this area flow
towards the Vistula. Antoniewicz, 1966, 20,
continues: "The second zone would cover the next
area with approximately the following provinces:

Warmia as well as Great and Little Bartha. The
Pomezanian dialect spread over this zone but, at
the same time, the hydronymia ending with -ape,
unknown in the first zone, occur here (for
example Węgorapa (etc.). In the third zone
(Sambia, Natangia and Nadrovia), the Sambian
dialect has been used; similar hydronymia to those
of the second zone can be noticed here, but
Nadrovia shows derivatives ending with -upe which
are chronologically later, being an evidence of
Lithuanian colonisation which started in the
Middle Ages."

1.300.   About the year 1230 the Teutonic knights
invited by the Masurian duke Konrad began an
invasion against the Old Prussians in Colmensis
and soon after Pomesania (1236) and Pogesania
(1237) were subjugated. In 1240 Varmia and part
of Nattangia and Barthia were devastated. In
1242 there was an uprising which was ended with
the so-called Treaty of Kristburg (February 9th,
1249). The Teutonic knights took power in all of
Nattangia and Barthia. In 1257 Samland and part
of Nadrovia were forced to surrender. In the
year 1260, encouraged by the defeat of the Knights
of the Cross by the Lithuanians the Old Prussians
rose up again against the Teutonic knights, the
Nattangians under the leadership of Henricus Monte,
the Sambians under Glande, the Varmians under
Glappus, the Pogesanians under Auctume, the
Barthians under Diwanus. Their struggle finally
ended in defeat in 1274 after which the Teutonic
knights mopped up the remaining Old Prussian lands,
Nadrovia, Scalovia and Sudovia. In 1283 the Teutonic
knights forcibly resettled 1,600 Sudovians into
north-western Samland (from which we have the name
of this part of Samland, viz. 'the Sudovian corner
or enclave,' cf. German Sudauischer Winkel, Lith.
Suduvių kaṁpas.) (See 2.400.)

1.301.   Only one group of Sudovians, led by Scurdas
did not succumb to the Teutonic knights, but moved
into Lithuania.   In this very year (1283) the
Teutonic knights got everything between the Vistula
and the Nemunas (Memel) into their power and began
a fierce struggle with the Lithuanian Grand Duchy,
a struggle which only ended in the year 1410 at
Tannenberg with the defeat of the Teutonic knights
by combined Polish and Lithuanian forces under the
leadership of the Lithuanian Duke Vytautas the
Great.   But by this time the former Old Prussian
territories had been flooded by German colonists
and the Old Prussians themselves were for the most
part serfs on the lands of the German masters.
The Germans apparently made no effort to learn the
Old Prussian language and used interpreters constantly although there is documentary evidence that
they did make an effort to have the Lord's Prayer,
the Holy Mary and the Creed translated into Old
Prussian.

    The last grand master of the Teutonic
knights, Albrecht (1490-1568) secularized his state,
declared himself the Duke of Prussia and openly took
the part of the Reformation.

1.302.   It was indeed this Duke Albrecht under
whose auspices the Lutheran catechisms were translated into Old Prussian (see section on documents),
since there remained in the 16th century some
persons who could speak and understand only Old
Prussian, particularly in Samland, the area which
held out the longest against Germanization.
Mažiulis, 1966, 24, reports that Caspar Hennenberger
(1529-1600) wrote that the amber worker J. Fuchs,
in order to honor his guest Merten Windtmüller,
invited ten Sudovian dancers of which not one knew
the German language.

    The Old Prussian language began to die out
rapidly at the beginning of the 17th century.   In
the introduction to J. Rehsa's Lithuanian psalm

book (1625) we read that the Old Prussian language
is still used by a few people in Fischhausen,
Schaaken, Labiawa along the sea coast and by a few
people on the Curonian inlet. In 1679 Christopher
Hartknoch reported that there is not just one, but
a number of villages in which the Old Prussian
language is known. Kiparsky, 1970b, 258-259,
thinks that this statement is an answer to
Ján Amos Komensky (Comenius) who had lived in
Elbing (at that time under Swedish rule) from the
fall of 1642 to the beginning of 1648 and had
written that there remained only a single village
in which a few old people knew the Old Prussian
language.

In 1684 Christopher Hartknoch wrote that
not a single village was left in which everybody
understood Old Prussian, but that here and there
are a few people who understand the language. On
the title page of the copy of the IId catechism
which had been in the St. Petersburg Public Library,
but which has been lost to the scholarly public
since the end of World War I, there was an inscription: 'Diese alte Preusnische Sprache ist nuhnmehr
gantz und gar vergangen worden. Anno 1677 ein
einziger alter Mann auf der Curischen Nährung
wonend, der sie noch gekont, gestorben, doch sollen
noch solche daselbst sein' (This Old Prussian
language has completely died out. In 1677 a single
old man living on the Curonian Isthmus who had
known this language died, but they say there are
still some.) According to Mažiulis, 1966, 26,
probably Hartknoch's reports are more accurate,
although nobody at that time seems to have carried
out any investigations of the ethnic status of the
Prussian land. Still Mažiulis thinks that around
1700 there were a few Old Prussians who knew their
native language and perhaps even into the first few
decades of the 18th century, although the famine
and plague of the years 1709-1711 must have dimin-
ished them even more.

The Sudovians
(Jatvingians)

2.000.   According to Antoniewicz, 1958, the
Sudovians inhabited the northeastern Polish border-
land and their tribal center was near the modern
Polish town of Suwa/ki. These people are presumably
those mentioned by the Greek geographer Ptolemy
(ii.11.15) and in the Middle Ages they are mentioned
for the first time in the Nestor Chronicle (983).
   In 1283 they were almost completely wiped out
by the Teutonic knights. See 1.000 & 1.300.
Antoniewicz reports, 1958, 160, that archaeological
finds seem to show that the Sudovians lived in
small villages containing about fifteen houses and
that their economy was based on farming and stock-
breeding.

2.001.   The name Sudovian (Lith. Sūdavà) occurs in
the Latin variants Sudow-ite, Sudow-enses, Sudow-
ienses. Apparently the form Sūduva is also known,
cf. Latin Zudua, if it is not to be read *Sudvā.
From this form, i.e., from *Sudv-, perhaps the
other attested shorter form of the name arose, cf.
Latin Sudi (terra Sud-orum). (Mažiulis, 1966,
18-19.)

2.002.   Savukynas, 1963, 323-325, first of all
disputes M. Rudnicki's (1961) etymology of Sūduva.
Rudnicki connects Sūduva with Lith. šūdas 'feces,'
but Savukynas objects that none of the known Baltic
place names use this word in the sense of 'swamp.'
Neither does Savukynas accept the etymology offered
by Buga who derived the word from Indo-European
*sudhos (Lith. sãvas 'one's own') nor the etymology
proposed by R. Schmittlein, 1948, 60, who notes the
similarity between the name Sūduva and the word
Sudeta Silva (a region which was Celtic until the
Christian era). Savukynas says that the root sud-
of Sūduva is not to be separated from other Baltic
place names with the root Saud- Sud-/Sūd-.

The full-grade vocalism is found in such place
names as Lith. Saudó-gala (a river) and Saud-
ininkai (a village) and OP Saud-en and Saud-iten.
The zero-grade and the lengthened zero-grade forms
of this root are to be found in such forms as Lith.
Sud-énai (a village), Sud-uonià (a river) and are
to be connected with a Lith. word sūduvà, which,
according to Savukynas, with the meaning 'swampy
place, bog, fen,' is found in the card file of
the Lithuanian Academy Dictionary. The word is,
in turn, also to be connected with Latv.
sud-eksis 'gypsum.' In Proto-Baltic the root
*sū-d- probably denoted 'damp, submerged in water,
swampy' and perhaps is not to be separated from
Lith. surùs, OCS syrъ 'damp, moist.' The OP name
Suduva means then 'land of bogs, fens, swamps.'
Mažiulis, 1966, 19, in general agrees with this
analysis, but suggests that rather than denoting
a 'swamp or a bog' the word is just a river name.

2.003.   Interestingly enough, Otrębski, 1963ᵃ, 158,
apparently independently of Savukynas, also wrote
that the name Sudovian derives from the name of
the area *Sūdava which was based on the river name
*Sūda. According to Otrębski the Lithuanian river
name Suduonià is derived from *Sūdau-nia (in the
area of Marijampolė [now Kapsukas]).

2.004.   Nepokupnyj, 1971, 24, says that the lack
of Baltic appellatives with the root sud- and a
certain semantic uncertainty force us to hunt for
further Indo-European correspondences. Nepokupnyj
then suggests the following Germanic correspondences:
Swedish súdda, Low German suddeln 'to grease,'
Low German sudde 'swamp,' Icelandic suddi 'vapor,
dampness, drizzling, rain'.

2.005.   Next Nepokupnyj points out that Brückner
had suggested a connection of Polish maź 'grease' with
the name Mazowsze 'Mazovia.' Nepokupnyj notes
further mazia 'swamp,' mazać 'to daub, to smear, to

wipe ' as a stem for the earlier name *maz(ur).
He then quotes Hrabec, 1958, 235 to the effect
that the name Maz either refers to a people that
lived in the swamps and therefore were smeared
(with something) or to a topographical name which
denotes 'swampy region.'

The comparison between the meaning of
the words Sudovian and Mazovian is then obvious.
The first word contains a Baltic root meaning
'to smear' and the second word contains a Slavic
root with the same meaning.

2.006. According to Otrębski, 1963a, 158, the
name Jatvingians was used only by the southeastern neighbors, the Poles and the Russians.
They denoted thereby the immediately neighboring
member of closely related Baltic tribes in
addition to the totality of this nation. The
westernmost member of the group was the Sudovians
with whom the German knights had the most to do.
This explains why the name Sudovians was used in
the west and Jatvingians in the east to denote
the same group of people. Otrębski also believes
the name to be derived from a river name, thus:
*Jatuvingai 'those belonging to the tribe whose
settlement was known as *Jatuva on the river *Jata.'

2.007. Mažiulis also, 1966, 19, says that the
name of the country *Jat-va derives from a river
name, cf. Lith. Jot-ijà (river name in Lithuania)
and (concerning the suffix) *Lei-t(u)va
Lietuvà 'Lithuania.'

2.008. Kulikauskas, 1970, 13, recalls that Būga,
1961, 155, had said that the Jatvingians (Lith.
Jotvingiai) were also called Getai (Getta,
Gettarum, Getwese), the name being derived from
Jotva where the letter g was used to denote the
sound j. Written sources used the term for all
the Old Prussians and sometimes even for Lithuanians.

2.009. The name Jatvingian is mentioned in the
Russian chronicles beginning in the year 945 up to
1279 in various kinds of transcriptions (Nalepa,
1964, 11-13): jatvjagy,[6]jatvęgy, jatvjagŭ. The
Russian chronicle for the year 983 writes: ide
Volodimirŭ na Jatvjagy i vzja zemlju ixŭ
'Volodimir went against the Jatvingians and took
their land.' According to H. Łowmiański, 1966, 97,
the expression zemlja can mean either 'land' or
'the people inhabiting a certain territory,' and in
this case the chronicler certainly had in mind the
capturing of prisoners.

2.010. The Kievan chronicle under the year 1197
mentions the form Ętvęgy. (Nalepa, 1964, 11) The
Arab writer al-Idrīsī from the middle of the 12th
century gives the form Jintiar which may be corrected
to Jintiaz by putting the dot on the Arabic letter
r (Arabic r = ﻭ ; z = ﻭ). (Nalepa, 18) Sources from
the middle of the 13th century give Jentuesones and
Jentuosi (Nalepa, 20). Finally Nalepa, 23, writes
that he considers Slavic *Ję̆t-ьv-ęg-ŭ to be equivalent to a reconstructed Baltic *Ant-iv-ing-as.

2.011. Nalepa, 1964, 6, is of the opinion that
previous etymologies of the name Jatvingian which
connected the word with the words for 'crayfish,
spear, bull, or mare' are not worthy of any scientific attention. The best hypothesis in Nalepa's
opinion is the one which connects the name with a
river name. Nalepa, 8, notes that the name of the
river Czarna Hańcza is attested in its earliest form
in the form Anse from the year 1385. Nalepa then
quotes Falk, 1941a, 166-169, who connected the word
with Latv. uõts, uõte, diminutive uotīte, uotiņa
'a drainage channel through which, for example,
liquid manure flows from the cattle stalls.' As
Nalepa, 59, observes: "This explanation finds confirmation in physiographical features, the bed of
the Hańcza river is narrow and deep. Moreover, it
is confirmed by semantic parallels among river

names of the Slavs,..Such names as <u>Korytnica</u> 'trough river' should be taken into consideration."

2.012.   This etymology accords with a 'first principle' among many peoples of deriving ethnic names from river names. Nalepa, 1964, 60, says that the Sudovians originally inhabited a territory near the Sudonia river, a tributary of the Šešupė, a river north of the Suvalkija region. The Dainava tribal territory was situated between the Suvalkija region and the Nemunas. Polexia was on the river Łek which was the tribal territory of the <u>Pollexiani</u>.

2.013.   Nalepa believes that the Sudovians, Dainavians and Pollexiania formed a tribal union under the leadership of the Jatvingians. Nalepa would distinguish between the Jatvingians in the narrow sense of the word (those along the upper Hańcza river) and the Jatvingians in the broad sense of the word, i.e., including all of the aforementioned tribes. Nalepa, 1964, 60 writes: "Generally speaking they lived on the territories to the north of the Biebrza swamps, to the east of the Great Mazurian Lakes, to the west of the Niemen (Nemunas) river and to the south of the Romincka Wilderness and the great wilderness upon the middle Szeszupa river up to the Niemen river."[7]

2.014.   Nepokupnyj, 1971, 19, says that it was the Polish historian A. Kamiński, 1953, 74, who was the first to point out that three inhabited places in the Lvov area have the name <u>Jatvjagi</u>. Nepokupnyj says furthermore that this triple repetition of a Baltic ethnonym in the old south-western part of the Lvov area is even more striking since in the rest of the Ukraine there are no other examples of the use of the name <u>Jatvjagi</u> as any kind of geographical term.

2.015.   Nepokupnyj, 1971, 20, mentions that in a description of the campaign of Danil Romanovič against the Jatvingians there is a mention of the name Nebjasta. The stem of this name is a Baltic *Nebēst- which Nepokupnyj finds repeated in the name of the village Niebieszczany in the area of Lemkov in Poland.

2.016. Nepokupnyj, 1971, 21 notes that Buga, 1961, 601-602, had said that the ending -da in the six river names Golda, Grivda, Jasolda, Nevda, Siohda, Sokolda, the final element goes back to *-udā (> Slavic -ъda > -da) which is to be connected with the Baltic word for water, cf. Lith. vanduõ, Latv. ûdens. Nepokupnyj would add to this list the name of the swamp Udxovda located in the area between the rivers Grivda and Jasolda.

Another apparent indicator of former Jatvingian territory is the element -stok as the second element of a hydronym. (s- 'together', tok- 'flowing,' cf. Lith. sán-tak-a 'confluence'). The best example of that is probably the well known name Białystok. Names of this type are localized in the basin of the upper Narew (in all there are thirty-two).

2.100. According to Otrębski, 1963a, 160, the most important sources for the Jatvingian language are hydronyms and place names in the area formerly inhabited by the Jatvingians, and the character-istics of the Lithuanian, Polish and White Russian dialects now spoken in this same area. Thus the names of the southern Lithuania city Léipalingis and the neighboring forest Leipalótas, are clearly derived from *leipā = Lith. líepa 'linden.' Perhaps the morpheme -al- in *Leip-al-ingis and *Leip-al-otas is a variant of the suffix -av-, cf. the place name Šilavótas in the region of Prienai derived from šìlas 'pine forest.' The name Léipalingis denotes, of course, a place abundant in linden trees, cf. Pol. Lipowiec. Otrębski claims that these Jatvingian place names show the retention of the IE diphthong *ei and thereby show a feature

of Jatvingian in common with Old Prussian, cf. OP
*leipo 'linden' attested by the place name
Leypiten (1331). As is well known the IE diphthong
*ei is rendered by ie in the cognate Lith. líepa
and Latv. liẽpa. See also 11.011.

2.101.   Grinaveckis, 1965, 198, notes that in Old
Prussian etymological ei was always retained but
that in the dialect of Zietela we find words with
both ei and ie, e.g., sviekatà and sveikatà
'health,' šievà and šeivà 'spool, bobbin.' It is
difficult to see exactly what point Grinaveckis is
making here. If the rendering of etymological *ei
by ei or ie eventually depends upon stress, an
internal explanation, viz. the play of stress
between stem and ending could explain the vacillation in the rendering of etymological *ei.

2.102.   According to Otrębski, 1963a, 161, one
finds the Jatvingian reflexes ul, ur, for IE *ḷ *ṛ
respectively. As an important example of this
Otrębski gives the name of the lake Dùlgas in the
district of Lazdijai. Presumably this Lithuanian
word stems from the Jatvingian. Since the lake has
an elongated shape one supposes that the name
corresponds to the Slavic adjective for 'long,' cf.
Russ. dolgij, Pol. długi 'long' which seem to
represent a proto-form *dъlgъ < *dulgo- rather
than *dьlgъ < *dilgo-. This Jatvingian form is
distinguished from the OP adverb ilga, ilgi 'long'
(cf. also the lake names Ilgene, Ilgoue, etc.)
Lith. ìlgas, Latv. iĩgs 'long' not only by the -u-
in the sequence -ul-, but also by the initial d-
which is present in the Slavic and the Jatvingian,
but not in the other Baltic forms of the word.
Otrębski also affirms that Jatvingian dùlgas cannot
be a loanword from Slavic because of its initial
acute intonation. A loanword from Slavic into
Lithuanian should have the circumflex intonation.

2.103. Savukynas, 1966, 167, claims that the
hydronym Dùlgas should not be separated from the
name of the OP lake Dulgen mentioned in Gerullis,
1922, 32, nor from the Latvian swamp name Duļģis.
The stem dul-g is connected with the hydronmic
root dul- which has various determinatives: dul-b-,
dul-k-, dul-v- found in names such as Lith. Dùl-pis
(< Dùl-upis, a river name), Duĩ-k-upis, a river
name, Duĩ-b-is a lake name, Dul-v-as a river name,
the OP village names Dul-kam, Dulo-kaym, etc. We
also find Lith. duliava 'fog with drizzle,' dùl-k-ti
'to drizzle,' dul-v-ḗti 'to grow moldy, musty,'
duĩ-k-as 'fog,' Latv. dul-s 'dark,' duļ-k-e
'sediment, mud.' The morpheme -ga- in the hydronym
Dul-gas probably is the same as in Lith. stó-ga-s
'roof,' žió-ga-s 'grasshopper.' Thus the form is
Balto-Slavic and shows no special Jatvingian-Slavic
connection.

2.104. According to Otrębski, 1963a, 161,
Jatvingian s and z correspond to Lith. š and ž
respectively. For example, the right tributary of
the river Šešupė in the district of Marijampolė has
the name Kirsnà (gen. Kirsnõs), literally 'the black
(river).' In Lithuanian this should have had the
form *Kiršna. In the district of Leipalingis there
is a lake by the name of Azãgis, a name which corresponds to OP assegis 'perch' (EV-572) and Lith.
ež(e)gỹs 'perch.'

2.105. Savukynas, 1966, 169, points out that corresponding to Kirsnà we also find the Lithuanian river
names Kirš-inas, Kiršnó-upis, Kirš-valkis, and corresponding to Azãgis we find Lith. Ãžagis. Savukynas
says that we can attribute Kirsnà to West Baltic
(in this case to Jatvingian) only on the basis of
the fact that in Old Prussian ordinarily we find -s
after r, whereas in Lithuanian usually -š. On the
other hand it seems to me that we have no firm
assurance that the German scribes were able to
distinguish -s and -š after r. For example, on the

German side of the Elbing vocabulary we find
Vuerstant (42) 'fire-place' where the -s after r
is at a morphological boundary and seemingly
should be pronounced -s- before the following t-
as opposed to word 100 Irstebart 'first beard,
fluff' where the -s- in word-medial position
should presumably be pronounced differently. The
question is whether the German scribe could distinguish at all between the Baltic phonemes /s/
and /š/. In fact one may argue then that in such
a word as Werstian 'calf' in the Elbing vocabulary the -t- is written specifically because the
scribe heard a /š/ rather than /s/ and, not
exactly comprehending what it was he wrote the
/š/ as -st-. Thus a word such as Werstian should
perhaps be phonemicized as /veršan/ = Lith. veršis
'id.' Perhaps the same can also be said for
Prastian (corrected by Trautmann, 1910, 92, to
Parstian) which perhaps should be phonemicized as
/paršan/, cf. Lith. paršas 'pig.' Note that
Toporov, 1959a, 259, suggests that at one time
the passage of s > š under these conditions was
known in all the Baltic languages.

2.106. Savukynas, 1966, 169-171, lists six
additional place names which he considers to be
of Jatvingian origin: 1) Perš-as (lake name) cf.
Lith. Perš-okšnà derived from the IE root *perk̂-/
*pr̥k̂-, cf. Old English furh 'furrow,' Skt.
párś-āna- 'pit'; 2) Veis-iẽjis (lake name), cf.
OP Weyss-en (lake name), Weis-pelke (river name),
cf. Lith. vieš-muõ 'spring, shallow and narrow
place in a river where the water runs rapidly';
3) Zãp-sė (river name), Zap-sỹs (lake name), cf.
Lith. Žẽp-la all derived from the IE root *ĝhap-/
*ĝhep- cf. Avestan gafya 'pit, abyss,' Skt.
hāp(h)ikā- 'yawn'; 4) Zeb-rỹs (river name),
Zeb-riùs (river name), cf. Lith. Žeb-ẽrė (river
name), Žeb-okštà (lake and river name) all derived
from the IE root *ĝhab-/*ĝheb-, cf. Old Icelandic
gap 'wide opening, hole.'; 5) Zembrė which has a

parallel Lithuanian form Žeṁbrė (both are river names); 6) Zerv-ýlios (several lakes), Zerv-ýna (river name), Zerv-ýnos (swamp and village name), cf. Lith. Žerv-ýnos, and the Lithuanian verb žervénti 'to flow swiftly'.

2.107.   Grinaveckis, 1965, 196, says that certain of the traits of southern Lithuanian dialects are to be connected with Jatvingian features, Jatvingian being in Grinaveckis' opinion a dialect of Old Prussian. In the Zietela dialect (in the Djatlovo region of the Belorussian republic) in some words we find s̲ and z̲ in place of standard Lith. š and ž: zāsı̀s for standard Lith. žąsı̀s 'goose,' zēmė for standard Lith. žēmė 'land.'

In the south-western Dzukish dialect in the village of Ašašnikai (Varėna region) we also en- counter the confusion of the consonants s̲ and š on the one hand and z̲ and ž on the other hand: thus sónas for standard Lith. šónas 'side,' vazúoja for standard Lith. važiúoja 'travels,' šu katı̀ for s̲u katė 'with the cat.' Grinaveckis, 1965, 197, says that the confusion of the given consonants is undoubtedly a new phenomenon, but it could also have arisen under the influence of a mixture of Jatvingian and Lithuanian language elements.

2.108.   Another important characteristic of the Jatvingian language is the passage of the palatal consonants t́, d́ to ḱ, ǵ respectively. This peculiarity holds for contemporary Lithuanian dia- lects in Jatvingian territory, thus for the stand- ard language forms jautēliai 'oxen,' zõdis 'word' we find the dialect forms jaukēliai, zõgis. In connection with this Otrębski, 1963a, 162, also mentions the reverse phenomenon according to which kēlias 'path' and geležı̀nis 'iron' are represented by tēlias and deležı̀nis.

2.109.   In contrast to Eastern High Lithuanian (Aukshtaitish) Jatvingian retains the palatality of the consonant ĺ before e̲ and ė̲. Thus the place name

*Leipūnai (a morphological and semantic variant of
the name Léipalingis) is rendered by Pol. Lejpuny
with a palatal l, not *Ļejpuny or *Łajpuny.

2.110.   In the southwestern Dzukish dialect, the
neighboring central High Lithuanian dialect and the
dialect of Zietela there is a lack of the affrication in the etymological sequence *dj, *tj. This
lack of affrication is to be explained, according to
Grinaveckis, 1965, 198, by the fact that the southern
portion of the Lithuanian dialect area bordered on
the Jatvingian language which, like Old Prussian,
did not have affricates from the etymological
sequences *tj, *dj.

2.111.   Otrębski, 1963a, 164, finds that in
Jatvingian there are many words the morphological
structure of which corresponds better to Slavic than
to Lithuanian or Latvian. One example is, of course,
the adjective dùlgas mentioned above. The Jatvingian
word for 'white' is bilsas (cf. the lake names in
the district of Lazdijai Baĩtajis Bílsas vs. the
neighboring Juõdajis Bílsas), which is a variant of
Russ. belĕsyj 'whitish' (< *bĕl-es-).

2.112.   But Savukynas, 1966, 166, suggests that the
Jatvingian word Biĩsas derives from the IE root
*bhel-/*bhol-, a root which with the determinative
-s- has a number of correspondences in Lithuanian
hydronyms: bal-s- (Balsė, a river; Báls-is, a lake,
etc.). The root bal-/bel-/bil- is not to be separated from Lith. bãl-as/bál-tas 'white,' baĩ-svas,
Latv. bãl-s 'whitish.' Thus neither Dùlgas nor
Biĩsas show any special Jatvingian-Slavic connection,
but are both Balto-Slavic.

2.113.   Otrębski, 1963a, 163, points out two further
phonetic characteristics which, in his opinion, show
Jatvingian influence; (1) the appearance of a prothetic h- in the contemporary Lithuanian dialect of
Zietela, cf. hárti and hártojas replacing standard
árti 'to plow,' and artójas 'plowman, [8](2) in the

27

same dialect the disappearance of the consonant k (g) before a sequence of several consonants cf., e.g., áuštas 'high,' rúštas 'sour,' šáuštas 'spoon,' splūsna 'feather, pen' for standard Lith. áukštas, rūgštùs, (older and dialect rūgštas), šáukštas, plùnksna (dial. plūksna).

2.114. In the dialects of Zietela and Lazdūnai the present tense of Lith. dúoti 'to give' is conjugated with a -j-, cf. 3rd pres. dúoja 'gives,' just as in Slavic where we find, e.g., the 1st sg. pres. Pol. daję, OCS dajǫ 'I give.' In Otrębski's opinion, 1963a, 165, here again we have to do with a Jatvingian feature of word formation common to Jatvingian and Slavic, but not to Baltic.

2.115. Otrębski concludes 1963a, 166, that the Jatvingian problem has special significance for Polish philology. He maintains that among the Slavic languages Polish presents a problem in that it has features which are unknown both to the other West Slavic languages (Czech and Slovak) and to the East Slavic languages.

2.200. Otrębski, developing his thesis more thoroughly in 1964, lists nine features of Polish which, according to him, can best be explained by the existence of a Jatvingian substratum.

2.201. An older Polish pronunciation in which we find the vowel plus nasal consonant (instead of the nasal vowel) is indicated by the existence of such place names as Sandomierz (from the name Sądomir, later Sędomir) and in addition the older spelling of such expressions as sampierz = sąpierz 'opponent at law,' samsiad = sąsiad 'neighbor.' The state of affairs with regard to the nasal consonants concerns only eastern Poland which he would call provisionally the Jatvingian-bordering territory (pojaćwiński). On the other hand in Great Poland, Poland Minor and Silesia the inherited nasal vowels developed

normally as in the neighboring Czech: ǫ > u and
ę > 'a or 'e. Thus the well-known vacillation in
Polish dążyć 'to aspire,' duży 'great, large,'
gąz vs. guz 'lump, bruise,' guzik 'button,' etc.

2.202.   The penultimate stress is the result of the
re-analysis of word initial stress in disyllabic
words.   Such a state of affairs is to be found in
the Lithuanian dialect of Puńsk neighboring on the
old Jatvingian area.   When the Jatvingians adopted
the Polish language they kept in principle their
old penultimate stress on the words.   This stress
then spread to other parts of Poland.

2.203.   The pronunciation of Polish sz, ż, cz, dż
as s, z, c, dz, the so-called Masurismus originally
took place in the speech of the Polonized Jatvingians
where the old contrast of s, ś, sz was simplified.

2.204.   The merger of the Slavic prepositions iz
'out of' and sǫ 'with; from' gave z in Great Poland,
Poland Minor and Silesia.   This served as a point
of departure for the characteristic voicing of word-
final consonants before vowel and j, l, ĩ, r, m(ḿ)
in the aforementioned dialect areas.   On the other
hand the prepositions iz and sǫ merged as s in
north-eastern Poland on the basis of the fact that
the OP-Jatvingian counterpart was is = Lith. iš
'out of.'   This served then as a point of departure
for the characteristic devoicing of word-final
consonants before vowel and j, l, ĩ, r, m(ḿ) in
north-eastern Poland in the old Jatvingian area.

2.205.   In standard Polish the phonemes i and y
are clearly differentiated, but in the north they
have merged completely where we find sin 'son'
(= standard Pol. syn) and riba 'fish' (= standard
Pol. ryba), although the preceding consonants, s
and r in these words do not undergo palatalization.
Slavic y does not have a clear counterpart in any
of the Baltic languages and one may attribute this
merger in Polish to the Jatvingian influence.

2.206. The passage of ra- to re- in word-initial
position is illustrated by the Polish words redło
= standard radło 'colter,' rek = standard rak
'crab,' reno = rano 'morning.' A similar phenomenon
is well-known in the neighboring Lithuanian:
prẽkė = prãkė 'goods,' rẽzginės = rãzginės 'a
basket for transporting hay,' réiškus = ráiškus
'clear.' One must admit, however, that the historical circumstances do not in certain cases show
whether the a or the e is original. Thus it is
safer here to talk simply of a vacillation between
e and a after r.

2.207. In 1963a, 162-163, Otrębski wrote that the
palatal labials m, v, p, b were apparently unknown
to the Jatvingian language and therefore the
Polonized Jatvingians replaced the corresponding
palatal labials with sequences of labial plus
jod. Thus in northeastern Poland we find for
standard Pol. miasto 'city,' wiara 'faith,' piwo
'beer,' bierze 'takes' the forms mjasto, vjara,
pjivo, bježe respectively which undergo even
further changes to mniasto (or even niasto),
(v)ýara, pẋivo, bŕeže, or even źara, pśivo, bźeže
respectively. In 1964, 215, he still considered
the split of palatalized labial into labial plus
jod to be the result of Baltic influence, but then
he wrote that since we find a similar phenomenon
in Lithuanian and Latvian one may suppose that
this existed in Jatvingian as well.

2.208. Otrębski, 1964, 212-213, suggests that
the devoicing of w after voiceless consonant in
Polish could somehow be connected with a similar
phenomenon in Jatvingian, cf. the form Jatfi
found in a document from the year 1516. Otrębski
assumes the word Jatfa to be a form of the name
Jatwa from which the word Jatvingian is derived.
The same phenomenon is found in the dialect of the
Lithuanianized Old Prussian-Jatvingians, who,
according to the Hypatian chronicle were settled
by the Lithuanian prince Traidenis in the year
1276 partially in Grodno and partially in Słonim.

Otrębski, 1964, 213, quotes from Rozwadowski's
1901 (still unpublished) description of the dialect
of the Lithuanianized Prussian-Jatvingians and notes a
pronunciation of chw, sw, szw, tw, kw as chf, sf,
szf, tf, kf: chf'aras 'sick': Russ. chworyj;
sfi'atimas 'foreign' = standard Lith. svẽtimas,
ketf'irtas 'fourth' = standard Lith. ketviřtas.

2.209.   Characteristic of the Polish speech area
is the substitution of word-final -k for etymological -ch, cf., e.g., na nogak 'on the feet'
(= standard na nogach), tyk staryk 'of those old
(people)' (= standard tych starych), etc. Nowadays
this is an exclusively dialect characteristic spread
chiefly in south-western Poland Minor. But the
oldest examples of -k instead of -ch date from the
fifteenth century from Mazovia. One supposes then
that this feature existed at one time in the old
Jatvingian territory. The use of k for Slavic ch
is well known in other Baltic languages and one
can easily imagine that in word-final position the
-ch was more difficult for the Jatvingians to
master than in word-medial or word-initial position.

2.210.   In conclusion Otrębski notes that a great
deal more could be written about the inflection,
word-formation, and vocabulary by studying the
corresponding dialects. In addition to the
Jatvingians the Old Prussians must have taken part
in the formation of the Polish language but they
were in general to the north. As a language
closely related to Jatvingian, Old Prussian had a
similar influence on Polish, but beyond the
Vistula to the neighboring Kashubian language
which shared many characteristics with the northern
varieties of Polish.

     Finally one must realize that by the term
Jatvingian Otrebski understands not only the tribe
but the whole community of Baltic tribes which they
led or which they represented in historical sources.
Thus the problem of the Jatvingian territory in the

narrow and in the broad meaning of the word cannot
be solved considering the contemporary state of our
knowledge. Nevertheless one can say without the
risk of complete error that the chief settlements of
the Jatvingians were in the basin of the Narew.
Otrębski's 1964 paper having been read at the First
Conference of Historical Sciences in Białystok,
there was a considerable discussion following it in
the pages of the same periodical in which Otrębski's
article appeared, viz., Acta Baltico-Slavica I.
Antonina Obrębska-Jabłońska, 267, objects that the
passage of -ch > -k is found in Great Poland far
beyond the Jatvingian territory. Similarly Czesław
Kudzinowski, 268, objected that the phenomenon of
Mazurenie is not to be ascribed to Jatvingian
influence.

2.300. Nalepa, 1966a, 127, says that in view of
the fact that the Jatvingian language is so close to
its Old Prussian and Lithuanian neighbors and the
fact that many Jatvingian names have been
Lithuanianized, in the majority of cases it is
impossible to know whether a given place name should
be ascribed to Jatvingian or to Lithuanian. In
addition to Otrębski's list of features character-
izing Jatvingian, Nalepa would add Jatvingian o
and ōi as corresponding to Old Prussian ā and āi.
But even Nalepa admits that this might not be
completely convincing since the basis for such a
statement is late and uncertain and in addition
o and oi are also known in the OP dialect represented in the Elbing vocabulary. Since this particular feature is the only feature suggested by Būga
(1925, LXXVII, = 1961, 132-133) which would distinguish Jatvingian from Old Prussian, one must say
that convincing conclusions concerning the differences between the language of the Jatvingians and
Old Prussians are still lacking.

2.301. In this article Nalepa also notes that the
names Garbas and Garbaś (now in Suvalkija) are
Jatvingian names and are to be connected with the

OP garbis 'hill' (as opposed to Lith. kálnas id.').

Kuzavinis, 1968, 66, shows, however, that in southern Lithuania the root garb- 'hill' is found and he gives as an example the name Gar̃bus, the name of a hill located on the shore of Lake Liškiavis (in the village of Liepiškiai in the region of Lazdijai). Kuzavinis mentions that names with this root are also known in Latvia: Gar̃bas, a farmstead, Gar̃bēni, a hill, Garbenauka, a farmstead, which Endzelīns, 1956, 297, compares with Old Prussian Garbenyken and Garbow and Lith. Gárbēnai. From this it is to be concluded that the word is Common Baltic and indeed the appellative garbis 'hill' (written as grabis, EV-28) is a very old word which is to be compared with Lith. gárbana 'lock of hair,' gárbanoti 'to curl (hair),' gur̃bti 'to become strong, to flourish,' Old Church Slavic grъbъ 'spine (of a mountain),' Russ. gorb 'hump,' Icelandic korpa 'shrivel up.' If we consider the frequent vacillation between voiced and unvoiced consonants we might also connect Lith. kárpa 'wart' and Gk. koruphḗ 'summit.'

Kuzavinis, 1968, 66-67, says that Lith. Gar̃bus is to be considered a Jatvingian word because of the intonation. The Lithuanian intonation is just the opposite of the West Baltic intonation and in this case Lith. gárbana 'lock of hair' with the acute shows the Lithuanian intonation whereas Gar̃bus shows the Old Prussian (or Jatvingian). In addition, according to Endzelīns' theory of the correspondence between Lithuanian and Latvian intonations, if in Latvian we find Gar̃bas in Lithuanian we would expect *Gárbas (*Gárbus), not Gar̃bus.[9] The numerous toponyms with the common root (Garbow, Garbeninken, Lulegarbis, Mantegarbs) and the West Baltic substratum area allow one to consider Gar̃bus a word of Jatvingian origin showing a direct genetic bond with the common noun *garbis. (See also Kazlauskas, 1967, 243.)

2.302. Nalepa, 1966a, 129, also suggests that the
name Laksde mentioned around the year 1384 in the
Lithuanian Wegeberichte of the Teutonic knights is
of Jatvingian origin.[10] Nalepa, then, 130, supposes
the name to be the same as Old Prussian laxde
(EV-607) 'hasel bush' and cognate with Latv.
la(g)zda 'id.' and Lith. lazdà 'stick.' Nalepa
next, 131, points out the Latvian variants lazds,
lazda, lęzda, lęzds, lęgzda, lęgzds and then suggests a possible connection with the Lith. Lizdai
on the right bank of the Nemunas to the north-west
of the Merecz and the Lizdu ẽžeras there also.
Kazlauskas, 1967, 243, objects, however, that one
cannot connect the Lith. names Lizdai and Lizdu
ẽžeras with lazdà 'stick' since the former are
cognate with Lith. lìzdas 'nest.'

2.303. In 1964, 218, Czesław Kudzinowski wrote
that science has already given an answer to some
of the questions connected with the Jatvingians.
For example, we know for certain that the Sudovians
of Ptolemy (see 1.000) and the historical Jatvingians
are the same people. It is still a question, however, as to whether the Jatvingians had their own
independent language or whether it was a dialect and
if only a dialect was it a dialect of Old Prussian
or Lithuanian. Historical testimony, 219, agrees
only that the Jatvingian language is Baltic.
Peter of Dusburg in his Chronicon terre Prussie
includes the Sudovians with the Prussians, although
he undoubtedly had in mind only the legal and
governmental aspects of the question. He recog-
nized all conquered territories as being Old
Prussian. The famous Polish historian Długosz
wrote: "...cum Pruthenica et Lithuanica lingua
magna ex parte habens similitudinem et intelli-
gentiam."

2.304. The first linguist to occupy himself with
the position of the Jatvingian language among the
Baltic languages was A. Bezzenberger, who, on the
basis of onomastic studies, established a line

34

from Labiawa to Rastembork (the so-called
'Bezzenberger line'). To the west of this line
there must have lived Prussian-speaking tribes,
whereas to the east Lithuanians. The Jatvingians
were found in the latter group, thus Bezzenberger
declared himself in favor of the Lithuanian nature
of the Jatvingians. But G. Gerullis, his student,
came to the conclusion that the Old Prussians and
the Sudovians formed a cohesive group. Later
Gerullis wrote that the Jatvingian language was
the closest relative of Old Prussian. The famous
Lithuanian linguist, K. Būga, came to the same
conclusion on the basis of onomastic material,
although he did not exclude the possibility of
the existence of Lithuanian elements in Jatvingian
which, however, betrays a later Lithuanian
colonization. Kudzinowski, 219, claims that post
World War I linguists had a political axe to
grind, the Lithuanian J. Vileišis defending the
Lithuanian nature of the Jatvingians and G.
Mortensen-Heinrich defending the Prussian-Jatvingian
unity.

2.305. Kudzinowski himself, 1964, 220-225, laid
out a plan for further research involving archeologists and linguists, the linguists to investigate
the Baltic borrowings in the Mazurian dialect of
Polish. Kudzinowski, 223-225, gives some 82
examples of Mazurian dialect words which he thinks
might be of Baltic origin (the word following the
hyphen is Lithuanian): aću, aću boži - ăčiū
'thank you'; baĺbotać, boĺbotać 'to speak unclearly'
- balbatúoti; bambiza 'big unshapely person' -
bambizà, bambĩzas; dulki 'pollen from field plants'
- dùlkės, etc. Kudzinowski, 225, maintains that if
it turns out that only twenty or thirty of these
are of Baltic origin, it will still be quite a lot.
Most of these have a cognate in Lithuanian, but
this may be a result of the fact that we do not
know the corresponding Old Prussian word. In the
case of a word like iegla 'spruce, fir' - Lith.
ẽglė we know the word must be of Lithuanian origin

because the Old Prussian cognate addle is known.
In my opinion this isn't certain at all since we
don't know how the German scribe might have heard
the release of the pre-lateral stop. Kiparsky,
1970b, 260-261, suggests that tl- and kl- (and dl-
and gl-) may have been in allophonic variation with
each other in Old Prussian, see 5.620.

2.400.   Kulikauskas, 1970, 13, writes that there
are vast differences of opinion concerning the
territory originally inhabited by the Jatvingians.
At the end of the 13th century the Jatvingians
were completely defeated by the Knights of the Cross
and in the year 1283 their last leader, Scurdas,
left his country and crossed over to the right bank
of the Nemunas, into Lithuania. (See 1.300.)
In the former territory of the Jatvingians there
appeared the Slavs and other neighboring peoples.
The common opinion is that in the south their
settlements reached the Narew and Bug rivers, in
the east Brest, Lyda, Minsk and Drohiczyn, in the
west the Nadrovian and the Galindian territory and
in the north Lithuania. The northern boundaries
of the Jatvingians are particularly in dispute.

2.401.   Sedov, 1964, 36-51, would move the northern
border of the Jatvingian territory to the right
bank of the Nemunas. Basing himself on Būga's work
he would attribute to the Jatvingians the territory
in which there are the most hydronyms with the
suffix -da (Grada, Grūda, Uvèda, etc.) and in
which hill graves with stone structures (topped
by wreathes, etc.) exist from the 1st until the 13th
century A.D. This way of marking the graves
characteristic of the Jatvingians is found even
up to the 17th century.

2.402.   Disputing Sedov's placement of the northern
boundary of the Jatvingians Tautavičius, 1966, 165,
pointed out that in the northern part of the area
attributed by Sedov to the Jatvingians we find
about 450 river names one of the elements of which
is the clear Lithuanian form -upè 'river.'

Furthermore, according to Tautavičius, 169,
archaeological finds with the shaded
(hatched) variety of ceramics correspond well
with the southern boundary of the area of
Lithuanian river names. In addition the northern
and eastern borders of the Jatvingian territory
as established by Sedov do   not correspond with
such characteristic Lithuanian archaeological finds
as temple rings, narrow-bladed axes, sickles with a
turned-up end and certain kinds of necklaces
(Tautavičius, 180). Tautavičius would push the
northern and eastern border between the Jatvingians
and the Lithuanians considerably further to the
south. According to Tautavičius, 1966, 165, 180,
the Jatvingians lived to the south of the line
Vištytis-Žuvintas-Alytus.

2.403.   Much of Sedov's analysis is clearly
erroneous according to Vanagas, 1968, 145, who
shows that many of the names quoted by Sedov were
incorrectly analyzed from the point of view of
their morphological structure. For example, the
name Prabaudà has the prefix pra- (as in the name
Pra-mūšis) and the root baud- cf. the names Baudỹs
and Baudeikà. The river name Pagrinda is not to
be separated from the noun pagrindà 'foundation.'
By means of a map Tautavičius, 1966, 164, shows
that in all of Lithuania there are about 50 river
names with the ending -da and that they are spread
about over almost the entire territory of the
Lithuanian republic. It seems obvious that not
all the river names with the ending -da are of
Jatvingian origin.

2.404.   In his answer to Tautavičius, Sedov, 1968,
177, objects that many of the names on the map
given by Tautavičius are also incorrectly analyzed
from the morphological point of view, e.g., the
name Raudà in northwestern Lithuania is connected
with Lith. raudà 'lament' or raũdas 'brown'
Latv. rauda 'kind of fish, roach,' raudas 'lament'.
Vanagas, 1968, 147, admits that in the polemic
between Tautavičius and Sedov, the latter is

correct in assuming that such river names
as Raudà are formed from the appellatives but that
it was quite sufficient for Sedov to mention Lith.
raũdas 'brown, reddish,' raudẽ 'kind of fish,
roach' Latv. rauda 'id.' and that there was no need
to bring in Lith. raudà, Latv. raudas 'crying,
lament.' Vanagas suggests then that the very
polemics of the famous archeologists in connection
with the hydronyms ending in -da is an indication
that a mistake was made in the beginning in the
attempt to supplement the list of ancient
Jatvingian compounds with -da < *-udā as the second
element. The hydronymic appellative can be
reconstructed from the Jatvingian appellative *udā 'river'
only in case there had been a vowel -u- before the
consonant -d-. To resume, one may say that only
the six hydronyms mentioned by Būga 1961, 602, are
clearly Jatvingian. (See 2.016.)

2.405. Continuing the polemic, Sedov, 1968, 179,
says that the element -upė 'river' is a contemporary
Lithuanian word and cannot be used for the establishment of earlier ethnic boundaries. Sedov also
draws attention to Grinaveckis' 1965 study which
compares certain dialect features of Lithuanian to
Jatvingian. Sedov concludes, 185, that hydronymy
and dialectology indisputably testify to the fact
that southern Lithuania was originally a part of
the Jatvingian settlement area dated from the 4th
to 12th-13th centuries A.D. Stone kurgans in the
region between the Neris and the Nemunas are the
monuments of these Jatvingians. In general the
problem of the assimilation of the Jatvingian population to the Lithuanians can only be solved by
analysis of the monuments of the varied ethnic
population of the region.

2.406. Finally Tautavičius, 1968, writes that
he never denied the existence of Jatvingian monuments in southern and southwestern Lithuania, nor
did he deny the existence of a mixed population,
but he thinks that the area of the early tribes
should be defined by the predominant population,

not by the maximum extension of the tribe. Likewise it is perfectly true that the boundaries between tribes do not remain perfectly stable, but change from epoch to epoch.

2.407. Kulikauskas, 1970, 14, says that the most recent archaeological finds (1955-1966) have not attracted the attention of either V. V. Sedov or A. Tautavičius. Investigations of the trans-Nemunas archeological sites show clear relationships with neighboring territories. These trans-Nemunas monuments already had special characteristics in the first millenium A.D. This is clearly shown by the castle hill of Paveisninkai and investigations of the habitations near it. It is interesting to note that now in the territory of Paveisninkai the Dzukish dialect of Lithuanian is used. Surely this territory was inhabited by Jatvingians until the 13th century.

Kulikauskas concludes that the Nemunas never was any kind of ethnic boundary. The most recent research has shown that the trans-Nemunas archeological finds, the castle hills and the graves bind this area closely with the contemporary Sulvalkija region. The unifying elements were language, customs, beliefs, clothing and type of dwelling, etc.

2.408. Kulikauskas, 1970, 31, 32 concludes that it is impossible to distinguish clearly the territories of previous tribal units. The Jatvingians were made up of a group of different closely related tribes. Such a conclusion is suggested both by archeological data as well as written sources.

The historical term Jatvingians is frequently replaced by the term Pollexiani in J. Kadłubek's chronicle. In the writing of 1259 of Mindaugas we find the term Dainowe. In the chronicles of the Knights of the Cross we find Sudower land, Sudlant, Sudauen, terra Sudorum. (Kulikauskas, 1970, 32). Thus the establishment of a northern

39

boundary Vištytis-Žuvintas-Alytus is without
foundation. The territory north of this line
should be considered Sudovian territory, to the
south and east Dainava.   The Pollexiani inhabited
a part of the territory in the neighborhood of the
Poles.

2.500.   Nalepa, 1966b, occupies himself with the
Baltic tribe Pollexiani, Polexia, known in sources
from the end of the 12th and the 13th centuries and
denoting the Baltic tribe in the northeastern part
of Mazovia. In recent years the opinion has become
established that Pollexiani is the Polish name for
the Jatvingians and that the name is to be read
(in Polish) as Polesianie and Polexia is to be read
as Polesie, cf. Pol. po 'along, by,' las 'forest.'
First of all Nalepa notes that the Pollexiani is
not the name for the Jatvingians in the narrow
sense of the word, but in the broadest sense.

2.501.   Nalepa localizes Polexia as being to the
east of the Galindians whose location has been described above. See 1.190. The conclusion is then
that Polexia is in the region of Pojezierze Ełckie
(Mazury Garbate), i.e., the territory of which the
chief river is the Ełk. This name derives from Łek.
(The change in form was completed first in the city
name which derived from the river name Łek and then
the river name itself was changed to bring it into
conformity with the name of the city.) The name
Łek in turn was taken from Baltic *Lukas.

2.502.   In the name Polexia the letter x is to be
read as a combination of k plus s. The initial
morpheme is po-, the root morpheme is -lek- (the
name of the river), the suffix morphemes are -s-
and -ia and the meaning of the name is: 'the
region along the river Łek (= contemporary Ełk).
The formation can be compared to such other well
known names as Pol. Pomorze 'region along the sea,'
Powisle 'region along the Vistula,' Połabie
'region along the Elbe,' etc. Quite possibly the
original form was Baltic *Pa-luk-s-ija which was

adapted to Slavic *Pa-lŭk-s-ijo > *Po-lŏk-s-ьje > *Po-lek-ś-e > *Poļeksie or *Poļeksze which in Latinized form was rendered as Polexia.[11]

2.503. A further adaptation to the norms of Polish folk etymology led to the creation of the forms Polesie, Podlesie and finally Podlasie which could be understood in Polish as meaning 'along, near, the forest.'

2.600. In 1963b, 3, Otrębski noted that the name (nom.) Dainavà, (gen.) Dainavõs, (acc.) Daĩnavą at the present time is the name of about ten villages in the Lithuanian republic, mainly in the districts of Ukmergė, Varėna and Vilnius. The diminutive form Dainavẽlė serves as a name of three villages in the districts of Lazdijai and Trakai. In the 13th century Dainavà was the name of a Jatvingian area which is mentioned in the official documents of Mindaugas (1259) who set aside for the use of the order 'denowe tota, quam etiam quidam Jatwesen vocant...' Otrębski supposes that the Lithuanian villages with the names Dainavà, Dainavẽlė, etc. were settled at least in part by emigrants from this area.

2.601. In addition to the document we also find other evidence to lead us to believe that Dainavà is the old name of the Jatvingian territory. In the neighborhood of Zietela in the Slonim district there is a village known in Belo-Russian by the name Jac'viž, earlier Jat(ъ)vežь or Jat(ъ)vez' (1580), which has been known in Lithuanian since the earliest times by the name Dainavà. The Lithuanian grand duke Traidenis, the founder of the city Rajgrod called himself the prince Jatьvezskij and Dojnov(ъ)skij. The chronicles call the district which Traidenis ruled Dojnova Jatvežь (Jatvezь).

2.700. One notes that K. Būga, 1961, 790, and Savukynas, 1966, 172, connected the place-name suffix -ingė, -ingis, of which we find a concentration in southern Lithuania on both sides of the Nemunas, with the Jatvingians. Vanagas, 1968, 144,

41

objects, however, that toponyms with these suffixes
are also found in other areas of Lithuania.

2.701.   Vanagas, 1970, 37, says furthermore that in
linguistic and archeological literature the opinion
has become fixed that the suffix -uva is characteristic only of Lithuanian (or of Lithuanian and Old
Prussian) and -ava only of Latvian and Old Prussian
hydronymy. This opinion, according to Vanagas, 38,
is not absolutely accurate because in contemporary
Lithuania hydronyms in -av- are fairly commonly
found except in the central section of northern
Lithuania where they are almost completely lacking.
One should say rather that toponyms with the suffix
-ava are rather well represented among Lithuanian,
Latvian and Old Prussian place names, whereas the
ending -uva is restricted to contemporary Lithuanian
names.

2.702.   Vanagas, 1970, 38, writes that one of the
most striking features of the Panemunių Dzukish area
is the existence of hydronyms with a stressed final
-ùs; in addition only in southern Lithuania do we
find other toponyms with final stressed -ùs: e.g.
Lapšiùs, Pravažùs, Alytùs, etc. Almost all of
them are to the south of the Nemunas Neris line,
between Gelgaudiškis-Lazdijai in the west and Vievis
(Jeva) and Varėna in the east. The most interesting
thing to note, however, is that we find within this
same set of boundaries the following features, viz.
the existence of toponyms with s, z instead of š, ž
and toponyms with ei where from the point of view
of standard Lithuanian we would expect ie. It
would be hard to believe, according to Vanagas, 39,
that this is accidental. A map of a number of the
most important hydronyms shows that there is not a
single formant of hydronyms which is specifically
east or west of the Nemunas. Thus both the right
and the left banks of the Nemunas form a single more
or less unified hydronymic area. Thus Vanagas'
statement agrees essentially with that of
Kulikauskas mentioned above that in the past the

Panemunių Dzukish territory was, as it is today,
unified both ethnically and linguistically, see 2.408.
Vanagas concludes, 1970, 41, with the statement that
one of the clearest examples showing the existence
of a Jatvingian substratum in the toponymy both to
the east and to the west of the Nemunas river is the
existence of the lake named Gáil-iekas in the area of
Seirijai and the lake name Gáil-intas in the region
of Merkinė. Both of these names have the same root
gail- which is connected with OP gaylis 'white'
(EV-459). Vanagas says that there are many more
such toponyms reflecting an earlier substratum.

2.800.   V. N. Toporov, 1966a, 285, wrote that it
is doubtless the case that one would find Jatvingian
elements in the old territory of the southern borders
of the Jatvingians, viz., along the Narew river.
In this article Toporov investigates some forty
hydronyms from the upper reaches of the Narew right
down to the point where it enters the Biebrza river.
It would take too much space to repeat all of
Toporov's etymologies, so I shall merely give a
few examples here.

2.801.   Toporov, 1966a, 288, gives the Baltic root
med- 'tree, wood' (cf. OP median 'forest,' Lith.
mẽdis 'tree,' Latv. mežs 'forest') which furnishes
the name Miedzianka on the right bank of the Narew.
He notes also the OP names Medinen, Medeniken,
Medenouwe, etc., Lith. Mẽdinas, Medinė, Mẽdinis,
etc., Latv. Mednieki, Medn-upes, Mednava, etc.,
and in the basin of the Dnepr and Western Dvina
(names without -n-) Mjadziol, Mjadelica, Medela,
etc.

2.802.   On the left bank of the Narew we find the
hydronym Łoknica which can be compared to the OP
name Lockeneyn, Lith. Luknà, Lùknas, Lùknė, etc.,
Latv. Luknis, Lukna-ęzęrs, Lukna-purvs, etc.
Cf. also in the basin of the Dnepr Lokna, Malaja
Lokna, Lokneja, Loknja, Loknjanka and especially the
exact form - Loknica. Without -n- compare the
Jatvingian Łъkъ (variant Loukъ) from the Hypatian

43

chronicle for the year 1251. (Toporov, 1966a, 289.)

2.803. We also find the hydronym Derazina. The root *darg- is widely represented in Baltic hydronymy from the Dnepr to the territories west of the Vistula and is represented in the name Drohiczyn (< *Dargūtīnas), clearly connected with the Jatvingian element. Cf. in the upper reaches of the Dnepr the names Deražnja, Derežna, Derjažnja, Deraženka, etc., Lith. Derežna, Derěžnyčia, Dergintas, Dérgioniu ēžeras, Latv. Derdžanu-ezers, etc. (Toporov, 1966a, 290).[12]

2.804. Nalepa, 1971b, 117, writes that the term terrula Cresmen appears for the first time in 1259 in a document of Mindaugas. In this document, the authenticity of which has been much discussed, Mindaugas gave to the Inflantian Knights Jatvingia with the exception of certain lands, Skalvia and Samogitia with the exception of certain properties given to the bishop of Lithuania. For the second occurrence of the name Nalepa, 1971b, 117, quotes from the Chronicle of Peter of Dusburg: "De destructione territorii Sudowie dicti Crasime. Frater Manegoldus magister... intravit territorium Sudowie dictum Crasimam, vastando per incendiu et rapinam." The name is also known in the Russian chronicles in the derived forms krismencě, krismenci.

2.805. The area Cresmen has been variously located but the majority of the specialists in recent times have identified Cresmen with Krzyżewo because six kilometers to the west of Krzyżewo lies the village of Skomętno Wielkie on lake Skomętno, a name which recalls the name Skomand, captain of the Sudovians.

2.806 Nalepa, 1971b, 118, quotes the Słownik Geograficzny Królestwa Polskiego, Warsaw 1883, which describes Krzemieniucha or Krzemionka as the highest mountain in the area of Suwałki, about 10 versts northwest of the latter city in the fields of the

44

village Żywa Woda. Nalepa, 1971b, 119 continues, saying that Krzemieniucha rises about two and one-half kilometers from the left bank of the Hancza from which the Jatvingians have their name and the mountain is surrounded by early mediaeval Jatvingian cemeteries. Krzemieniucha is located almost in the middle of the Jatvingian territory. The evidence of material culture and history locates the land of Cresmen in the region of Krzemieniucha, but is it possible to accept a link between the two names? Unfortunately there is no early documentation of the name of the mountain. Nalepa, 1971b, 120, finds the earliest mention on a map from the end of the 18th century (ca. 1780) in the form Krzemienna Gura.

2.807.   The major problem to connecting the name Cresmen with Polish Krzemieniucha < *Kremen-jucha (the -jucha being an augmentative suffix) is the lack of the -s- in the Slavic cognate. In any case Nalepa, 1971b, 121, quotes Būga, 1961, 135, to the effect that the name Cresmen contains the Baltic root krēs-, kres- 'to sit down, to be seated,' cf. Lith. krãsė 'arm chair' with an apophonic -a- instead of -e- recalling the -a- of OP Crasima. The lack of the -s- in the Slavic form of the name is a result of an adaptation to the Slavic word *kremenь > Pol. krzemień 'flint.' We must remember also that the Slavic languages do not know the expression kresmen, at least today. On the other hand the name of the stone, flint, was well known, a necessary object of every-day use.

2.808.   Nalepa, 1971b, 123, concludes that the mountain Krzemieniucha (perhaps it had then the ancient Jatvingian name Cresmen) dominated central Suvalkija or ancient Jatvingia (in the narrow sense of the term). It is also possible that the name was used for the surrounding territory as well, cf. the early sources which mention the 'territorium Sudowie dictum Crasima, terrula Cresmen.' The Russians called the inhabitants of this land

45

<u>Krismenci</u>. From this land came the Jatvingian prince
Skomand, the tragic creator of the Jatvingian state
which was destroyed by the Teutonic Knights in 1283.

Jatvingian Place Names

2.809. Zdancewicz, 1963, 236f, suggested that the
Polish place name <u>Sejna</u>, Lith. <u>Seinà</u> was derived from
the Jatvingian term <u>seina</u> 'wall, border' cognate with
Lith. <u>síena</u> 'id.' In Jatvingian, as in Old Prussian,
the etymological diphthong <u>ei</u> was retained and did
not pass to <u>ie</u> as it did sometimes in East Baltic.

2.810. Nalepa, 1969, 190, objects that the meaning
'wall' does not appear in the list of approximately
19,000 hydronyms of the Vistula basin. Nalepa then
proposes that the name be derived from Baltic *<u>šeinas</u>
a word represented in Lith. <u>šiẽnas</u> (cf. also Russ.
seno, Pol. siano 'hay'). Nalepa also quotes some
parallels from Polish in which the root for 'hay'
has served as the basis for place names, e.g.,
<u>Sienna</u>, <u>Siennica</u>, <u>Sienno</u>, etc. In addition parallels
are to be found in Lithuanian: <u>Šienéperšis</u>,
<u>Šiẽnupis</u>; cf. also in East Prussian <u>Sajna</u>, river name,
<u>Sajno</u>, lake name, etc. The river name <u>Sejna</u>, the
lake and the city <u>Sejny</u> are names of Jatvingian
origin. Their Jatvingian nature is characterized by
two features, (1) the presence of <u>s</u> (for Proto-Baltic
<u>š</u>) and (2) the retention of the diphthong <u>ei</u>. This
conclusion accords with the fact that we encounter in
the neighborhood other names of Jatvingian origin, e.
g.. <u>Berzniki</u>, <u>Zelwa</u> (both near Sejny) and <u>Azãgis</u>,
<u>Léipalingis</u> and <u>Kirsnà</u> in Lithuania.

2.811. Otrębski, 1963b, 5, writes that the name
<u>Deimenà</u>, a branch of the river Pregel' between
<u>Tepljava</u> (Ger. <u>Tapiau</u>) and <u>Labguva</u> (Ger. <u>Labiau</u>) and
an abbreviated form of the name, viz. <u>Deimẽ</u> are Jatvingian.

2.812. Otrębski, 1962, 148-149, writes that in
northeastern Poland southwest of Augustów (Lith.
Augustavas) there is a lake bearing the name <u>Tajno</u>

(Lith. Taĩnas), undoubtedly Tainas in Jatvingian.
Otrębski claims that Tainas is a variant of OCS
tina 'dirt, mud,' Old Czech tina 'mud; morass.'
In OCS texts we also find timĕno 'mud' and timĕnьje
'mud, swamp.' The root of Jatvingian Tainas,
Slavic tina, *timen- is the same as in Slavic
*tajati, *tajǫ 'to melt' which presupposes an IE
*tā-i. Otrębski says that in Tai-nas the original
root form *tə-i- is found, whereas in Slavic *ti-na
and *ti-men we find the Indo-European root variant
*tī-< *tə-i-. The root *tī- is also known in the
river name Týtuva as well as in the derived city
name Týtuvėnai, Týtavėnai (Pol. Cytowiany) in the
district of Kelmė. Otrębski, 1962, 149, writes
further than in addition to *tā-i- with an -i-
extension there also existed an extension with -u-
which gave an expanded root form *tā-u- represented in Germanic *þaujan, cf. Old Norse þeyja,
OHG douwen, dewen, Modern German tauen, Anglo-Saxon
þawian, English to thaw. The root *tā-u- is also
known in Baltic, cf. above all the river and place
names Tóvė (German Tawe, a city, Tawelle, a river)
in East Prussia from *tāv-ė. In any case Otrębski
concludes that the close bond between Jatvingian
Tainas and OCS and Czech tina (as well as OCS
timĕno, timĕnьje) can be regarded as a proof of
the fact that Jatvingian vocabulary was very close
to Slavic. Otrębski even makes the rather surprising statement that Jatvingian vocabulary was
closer to Slavic than to Lithuanian.

2.900.   Toporov, 1966b, 143, points out that information concerning Jatvingian mythology is extremely
scanty, consisting chiefly of a few names of gods,
the etymologies of which are quite unclear or
mysterious, and some minimal information according
to which we can make some judgements about certain
elements of their ritual practices. Here Toporov
gives several sources for the judgements concerning
Jatvingian mythology. One of these sources is the
Hypatian chronicle and a second is a note made in
1261 by the Russian copyist of the Russian translation of the Chronicle of John Malalas. In this

note we find the story of a certain Sovij who once caught a wild boar from which he extracted nine spleens. He gave these to his children and asked them to cook the spleens. But the children ate the spleens and Sovij became angry and tried to descend to hell through eight gates. He did not succeed, but one of his sons showed him the ninth gate through which he got into hell. Leaving his angry brothers the son went to search out his father whom he found in hell and for whom he made a couch and whom he then buried in the ground. The following morning Sovij told his son that he had been eaten by worms and vermin. On the next night the son put his father Sovij in a tree, but in the morning it turned out that he had been eaten by bees and mosquitoes. Then the son burned Sovij and in the morning on being questioned by his son, Sovij replied that he had slept like a child in his crib. This tradition is ascribed to the Lithuanians, Jatvingians and Prussians and suggests an origin for the custom of cremation among the early Balts.

2.901. It turns out that Sovij is closely bound to the idea of fire, to the name sovica as a name for peoples practicing cremation and also to the sun. (In the most varied traditions the wild boar appears as the zoomorphic incarnation of the sun.) Sovij had a smith by the name of Teljavel' who forged the sun for him and thus we can imagine that Sovij is the parent or creator of the sun and Teljavel' is the person who actually makes the sun.

2.902. Both in the Hypatian chronicle and in a supplementary quotation from John Malalas we find reference to Svarog whom Toporov 1966b, 147, identifies as the father of the sun (=Dažbog).

Toporov,1966b, 148, also suggests the reconstruction of a general myth for certain Baltic and Slavic tribes, a myth in which a father and a son participate. These are connected with fire and the sun and by the same token with the establishment of a certain tradition (manner of burial, types of smithying, smith-work, marital relationships). Among the important details of this schema one might find the form of a miraculous wild boar, the presence of nine gates, etc. Perhaps the name Sovij was somehow connected with the name Svarog (cf. the variant Sovarog in the Hypatian chronicle) in the linguistic consciousness of the scribe and the name Sovarog for speakers of Baltic languages with names of the type Sawarycke 'one's own lord.' As far as the name Sovij is concerned one might suggest a connection with the Indo-European root for 'sun,' *sāuē- (*sŭ, *sye-). See Toporov, 1966b, 148.

3.000 The position of Old Prussian in the Baltic language family is not completely clear. Endzelīns, 1970, 59, concludes that since there are so many differences between West Baltic (Old Prussian) on the one hand and East Baltic (Lithuanian and Latvian) on the other hand, it would not be possible to write a grammar of Proto-Baltic in the same sense that one could write a grammar of Proto-Slavic. One could imagine theoretically that the dialect of Proto-Indo-European from which Old Prussian developed stood as near to the dialect from which Proto-Germanic developed as it did to that dialect from which the East Baltic languages developed.

3.001 Among the characteristics of Old Prussian, Fraenkel, 1950b, 26, notes that an etymological ei is retained in Old Prussian, but passes to ie in Lithuanian and Latvian under the stress, e.g., Lith. diẽvas 'god,' as opposed to deivė̃ 'goddess; fairy.' We find, however, in contrast OP deiw(a)s, deywis (EV - 1) 'god.'

3.002 Fraenkel, 1950b, 27, also says that a portion of the Old Prussian dialects change Indo-European and Proto-Baltic *ē into ī, cf. OP bītas īdin 'evening meal' beside Lith. ésti, Latv. ēst 'to eat.' I would suggest, however, that the rendition of Proto-Baltic *ē by orthographic ī is either the result of a misinterpretation on the part of the scribe, or else it shows a phonological change in the process of taking place, see paragraph 5.002.[13]

3.003 Some of the Old Prussian dialects, according to Fraenkel, 1950b, 28, have retained the etymological sequence tl, dl, whereas Lithuanian and Latvian have changed this into kl, gl, cf. OP ebsentliuns 'designated,' Lith. žénklas 'sign.' The interpretation of OP tl, dl is open to question, see Kiparsky, 1970b, 260-261 and paragraph 5.620.

3.004 According to Fraenkel, 1950b, 28, the Indo-European neuter is retained in the Elbing vocabulary and perhaps there are traces of it in the I and II catechisms, although the IIIrd

catechism has for the most part masculine for the
old neuter. Fraenkel, 28, says that the nom. pl.
malnijkiku 'children' is a neuter plural, but I
am highly suspicious. I would assume rather a
misspelling for a masc. nom. pl. /malnīkikai/,
see paragraph 5.200. Fraenkel also says that
OP crauyo (EV - 160) and krawia (IIIrd catechism)
'blood' are neuter plurals and he compares the
forms Greek haímata, Old Church Slavic krᵻvi
'blood' (both in the plural).
3.005 Fraenkel, 1950b, 30, points to the contrast
between OP newīnts 'ninth' with an initial n-
(cf. Gothic niunda 'id.') vs. Lith. deviñtas,
Latv. devīts 'id.' Lith. trēčias, Latv. treš
corresponds in vocalism to OCS trettьjь 'id.'
whereas OP tirt(i)s seems to correspond with
Sanskrit tr̥tīya- (with ir from r̥).
3.006 Fraenkel, 1950b, 31, says that the Old
Prussian pronominal declension is much more
conservative than that of Lithuanian and Latvian,
cf., e.g., the OP masc. dat. sg. stesmu (like
Sanskrit tasmai), but in Lith. tám(ui), Latv.
tam there is no s before the m. The word for
'self' is pats in Lithuanian and Latvian and
this can be compared with Sanskrit páti- and
Greek pósis 'master.' On the other hand Old
Prussian has the word subs 'self,' the zero-grade
form of the root *svebh-, *svobh- which we also
find in Old Church Slavic svobodь 'free.'[14] It
seems likely to me, however, that the form *pats
is represented in Old Prussian, see Bezzenberger,
1878, 139, and paragraph 4.705. Fraenkel
continues, pointing out that we encounter the
OP reflexive dative sebbei 'to oneself,' 2nd sg.
dat. tebbei 'to you (sg.)' as opposed to Lith.
sáu, táu and Latv. sev, tev, respectively.
3.007 The Old Prussian imperative weddeis
'lead' corresponds with Slavic vedi 'id.',
according to Fraenkel, 1950b, 33. Latvian
imperatives are formed partly on the optatives,
but the usual Lithuanian imperative is in -k.[15]
The Old Prussian infinitive ends in -tun (which
corresponds to the Lithuanian supine in -tu̧), -t
(corresponding to the infinitive endings, Lith.
-ti, Latv. -t, Slavic -ti) or -twei, the dative

51

of a stem in -tu.
3.100 Mažiulis, 1966, 11, gives four characteristics which define the position of Old Prussian
among the Baltic languages: (1) Old Prussian is
the closest relative of Lithuanian and Latvian,
(2) Old Prussian has fewer linguistic features
in common with the Lithuanian and Latvian
languages than the latter two languages have with
each other, (3) Old Prussian has retained more
archaisms than Lithuanian and Lithuanian has
retained more than Latvian and (4) Old Prussian
is closer, at least in vocabulary, to Lithuanian
than to Latvian. Mažiulis points out further
that the Old Prussians themselves are closely
bound to the other Baltic peoples by culture,
religion, traditions and common borders. This is
illustrated by Vytautas the Great's demand after
the defeat of the Teutonic knights at the battle
of Tannenberg (1410): "Prussia was also my
father's land and as the inheritance from my
father I demand it even up to the river Osa."
3.200 Otrębski, 1965, 79-81, wrote that at a
certain period Slavo-Baltic, as he describes it,
was divided into three main dialects, East Baltic
(including Lithuanian and Latvian in the north-
eastern area), West Baltic (Old Prussian and
Jatvingian in the southwest) and Slavic (in the
south). West Baltic was rather a bridge between
East Baltic and Slavic. Usually the lexical
differences between Lithuanian and Old Church
Slavic are emphasized, but Otrębski considers it
useful to point up the differences between East
Baltic (Lithuanian and Latvian) and Old Prussian
on the one hand, and the correspondences between
Old Prussian and Slavic on the other hand: OP
lauxnos (EV - 4) 'stars,' OCS luna, Polish łuna
'moon,' vs. Lith. žvaĩgždės 'stars'; OP assanis
(EV - 14), Polish jesień, Russian osen' 'autumn'
vs. Lith. ruduõ; OP seydis, Serbo-Croatian zîd
'wall' vs. Lith. síena; OP genno (EV - 188), OCS
žena 'wife' but Lith. móteris 'woman,' žmonà
'wife'; OP awis (EV - 177), Czech ujec, Polish
wuj, wujek 'uncle'; OP tisties (EV - 184), OCS
tьstь, Polish teść 'father-in-law, wife's father'
vs. Lith. šẽšuras 'father-in-law' (ordinarily

šẽšuras denotes the 'husband's father,' whereas
Lith. úošvis denotes either the wife's or the
husband's father, so it is difficult to understand Otrębski's point here - WRS); OP curwis
(EV - 672), kurwan 'ox,' Old Polish karw 'old,
lazy ox,' but Lith. jáutis 'id.'; OP salowis
(EV - 727), Russian solovej, Polish słowik, but
Lith. lakštiñgala 'nightingale'; OP insuwis (EV -
94), OCS językъ 'tongue,' but Lith. liežùvis[16]
'id.': OP musgeno (EV - 74) 'marrow,' OCS mozgъ,
Russian mozg 'marrow, brain' vs. Lith. (pl.)
smãgenys, smẽgenys 'brains'; OP strigeno (EV -
73) 'brain,' Russian steržen' 'marrow; resin';
OP geits 'bread,' OCS žito 'grain,' Polish żyto
'rye,' vs. Lith. dúona 'bread,' (nom. pl.) rugiaĩ
'rye'; OP som-pisinis (EV - 340) 'rough bread,'
OCS pьšenica 'wheat,' Lith. (nom. pl.) javaĩ
'grain'; OP babo (EV - 263), Polish bob 'bean'
but Lith. (nom. pl.) pùpos 'beans'; OP wutris 'smith'
(EV - 513), autre (EV - 514) 'forge,' OCS vъtrь
'faber ferrarius, faber lignarius' vs. Lith.
kálvis 'smith'; OP dalptan (EV - 536) 'a pointed
instrument of iron and steel for making holes,'
Polish dłoto, Russian doloto from *dolb-to
'chisel,' but Lith. káltas 'chisel'; OP eyswo
(EV - 159), OCS jazva, but Lith. žaizdà 'wound';
OP kailūstiskun 'health,' OCS cělъ 'whole' but
Lith. sveĩkas 'healthy'; OP arwis 'true, certain,'
OCS ravьnъ 'even, like' vs. Lith. tìkras 'sure,
certain,' lýgus 'even, level'; OP and Jatvingian
kirsna-, OCS črъnъ vs. Lith. júodas 'black'; OP
aumūsnan 'washing away, ablution,' OCS umyti 'to
wash away,' but Lith. praũsti, pláuti 'to wash.'
3.201 Furthermore, Otrębski, 1965, 81, writes
that frequently a word occurs in Slavo-Baltic
with two nuances of meaning and the Old Prussian
and Slavic meanings go together, as opposed to
the meanings which we find in East Baltic. E.g.,
OP austo 'mouth, muzzle' at least in principle
is the same word as Lith. úostas, Latv. uosts,
uosta 'harbor' and corresponds to Slavic usta
'mouth'; OP wetro (EV - 53) corresponds formally
to Lith. vėtra, Latv. vētra 'storm,' but the
Old Prussian word means 'wind' just like OCS
větrъ and Polish wiatr, etc.

3.202 According to Otrębski, 1965, 81-82, the
East Balts (Lithuanians, Latvians, etc.) lived
for a certain period separated from the West
Balts (the Old Prussians, Jatvingians, etc.) as
a result, probably of the incursions of Finnic
peoples (Livonians, etc.). During this period
the languages of the East Balts tended to become
more different from West Baltic and Slavic.
Later, as the result of the denationalization of
these Finnic peoples the East Balts came into
direct contact again with the West Balts and the
Slavs. From then on the Balts lived in close
contact with the Slavs and they understood each
other's languages without difficulty and each
could easily adopt the language of the neighbor.
Indeed a significant portion of the politically
divided Balts were Slavicized by the better
organized and culturally superior Slavs. There
was, however, no simple acceptance of the Slavic
language, which in many respects had already become quite different from the Slavo-Baltic proto-
form. As a result of this there arose new Slavic
languages, viz., Belorussian and a special Polish
dialect. To this can be attributed the palatalization of t', d' (before e, i, ě) to c' , dz'
as a result of the Jatvingian pronunciation of
t' and d' as k' and g'. (See paragraph 2.108.)
Perhaps also the Russian phenomenon of akanje is
to be ascribed to the Baltic substratum. The
Slavo-Balts pronounced Slavic short o as an å
which came to be pronounced o in a stressed
syllable.
3.203 Stang, 1966, 13, and 1971, 78, notes that
in certain cases the Old Prussian vocabulary
agrees especially with that of Germanic. Stang
lists the following examples: kaāubri 'thorn,' [17]
Old Saxon hiopo 'briars,' Old Swedish hiūpon
'hip, haw,' Norwegian dialect njupa and hjupa,
Danish hyben; kalis (EV - 569) 'sheat-fish,'
Old High German wels, Old Norse hvalr 'whale'
(it may be of interest to note here that J.
Kazlauskas once suggested in a letter to me that
OP kalis, in spite of its resemblance to Finnish
kala 'fish' may be related to Lith. kalýbas 'dog
with a white ring about his neck,' kalývas, same

meaning as above or 'pure white'; Kazlauskas'
suggestion seems correct to me), see also
paragraph 10.045; layso (EV - 27) 'clay,' Old
Norse leira 'mud-flat'; nautei (dat. sg.)
'need,' Gothic naups; twaxtan (EV - 553) 'bath-
ing-switch,' Gothic þwahan 'to wash,' but see
paragraph 10.110; warsus (EV - 91), Old Norse
vǫrr 'lip,' Gothic waírilos 'lips'; doacke (EV -
732) 'starling,' Old High German taha(la) 'jack-
daw'; druwīt 'to believe,' Old High German
trū(w)ēn, but see Marstrander, 1945, and
paragraph 10.029.

Stang, 1966, 13, asserts that one cannot draw
firm conclusions from these examples, but that
the agreements show that the West Baltic dialect
was in closer contact with the neighboring
western languages than the East Baltic dialects
were.

3.300 Duridanov, 1969, analyzes a considerable
number of Dacian and Thracian words which he
compares with Baltic words and decides that in
prehistoric times Baltic, Dacian and Thracian
tribes lived side by side (i.e., around 3,000
B. C.). It would be impossible to repeat all of
Duridanov's etymologies here, but I will give
just a few examples.

3.301 Duridanov, 1969, 20, compares OP berse
(EV - 600), Lith. béržas, Latv. bȩ̃rzs 'birch,'
which is well known in Baltic hydronymy, cf.,
e.g., the river names Lith. Bérž-upis, Latv.
Bȩ̃rz-upe, the lake name Lith. Béržuvis, with
Dacian Bersovia, a čity in the southwestern part
of Dacia.

3.302 According to Duridanov, 1969, 21, Dacian
Boúttis, a castle in the district of Skassetana,
Dacia mediterranea, Boutae, the southern entrance
to Dacia (cf. Jordanes, Getae) can be compared
with OP buttan 'house,' Lith. bùtas 'apartment.'

3.303 Duridanov, 1969, 21, says that OP braydis
(EV - 650) 'elk,' Lith. bríedis 'stag, hart; elk,'
Latv. briêdis 'deer, stag; hart' go back finally
to an Indo-European root *bhrendis and are to be
connected with the Thracian place name Brentopara.
Also to be compared are Messapian bréndon ·
élaphon (Hesychius). But see also para. 10.020.

3.304 Duridanov, 1969, 34, compares Thracian
Iuras, a coastal river in western Thracia in the
area of the Strandža mountain range between
Halmydessos and Thynias (now Cape Ineada on the
Black Sea) with OP iūrin, Lith. (nom. pl.) júros,
Latv. (nom. pl.) jūras 'sea.'
3.305 Further examples come from Duridanov,
1969, 99 et passim.

Thracian	Old Prussian
(place names)	
Díggion (castle in Hebrus district)	Dinge (forest)
Kabúlē (city in Thracia northeast of Izvor)	Cabula = *gabula (river name)
Purdae (place in Agaean Thracia between Akontisma and Topiron, northwest of the mouth of the Nestus)	Porden, Purde (lake name), Purden (place name)
Rumbo-dona (place in Agaean Thracia, now Geniseja)	Rumbow (ford)
(personal names)	
Kersēs (Thracian king 'Kersi-baulos')	Kerse, Kerso (personal name), cf. Lith. kéršas 'piebald, flecked with black and white'
Sparkē	Sparke

Dacian

Balauson (castle in the   Bolausen (place name)
  district of Skassetana,
  Dacia mediterranea;
  both the Dacian and
  Old Prussian words have
  the Indo-European root
  *bhol- 'white,' cf.
  Lith. balà 'swamp,'
  báltas 'white')
Galtis (place on the   Galten-garb, Galtgarbe
  river Alutas in Dacia;   (place name)
  t-extension of Balto-
  Slavic root *gǎl- 'ice-
  covering')

56

Dacian	Old Prussian
Drasdea (castle in the area of Nicopolis)	Drasda, Drosten (place name; cognate with OP tresde [EV - 728], Lith. strãzdas, Latv. strazds Russian drozd 'thrush')
Hresidína (castle in Scythia minor)	Resedynen, Resdynen (place name; the initial element is cognate with Sanskrit rasā 'moisture, humidity,' Lith. rasà, Old Church Slavic rosa 'dew'
Scaugdae (tribal name)	Skawdegede (personal name; initial element possibly derived from root cognate with Lith. skaudéti 'to hurt'; second element from root cognate with Lith. gedéti 'to mourn'
Burtinus (personal name)	Burthe, Burtin (personal name)
Sausa (personal name)	Sause (personal name; cognate with Lith. saũsas, Latv. sàuss, Old Church Slavic suxъ 'dry')[18]
Skabēs (personal name)	Skabeike, Skabeyke, etc. (personal name, cf. Lith. skabùs 'sharp,' Latv. skâbs 'sour')
Tautomedes (personal name, probably a compound, cf. the Old Prussian cognates)	Thawthe, Mede, Medis (personal names, cf. also OP tauto [EV - 793] 'land')

3.306 Duridanov gives the following statistics resulting from his word comparisons (1969, 100):

(I) Dacian and Baltic:
  a. firmly established comparisons 60
  b. probable comparisons 16
(II) Thracian and Baltic:
  a. firmly established comparisons 56
  b. probable comparisons 19
(III) Thracian, Dacian and Baltic 14

3.400 Milewski, 1947, 21, wrote that in the Middle Ages the Lechitic tribes of the Cassubians (Kashubians), Kujavians and Mazovians in the region of the lower Vistula and Osa, the upper Drwęca, in the lake region and further above the Biebrza and Narew had a common border with the Old Prussian and the Jatvingian tribes, which, at the same time, along with the Lithuanians, Latvians and Curonians, formed a large Baltic linguistic area. Milewski finds that there was a reciprocal influence between the Lechitic and the Old Prussian languages. Of the some 1800 Old Prussian expressions which have been retained in the various texts, about 11 per cent are either borrowings from Polish-Pomeranian dialects or derivatives of such borrowings.

3.401 First Milewski tries to establish from which Slavic language the borrowings enter into Old Prussian. For example, we find OP silkas (EV - 484) from Lith. šiĩkas, which, in turn, came from Old Russian šьlkъ 'silk'; OP wogonis (EV - 366) 'bowl with a vaulted top' from Old Lith. vogõnė 'round, wooden bowl,' cf. Belo-russian vahán 'bowl' (although of Slavic origin this word is not known in the Lechitic languages), etc.[19]

3.402 Milewski, 1947, 22, then says that as far as the great majority of Lechitic borrowings are concerned it is impossible to decide whether they are of Polish or Pomeranian origin. They date from a distant past when the differences between these dialect groupings were not great and our knowledge of them is very insignificant. One should note also that the Polish and Pomeranian influences merged into one whole just like the Polish and Russian influences have merged for Lithuanian.

3.403 Nevertheless one can establish some words as being of clear Pomeranian origin, because in some circumstances the Pomeranian dialects did not undergo the liquid metathesis of the other Slavic languages. Therefore one assumes that borrowings containing unmetathesized talt and tart are probably Pomeranian borrowings, cf., e. g., OP salmis (EV - 420) with Polish szłom

'helmet' from Proto-Slavic *šelmъ, which, in turn,
comes from Proto-Germanic *xelmaz; OP waldwico
(EV - 406) 'knight, warrior, minor nobility'
with Polish włodyka 'member of small gentry' from
the Proto-Slavic stem *vold- 'to possess, to
rule'; OP tarkue (EV - 449) 'harness strap for a
horse' with Polish troki 'strap,' Russian toroká
'saddle-bow straps.'

3.404 According to Milewski, 1947, 24, in the
Middle Ages Pomesania was on the periphery of the
Old Prussian area and received the first waves
of the Lechitic peoples from Pomerania rather
early. (See paragraph 1.120.) On the other hand
the agricultural Sambia (Samland), thickly popul-
ated and at that time the center of the Old
Prussian ethnic group, was free from Polish
colonization. Thus the first recipients of
Lechitic expressions were the Pomesanians who
passed them on later to the Sambians. One
could anticipate a greater number of Polish
borrowings in Pomesanian than in Sambian and one
could assume that Polish borrowings in Sambian
came through the mediation of Pomesanian. On
the other hand Milewski, 1947, 26, suggests that
this may have been only one of the routes through
which Polish words could have penetrated into
Sambian, since we find in Sambian supūni 'lady,
mistress,' a word foreign to Pomesania. Obviously
this came by another route, possibly from the
Mazovian lakes.

3.405 Milewski, 1947, 26-27, says that some of
the Christian terminology came from Polish along
with the new concepts. Some words borrowed from
Polish merely show, however, that the latter
language had more prestige than Old Prussian,
since the concepts certainly had already existed
in Old Prussian. Thus in the Pomesanian dialect
(here represented by words from the Elbing
vocabulary) the concept for 'head' was certainly
originally expressed by the word galwo (= Lith.
galvà 'id.,' cf. also [EV - 78] pergalwis 'nape
of the neck'), although in the Elbing vocabulary
galwo (EV - 504) is translated to mean 'the
upper part of the shoe' whereas the borrowing
from Polish, viz., glawo (EV - 68) has been

59

established with the meaning of 'head.'[20] (It
appears to me, however, that Bezzenberger's
opinion, 1904, 159, that glawo is just a misinterpretation on the part of the scribe is
probably right.) Milewski, 1947, 27, cites as
another example of his thesis the fact that both
Proto-Lechitic šołmъ (Polish szłom) and OP kelmis
(EV - 474) originally meant 'helmet' since both
were borrowed from Proto-Germanic *xelmaz, but
the borrowing from Lechitic, viz., OP salmis
(EV - 420) 'helmet' established itself in the
Pomesanian dialect, whereas the native kelmis
came to mean 'hat.'[21]Milewski's third example is
OP smoy, a native word which means just 'man,'
as opposed to OP ludis (EV - 185; borrowed from
Polish ludzie) which means 'head of a household.'
Milewski continues further, 1947, 27-28, saying
that the semantic shift supposed by the existence
of OP supūni 'mistress' to supana (GrA - 67)
'betrothed' was only possible on the background
of the medieval cult of woman and denoted an
elevation in worth.
3.406 Milewski says further that it is characteristic that such a change in meaning took place in
the Pomesanian rather than in the Sambian
dialect. Thus, for example, Polish sąd originally
meant 'judgement, court, punishment,' but when
borrowed into Old Prussian we find sūndan
'punishment' along side of the native OP līgan
'court.' In Milewski's opinion this shows that
in the centrally located Sambian dialect Polish
did not have the same prestige, since the Polish
borrowings penetrated into Sambian through other
Old Prussian dialects.
3.407 In addition to a careful analysis of all
the Polish borrowings in Old Prussian, Milewski,
1947, 42, tries to establish a chronology of
borrowings in the light of the historical
phonology of Polish. For example, the oldest
borrowings reflect Slavic ъ as u and ь as i, cf.
e.g., OP tuckoris (EV - 454) 'weaver' from Proto-
Slavic * tъkar'ь, etc. Milewski says that in
view of the archaic form of the borrowings, they
must have gone into Old Prussian at the very
latest in the ninth century. I would doubt the

probative value of this particular word since
initial *tk- is not an admissible phonemic
sequence in Old Prussian anyway. Some vowel
would have to be inserted between the initial t-
and the immediately following -k.
3.408 Milewski, 1947, 43-44, believes that
Slavic y was originally pronounced something like
ui and that such a pronunciation is indicated in
OP suiristio (EV - 692, corrected from sutristio)
'whey' < Polish serzysko (Slavic *syrisko, loc.
sg. *syriščě), OP zuit 'enough,' cf. Polish syt
'full,' OP waldwico (see para. 3.403) in which
-wi- = -ui-. I doubt that the Old Prussian
rendering proves a diphthongal pronunciation for
Slavic. For the Balts the closest rendering of
a high central unrounded vowel is the Baltic
sequence /ui/.
3.409 One of the most characteristic features
of the Polish Pomeranian dialects is the shift
of ě and e to a and o respectively before the
hard consonants t, d, s, z, ł, r, n. Already at
the end of the ninth century we find the name of
the Silesian tribe Dziadoszan written as
Dadosesani by the Bavarian geographer, according
to Milewski, 1947, 45. At the same time in the
Old Prussian texts we find a series of expressions
of Lechitic origin which do not show the shift
of ě to a. Milewski includes here OP swetan (EV -
792) 'world' as well as swītan from the IIIrd
catechism (cf. Polish świat 'id.'), OP mestan
(EV - 796) 'city' from Proto-Slavic *město, cf.
Polish miasto 'city.' On the other hand we find
the same word in the form myasta (GrA 2,
corrected from maysta). The passage of e to o
is noted in OP schostro (GrA 70) 'sister' from
Polish siostra.
3.410 Another indicator of the date of borrowing is furnished by the history of the Polish
nasal vowels. From the beginning of the 13th
century the Proto-Slavic nasal vowels had merged
as ą. Towards the end of the 14th century ą̄
began to move in the direction of ǫ and its short
counterpart in the direction of ę. Thus we find
in the words mynsis (EV - 380) 'fat' and ratinsis
(EV - 368, 540) 'chain' from Old Polish *m'ęž >

miąż(sz) 'flesh' and Old Polish *r'et'ędz, Modern
Polish rzeciądz, wrzeciądze 'hasp.' On the other
hand in OP wumbaris (EV - 556) 'pail, bucket' we
see the retention of the back rounded nasal vowel,
cf. Modern Polish węborek 'id.' See Milewski, 1947,
47.
3.411 Milewski, 1947, 48, claims that such a word
as OP curtis (EV - 700) 'greyhound' was borrowed
from Old Polish at a time when the r̥ sounded
something like ur before it became ar (sometime
after the end of the first millenium A.D.), cf.
Modern Polish chart 'id.' (But see Schmid,
1958b and paragraph 10.022.) On the other hand
OP karczemo (EV - 382) 'tavern, public house'
must have been borrowed from Polish at a time
after the passage of *r̥ to ar, but prior to the
loss of the Slavic jers. According to Milewski,
Polish karczma is from Proto-Slavic *kr̥čьma.
3.412 Milewski, 1947, 49, claims that OP t and
d in place of Proto-Lechitic t' and d' must show
a word to have been borrowed in the first millenium
A.D., e.g., OP tisties (EV - 184) 'father-in-law,'
cf. Old Polish cieść from Proto-Slavic *tьstь.
If the word had been borrowed at a time when t
and d had become t' and d', then we would find a
velar stop, cf., e.g., OP rikisnan (EV - 107)
'back' apparently borrowed from an Old Polish
*r'it'ez'n'e reconstructed on the basis of Czech
řitézně and Modern Polish rzyć 'buttocks.' In
this word OP k represents the Polish t' which
must have already been pronounced differently
from the way it was when it was borrowed as OP t.
3.500 Sabaliauskas, 1966, 110-113, wrote that
the question of Prussianisms in Lithuanian is
complicated and poorly investigated. It is
quite possible that some words of unclear origin
are Old Prussian, but frequently it would be
impossible to show this, because the word might
not be attested either in place names or in any
of the few Old Prussian texts. In addition, the
fundamental means of establishing such borrowings,
viz., phonetic criteria, do not give much help,
since the Old Prussian and Lithuanian languages
are so close. According to Sabaliauskas, 1966,
110, Būga claimed that the Lithuanian words alùs

'beer,' ýla 'awl,' midùs 'mead,' šárvas 'armor'
came from Germanic into Lithuanian through Old
Prussian.
3.501 According to Sabaliauskas, 1966, 110,
a number of Prussianisms in Lithuanian are found
in the works of Bretkūnas, e.g., ausinas 'gold'
(= standard Lith. auksìnis), auskalis 'goldsmith'
(= standard Lith. auksakalỹs), cf. OP ausis (EV -
523) 'gold'; balgnas 'saddle' (= standard Lith.
baĩnas 'id.'), balgnuoti 'to saddle' (= standard
Lith. balnóti 'id.'), cf. OP balgnan (EV - 441)
'saddle,' etc.

In the meaning of 'yeast' Lith. dragès is
known in the works of Bretkūnas (cf. OP dragios
[EV - 386] 'yeast'), but the word is also known
in Lithuanian dialects with the meaning 'sediment
created when fat is removed from smelts (fish).'
Latv. dradži 'sediment from melted fat' is also
known. These words are connected with Russian
drožži, Polish drożdże, Old Icelandic dregg
'yeast.' But the relationship between Lith.
drãgès, Latv. dradži and OP dragios is not quite
clear. Most likely this is a common Baltic word
which developed new meanings in Lithuanian and
Latvian, retained the old meaning in Old Prussian,
but came from Old Prussian again into Lithuanian
with the meaning 'yeast.'
3.502 Būga, 1958, 478, had assumed that Lith.
jušė 'fish soup,' with which one can also compare
Slavic juxa (cf. OP iuse [EV - 377] 'bullion,
meat soup') and Lith. kriáušė, kráušė 'pear'
(cf. OP crausy [EV - 617] 'pear tree'; crausios
[EV - 618] 'pears') were borrowings from Old
Prussian, since the words stem from East Prussian
Lithuanian dialects and we find š instead of s,
i.e., š < *sy, viz., *yūsyē (> *yūš'ē), gen. sg.
*krausyas > *kraušyās. Sabaliauskas, 1966, 111,
also notes the Old Prussian place names Crawsyn,
Krawsselawken and casts doubt on the Old Prussian
origin of the Lithuanian word, because we also
find Latv. krausis, although he notes that the
word is found only once in an area not far from
the Lithuanian border (in the region of Barta).
The Old Prussian name for the pear fits well with
the area of the Slavic names with initial k-,

cf. Bulgarian kruša, Serbo-Croatian krȕška,
Polish krusza, Upper Lusatian krušva, Lower
Lusatian kruša.

3.503 Sabaliauskas, 1966, 111, thinks that Lith.
malūnas 'mill' may well be a Prussianism, since it
occurs for the first time in Lithuanian in the
Bretkūnas Bible translation where it is glossed with
a Slavic word (...akmo maluna [melniczas] 'millstone' Luke 17, 2). Apparently Bretkūnas, who
knew, of course, Old Prussian, thought that the
Lithuanians might not know this word. Lith.
malūnininkas 'miller' may have been created by D.
Klein who apparently knew Old Prussian, since in
the matriculation list of the University of
Königsberg we find the inscription: D. Klein,
Tilsensis. Borusus (i.e., Prussian). In Old
Prussian, of course, we find the words malunis (EV -
316) 'mill,' malunakelan (EV - 321) 'mill wheel,'
malunastabis (EV - 319) 'millstone.'

3.504 Lith. pãvirpas 'poor fellow,' nom. pl.
pavirpaí 'simple people, folk' is considered by
most investigators to be a borrowing from OP powirps
'free' (i.e., it denotes a laborer who is not
bound to the soil), according to Sabaliauskas,
1966, 112. See also paragraph 10.087.

3.505 Lith. pydyti is usually compared with OP
pīdai 'carries,' pidimai 'we carry,' but still,
according to Sabaliauskas, 1966,, 112, the meaning
of Samogitian pýdyti could have developed even
without Old Prussian influence, cf. Samogitian
pýdyti, Latv. pîdît 'to chase' the meaning of which
arose from the interjections pý, pỹ. From the
meaning 'to chase fast' the meaning 'to carry
rapidly with difficulty' could have arisen. The
word pýdyti is used with the latter meaning in
Samogitian dialects, cf. also pýdyti 'to drag a
wagon from a swamp with difficulty' from which the
meaning 'to carry' may have come.

3.506 Lith. ušės 'week, birth,' ušininkė, ušiaunykė,
ušaunykė 'woman in child birth,' ušios 'bearing of
children' is probably borrowed from Old Prussian,
cf. OP usts, uschts, wuschts 'sixth.' Sabaliauskas,
1966, 113, says that in a manuscript dictionary
from Königsberg (now Kaliningrad) one finds ušės
with the meaning 'week.' This meaning developed

64

on the model of the German word Woche 'week.' In
German the plural die Wochen 'the weeks' can be
used with the meaning 'time of birth,' cf. German
in Wochen sein (liegen), in Wochen kommen 'to bear,
to give birth.' Sabaliauskas notes that the geography of this word confirms its Old Prussian
origin. The native Lithuanian forms are šéšios,
šešiáuninkė which have the Latvian correspondences
sešas 'bearing, giving birth' and sešiniece,
sešniece 'woman in child birth.'
3.507 Sabaliauskas, 1966, 110-113, also discusses
other Lithuanian words which may be of Old Prussian
origin: burvalkas 'suburb,' (cf. OP burwalkan
'yard'), giegalas 'diver' (cf. OP gegalis [EV -
759] 'small diving bird'), pušnìs 'fisher's boots,
high-top boots' (cf. OP pusne [EV 499] 'boot'),
saliūbas 'marriage, wedding' (cf. OP salūban 'id.'),
saváitė 'week' (cf. OP sawayte [EV - 16] 'week').
The word saváitė was encountered in East Prussian
Lithuanian writings and was popularized in the
journal of the Lithuanian national renaissance
Aušra in the last century and from there it spread
to the standard language. We find possissawaite
(EV - 20) 'Wednesday' on the model of German Mittwoch (cf. Lith. pùsė 'half'), but this latter word
was shortened to pussewaite in East Prussian
Lithuanian dialects. As a result of a misunderstanding from pussewaite (pusse = 'half') a new
word for 'week,' waite was created. But according
to Sabaliauskas, 1966, 113, both Nesselmann and
F. Kurschat in whose dictionaries this word appears
say that the word is hardly known. In fact, as
Sabaliauskas points out, Nesselmann himself, 1873,
138, said that the word waite should be removed
from his Lithuanian dictionary.[22]
3.508 There are apparently several Prussianisms
in Latvian also according to Sabaliauskas, 1966,
113. He lists Latv. ķermenis 'body' (cf. OP
ķērmens 'id.'), vaidelis 'pagan priest' (cf. OP
waidelotte). Most probably Latv. glīsis 'amber'
comes from Old Prussian through Curonian, cf. the
OP glēsum mentioned by Tacitus.
3.600 Bielfeldt, 1970, 46-48, gives a list of
German words taken from Old Prussian and used in
the documents of the Teutonic knights between the

14th and 16th centuries: <u>dassumptin</u> 'tenth' -
OP <u>dessimpts</u> 'id.'; <u>sweike</u> 'work horse' (see
Trautmann, 1910, 443); <u>(jor)porlenke</u>, <u>parlenke</u>
'(yearly) tax,' cf. Lith. <u>perleñkis</u> 'portion due,
share owed'; <u>sunde</u> 'cash fine' - OP <u>sundan</u>
'punishment,' cf. Polish <u>sąd</u> 'court' which
Bielfeldt, 1970, 46, compares with Lith. <u>samdas</u>
'hire'; <u>sorgalio</u> 'wages, compensation (for pro-
tection)'; <u>porrepil</u> 'contribution for military
expeditions,' cf. Lith. <u>répti</u> 'to include';
<u>palleyde</u> 'subject's estate, what he leaves behind'
is compared with OP <u>polaikt</u> 'to remain,' but it
would seem to me that from the phonological point
of view it would be preferable to connect the word[23]
with Lith. <u>paláidas</u> 'loose, untied, detached' and
<u>paléisti</u> 'to let go, to let slip, etc.'; <u>waidelotte</u>,
<u>waideler</u> 'pagan priest'; <u>craysewisse</u> 'oats' - OP
<u>crays</u> (EV - 289) 'hay'; <u>slusim</u> 'tax, tribute'
(Bielfeldt, 1970, 46, refers to Fraenkel, 1955, 836,
where Fraenkel quotes the by-form <u>slũžmà</u> [of
<u>slũžbà</u>] and it is apparently to this form which
Bielfeldt refers - presumably a similar form
existed in Old Prussian and this form gave rise to
the German form noted by Bielfeldt); <u>witing</u> 'servant
of the order who is of Old Prussian origin' OP <u>witing</u>
cf. Russian <u>vitjaz'</u> 'knight; hero,' Old Norse
<u>vikingr</u> 'viking, pirate,' etc. According to
Bielfeldt, 1970, 46, the German word <u>dwarnik</u> 'farm-
steward' first reached Baltic from Slavic, but
differently from Baltic German <u>dwornik</u> 'house-boy,'
it did not come into German directly from a Slavic
language.
3.601 According to Bielfeldt, 1970, 46, German
<u>Zerm</u>, <u>Zarm</u> 'funeral meal, obsequies' is attested
from the 15th to the 17th centuries (cf. OP <u>sirmen</u>,
Lith. <u>šermens</u> 'funeral meal'). Bielfeldt, 47, also
mentions <u>kaddig</u> 'juniper' and <u>pawirpen</u>, <u>powirpen</u>
'hired worker.' Likewise he says that <u>Talk(e)</u>
'voluntary aid, help; banquet' is known in East
German texts in the years 1450 and 1525, cf. OP
<u>tallokinikis</u> (EV - 408) 'free man,' Lith. <u>talkà</u>
'common labor which is rewarded by a banquet
afterwards.'
3.602 Word geography suggests that the following
German words are of Old Prussian origin, although

they are not attested beyond the 19th century:
pintsch, pinsch 'match, tinder' - OP pintys (EV -
372) Lith. pìntis 'tinder'; margéll, marjéll 'maid-
en' - OP mergo (EV - 192), Lith. mergà 'girl'
(this word has spread via East Prussia into Danzig,
Poznan and Silesia and is occasionally found in the
colloquial language); kujel 'boar' OP cuylis (EV -
683; corrected from tuylis), Lith. kuilỹs 'id.';
palwe 'heath' - Lith. plýnas 'bare, treeless,' see
also Sabaliauskas, 1974, and paragraph 9.060; duck,
dogg, dock 'polecat' - OP duckis (EV - 669)
'hamster.'

4.000 The major documents in Old Prussian are the
Elbing vocabulary (EV), Simon Grunau's vocabulary
(Gr) and the I, II and IIIrd Old Prussian
translations of Luther's catechisms. For an
exhaustive treatment of the phonology and morphology
of the catechisms see Schmalstieg, 1974. Besides
these five major documents there are also some
fragments, place names (see Gerullis, 1922) and
personal names (see Trautmann, 1925).
4.100 The Elbing vocabulary is a part of the so-
called Codex Neumannianus which dates from around
1400 and is apparently a copy of the original,
which was composed at the beginning of the 14th or
the end of the 13th century. According to Marchand,
1970, 112, "The Elbing vocabulary presents the
usual kind of conceptual dictionary found in
medieval Latin and German manuscripts... Its only
unusual features are those which bespeak the
Prussian condition, e.g., words for 'sled,' 'fire-
hole,' etc. It is most certainly not, as Berneker
and, following him, Trautmann would have us believe,
drawn up for legal purposes. One wonders what legal
purposes 5 sebengest'ne 'Pleiades,' 38 stopassche
'powdery ashes,' 612 vulbem 'stink-tree,' for
example, might have served." Marchand gives the
following categories: 1. God and the heavens, 2.
time and weather, 3.earth, 4. fire, 5. air, 6.
water, 7. man and his parts, 8. family and
relations, 9. house, 10. farming, 11. wagon and
sled, 12. mill, 13. breads, 14. kitchen and
utensils, 15. potables, 16. government & soldiery,
17. saddler, 18. weaver, 19. tailor, 20. shoemaker
21. smith, 22. bathing, 23. fish, 24. woods, 25.
animals, 26. domestic animals, 27. milk, 28. hunter,
29. birds, 30. crawling things, 31. orbis mundi.
4.101 This Codex Neumannianus was found by F.
Neumann (1792-1869) in the estate of the Elbing
merchant A. Grübnau (1740-1823). In 1868 Neumann
transmitted it to the Elbing city library where it
was retained until World War II, but according to
Mažiulis, 1966, 27, the whereabouts of this
valuable manuscript is now unknown. Mažiulis
writes that this codex has four parts: 1. the

Lübeck law, 2. the Pomesanian law, 3. the old
Polish law and 4. the Elbing vocabulary. The codex
has 186 pages, the last page of which, page 186 is
blank. The Elbing vocabulary occupies the last 17
written pages, viz. 169-185. On p. 185 its author
wrote: "Explicit per manus Petri Holczwesscher De
Mai'en Burg."

4.200 Mažiulis, 1966, 31, describes Simon Grunau's
vocabulary as a vocabulary of about 100 Old Prussian
and German words which Grunau put into his
Preussische Chronik (written between 1517 and
1526) in order to illustrate the Old Prussian
language of which he himself claimed to have a
small knowledge. The original has not survived,
but Mažiulis describes the copies in the following
manner. GrA which was in the Königsberg university
library is a 17th (or beginning of the 18th)
century copy; GrC (a copy made about 1750) formerly
in the Königsberg government archives; GrH, the copy
published by K. Hartknoch.

4.201 In 1949 Eduard Hermann published a copy of
a manuscript version of Simon Grunau's vocabulary
found in the Göttingen university library. This
copy, called GrG by Mažiulis, differs somewhat
from the best previously known version GrA. GrG
dates from the 16th century, whereas GrA dates from
the 17th century.

4.202 GrG is a German-Old Prussian vocabulary
(not Old Prussian-German like GrA). According to
Hermann, 1949, 161, the reason for this is that the
archetype of GrA had been influenced by the Elbing
vocabulary, whereas the purpose of the archetype of
GrG was to show that Old Prussian was a foreign
language and therefore to start from the known and
to go to something unknown. Hermann, 160-161,
says that the order of the words is older in GrG
than in GrA and there are a few words in GrG which
are not to be found in GrA, thus, Meinse 'meat,
flesh' (15), Soye 'rain'(46), nackt 'night' (58),
mynkus 'belly, paunch' (63), Kreitzno 'pitcher' (77),
ny thuer thu 'don't you have it?' (89), Dam thor
'I will give it to you' (90), Kayat thu 'where will
you go?' (94). Words lacking in GrG are: wisge
'oats' (11), schostro 'sister' (70), kyrteis
'strike, hit' (78), tickers 'judge' (82), merguss

'maid' (88), saydit 'may (God) watch over you'
(93), pirmas 'at first' (94), eykete 'come here'
(95), iest 'he is' (98), gosen (for goven) 'bit of
excrement' (99). Hermann points out that among
these words there are three Polish words, viz.,
schostro, iest and gowen and two Lithuanian words
merguss and eykete. Supposedly the author of the
original of GrG intentionally removed these foreign
words. On the other hand he did not replace them
with pure Old Prussian words. merguss, of course,
was unnecessary because merga (GrG 52) sufficed.
tickers 'ein richter' (originally, of course,
'a judge,' but probably understood as 'rechter,'
i.e., 'righteous man') was unnecessary because of
dyrsos gyntos = German from man 'a good man.' GrA
saydit is unclear to linguists; perhaps it was to
the editor of GrG also. Finally, according to
Hermann, 1949, 160, the words kyrteis 'strike' and
pirmas 'first' were unnecessary, the latter because there was no word for 'second' either. Since
the word for 'brother' was lacking the word schostro
could be omitted also. Thus only the word wisge
'oats' seems to be a real lacuna.
4.203 Hermann, 1949, 161, decides that Simon
Grunau, whose speech was inclined to Low German,
could not have been the author of the GrG prototype,
since we find on the German side the High German
form apffell (GrG 91) as opposed to eppil (GrA 84)
'apple.' Hermann says that the strongest proof is
GrG 17 Treuge 'dry,' the phonological form of which
is limited to a small area of High German. In
addition GrG 32 Erbeis 'pea' with a -b- as opposed
to GrA arwes speaks in favor of a southern origin
for GrG.
4.204 Hermann, 1949, 162, lists some of the
mistakes of GrA along with the correct transmission
found in GrG. Thus GrA translates OP gayde (9) as
German (Ger) Gerste 'barley' and OP mayse (10) as
Ger Wesze 'wheat,' a clear reversal of the correct
translations found in GrG where OP gaide (13)
translates Ger Weisse 'wheat' and OP Maise translates Ger Gerste 'barley.' Bezzenberger, 1874b,
1245, had already corrected GrA 30 meida ≠ Ger
hechtt 'pike (fish)' to lieda. In GrG Ger Hecht
(70) is translated as OP lyda. In GrA OP gnabsem
(32) is translated as Ger henff 'hemp, whereas in

GrG Ger hanfsam is the correct translation for OP
gnabsem (66), which really means 'hemp seed.'
Mažiulis, 1966, 251, reads GrG 66 as containing
Ger hanfsaet. GrA 51 gotte is translated by Ger
ein Haus 'a house' whereas GrG 26 has the correct
OP botte, cf. Lith. bùtas 'apartment.' GrA 68 OP
haltnyka is translated as Ger kindt 'child.'
Probably intended is the Slavic loanword which
begins with m- (cf. Russ. mal'čik 'boy,' etc.);
GrG 53 has OP maltnicka. GrA 72 has OP aucte =
Ger potter 'butter.' GrG 61 has OP ancte, surely
the correct form, cf. (EV - 689) anctan = Ger
puttir 'butter.' GrA 85 OP moska is rendered by
Ger leimet, the meaning of which is unclear
according to Endzelīns, 1943, 212. GrG 73 Ger
Wimat = OP mosla; Wimat is Middle High German
wirmât, wimmet 'vintage.' According to Hermann,
162, OP mosla could be connected with OCS mъstъ,
Ger Most 'must.' GrA 86 has angle = Ger nolden;
GrG 75 has augle = Ger Nolde 'a weed with pink
blossoms and a red root, Sherardia arvensis'
Because of its rapid rate of reproduction it was
dubbed augle and the word is to be connected with
OP auginnons 'grown up' and Lith. áugti 'to grow.'
4.205 Fraenkel, 1950a, 120-121, approves of
Hermann's 1949, 163, analysis of GrG 50 gema =
Ger Fraw which supports the reading gemia of GrA
21. The latter is supposedly remodeled on analogy
with the Baltic root gem- 'to be born,' cf. Lith.
gìmti, Latv. dzimt 'to be born,' OP gemmons 'born.'
I find this solution hardly credible and attribute
it to the philologists' desire to believe in the
scribal rendition. It seems to me much more likely
that both forms are merely an error for *gena,
cf. OP genno (EV - 188). In my opinion Trautmann's
1910, 337, correction to genna still stands.
4.206 Hermann, 1949, 164, quotes Dam thor = Ger
Ich wils euch geben (GrG 90) and says that dam =
Lith. dúomi 'I give' and that thor is an abbreviated
form of turri 'have, has' without the final -i and
that the expression is to be translated as 'I give
it, I have it.' Fraenkel, 1950a, 121, suggests,
however, that tur is not a form of turīt 'to have,'
but rather is to be compared with the Latvian
adverb tur 'there,' which was created in turn as

a counterpart for kur 'where, where to.' The
meaning is then, in Fraenkel's opinion, 'I give it
there.' I personally prefer Mažiulis' 1966, 251,
correction of the expression to Dam thoi. One
might wonder whether thoi is not perhaps an enclitic
dative singular, cf. Old Church Slavic ti and
Sanskrit te, both of which could be reconstructed
as *toi. The fact that Old Prussian has a 2nd sg.
dat. tebbei 'to you (sg.)' also is no hindrance,
since both Old Church Slavic and Sanskrit have also
full forms of the dative, cf. OCS tebě and Skt.
tubhyam.
4.207 Hermann, 1949, 164, says that kayat thu =
Ger Wo wiltu hin 'where do you want to go?' contains kay 'where' and -at (= the Latvian preposition
at 'to') used postpositively. There is no verb
and thu denotes 'you (sg.).' Fraenkel, 1950a,
121-122, objects that at- in Baltic is only a
prefix and only here and there used as a preposition
in Latvian. Fraenkel suggests that when one takes
into consideration GrA 83 ny koytu = Ger wiltu nit
'won't you,' ny koyto GrG 100, iquoitu from the
IIIrd catechism one should correct kayat thu to
kay kaithu. The repetition of the initial letters
brought about the remodeling and t and i are
similar in GrG. I personally would suggest that
kayat was a scribal error for *kayta and that the
whole expression is to be phonemicized as /kai
tu/ and translated as 'do you want?' The word for
'where' has just been omitted in transmission.
4.208 Hermann, 1949, 164, quotes GrG 95 as: Behut
dich Got - (OP) Warbo thi Dawes 'may God protect
you.' Hermann divides up the first OP word into
war = wara, which, he says, is a 3rd person
indicative used in hortative meaning and is from a
previously unknown verb warton 'to protect' and bo
'surely.' Likewise, according to Hermann, the word
thi 'you (sg.)' is new to the Old Prussian
vocabulary. I would suggest that thi is either a
scribal error with no final -n, cf. tien, tin
attested in the catechisms and which I have
phonemicized as either /ten/ or /tin/ (1974, 139),
or else that it represents an allegro form in which
the final nasal was not pronounced.
    Fraenkel, 1950a, 121, corrects the first word
of the expression to warto, cf. Lith. dialect

varta from Pol. warta 'guard.' OP warto, in
Fraenkel's opinion, is a denominative just like
Pol. wartować 'to keep guard.' The only difference
is that warto has an -aiŏ- suffix corresponding to
the fundamental word.

I would suggest even a third explanation. I
propose that OP warbo is actually a borrowing from
German werben. According to Kluge, 1967, 853, the
original meaning of the word is 'sich drehen,' but
he also gives the meaning 'sich bemühen,' so one
might imagine an expression meaning 'may God exert
himself for you, may God turn his attention to
you,' for the Old Prussian expression. Another
possibility is that werben in the sense of 'to
recruit' may have been borrowed into Old Prussian
and have taken on the meaning 'to take into the
service of.' Thus the sense might have been 'may
God take (recruit) you into his service.' The verb
is known in Polish as werbować and Russian
verbovat' 'to recruit.'24
4.209 Hermann, 1949, 166, writes that GrG is a
perfect clean copy on the best paper and in a
leather binding. Then Hermann poses a number of
questions: Who caused the manuscript to be
produced and who suggested the inclusion of the
extract from Grunau? Why are none of the numerous
misprints corrected? How did the manuscript come
to Göttingen? Was the donor Bishop Mörlin of
Samland who was superintendent for a long time in
Göttingen? This last supposition seems likely
because at the founding of the University of
Göttingen the basic holdings of the university
library were created by combining the libraries of
the former gymnasium and churches.
4.210 Rosenkranz, 1957, 113, in his analysis of
Hermann's 1949 edition of Simon Grunau's
vocabulary (GrG) notes that some of the criticisms
of Grunau made by Endzelīns, 1944, 13-14, are
at least partially unjustified. Thus Endzelīns
said that some words are written without endings
or with mutilated endings. On the other hand GrG
has mangos Sones 'whore's son' as opposed to GrA
mangoson and instead of GrA maytter 'rogue' we find
GrG Maiters.
4.211 Rosenkranz remarks further that it is

73

indisputably true that the order of the words in GrG is significantly nearer the original than in any of the other texts. On the other hand, he concludes, 1957, 116, that the reconstructed form of the original of GrA is quite different from the text of GrG and it seems that both GrA and GrG are separated from the archetype by a number of intermediate texts. It seems that in many places both groups of words and sentences were omitted. By combining the data from both texts one can make sense and even reconstruct a conversation from daily life. According to Rosenkranz, 1957, 117, fn. 17, it is unclear who assembled the material of the vocabulary. Apparently it comes from conversations from daily life; in any case it hardly seems to have been used for ecclesiastical or administrative purposes. It also seems unlikely that it was put together by Grunau himself, since then the clearly practical aspects could not be explained. Most probably Grunau had shortened and remodeled an already existing conversation book.

4.212 In 1968b, Valentin Kiparsky mentioned that his former teacher at the University of Helsinki, Prof. J.J. Mikkola, had once shown him an Old Prussian catechism bound together with another smaller work. Mikkola had mentioned that the book was a bibliographical rarity, but unfortunately Prof. Kiparsky could not remember to whom the book had belonged and where it had been kept. In 1959, Prof. Kiparsky had received a letter from Mrs. Sigrid Bigalke, the daughter of the famous Balticist, Georg Gerullis. Mrs. Bigalke wrote that in her father's copy of Trautmann's Die altpreussischen Sprachdenkmäler there was a note to the effect that an additional copy of the Old Prussian IInd catechism was located in Helsinki according to Mikkola. In 1968 this bibliographical riddle was solved.

4.213 In 1970a, 219, Kiparsky wrote that during the cataloguing of the manuscript division the librarian Henrik Grönroos and the assistant librarian Jarmo Suonsyrjä (a man with training in Baltic studies) ran across a large manuscript volume entitled Monumenta Prussica I (Signature A ö IV 9), which had apparently stood untouched since the time of

Mikkola. This volume is one of the ca. 24,000 books and manuscripts which were given to the Helsinki university library in 1901 by captain Aleksandrov, an illegitimate son of the grand duke Konstantin Pavlovič (1779-1831), a younger brother of Alexander the First. It is impossible to trace the volume any further back.

4.214 It consists of 1,325 compactly written pages and two folded sketches (plans of the Königsberg library). The author is a certain 'T. S. B. Regiomontanus,' most probably a Königsberg librarian, a man who had apparently planned to publish the manuscript, since there are instructions for the printer. Kiparsky, 1970a, 220, gives a complete description of the contents of the volume, but notes that Mr. Suonsyrjä intends eventually to investigate this text more thoroughly.

4.215 Probably the most interesting thing about this manuscript is that it contains another copy of Simon Grunau's vocabulary, but with Latin translations of the Old Prussian words rather than German translations. In his 1970a, 220-222, article Kiparsky reprints the vocabulary keeping to the same lines as in the manuscript. For this manuscript Kiparsky suggests the letter F (which we will call GrF here in order to be consistent with the system used for the other manuscripts), because previously the letter F was missing in the alphabetical order from A - H and because the manuscript is kept in Helsinki, Finland.

4.216 Kiparsky, 222, writes that GrF is obviously based on GrA rather than GrH, the latter being unknown apparently to the author of GrF. In any case in those cases where GrA and GrH differ, GrF agrees with GrA. Naturally GrF cannot derive from GrC which is dated almost 60 years later, but certain errors common to GrC and GrF seem to indicate a common source.

4.217 The unknown author of GrF apparently translated Grunau's German into Latin himself and thereby introduced certain errors which are either the result of his ignorance of obsolete or dialect words or else the result of the lack of a good Latin translation.

For example in order to translate OP Ruggis

the author of GrF used Latin Ador 'spelt' instead
of the correct Latin Secale, i.e., German
rockke 'rye.' OP Pogeys which is translated in
GrA as trinck 'drink' is translated in GrF as
Latin Potus. OP Pogeys is certainly a second
singular imperative meaning 'drink.' Presumably
the author of GrF assumed that German trinck was a
noun rather than a verb and thus he chose incorrectly
the Latin noun Potus rather than the appropriate
form of the verb.
4.218 In his Prussian Chronicle Simon Grunau also
gives a distorted version of the Lord's Prayer,
which Grunau claims to be a magic prayer used by
the Old Prussian heathen priests. Below I give the
prayer in the form which is found in Hermann, 1948,
20, as quoted from Blese, 1947, 25:
  Nossen Thewes
Cur thu es delbas Sweytz gischer tho wes wardes Penag
  munis Thol,
be mystlastilbi Tholpes prahes Girkade delbeszisne
  tade symmes Semmes
Worsunij dodi mommys An nosse igdemas mayse, unde
  Gaytkas Pames
mumys Nusze nozeginu Cademes Pametam musen
  Prettaune kans.
Newede munis lawnā Padomā swalbadi munis No wusse
 _ Loyne Jhesus
ame.
4.219 Already in 1845, xvi, Nesselmann had written
that this prayer shows that Grunau, who had said
that he knew a little Old Prussian, apparently
didn't know very much. Although there are a few
words which might appear to be Old Prussian, such
as Nossen Thewes 'Our Father,' semmes 'land,' and
wede 'lead,' Nesselmann says that the whole thing
is more probably a corrupted and incorrectly
transcribed Latvian translation. Evidence of this
is to be found in the following words which
Nesselmann considered to be Latvian rather than
Old Prussian (forms in parentheses are Nesselmann's
normalizations): Thewes (tehws) 'father,' delbas
(debbessis) 'heaven,' sweytz (śwehts) 'hallowed,'
thowes wardes (taws wards) 'thy name,' penag
(nahk) 'come,' mums 'us' (Hermann, 1948, 20 has
munis), prahes (prahts) 'will,' semmes 'earth,'

76

dodi 'give,' mayse 'bread,' pames 'forgive,'
pametam 'we forgive,' prettaunekans (parradneekem)
'debtors,' wede 'lead,' lawna 'evil,' wusse
(wisse) 'all,' loyne (launa, loune) 'evil.'
4.220 Hermann, 1948, examines each word of the
Lord's Prayer given above and he comes to the
conclusion that the prayer is indeed in Old
Prussian rather than Latvian. 1. Nossen is the
genitive of mes 'we' and has cognates in the Old
Prussian IIIrd catechism. 2. In thewes 'father'
final -es is weakened from -as, and we also find
with this meaning OP tawas, but thetis (EV - 171)
'grandfather' and thewis (EV - 176) 'father' also
have a stem vowel e. 3. cur 'where' used for 'which'
as in many languages, e.g., Lithuanian. 4. thu es
'thou art' follows perhaps the German construction
as in the Old Prussian catechisms. In this text,
according to Hermann, 1948, 21, the form thu is
necessary, since the shortened form es 'art' is used
which could not have been distinguished from est
(3rd sg.) in position before the following d- of
debbes. 5. debbes 'in heaven' is probably in the
locative case of the consonantal declension with a
change of meaning as in Latvian and Slavic from
'clouds' to 'heaven.' Old Prussian has dangus
'heaven' in both the Elbing vocabulary and the
catechisms. 6. sweytz 'holy, hallowed.' Hermann,
1948, 21-22, suggests that in the original there
may have been a form swentz with the n marked by
a hook as in dangonsun in an Old Prussian fragment
of the Lord's Prayer, a photocopy of which appears
in Mikalauskaitė, 1938, 103 [not 101, as noted by
Hermann, 1948, 22]. The stroke of the letter t may
have touched the hook and appeared to be a y to a
later copyist. Thus the form is to be restored as
swentz and compared to swints 'holy' attested in
the catechisms. 7. gischer 'be' or 'may it remain
[until the end].' According to Hermann, 1948, 22,
the form is to be read as jiz-jīr(a) from iz-īra,
cf. Lith. iš-būti 'to remain until the end' (the
3rd pres. of Lith. iš-būti would be, however,
either iš-buna or iš-buva in the standard language,
not *iš-yra - WRS). But, according to Hermann,
gischer, with an -e- instead of -i-, is to be
understood as a 3rd pres. indicative with

voluntative meaning. 8. thowes 'thy' as in East
Baltic formed from the genitive, which is tàvo
'thy' in Lithuanian and tava in Sanskrit. Formerly
in Old Prussian only twais 'thy' from Indo-European
*tuoi was known. 9. wardes 'name' again as in East
Baltic. Otherwise Old Prussian has wirds 'word'
and emmens 'name,' the latter being an old neuter
which was transferred to the masculine gender. In
this Lord's Prayer along with the neuter gender the
old word for 'name' was lost and the semantically
related wardes was introduced, according to
Hermann, 1948, 22. The semantic proximity of the
concepts for name and word is illustrated by
Greek ónoma which has shifted in meaning from
'name' to 'word.' 10. penag 'come' with g instead
of k before the following voiced m-. pe- is to be
derived from earlier *pei which in turn must go
back to pre, prei-. -nag is cognate with Latv.
nākt 'to come,' a very common word, which is known
in Lithuanian as nókti 'to become ripe.' Hermann
writes, 1948, 22, that this might not be the only
example of this word in Old Prussian. He claims to
see the first three letters, viz., pei- in
Mikalauskaitė's, 1938, 103, photocopy of the Old
Prussian Lord's Prayer fragment. 11. munis 'us'
comes closest to OP nūmas attested in various
spellings in the IIIrd catechism. Hermann thinks
that the initial m- in the nom. pl. mes 'we' and
acc. pl. mans may have been the impetus for the
metathesis of the nasals. 12. thowe 'thy' is the
nom. sg. fem. possessive pronoun with -e from -a.
13. mystlastibbi 'kingdom,' according to Hermann,
1948, 23, could be corrected to mystlastippi; one
can find vacillations between p and b elsewhere in
Old Prussian. The second element of the word,
-stippi, recalls OP postippin 'whole, all.' Thus
the word stippi could have meant 'totality, entire-
ness.' The initial element of mystlastibbi, viz.,
mystla- can be connected with OP mistran 'prince,'
particularly 'grand master of the order.'
(Hermann, 23, notes that in some handbooks of
paleography one can find a variety of r which is
similar to a variety of l.) Thus the word is to be
reconstructed as mistrastippi and originally
denoted something like 'prince-totality, master of

the order-entireness' and was an elegant translation
of the word for 'kingdom.' Hermann continues with
equally ingenious interpretations to support the
Old Prussian as opposed to the Latvian character of
the text. I am rather suspicious of these interpretations.

Furthermore Hermann, 1948, 27, claims that the
1526 Lord's Prayer must be taken from its position
as the oldest complete monument of Latvian
literature and put in its rightful position at the
peak (an der Spitze) of Old Prussian texts.
4.221 Hermann asserts, 1948, 26, that Grunau was
a falsifier who undertook his falsifying in order
to damage the adherents of the new faith (i.e.,
Protestantism - WRS) and to strengthen the claims
of the king of Poland against the Protestant duke.
Thus in order to depreciate a Lord's Prayer
presumably composed by a Protestant, he invented
the incredible story of his encounter with the Old
Prussian sacrifical priests.
4.222 I give herewith my English translation of the
Latin version as reported by Kiparsky, 1970a, 225:

"For I myself have seen that the Prussians do
not yet use the German language in their incant-
ations. I came across this affair quite by accident
for they are silent and conceal all. I entered into the house of a certain village and found many
men and women in a meeting. A certain old peasant,
their Vaidelota, was preaching a sermon to them.
They all ran up to me with their knives in order to
kill me. The Vaidelota, who encouraged them
verbally, also took part. I thank the god of gods
that I knew a little Old Prussian in which I prayed
them to grant me my life which they were on the
verge of taking. When they heard their language,
they were overjoyed and they all sang sta nossen
rickie, nossen rickie. I was forced, however, to
take an oath on the authority of Percunas not to
mention this to the bishop, who was their lord, and
I swore and gratified those taking part in the
ceremony. Then the Vaidelotas built a high seat
and chair so that it would be near the ceiling.
And they gave their sermon."
4.223 Arguing against Hermann, Schmid, 1962, 262-
263, shows that at least 20 words from Simon Grunau's

Lord's Prayer can be well understood from the point of view of Latvian, but which are in no way clear from the point of view of Old Prussian. 1) Thewes 'father': Latv. Thews (in the 1586 Lord's Prayer) as opposed to OP tāwa in the equivalent position in the IIIrd catechism. 2) Cur 'who' (relative pronoun): used as relative in both Lithuanian and Latvian but in Old Prussian only kas is attested. 3) Es 'thou art': Latv. es as opposed to OP essei (asse, æsse, etc.). 4) Delbas (to be corrected to debbas) 'in heaven': Latv. debbes 'id.' (1586) as opposed to OP endangon. 5) Sweytz 'hallowed': Latv. svēts, svētīts as opposed to OP swints or swintints respectively. 6) Thowes 'thy': Latv. tows (1586) standard Latv. tavs as opposed to OP twais. 7) Wardes 'name': Latv. wārdtcz (1586) standard Latv. vārds as opposed to OP emnes. 8) Penag 'come': Latv. pienāk 'may (it) come' (in the 1586 Lord's Prayer we read enakas), today lai nāk 'may (it) come' as opposed to OP perēit, pergeis, pareysey. 9) Mumys 'us (dat.)': Latv. mums as opposed to OP noumans. 10) Prahes 'will': Latv. prātcz (1586) standard Latv. prāts as opposed to OP quāits. 11) Worsunij 'on': Latv. wūrsson (1586) standard Latv. virs as opposed to OP no, na. 12) Dodi 'give': Latv. dode (cf. Lith. dodi in Mažvydas, standard Latv. dod) as opposed to OP dais. 13) Igdemas = ikde(i)nas: Latv. ik dienas 'each day'; Old Prussian makes use of deinennin, deininan 'daily' in the corresponding passage. 14) Mayse 'bread': Latv. mayse (1586) standard Latv. acc. sg. maizi) as opposed to OP geiti(e)n. 15) Pames, pametam 'forgive, we forgive': Latv. pammet, pammettam (1586) standard Latv. pamet, pametam as opposed to OP etwerpeis, etwērpimai with similar meaning. 16) Nozeginu 'sin, trespass, debt' corresponds to Latv. noziegums as opposed to OP auschautins (acc. pl.). 17) Newede 'do not lead': Latv. nhe wedde (1586) standard Latv. ne ieved as opposed to OP ni weddeis. 18) lawnā padomā 'temptation' (literally 'evil thought'): Latv. ļauns 'evil' and padoms 'thought' (neither Old Prussian nor Lithuanian has a similar construction here. 19) No wusse Loyne 'from all evil'

corresponds to standard Latv. no visa ļauna 'from
all evil' as opposed to OP esse wissaṇ wargan. 20)
Vnde 'and': Latv. unde (1586), today un, as opposed
to OP ir and bhe (cf. Lith. ir and bei 'and').
4.224 Schmid argues convincingly, in my opinion,
that the prayer is not in Old Prussian, but he
does find one aspect of Hermann's argument worthy
of consideration, viz., that Simon Grunau's Lord's
Prayer is not Latvian. Schmid, 1962, 265-270,
then directs his attention to the word prettaunekans
'debtors' (dat. pl.). He feels that Bezzenberger's
1875, 56, connection of this word with Latvian
pretinieks, pretenieks 'adversary, opponent' was right.
Latv. forms in -nieks correspond to Lithuanian
forms in -ninkas and there exist in Lithuanian
many words with the suffix -ninkas added to the
etymological verbal stem -auti giving a common
Lithuanian suffix (or sequence of suffixes)
-auninkas. In addition Lithuanian verbs in -auti
frequently correspond to Latvian verbs in -uot, e.
g., Lith. skaláuti, Latv. skaluot 'to wash,' Lith.
úogauti, Latv. uoguot 'to gather berries.' Thus on
the basis of the existing Latv. pretuoties 'to
oppose, to resist' one can reconstruct a *pretauti
which must have stood as the base from which
prettaunekans was derived. Schmid, 1962, 267,
then draws the conclusion that prettaunekans must
belong to a Latvian dialect (or to a language which
is very close to Latvian), in which derivatives
with -auti were still present at the beginning of
the 16th century. Since the basic word pret
excludes Lithuanian, Old Prussian and Jatvingian
on the one hand and on the other hand the twenty
points already given demonstrate the proximity of
Latvian, where, however, the verbal class in -auti
no longer exists, Schmid decides that the word
comes from a Curonian Latvian dialect and that the
Lord's Prayer is either in this dialect or in the
Curonian language itself.
4.225 Finally Schmid, 1962, 271, draws five
conclusions: 1. In phonology, morphology, syntax
and choice of vocabulary this Lord's Prayer shows
a certain independence from the Latvian
translations of the Lord's Prayer dated from the
middle of the 16th century. a. It seems likely

that -ei- is retained, that tautosyllabic -n-
remains and that u tends towards o. b.The nom. sg.
of the a-stems appears as -es: thewes 'father,'
wardes 'name.' The dat. pl. ends in -ans < *-ams.
c. The syntax is less influenced by German, e.g.,
there is no definite article and the locative is
used without a preposition, cf. delbas (=debbas)
'in heaven' as opposed to Latv. eckschan debbessis
(1550), exkan debbes (1586); lawnā padomā as
opposed to Latv. exkā kārdenaschenne (1615). d.
In the choice of words we find kade - tade 'both...
and' as opposed to Latv. kā - tā. The word
mystlastilbi 'kingdom' (to be read as *mylastibbe
[literally] 'love') is used for Latv. walstibe.
The expression lawnā padomā is used for
kārdenaschenne, etc. 2. A number of features show
that the language of the document is not central
Latvian (Zemgalian). 3. All of the phonological
characteristics of point 1a. seem to indicate
Curonia as the place of origin. With the exception
of the tendency to open u to o all of these
characteristics are archaisms in comparison with
standard Latvian. 4. The age of the text and the
lack of provable Curonian texts do not let us decide
whether this language is Curonian influenced by
Latvian or whether it is a very archaic version of
Latvian influenced by Curonian. 5. This is surely
not an Old Prussian text.
4.226 Kiparsky, 1970a, 225-226, calls attention
to the fact that in GrF we also find Simon Grunau's
Lord's Prayer. In other manuscripts the first two
words, Nossen Thewes certainly appear to be Old
Prussian, but in this manuscript the first two words
are missing completely so the text does have a more
Latvian aspect. Like Schmid, Kiparsky doubts that
the text is Old Prussian. I reproduce it here
from Kiparsky, 1970a, 226: Cur thu es delbas
zweytzgisch er thowes wardes, penag mynys thowe
mystlalstibe. Tolpes pratres girkade delbeszisnae
tade symmes semmes worsumi. Dodi mommijs an
igdemas mayse unde gaytkas pames muniins nusse
nozegimi cademes pametam musen prettaune kans
nevede munis lawna padoma svalbadi munis nowusse
layne. Jhesus amen. The previously known
manuscripts had mystlastilbi, which Bezzenberger

had corrected to mystlastibbi and Hermann to
mystlastippi. In GrF we find mystlalstibe in
which we see the Latvian word (v)alstība
'government; kingdom,' according to Kiparsky,
1970a, 226, who writes further that mystl is
probably a mistake for wysse, which corresponds to
Latv. visa 'all.' The meaning of mystlalstibe
(= wysse (v)alstība) would be 'entire kingdom.'
The word prettaunekans is, in Kiparsky's opinion,
Latv. *pretavniekam(s) 'enemies, opponents'
instead of the usual pretiniekam 'opponents' (dat.
pl.). Ordinarily the Latvian Lord's Prayer uses
the expression parādniekam 'debtors, guilty ones'
in this context. It seems to me that Kiparsky's
analysis is perfectly correct.
4.300 In 1972, 147, Robinson announced the
discovery of one copy each of the first two Old
Prussian catechisms in the Niedersächsisches
Staatsarchiv in Göttingen. These are bound
together with the Old Lithuanian Rhesa Psalter and
are catalogued as no. 52 in the special Baltic
collection of that library. In the British Museum
Library Robinson found still another copy of the
Ist catechism, the call number of which is C. 40.
e. 52, formerly 3505. e. 38. and the year of
accession is 1857. Robinson was unable to learn
how the British Museum Library had acquired this
copy. He claims that it agrees in every particular
with the copy in the facsimile edition of Mažiulis,
1966, 81-95. In sum then, eight copies of the Ist
catechism are now known to exist. Robinson also
announced the discovery of a third copy of the
Old Prussian IIIrd catechism (call numer 17) in the
Niedersächsisches Staatsarchiv in Göttingen, but
he was unable to determine the former Königsberg
call number.
4.400 Jansons, 1965, examines the report that
William of Modena had translated the grammar of
Donatus into Old Prussian. First Jansons, 25-26,
quotes the passage from the Frankish chronicler
Albericus concerning the events of the year 1228:
"In Prussia, which is beyond Poland, Bishop William
of Modena, papal legate, with his wisdom and
intelligence, not with his bravery, attracted many
pagans to the faith and learned their language

quite well. In addition, with great effort he
translated the principles of the grammatical art,
i.e., Donatus, into that foreign language. In this
year by this means five pagan provinces in these
parts were acquired, viz., Prutia (Prussia),
Curlandia (Curonia, Kurland), Lethonia (Lithuania),
Withlandia (Vidzeme), and Sambria (Samland,
Sambia)."

4.401 Albericus, usually known as Albericus de
Trois-Fontaines (a Cistercian monastery in France)
was a 13th century chronicler, much of whose work
is considered fanciful and unreliable. In the
final portion of his work, where he mentions events
which took place during his life time, he is,
however, considered reliable. (The author of the
text mentioned by Albericus, Donatus, was a Latin
grammarian of the 4th century whose grammar was so
widely known that the name became almost synonymous
with Latin grammar. Donatus' grammar existed in
two parts, the Ars minor [an elementary grammar]
and the Ars maior [a larger grammar].)

4.402 Jansons, 1965, 26, writes that there exists
a considerable literature about William of Modena.
The latter is considered one of the most capable of
papal diplomats of his time in northern Europe.
He arranged the affairs of the Catholic church not
only in Prussia, Latvia and Estonia, but also in
Sweden and Norway. He worked in the Baltic in the
years 1225-1226, 1234, 1238, 1242, 1244 and 1251
and according to Henry of Livonia he preached to
the Livonians and the Latgalians.

4.403 Jansons, 1965, 30, claims that if we read
Albericus' text carefully and compare the testimony
found there with other testimony from that time we
must note the discrepancies in the chronology.
Albericus' information about William comes under
the year 1228, but the rather superficially
described events, i.e., the plans for the
subjugation of Prussia, Curonia, Vidzeme,
Lithuania and Samland are connected with William's
mission to Livonia in 1225 and 1226.

Jansons, 1965, 31, writes that he does not
believe that William of Modena had spent a
sufficient amount of time in Prussia in order to
learn the language and to translate a grammar into
the Old Prussian language. As papal legate he had
many diplomatic tasks and we do not know whether
he produced any other literary works or not. We
know only of his activity as a speaker and preacher.
4.404 Jansons, 31, asks then whether Albericus
was not mistaken. Perhaps Albericus knew of
William of Modena, but Albericus may have written
of William's first trip to Livonia, i.e., to Latvia
and Estonia during which time the translation of
the grammar was made, not into Old Prussian, but
into Zemgalian or some other contemporary
language. Quite possibly William had the help of
Henry of Latvia, who knew Latvian, Livonian
and perhaps Estonian, and who had worked as a
translator for the Lateran council in Rome.
Perhaps this grammar was then later ascribed to
William of Modena.
4.405 Jansons, 31, then says that some kind of
grammatical notes and elementary vocabularies
were necessary not only for teaching the Christian
faith to the young people by teachers and
interpreters, but also for the German preachers.
It is not credible that the German clergy who from
day to day had to speak Livonian, Latvian and
Estonian did not have some notes. Jansons, 32,
bolsters his case by saying that analogy with
other nations leads one to think that there was
writing in Latvian in the 13th century and perhaps
earlier. He compares the case of Gothic in which
Ulfilas wrote already in the 4th century and he
mentions the Russian birch bark writs from the
11th century. Therefore Jansons, 1965, 33,
says that it is inconceivable that the Baltic
peoples who lived as such close neighbors would
not have known the Russian birch bark writs and
would not have used this method of writing for
themselves. He writes further, 34, that it is no
surprise that none of these texts have been
retained until today, because some were written on
cheap, insubstantial material, e.g., birch bark,
and others became unnecessary, difficult to read

85

and were simply destroyed.

4.406 Jansons is certainly right in saying
that the translation by William of Modena may not
have been made into Old Prussian, but there would
seem to be no more reason for believing the
translation to have been made into Latvian than
into any other language of the Baltic area.
Janson's claims on the basis of the fact that other
nationalities had writing are, however, so general
that they could be applied to all the nationalities
of the world with outside contacts at that time.

4.500 In 1969, 275-276, A. Sjöberg reported on
the existence of an Old Prussian fragment in the
1583 Onomasticum published in Berlin by the
alchemist Leonhard Thurneysser. The book is a
dictionary of foreign words from ancient and
mediaeval sources on medicine and alchemy. The
words are reproduced first in their original script
and next in Latin transcription and then supplied
with a detailed explanation in German and frequently
the original source for the word is given.

4.501 Under the heading Deves one finds the
proverb: Deves does dantes, Deves does geitka which
is explained as meaning that since God gives bread
he also gives teeth so that one can bite the bread:
"Diss ist recht Preussisch geredt und bedeutet so
viel als Giebt einem Gott Brot, so gibt er ihm auch
Zehne darzu, darmit ers beissen kan." Niedermann,
Senn, Brender, 1932, 106, give an equivalent
Lithuanian proverb: Diẽvas dãvė dantìs, Diẽvas
duõs iȓ dúonos 'God gave teeth, God will give
bread also.'

4.502 Sjöberg, 276, compares the form Deves with
dewes found in Simon Grunau's vocabulary. He
quotes the form dantis from Trautmann, 1910, 317
and says that the ending -es is difficult to
explain since we would expect perhaps *-ins as the
accusative plural form. Sjöberg suggests that
does = dãs and is a 3rd future form corresponding
exactly to Lith. duõs 'will give.' The first does
may also be a 3rd future, but Sjöberg, 276, quotes
Endzelīns,1944, 179, to the effect that one would
reconstruct for Old Prussian an imperfect das(t)
'he gave,' which, however, merged in form with the
3rd future and therefore became unsuitable.

We cannot tell whether the first <u>does</u> is a future or an imperfect without knowing when the proverb was invented.

4.503 The form <u>geitka</u> 'bread' is also difficult to explain according to Sjöberg, 276. One finds various renderings in Simon Grunau's vocabulary. e.g., (GrG) <u>gaitke</u>, according to Hermann, 1948, 152, (GrG) <u>geitke</u>, according to Mažiulis, 1966, 250, (GrA) <u>geytko</u>, according to Trautmann, 1910, 94, (GrF) <u>Gaytko</u> and <u>Geytko</u>, according to Kiparsky, 1970a, 221. Sjöberg, 1969, 276, says that the most likely possibility is that the word is in the genitive singular just like the corresponding Lith. dúonos. As one can see from 4.601, below I am in complete agreement with Sjöberg's suggestion.

4.600 In 1974 at the fourth meeting of the Association for the Advancement of Baltic Studies in Chicago the discovery of a new fragment in Old Prussian was announced by Prof. Valdis Zeps of the University of Wisconsin. The text has been tentatively transcribed by Zeps as follows:
(1) Kayle rekyse. (2) thoneaw labonache thewelyse (3) Eg. koyte. poyte (4) nykoyte . penega doyte.

A facsimile is provided in Schmalstieg, 1974 and McCluskey, 1975. The translation seems to be:
(1) To your health, sir! (2) You are not a good fellow (or: Aren't you the good fellow?)
(3) If you want to drink (and) (4) do not want to pay money.

4.601 The translation is still far from certain. Parts 1, 3 and 4 above are fairly clear, but part 2 does offer difficulty. The following comments are almost a direct quote from McCluskey, 1975.

The word <u>kails</u> in various spellings is attested by Meletius (Mažiulis, 1966, 31), also as a drinking toast, but possibly a greeting in general. The final -<u>e</u> suggests voc. sg. See 11.200.

<u>rekyse</u> 'master, lord': <u>rekis</u> is one of the attested spellings of the word, which Endzelīns, 1943, 239, would normalize to <u>rīkīs</u>. Other attested spellings include <u>rikijs</u>, <u>rickis</u>, <u>rykyes</u>, <u>reykeis</u> and <u>rikeis</u> and I have suggested, 1974, 54, a phonemicization /rīkej[a]s/, although such a phonemicization must remain highly speculative just like everything else about Old Prussian. The final

-e̱ is problematic, unless we can suppose that the
author of the OP text had some vague notion that
the OP vocative singular ending was -e̱ and added
this ending directly to the nominative singular.
In this case one would suppose that the author was
not a native speaker of Old Prussian, although my
supposition about the genitive singular below
would almost require that the text have been
written down by a native.

Eg ko̱yte 'if you want' possibly should be
equated in its entirety with i̱quoitu 'wenn du
willst.' See Endzelīns, 1943, 183 and Schmalstieg,
1974, 174. The reading 'when he wants' is not
ruled out, since quoite̱ is well attested as the
3rd person form. I have phonemicized this as
/kaitá/ in 1974, 174.

po̱yte 'drink' and do̱yte 'give' we have
translated as infinitives, even though the closest
attested infinitive ending is -twei. The 2nd
pers. pl. imperative is the best formal match;
such an interpretation, however, would necessitate
the reading 'if you want, drink! -- [if] you don't
want -- give money!' It is difficult to imagine a
situation in which this phrase would be
appropriate.

nyko̱yte 'you do not want' is most nearly
paralleled by Grunau's ny ko̱yto 'wiltu nicht.'
(Mažiulis, 1966, 252.)

If one assumes that the OP *o̱-stem genitive
singular ended in -a̱s, as Trautmann, 1910, 216
and Endzelīns, 1943, 58, did, then the form penne̱ga
'some money' offers a problem. One would expect a
partitive genitive here. It may be noted, however,
that Sjöberg, 1969, 276, has apparently found a
partitive genitive in the fragment reported above
in 4.503. An *o̱-stem genitive ending in -a̱ would
fit very well with the evidence of the Slavic
languages (-a̱) and the Baltic languages, Latv. -a̱
and Lith. -o̱ (< *-a̱)

One can also bring as supporting evidence
Leskien's explanation (1876, 33-34) of the Old
Prussian sentence (recorded in Trautmann, 1910, 55,
lines 33-34): tu turei stesmu kurwan kas arrien
tlaku ni stan austin perreist - Du solt dem Ochsen
der da Dreschet nicht das maul verbinden 'Thou

88

shalt not bind the mouth of the ox which threshes.'
According to Leskien the phrase arrien tlāku may be
equivalent to Lith. āria añt laũko 'plows on the
field.' Leskien calls this a 'gewagte Vermuthung'
in view of the corrupt nature of the text, but it
appears that Leskien's interpretation could well
be correct. Since the German pastor did not
understand the text at all he did not have any
chance to 'correct' the true Old Prussian *o-stem
genitive singular form. Thus (t)lāku could be
normalized to *laukā, and we would then have a
third example of the *o-stem genitive singular
form.[25] (The -u after the velar is merely a
reflection of the German scribe's interpretation
of *-ā after a velar consonant, see Schmalstieg,
1974, 9-10.) Thus I am inclined to believe that
the *o-stem genitive singular case in -as is merely an invention of the German pastors. All of us
have met persons who have learned incorrectly some
form in a foreign language and persist in using
this form even though it is incorrect. In addition
one should note the relative cultural position of
Old Prussian vis-à-vis German. Surely the German
was interested only in making himself understood in
Old Prussian and was not interested in the niceties
of Old Prussian morphology. For a further
discussion of the *o-stem genitive singular see
paragraphs 6.011-6.015.

The word thewelyse 'fellow' has the same root
as Lith. tévas, Latv. tēvs 'father' and OP thewis
[EV - 176] 'vetter,' which Trautmann, 1910, 448,
explains as 'father's brother,' i.e. 'uncle.'
The same suffix is found in OP patowelis [EV - 179]
'stepfather.' For the semantics one can compare
Latv. tēvainis 'burly fellow.' The final -e is
unclear. See I1.200.

labonache seems to contain the root which we
know in Lithuanian as lãbas, Latv. labs 'good.'
The rest of the word (suffix?) is obscure.[26]

thoneaw is obscure throughout. The
translation represents an attempt to read the word
as consisting of the 2nd sg. pronoun tu 'you' plus
a 3rd person negative of the verb 'to be,' not
attested, but extrapolated from Latv. nav 'is
not.' Needless to say this interpretation is

quite precarious. Stang (personal communication) thinks that <u>thoneaw</u> might be a proper name. If so, then the couplet may be about the scribe himself, e.g., 'To your health, sir! Tony is a fine fellow, if he wants to drink and doesn't want to pay money.'

It should be pointed out also that the half-lines rhyme: <u>rekyse</u> and <u>poyte/doyte</u>.

4.602 The epigram appears on folio 63ra of MS Basel, Öffentliche Bibliothek der Universität Basel F.V. 2. and immediately follows the <u>Questiones Super Quattuor Libros Methororum</u>, a work written by Nicole Oresme, dated 1369, and immediately precedes the undated <u>Registrum quartium</u> [sic] <u>librorum Methororum</u>. The text may be the earliest dated text of Old Prussian, although the Elbing vocabulary may represent an older state of the language, see Mažiulis, 1966, 27, but the date is not certain since it refers to the completion of the text preceding the colophon, and not to the colophon itself.

The earliest recorded owner of Basel MS F.V. 2. was the physician Peter of Ulm the younger (fl. 1427-1462) who obtained this manuscript at some point in his travels and finally sold it to the University of Basel where it is today. According to McCluskey, 1975, 'An analysis of the text of Oresme's <u>Questiones</u> on Aristotle's <u>Meteorologica</u>, performed in the process of preparing a critical edition, indicates that Basel F.V.2 can be placed in a group of codices that emanated from the University of Prague in the last third of the 14th c.' Since this was a cosmopolitan university it would not be surprising to find a scribe there who knew Old Prussian.

4.700 Mažiulis, 1966, 29-30, lists a number of glosses which are useful in the study of Old Prussian and refers to Trautmann, 1925 and Gerullis, 1922. Among the examples given by Mažiulis are: <u>Ansnicz</u>, <u>Ansnit</u> 'eyn eychwalt (an oak forest,' cf. Lith. ažuolýnas 'id.'; <u>Gaila</u> '(Pol.) <u>Bialla</u> (white)'; <u>Gailgarben</u>, <u>Geylegarben</u> 'Weissenberg (white mountain)'; <u>Gerten</u> alias <u>Huns[felde]</u> 'hen's [field]'; <u>Ilgenpelke</u> - Der lange Bruch, cf. Lith. ilgà pélke 'long swamp'; <u>Iwogarge</u>

'huwinboum (owl's tree)'; Kuke or Chucumbrast
'devil's ford,' cf. Lith. kaũkas 'goblin, gnome'
and brastà 'ford'; Panyen 'swamp'; Rugkelayke
(= *-lauke?) or Rokelawken 'Krebisdorff (crab's
field, village)'; Sawliskresil 'Sonnenstuhl (sun
chair)'; Stabynotilte 'lapideus pons (stone
bridge)'; Tapelawke or Taplawken 'Warmfelt (warm
field)'; Tollauken 'Breytenveld (distant field),'
cf. Lith. tolùs 'distant'; Treonkaymynweysigis
'trium villarum pratum (the meadow of three
villages)'; Umpna or Umne 'clibanus (oven)';
Wagipelki 'palus furum (thieves' swamp),' cf.
Lith. vagìs 'thief' and pélkė 'swamp'; Wosispile
'Ciginburg (goat's fortress, castle),' cf. Lith.
ožỹs 'goat,' pilìs 'castle.'
4.701 Mažiulis, 1966, 30, mentions Mikalauskaitė's
1938, analysis of the pre-Reformation fragment of
an Old Prussian Lord's Prayer. According to
Mikalauskaitė, 1938, 102, this fragment is in the
ms. boruss. 1 [8], which, at least in her time, was
in the Berlin Staatsbibliothek. Mažiulis, 1966,
30, gives the text as follows: Towe Nũsze kãss esse
andangonsṽn swyntins which was translated apparently
directly from Latin pater noster, qui es in coelis,
sanctificetur rather than from the German. One
notes that in those versions translated directly
from German the 2nd sg. personal pronoun is
encountered, cf., e.g., from the Ist catechism
(Trautmann, 1910, 7, line 4): THawe nuson kas thu
asse andangon - Our Father who (you [sg.]) art in
heaven' just like the German: VAter unser der du
bist jm himmel (Trautmann, 1910, 6, line 4).
4.702 Mažiulis, 1966, 30, mentions also Hieronymus
Meletius' account, Warhafftige Beschreibung der
Sudawen auff Samland/ sambt ihren Bock heyligen und
Ceremonien (True description of the Sudovians in
Samland [Samogitia] along with their goat sanctification and ceremonies) which came out in two editions
around the middle of the 16th century (although the
exact date, place and press are not indicated). This
book contains a few phrases and sentences in the
Old Prussian dialect of the Sudovian enclave, see
paragraphs 1.300 and 2.400. Mažiulis, 1966, 30-31,
gives the most important phrases (with variants):
Ocho moy myle schwante panicke

das ist/ o mein liebes heiliges fewerlein 'Oh,
my dear holy fire (diminutive)' [variants: O hoho
Moi mile swente Pannike; O ho hu Mey mile swenthe
paniko; O mues miles schwante Panick]. Kellewesze
perioth/ Kellewesze perioth/ das ist der treiber
(i.e., Wagentreiber) ist kommen 'the driver (i.e.,
the wagon driver) has come [variants: kellewese
periothe; kellewese parioth]. Bezzenberger, 1878,
137, analyzes kellewese as kele-(kelia-)vese, cf.
Lith. kẽlias 'way, path,' vèžti 'to transport,'
važiúoti 'to ride, to travel,' i.e., 'road
traveler.' Būga, 1961, 133, suggests OP kela-veze
in which kelan 'wheel' is represented in the nom.
pl. *kelō 'wheels,' i.e., 'wagon.' For perioth
cf. Lith. par- 'through, by' and jóti 'to ride.'
We also find in Meletius (according to Mažiulis,
1966, 31) trencke trencke 'stos an, stos an, i.e.,
kick (on the door with the feet),' cf. Lith.
treñkti 'to strike; to slam.'
4.703 Other examples are: Abklopte '[bridal]
wreath, crown' [variants: Abglopte; abgloyte -
Nesselmann, 1873, 1, says that the latter form is
probably a misprint]. Mažiulis, 1966, 31 quotes
Meletius (Vilnius copy): 'setzen jr ein krantz auff
mit einem weissen tuch benehet das heissen sie
Abklopte' - they put a wreath sewn with a white
cloth on her which they call Abklopte. Kailess
noussen gingis Ich trincke dir zu unser freundt
but more exactly in English probably 'Hail,
[or hello], our friend' [variants: Kails naussen
gnigethe; Kayles mause gygynethe; Kailes nanse
geigete]. Būga, 1961, 132, reads gingis as
gignis = gińis. Forms with -ethe, -ete are
diminutives.
4.704 We also encounter: Geygey begeyte pockolle/
Laufft laufft jr Teuffel which Mažiulis, 1966, 31,
translates as Lith. bėkit, bėkit, velniaĩ 'run,
run, devils.' [variants: Beigeite beigeite
puckolle; Beigeite beygeyte peckolle; Geygeythe
begoythe peckelle; Geygeythe, Begaythe, Pekelle;
Begaythe, Pokulle; geigete begeigete Packolle],
cf. the Slavic imperatives in -ite <*-oite.
Kayles, poskayles enis perandros, described in
German as 'vnd heben an zu sauffen,' but which
Mažiulis translates as (Lith.) sveĩkas pa sveĩkas

víenas per añtrą 'hello and hello, one after
another. [variants: Kayles, postkayles eins
periandros; Kails poskails ains par antres;
Kailes puszkailes ains Petantros; Poss Kayless
kayles eines perenteres.]27
4.705 Unfortunately neither Mažiulis, 1966, nor
Būga, 1961, mention Bezzenberger's 1878, 139,
explanation that Kayles poskayles...etc. is to be
transcribed as kails! pats kails! The first word,
kails, is, of course, cognate with OP kailūstiskun
'health' and is to be translated as 'hail [or
hello]'; pats = Lith. pàts 'oneself.' The whole
expression then is 'Hello [or hail]. Hello
yourself!' and is a greeting formula, possibly used
during drinking bouts.
4.710 In his analysis of the Basel epigram
Mažiulis, 1975, 125, writes that these two lines are
written in dactylic hexameter, although the dactyls
and spondees are rather artificial. The accented
lines are shown here by the underlining:

Kayle rekyse ˙ thoneaw labonache thewelyse

Eg ˙ koyte ˙ poyte ˙ nykoyte ˙ pēnega doyte

Without the addition of the final -e in the words
rekys-e and thewelys-e the hexameter of the first
line would not work out, or to put it more exactly it would be almost completely spondee. One
should not be surprised at this addition of an -e
when we take into consideration the fact that the
Basel epigram is an ironic-humorous text composed
by some student and therefore having perhaps some
of the jargonisms and puns of the student language.
This seems to me to be an excellent suggestion and
it also leads one to suspect that there may have
been further distortions in the text to add to its
humorous quality. See also 11.200.
    In any case Mažiulis would correct the first
word kayle into *kayls or *kayles with a loss of
the final -s. The form kayle in place of the
expected *kayls may also have been influenced by
Latin (salv-)e 'hello' (2nd sg. imperative) and by
the fact that the form kayle (with two syllables)
fits the hexameter better than *kayls. Mažiulis
writes further that rekys-e (with the added -e) is
to be read as rīkīs 'sir, gentleman' and is a

nominative singular form used for the vocative.
4.711 The sequence thoneaw is to be divided into
tho = *tu 'thou, you (sg.)' and neaw = n'au (the
letter -e- here denotes palatalization of the
preceding consonant, cf. pannean [EV - 288] 'mossy
fen' = *pan'an). OP *n'au is to be derived from
*ni 'not' + *jau 'already, still,' cf. OP iau
attested in the IIIrd catechism. This OP *n'au
denoted Lith. 'nebe,' German 'nicht mehr,' English
'no more.' Cf. also Lith. dial. niau < ne + jau.
The Acad. Dictionary, Vol. 8, 762, gives the
example: Niaŭ našlys nežino, ką anas be pačios?
'Doesn't the widower know yet that he is without a
wife?' If the first element of this sequence,
i.e. tho- is really equivalent to *tu, as seems
quite possible, then Mažiulis' suggestion for the
second element, i.e., -neaw is excellent.
4.712 In labonache Mažiulis finds that the first
element is lab-, cf. Lith. lãb-as, Latv. lab-s
'good.' The second element -onache represents
some kind of suffix. It is difficult to make out
this suffix since the -o- after the labial may
stand for OP *-a-, cf. OP wo-bse (EV - 789) 'wasp' =
Lith. dial. va-(psà). Mažiulis suspects, however,
that the form labonache stands for *lab-ans,
derived from an earlier OP *lab-nas or *lab-anas
(nom. sg. masc.), which means something like
'good.' Mažiulis says that perhaps one should be
careful about reconstructing an OP *lab-nas since
it would have only one cognate form in other Baltic
languages, viz., the Lith. lãb-nas attested in one
of the districts of Liškiava (these belong to the
former Sudovian territories!). In Mažiulis'
opinion OP *lab-nas could have become *lab-n(a)s >
*lab-ans (cf., e.g., OP *(aliks)-nas 'alder tree'>
*(aliks)-n(a)s > *(alisk)-ans). Similarly a form
*lab-anas could also have passed to *lab-ans.
Later an OP *lab-ans could have given OP *lab-ants.
And from *lab-ants a form *laban^{a}ts > *labanats with
an anaptytic vowel -a- between the -n- and the
final -ts could have developed. The consonant -t-
could easily be written with the letters *-th- =
-ch- (the letter t is frequently confused with c
in medieval manuscripts) and in place of the
letter *-s we find -e, which, in addition, fits the

hexameter structure better. Perhaps then
labonache = *lab-ans is from *lab-anas, which has
the Old Prussian diminutive suffix -ana-. Thus
labonache thewelyse = Lith. gerùtis dėdẽlis 'good
old uncle, good fellow,' etc. The word thewelyse
has the added -e and reflects OP *tēvelis (nom.
sg.) a form with the diminutive suffix -el-
derived from *tēvis = thewis (EV - 176) 'uncle
(on the father's side).'
4.713 The sequence Eg. koyte calls to mind the
OP expression iquoitu = *ik + quoi + tu = Lith.
jéigu nóri tù 'if you (sg.) wish.' Mažiulis
believes that this OP *ik 'if' should probably be
read as *īk. As a result of considerations of
areal linguistics one would not wish to connect
the Basel epigram eg 'if' with Lith. dial. ẽgu
which is attested only once in the Acad. Dict.,
Vol. 2, 1053, from the region of Panevėžys.
4.714 Mažiulis continues further saying that the
word koyte is not to be separated from koyto
(GrG 100) = koytu (GrA 83) = (*ik +) quoitu (IIIrd
catechism) and quoi tu (also IIIrd catechism) 'do
you wish?'. It would perhaps be possible to
identify koyte directly with OP quoite (IIIrd
catechism) 'he wishes,' but then we would expect
the author to have written not koyte but koyte to
(with *to = *tu 'you (sg.),' i.e., the subject.)
In Mažiulis' opinion the author would have done
this because the subject of the verb is not dropped
in Old Prussian texts and not only as a result of
German influence. Thus in the sequence -te of
koyte Mažiulis sees *-tu, i.e. 'you (sg.).' This
was probably pronounced as an enclitic in Old
Prussian. The rime with the following word poyte
may have had some influence on this transformation
also.
4.715 From the context it would seem that the word
poyte should be an infinitive denoting 'to drink,'
but in Old Prussian the attested forms of the
infinitive of this verb are pout and poutwei (both
in the IIIrd catechism). Mažiulis suggests that
at the time of the preparation of the Basel
epigram these two infinitive forms would probably
have been *pot and *potvei respectively. Perhaps
the digraph -oy- is written for riming with the

preceding koyte. The word nykoyte is the same as
koyte except for the preceding prefixed negative
ny- 'not, don't.'
4.716 Mažiulis suggests that pennega = *penniga
has lost the final -n and is to be corrected to an
acc. sg. *pennigan. I disagree with this completely and would rather see a partitive genitive here
as I have mentioned above in 4.601. See also
paragraph 6.015.
4.717 Mažiulis writes that doyte denotes the same
as dāt and datwei 'to give' (both attested in the
IIIrd catechism). In his opinion doyte reflects
*dōt, but the author of the Basel epigram wrote
doyte to rime with the preceding nykoyte. Still
the best formal match for poyte seems
to be the 2nd pl. imperative forms (I) pugeitty,
pogeitty, (II) puieyti, puietti, (IIIrd catechism)[28]
poieiti. Likewise the best formal match for doyte
would seem to be the 2nd pl. imperative daiti,
daiti attested in the IIIrd catechism.

In paragraph 4.602 I wrote that it would be
difficult to imagine a situation in which an
interpretation: 'if you want, drink! -- [if]
you don't want, give money!' would be appropriate.
But if we extend Mažiulis' own suggestion that this
text is some kind of student joke, then perhaps the
significance of the text is incomprehensible to us
because we are too far removed from the cultural
context which gave rise to the epigram. Still
another possibility is that the text is to be reconstructed as: Eg koyte poyte ˙ nykoyte penega
*(ny-)doyte 'if you want, drink! if you don't want,
don't give any money.' Perhaps there is a missing
*ny- before the doyte, or perhaps the use of
penega in the genitive even implies a negated verb,
so that it was unnecessary to prefix the *ny- to
doyte. The problem still remains, however, as to
why we have a singular *tu 'you' in the first line
and plural forms in the second line, unless some
kind of student joke is envisioned.[29]

On the other hand perhaps it is better to read
both poyte and doyte as infinitives.
In the last paragraph Mažiulis writes that the
figure of the person drawn in the text has a
banner or a drinking horn in his hand on which is

written the inscription <u>Jesus</u> <u>ich</u> <u>leid</u>. Mažiulis
says that this is a rather strange inscription for
such a situation. I find nothing strange here at
all. The young man is undoubtedly recovering from
a drinking bout and has a severe hangover. This is
what prompts the expression of suffering.[30]

Mažiulis concludes that having purified the
epigram from the student puns which were inserted
to make the hexameter and rime, one may say that
the epigram is a rather accurately transcribed
Old Prussian text. Thus one is forced to conclude
that the author was **indee**d an Old Prussian himself.

5.000 Althougn it is undoubtedly immodest, I
believe that it will be easier for the reader to
understand my own bias and my own framework for
criticizing the other approaches to Old Prussian
if I explain my own theories first.

5.001 In 1959a I assumed that the Old Prussian
graphemes e and a denoted a single phoneme /a/,
the e frequently denoting a preceding palatalized
consonant and the a frequently denoting merely a
preceding unpalatalized consonant. (The parallel
with Lithuanian is obvious.) Although there is
considerable orthographic vacillation, I assumed
this to be unimportant, since it was the nature
of the preceding consonant which carried the
phonemic burden. At this time I suggested that
concomitant with the loss of the phonemic contrast
between /e/ and /a/ in post-consonantal position
the contrast was being lost in word-initial
position also. I then compared the Old Prussian
situation with that of Russian (where o- took the
place of e- in tonic or pre-tonic syllable) and
suggested that OP a- was substituted for e-,
whereas e- was retained in unstressed position.
I wrote then, 1959a, 194: "Initial e- is
frequently found in prefixes (which would often be
unstressed), e.g., et- (prefix of separation), ep-
(translating German be-), en 'in,' but initial a-
is frequently found in words which may have had
the stress on the initial syllable, e.g., assaran
'lake' (cf. Lith. ẽžeras), assanis 'fall' (cf.
S.Cr. jȅsēn), aswinan 'mare's milk' (cf. Lith.
ašvà [accentuation class 2], Skt. áśvā), addle
'fir' (cf. Lith. ẽglė), alne 'female hind' (cf.
Lith. élnė..."

5.002 In 1964 I undertook a phonemicization of
the IIIrd catechism (Enchiridion) for which I
tried to establish a short-vowel system with three
vowels:

$$i \qquad\qquad\qquad u$$
$$a$$

and a long vowel system with five vowels:

$$\bar{\text{i}} \qquad\qquad\qquad\qquad \bar{\text{u}}$$
$$\bar{\text{e}} \qquad\qquad \bar{\text{o}}$$
$$\bar{\text{a}}$$

I assumed then that the orthography allowed us to
see a phonemic shift in statu nascendi, i.e., the
old long vowel system [1] sketched above was
giving way to an innovating vowel system [2].
The shifts in question were:

Conservative >   Innovating
A. [1] /ē/ >   [2] /ī/
B. [1] /ō/ >   [2] /ū/
C. [1] /ī/ >   [2] /ei/ or /ai/ [?]
D. [1] /ū/ >   [2] /ou/ or /au/ [?]

Examples:
A. [1] semmē 'earth' = Lith. žĕmė 'id.' (< *-ē);
[2] sīdons, sīdans 'sitting,' cf. Lith. sésti 'to
sit down' (< *sēd-).
B. [1] no-seilis 'spirit' > [2] nu-seilin
C. [1] gīwan 'life' > [2] gēiwan
D. [1] būton 'to be' > [2] boūton, baūton
The innovating vocalic system was then:

$$\bar{\text{i}} \;(< /\bar{\text{e}}/) \qquad\qquad\qquad\qquad \bar{\text{u}} \;(< /\bar{\text{o}}/)$$
$$\text{ei} \;(< /\bar{\text{i}}/)31 \qquad \text{ou, au} \;(< /\bar{\text{u}}/31$$
$$\bar{\text{a}}$$

5.003 In 1964, 219, I wrote: "As far as I can
determine any of the consonantal phonemes (except
/j/) may be either palatalized or unpalatalized:
Labials   /p,b,m,v/
Dentals: /t,d,n/
Dental spirants: /s,z/
Palatalo-alveolar spirant: /š/
Velars: /k,g/
Semivowel: /j/
Liquid: /l/
Trill: /r/"
5.100 Stang, 1970, 122 and 1966, 39, noted that
instead of *-kūn, *-gūn < *-kān, *-kōn, *-gān in
the Ist and IInd catechisms one finds -guan, -gwan
and in the Ist catechism -kun (4 X), and -kon (2
X). He proposes then a development of *-kān, *-kōn,
*-gān > *-kǭn, *-gǭn > *-kuon, *-guon and that from
these in some dialects there arise -kuan, -guan
and in other dialects -kun, -kon, which come
perhaps from a shortening of *-kuon. A few

99

examples from the Ist catechism: mergwan 'maiden,'
pattiniskun 'marriage'; the IInd catechism mergwan,
griquan (gen. pl.) 'sins.' In the IIIrd catechism,
however, we find -kan, -gan (only exceptionally
-kun) and the latter forms show an analogical
substitution of -kan for *-kuan. A form such as
alkīnisquai 'sorrow, trouble' found in the IIIrd
catechism is thought to be analogical to the
accusative *alkīnisquan. Although forms in -quan,
-gwan do not occur in the IIIrd catechism, Stang,
1970, 124, says that they must have been in the
dialectal area where Abel Will or his helper could
have heard them.
5.101 In the IIIrd catechism, according to Stang,
1970, 124, we encounter the nom. sg. fem. and nom.
pl. masc. quai 24 times.[32]The nom. sg. fem. derives
from *kā > *kū with the addition of the particle
-ai. Since in all three catechisms *-kān > *-kwan,
the acc. sg. fem. of kas would have been *quan and
an analogical substitution of the initial element
into the nominative would have led to the creation
of quai, we have here an alternative way of
explaining this form according to Stang, 1970, 125.
The initial qu- spread to the masc. nom. pl. quai,
to the interrogative-relative adverb *kei, which
became quei 'where' and from quei to *kendau >
quendau 'whence' and from quendau to *sten,
*stendau and *stē, which became, respectively,
stwen 'there,' stwendau 'from there,' and stwi
'there.' In the addenda in 1970, 129, Stang says
that he now considers it unlikely that the nom.
sg. fem. quai played any role in the creation of
the nom. pl. masc. quai. He says further that he
now believes that the interrogative adverb quei
'where' derives from *kŭ (cf. Vedic kŭ, Avestan
kū, Skt. kutra) plus the -ei taken from other
adverbs.
5.102 With all due respect to the great Prof.
Stang, whose work has been profoundly influential
on me and who is undoubtedly one of the greatest
Balticists who has ever lived, I disagree in every
respect with his analysis and I propose my own
herewith.
5.200 In 1968a, I proposed that, as in many
languages with phonemic palatalization, in Old
Prussian there was non-phonemic labialization of

consonants before back rounded vowels, a
labialization which was sometimes perceived and
sometimes not perceived by German scribes. I
repeat here a few examples from my 1974, 9-10,
study:

Labialization unmarked	Labialization marked
Nom. sg. masc.	
kawijds (interrogative and relative pronoun)	kuwijds
Nom. sg fem.	
aucktimmisikai[33] 'authority'	aucktimmiskū
Acc. sg. fem.	
mērgan 'maiden'	mergwan (I and II)
Acc. sg. fem.	
prābutskan 'eternal'	prabitscun (I)
	prabusquan (II)
Acc. sg. fem.	
crixtianiskan 'Christian'	crixtianiskun
	krichstianisquan
Adverbs	
deineniskai 'daily'	deinenisku
laimiskai 'richly'	laimisku
perarwiskai 'certainly'	perarwisku
Prefix pa-	
pagauts 'conceived'	pogauts
pakūnst 'to watch over'	pokūnst
Verbs	
asmai 'am'[33]	asmu, asmau
polīnka 'remains'	polijnku

5.201 Over the years, however, I have come to the
conclusion that all theories about Old Prussian
phonology are highly speculative. Thus I am
increasingly critical not only of my own theories
outlined above, but also of the theories of others
concerning the phonology of the extinct Baltic
languages. It is difficult enough to say something
beyond dispute about the contemporary spoken

languages, so I assume it to be even more
difficult to say anything about the dead languages.
I am not against the attempts to do this, but
analyses of dead languages should always be
considered highly tentative. I am especially
dubious about excessive reliance on the written
evidence of the texts. As I wrote in 1974, 305,
"I have tried to determine the reason why so many
linguists and philologists have put such great
faith in the accuracy of the orthographic systems
of dead languages. One reason is, of course, that
it is only the orthographic systems which allow
us to reconstruct anything of the language.
Another reason is the fact that correct use of
language is a very important cultural value to
those in the academic world, i.e., precisely those
who are studying the dead languages. Thus it is
extremely difficult to break out of this cultural
ethnocentrism which expects everyone to value
correct language use as much as do the academics.
I share the prejudices concerning 'acceptable' and
'unacceptable' types of language use, but I am not
convinced that everyone shared these prejudices at
all times in human cultural history. I fear that
the academic world has become so separated from
the rest of the world as to be unable to understand
how other individuals could value messages couched
in what to us is 'unacceptable' orthography or
grammar."34

5.300 Mažiulis, 1963a, 191, writes that following
the labials m̱, v̱, p̱, ḇ and the velars g̱ and ḵ the
opposition between those proto-Baltic vowels which
gave Lith. ō and Latv. ā on the one hand and Lith.
and Latv. uo on the other hand was neutralized.
Thus, for example, in the Old Prussian catechisms
we find mū-tin 'mother' beside Lith. mó-tė and
Latv. mā-te on the one hand and OP pū-ton 'to
drink' beside Lith. puo-tà 'feast' and Gk. pō-nō
'I drink' on the other hand. Mažiulis reasons that
the vowel ū could not have derived from *ā (since
the latter could not have passed to ū). Such an
ū, in Mažiulis' opinion, goes back to a rather
back and to a certain extent labialized proto-
Sambian low vowel which we might denote with the
letter ɔ̄ . Therefore there is reason to think
that this ɔ̄ was rather close to the old *ō (which

102

corresponds to Lith. and Latv. uo). This could
explain why in the Pomesanian dialect of the
Elbing vocabulary we find *brō-tē passing to word
173 brote 'brother' and * mō-tē passing to word
170 mothe. Other examples speaking in favor of
the existence of a proto-Sambian *ō are soa-lis
(EV - 293) 'grass,' but in the IIIrd catechism
sā-lin (cf. Lith. žo-lė̃, Latv. zâ-le 'id.'), menso
(EV - 154, 374) 'meat' but mensā in the IIIrd
catechism (cf. Latv. mìesa). Also in favor of the
theory of a rounded ō is the existence of labial
prothesis with this vowel, cf. wosee (EV - 676)
'goat' beside Lith. ožỹs and Latv. âzis.
5.301 Mažiulis, 1963a, 192, establishes three
categories for the appearance of the graphemes oa
and o in the Elbing vocabulary: 1) to denote a
sound corresponding to Lith. ō and Latv. ā, e.g.,
soalis 'grass' (see above), OP moazo (EV - 178)
'aunt,' cf. Lith. móša 'husband's sister,' Latv.
māsa 'sister'; 2) to denote a sound corresponding
to Lith. and Latv. a in certain diphthongs, e.g.,
OP roaban (EV - 467), Lith. raĩbas 'variegated,
striped,' OP doalgis (EV - 546), Lith. dalgis
'scythe'; 3) to denote a vowel following labial
consonants (including a prothetic w-), e.g.,
OP gramboale (EV - 781) 'beetle, chafer,' Lith.
grambuolỹs, grámbuolė 'cockchafer,' OP woasis
(EV - 627), Lith. úosis, Latv. uôsis 'ash.' In
all of the three aforementioned environments in
addition to the graphemic sequence oa the grapheme
o is also used: 1) brote, cf. Lith. broter-ė̂lis,
Latv. brāter-ītis; 2) OP wormyan (EV - 463) 'red,'
Lith. varmas 'insect'; 3) podalis (EV - 351)
'worthless pot,' Lith. puodãlis, púodas 'pot,'
Latv. puôds, etc. Mažiulis suggests that the
graphemes oa and o can denote the open ō and that
the o can denote not only ō but also *o, a short
ɔ or even in some cases u. The contrast of *ō
vs. ō was retained after consonants other than
labials and velars.
5.302 Examples of the retention of the old close
*ō are furnished by the preposition no 'on'
(cf. Lith. nuõ 'off, from'), the genitive plural
ending -on as in nus-on, nous-on, noūs-on 'of
us' < *-ōn, the formant -ōn- as in per-ōn-iskan
'parish, community,' and the formant -om- as in

103

tikr-ōm-iskan 'right.' Mažiulis, 1963a, 195, also
notes that in addition to no 'on' we also find the
spelling na and that in addition to the genitive
plural ending -on we also find the spelling -an as
in nus-an 'our, of us,' iōusan 'your, of you.'
Mažiulis then suggests that the relationship no:na
and -on:-an is a function of the stress, the former
being the stressed form and the latter the
unstressed. I personally am highly suspicious of
such reliance on the orthography and would rather
see here just chance orthographic variation.
5.303 According to Mažiulis, 1963a, 195, in place
of the expected grapheme o we find a corresponding
to an earlier *ɔ̄ in the word dā-ts, dā-ts 'given,'
dā-twei 'to give,' Lith. dosnùs 'liberal,
generous,' Latv. dāsns 'id.,' dā-stît 'to give
away thoughtlessly.' Mažiulis then writes, 196,
that this is a result of the fact that this verb
was originally in the mobile accentuation class and
in some forms at least the root vowel *ō was
unstressed. Under these conditions the *ō passed
to *ɔ̄ which was (in Prague school terms) the
archiphoneme (or the result of neutralization in
unstressed position) of the two phonemes *ō and
*ɔ̄ . The neutralized vowel *ɔ̄ was then
transferred to those forms of the verb in which
the vowel was originally stressed and thus *ɔ̄
replaced the earlier *ō. This explains then the
appearance of OP dā-twei 'to give' with an ā
instead of an *ō which might be expected on the
basis of Lith. dúoti, Latv. duot 'to give.'
5.304 In my opinion such an explanation might have
been somewhat more convincing with examples of
similar substitutions from other languages. The
parallel with Russian is obvious. One could hunt
for examples in which the [a]< /o/ in unstressed
position was generalized at the expense of the
morphophonemic /o/. The only examples which come
to my mind are counterexamples. Thus the masculine
singular past tense of Russ. rasti 'to grow' has
not become */ras/, but remains /ros/. The Russian
prefix raz- is usually [roz-] in stressed
position. There must be examples of the
generalization of an [a]< /o/, but none come to
mind at present.[35]

5.305 Other explanations for this OP $\bar{a}$ in $\underline{d\bar{a}twei}$ have been given. I suggested, 1964, 219, a laryngal explanation, viz., $*deA^W- > *d\bar{a}v-$ in pre-vocalic position with a generalization of the $*\bar{a}$ to preconsonantal positions. I might suggest now that an OP stem $*dav-$ (cf. Lith. $\underline{d\tilde{a}v-\dot{e}}$ 'gave') had existed at one time, and that on the basis of a contamination between $*d\bar{o}-$ and $*da(v)-$ a new stem $*d\bar{a}$ was created. See Schmalstieg, 1973a, for a suggestion that the Indo-European diphthong $*\underline{ou}$ (or $*\underline{au}$) was monophthongized to $*\bar{o}$ in preconsonantal position. One might suggest alternatively that the $\bar{a}$ of $\underline{d\bar{a}-twei}$ may be the result of Slavic influence.[36]

5.306 Finally, however, Mažiulis, 1963a, 196 establishes a proto-Prussian phonemic system as follows:

Long vowels		Short vowels	
$*\bar{\imath}$	$*\bar{u}$	$*i$	$*u$
	$*\bar{o}$		
$*\bar{e}$	$*\bar{\jmath}$	$*e$	$*\jmath$

5.307 For Common Baltic Kazlauskas, 1962, 19, proposes a very similar system:

$*\breve{\bar{\imath}}$		$*\breve{\bar{u}}$
		$*\bar{o}_1$
$*\breve{\bar{e}}$		$*\breve{o}_2$

5.308 In his criticism of the systems proposed by Mažiulis and Kazlauskas, Burwell, 1970, 12-13, quotes both Trubetzkoy, 1939, 102, and Hockett, 1955, 83, to the effect that it would be at least unusual for a vocalic system to exist with more back rounded vowels than front unrounded vowels. Burwell quotes Martinet, 1939, 30-40, as saying that as a result of the "asymmetrical shape of the vocal organs less room is provided for the formation of back vowels than of front vowels." (Burwell, 1970, 14.) In addition Burwell draws attention to the fact that the difference in the frequency in the first two formants of back vowels is less than the difference in frequency between

105

the first two formants of front vowels.
5.309 Burwell, 1970, 16-17, proposes the
following development for the vocalic system of
the Elbing vocabulary:

(A.) Late Indo-European: $*\breve{\bar{\imath}}$ $\breve{\bar{u}}$

$\breve{\bar{e}}$ $\breve{\bar{o}}$

$\breve{\bar{a}}$

(B.) Common Baltic: $*\breve{\bar{\imath}}$ $\breve{\bar{u}}$

$\breve{\bar{e}}$ $\breve{\bar{o}}$

$\breve{\bar{a}}$

(C.) Old Prussian (Elbing vocabulary)

(1.) (a.) $\breve{a} \nwarrow \!\!\! \searrow$ $\bar{a}_2$, a

(b.) $\breve{e} \nwarrow \!\!\! \searrow$ $\bar{e}_2$, e

(2.) (a.) $\bar{a}_1$ is raised and merges with $\bar{o}$.
(b.) $\bar{e}_1$ is raised and correlates with $\bar{o}$.

$\breve{\bar{\imath}}$ $\breve{\bar{u}}$
$\breve{\bar{e}}_1$ $\breve{\bar{o}} < *\bar{a}_1$ [37]
$\breve{\bar{e}}_2$ $\breve{\bar{a}}_2$

(3.) (a.) $\bar{o} > ua$
(b.) $\bar{e}_1 > ie$

$\breve{\bar{\imath}}$ $\breve{\bar{u}}$
$\breve{\bar{e}}$ $\breve{\bar{a}}$

5.310 In Burwell's opinion then the diphthong
/ua/, which was foreign to the German spoken during
this period, was rendered by orthographic o, since
the first element of the diphthong was absorbed by
the preceding consonant and the second element
[a] was interpreted with the labialization of the
preceding consonant. Burwell, 1970, 17, writes:
"In those few cases where an a does appear, it can
simply be assumed that the initial component of
the diphthong was seen as belonging to the
preceding consonant, but that the second element
escaped misinterpretation. Finally, the
representation of /ua/ by oa is perfectly
understandable in view of the phonetic similarity
of [u] and [o] in the first place and, in the
second place, because of the tendency of a heavily
labialized foregoing consonant to obscure the

distinction between the two."
5.311 Burwell, 1970, 18, rejects the possibility
that the spellings with o for expected a are the
result of the misinterpreted consonantal labialization since we find o consistently as the marker
of *ā-stem nouns, whereas we encounter -an
consistently as the final syllable of the 64
neuter substantives and adjectives (e.g., golimban
'blue,' assaran 'lake'). Burwell also suggests
that the phoneme /o/ may have existed in the Slavic
loanwords of the Elbing vocabulary. It seems to
me, however, that it would have been possible to
stop with Burwell's system (C2) above and come out
with approximately the same result. There would
be no need to assume the diphthongization which he
does.
5.312 Mažiulis, 1971, 101, has three fundamental
criticisms of Burwell's 1970 paper: 1.A more
exhaustive analysis of the facts of the Elbing
vocabulary (or, at least, the conclusions from such
facts) would have been desirable. 2.The fact that
an investigation of the vocalism of the Elbing
vocabulary is necessarily connected with an
investigation of the vocalism of the dialects of
the Old Prussian catechisms has been left out of
consideration. 3.An important element has been
omitted, viz., the reconstruction of the vocalic
system of the Old Prussian dialects of the
catechisms for the time of the composition of the
Elbing vocabulary. Mažiulis also objects to the
conclusion that Baltic *ō and *ā merged as *ō in
the dialect of the Elbing vocabulary.
5.313 Mažiulis, 1971, 102, then draws attention
to Būga's, 1961, 106, conclusion that the ā in the
Old Prussian catechisms (supposedly written in the
Sambian dialect) is completely new, since in its
place in the 13th, 14th and 15th centuries we find
such Sambian place names as Auctowangos, Grindos
(nom. pl. fem.), Byoten, Beyoten, Dywone-lauken,
Soke 1258, Schokym 1299, Scoken terra 1326, German
Schaaken, Wobsdis 1331 'eyn luchs,' cf. Lith.
opšrùs, Latv. âpsis (âpša) 'badger,' Wosenbirgo,
Wosispile, cf. Lith. ož̃ỹs, Latv. âzis 'goat,' etc.
5.314 But it seems to me that one cannot take the
spellings of the place names so seriously in view
of the frequent vacillations such as the following

listed by Gerullis, 1922, 270. [38]
(1) Wogenis, Ugeyne (today Uggehnen)
(2) Uppin, Woppe (today Oppen)
(3) Wundithen, Wondithen (today Wonditten)
(4) Wutterkaym, Woterkeim (today Wotterkeim)
(5) Warmediten, Wormedith, Wurmdit (today
    Wormditt)
(6) Warkaym, Workaym, Wurkaym (today Workeim)
    (Gerullis, 1922, 208)
(7) Worelauke, Wurlauks, Worlavken, Wurlauken
(8) Wormen, Warmen
(9) Worwayn, Wurwaynen
(10) Worennye, Wrenie, Vuoronnye, Vuoreine,
    Worenyge, Werennye, Worennie,
    cf. Lith. Varėnà.

5.315 Under the heading for the name Worit ,
Gerullis, 1922, compares Lith. Vorýtė, the name of
a brook, and proposes that the Old Prussian word
derives from a root cognate with Lith. võras 'old'
(with the addition of the suffix -ĭt-). In the
IIIrd catechism we encounter the OP urs 'old,'
which is also thought to be cognate with Lith.
võras < *vãras. See Schmalstieg 1974, 13.

5.316 Marchand, 1970, 113, notes that
Ordensdeutsch is a mixture of East Middle German
as the basis with Upper and Low German which
became common in the Ordensland. Marchand remarks
further, 114, that it is typical of a Middle
German dialect for a and o to be confused. Thus
one can hardly take the evidence of the place
names written down by Germans any more seriously
than the orthographic evidence of any other Old
Prussian documents. See also 5.605.[39]

5.317 Mažiulis, 1970, 11-15, essentially repeats
the arguments propounded in 1963a and 1965,
now proposing the proto-Old Prussian vocalic
system (= Late Common Baltic) as given below:

Long vowels		Short vowels	
*ū	*ī	*u	*i
*ọ̄			
*ō	*ē	*o	*e

On the basis of the evidence of Baltic loanwords
in Finnish, such as Finnish v-uo-ta < East Baltic
*(v)ō- (= Latv. â-da, Lith. ṓ-da 'skin.') and

Finnish l-o-hi< East Baltic *-ŏ- (= Latv. l-a-sis,
Lith. l-ắ-šis 'salmon'), Mažiulis, 1970, 16,
claims that this proto-Old Prussian system was
probably the same as the late Common Baltic vowel
system. See 11.300.
5.318 Mažiulis, 1970, 16-17, does, however,
recognize one serious question, viz., how does the
quadrangular system of late Baltic develop from
the five-vowel triangle of Indo-European:

ū		ī		i		i
	ō		ē		o	e
		ā				a

Mažiulis then suggests that the development of
Indo-European *ā in the direction of Lith. ō is a
development shared with Old Prussian and that the
Indo-European vowel *ō couɩd give not only Lith.
and Latv. uo, but also Lith. ō, Latv. ā (ō) and in
the Old Prussian catechisms a after consonants
which are not labials or velars.
5.319 Mažiulis, 1970, 18, then gives his own
version of Kazlauskas', 1962, 24, statement of
the early Baltic vocalic system:

Stressed position
(system alpha)

Long vowels			Short vowels	
ū		ī	u	i
ọ̄		ẹ̄		
ō			o	e

Unstressed position
(system beta)

ū		ī		u		i
ō		ē				
	ā			a		e

5.320 Next Mažiuⅼis, 1970, 18, quotes Kazlauskas
to the effect that as a result of apophonic and
other phonetic as well as morphological factors the
system of the stressed vowels (system alpha)
became established in the unstressed position
(system beta). Now I remember discussing this very
matter in Vilnius in 1970 with Kazlauskas before
the untimely death of the latter. At this time in

life I was a confirmed structuralist and I pointed
out to Kazlauskas that in phonemic terms there
could be no contrast between the vowels of the
stressed and unstressed positions, since they were
merely allophonic variants of each other.
Presumably native speakers do not hear the
difference between allophonic variants, so
essentially there were not two contrastive systems,
but only one system and that from the phonemic
point of view it did not make any difference
whether one wrote the ŏ of his system alpha or the
ā of his system beta. I suggested, however, that
since there is a tendency for languages to have
balanced vocalic systems, I would prefer his system
beta as a more likely representation of early
Baltic than his system alpha. At this time
Kazlauskas had no answer to my comments, but
promised to look up Endzelīns' thought on the
nature of the o or a in early Baltic. A few days
later Kazlauskas told me that Endzelīns had said
that it made no difference whether one wrote o or
a. At that time Kazlauskas did not cite his
source and I did not ask. I think, however, that
Kazlauskas was impressed by my arguments, but it
must be remembered that I am relating this entirely
from my personal memory of an incident which took
place some four years ago. I am convinced,
however, that Kazlauskas was not a dogmatic person
and was willing to change his views if he saw there
was reason for a change. Had he written more on
this subject, I believe that he would have taken
my comments into consideration even if he did not
change his fundamental outlook on the early Baltic
vocalic system.

5.321 Between the early Baltic vocalic system and
the late Baltic vocalic system Mažiulis
intercalates an old Baltic vocalic system in which
an open ē was created as a result of apophonic and
perhaps other reasons. In other words *o̧:*ẹ as
*ō̧:x; *o̧:*ō̧ as *ẹ:x; *ō̧:*ō̧ as *ẹ̄:x or *ō̧:*ẹ̄ and x =
ē. The old Baltic vocalic system was then:

Long vowels		Short vowels	
*ū	*ī	*u	*i
*ō̧	*ẹ̄		
*ō	*ē (analogical)	*o	*e

110

At this point Mažiulis, 1970, 18-19, adds that
the late Common Baltic vocalic system given above
(5.317) is neither complete nor regular
(dėsningas), since ordinarily in the languages of
the world vocalic systems are such that the number
of back vowels does not exceed the number of front
vowels. Thus one must consider the long vowel
system of late common Baltic 'irregular' and
perhaps a transitory system between the long vowel
system of old Baltic and the early specifically
Latvian and Lithuanian vocalic systems (i.e., with
an already monophthongized *ei). Mažiulis, 1970,
19, continues, "The transition from the old Baltic
to the late Baltic system of long vowels could have
been determined by the circumstance that in the old
Baltic vocalic system the opposition *ǭ:ę̄, having
no correlates in the short vowel system could not
be stable for long. The vowel *ę̄ had to pass to
the vowel *ē... Thus the long vowel system of late
Baltic could arise with a 'case vide' (a long mid
front vowel), a system which, because of its
irregularity, had to become regular rapidly: the
'case vide' was filled in East Baltic by the new
*ę̄ which arose from *ei." Later in the various
Baltic dialects Baltic *ō (< Indo-European *ā)
developed into Lith. dialect ā, Latv. ā and OP ā
in the dialect of the catechisms.
5.322 Although my purpose here has been to
discuss the phonology of Old Prussian, I have had
to introduce some East Baltic phonology in order
to explain Mažiulis' and Kazlauskas' views of Old
Prussian. I cannot refrain now from introducing
my own views of the development of the East Baltic
vocalic system since my views do not require an
'unbalanced system' for any stage of the
development of the vocalic system from Indo-
European to East Baltic:

I. Indo-European

ĭī̆   ŭ
        ĕ̄   ŏ̄
              ă̄

II. Common Baltic (Balto-Slavic?)
ĭī̆   ŭ
        ē   ō (merger of *ŏ
              ā   and *ă)

111

III. Common East Baltic

$\overset{\smile}{\underset{}{\bar{\imath}}}$ $\overset{\smile}{\bar{u}}$

$\bar{e}_2$ (< *ei and perhaps *ai) $\bar{o}$

$\overset{\smile}{e}$ $\overset{\smile}{a}$

IV. Common East Baltic
(showing the diphthongization of *$\bar{e}_2$ > ie and *$\bar{o}$ > ua)

$\overset{\smile}{\bar{\imath}}$ $\overset{\smile}{\bar{u}}$

ie (< *$\bar{e}_2$ < **ei, **ai[?])   ua (< *$\bar{o}$)[40]

$\overset{\smile}{e}$ $\overset{\smile}{a}$

V. Common East Baltic
(initial element of ie > i, second element > e;
 initial element of ua > u, second element > a)

$\overset{\smile}{\bar{\imath}}$ $\overset{\smile}{\bar{u}}$

$\overset{\smile}{e}$ $\overset{\smile}{a}$

VI. Lithuanian
(In Lithuanian the old short *a and *e were split
into short and long variants and the etymological
sequences of */an/ and */en/ plus spirant passed to
/$\bar{a}$/ and /$\bar{e}$/ respectively creating a new contrast
of /a/ vs. /$\bar{a}$/ and /e/ vs. /$\bar{e}$/. Examples are
standard Lith. màno 'my, mine' vs. mãno 'thinks,'
and mès 'will throw' vs. mẽs 'we.' At the same
time the old /$\bar{a}$/, still attested in Mažvydas,
passed to /$\bar{o}$/ and the old */$\bar{e}$/ passed to /ė/.)

$\overset{\smile}{\bar{\imath}}$ $\overset{\smile}{\bar{u}}$

ė (< *$\bar{e}$) $\bar{o}$ (< *$\bar{a}$)

$\overset{\smile}{e}$ $\overset{\smile}{a}$

VII. Latvian
(In Latvian the old *$\bar{e}$ was split into a low and a
mid variant depending upon the nature of the
following syllable and the new $\bar{o}$ was introduced
only from borrowed words.)

$\overset{\smile}{\bar{\imath}}$ $\overset{\smile}{\bar{u}}$

$\overset{\smile}{\bar{e}}$ $\overset{\smile}{\bar{o}}$

$\overset{\smile}{ę}$ $\overset{\smile}{a}$

5.323 I do not think that the rendering of Indo-
European *$\bar{a}$ by orthographic o in the Elbing
vocabulary, as orthographic u after labials and

velars in the Old Prussian catechisms and as $\bar{\text{o}}$ in standard Lithuanian is sufficient reason for presupposing rounding of Indo-European *$\bar{\text{a}}$ in proto-Baltic.[41]One could imagine the Elbing vocabulary vocalic system as pictured by Burwell in C2 (see 5.309) above, i.e., with a split of the former short *a and *e into new short and long $\bar{\text{a}}$ and $\bar{\text{e}}$ as in Lithuanian.[42]The old Indo-European *$\bar{\text{a}}$ was then raised and rounded as in Lithuanian and was rendered as orthographic o or oa, the oa denoting that the process of change from *$\bar{\text{a}}$ was still in statu nascendi. Endzelīns, 1951, 125, notes such an intermediate stage in the passage of $\bar{\text{a}}$ to $\bar{\text{o}}$, which, interestingly enough, he writes as oa, in certain Latvian dialects. Presumably the Indo-European short *a in certain diphthongs had been lengthened and was undergoing the same fate as the Indo-European etymological *$\bar{\text{a}}$ and this accounts for such spellings as doalgis (EV -546), cf. Lith. dalgis 'scythe.' As does Levin, 1972, 152, I assume that in proto-Pomesanian, at least, and most probably in the other Old Prussian dialects *$\bar{\text{o}}$ merged with *$\bar{\text{a}}$. The oa of gramboale (EV - 781) beside Lith. grambuolys 'cockchafer' also derives then from proto-Old Prussian *$\bar{\text{a}}$ < Indo-European *$\bar{\text{o}}$.[43]

5.324 As far as the u in the dialect of the Old Prussian catechisms is concerned, in all probability in most cases it merely shows a scribal rendering of labialization of the preceding consonant, see 5.200. It should be pointed out also that although we do not know for certain the influence of Middle Low German on Old Prussian, there must have been some, since there are some Middle Low German loanwords in Old Prussian. Trautmann, 1910, XVI, quotes höfftmannin 'captain' from Middle Low German hövetman and instran (EV - 133) 'fat, grease' from Middle Low German inster, etc. Lasch, 1914, 96, shows that Middle Low German /uo/ was frequently written as u. It is a fair assumption then that in some cases orthographic u may have denoted /ua/. One may compare the IIIrd catechism words gallū, gallu 'head' with galwas-dellīks 'chief article.'[44] Presumably gallū is in the nominative singular and

stands for something like /galvā/, cf. Lith. galvà
'head.' The initial morpheme of the CP compound
galwas-dellīks 'chief article' is probably to be
phonemicized as /galvās/, i.e., it is a genitive
singular of /galvā/, cf. the Lith. gen. sg. galvõs
(< *galvās). In other words we find the same
phonological sequence written as -ū, -u and as
-wa-.
5.325 In every language vocalic systems are
constantly in the process of change and there is no
need to assume that a rounded vowel of an attested
language need reflect a rounded vowel at an earlier
stage of that language. There is nothing
surprising about a shift of /ā/ to /ō/ in
principle. One may note, for example, that the
modern English word stone derives from Old English
stān in which the ā derives from a diphthong ai,
cf. Gothic stains. Likewise Labov, Yaeger and
Steiner, 1972, 158, report on a vocalic chain
shift in New York City in which /ah/> /oh/> /uh/.
Essentially then, it is quite unnecessary to
connect the Old Prussian and Lithuanian roundings
in the rendering of Indo-European *ā. These were
undoubtedly independent, although perhaps parallel,
developments in the individual languages. Rather
it is necessary to study the possibilities of chain
shifts within the vocalic systems of each language.
5.400 Stang, 1966, 25, notes that in the Elbing
vocabulary one frequently finds o for a and says
that in twelve of the fifteen cases which he
considers the most certain the o follows a labial
or a guttural (I would prefer the term velar to
guttural). Several examples from those which
Stang gives are the following: bordus (EV - 101)
beside Latv. bārda, Lith. barzdà 'beard'; golis[45]
(EV - 168), IIIrd catechism gallan 'death,' cf.
Lith. gãlas 'end'; gorme (EV - 41) 'heat,' cf. Skt.
gharmáḥ, Latin formus, Old High German warm;
wormyan (EV - 463), IIIrd catechism urminan 'red,'
Lith. varmas 'gnat.' Stang, 1966, 26, says that in
Pomesanian the first element of the diphthong was
lengthened and the lengthened a tended towards an
o pronunciation. This tendency was perhaps
clearest after velars and labials. Stang remarks
then that this agrees with Gerullis', 1922, 214,
observations concerning the place names.

5.401 Stang, 1966, 26, states that in the IInd
catechism the a is written often as e, æ, ae
following dentals in final syllables. He gives the
following examples: 1. -aey for -ai: Staey,[46]
Pallapsaey; 2. -en for -an (omitting the cases
after j): sten (3X), nienbænden, butten,
tanæssen, aynen, syndens, wyssens, etc. He
proposes then that a reduction of -an (< *-an,
*-ān) to -ən in unstressed final syllable took
place. This -ən was expressed by -en. Stang says
also that a reduction must have taken place in the
gen. sg. menses 'flesh' since in Old Prussian the
a-stem nouns have a short a in the genitive
singular and probably also root stress in words
belonging to the mobile accent class, cf. OP ālgas
as opposed to Lith. algõs 'salary.'
5.402 Likewise the IIIrd catechism, in Stang's
opinion, 1966, 27, gives evidence for the reduction
of a in unstressed final and medial syllables,
e.g., kad(d)en 'when,' dabber 'still,' laisken
'book,' sacramenten, winnen 'weather,' waldunen
'(co-)heir,' kittewidei 'otherwise' beside
kittawidin, etc. In my opinion, of course, all of
the preceding examples merely reflect the
inaccuracies of scribal practice.
5.403 According to Stang, 1966, 32, in Old
Prussian there are a number of examples of a- from
e- both in the catechisms and in the Elbing
vocabulary. In the verb 'to be' in addition to
the usual forms in as- there are also some in es-,
e.g., in the IIIrd catechism essei (1X), estei
(1X), in the IInd catechism æsse (1X), æst (3X),
and hest (1X) which show clearly that the passage
of e to a took place originally before a back
vowel and then spread secondarily to other
positions. I have proposed my own explanation in
paragraph 5.001.
5.404 Stang, 1966, 49, suggests that in OP no
'on' (< nō) we find a short o. In those dialects
which are the basis of the Ist and IInd catechisms
the o, which was a new sound not firmly rooted in
the phonological system, became a. In the dialect
which served as the basis of the IIIrd catechism we
must accept the existence of a short o sound, cf.
OP tols (1X), acc. tollin (1X) 'duty, toll.'

In 1968b, 391, I asked: "If indeed the unstressed
/ō/ were shortened to [o], one might ask how this
distinction became phonemic. Supposedly the [o]
in unstressed position would be only an allophonic
variant of /ō/ in stressed position." I am not so
certain now as I was then of the efficacy of
phonemic theory. Still I would see the shortening
of an unstressed long vowel as merely automatic if
there were no phonemic merger with some other
vowel involved in the question.
5.405 Stang, 1966, 48, writes that the -on in
noūson 'our,' iouson 'your,' stēison 'of it'
retains the proto-Baltic ō and that o before n was
shortened at a later date. In 1968b, 391, I
stated: "Now the forms nuson and nouson are found
in the First and Second Catechisms respectively.
If it is probable that there was an /o/ in this
position in the First and Second Catechisms, why
couldn't the sound which developed from the
shortening of the /ō/ in no have fallen together
with this /o/ instead of passing to /a/? It may be
pointed out here that the word noūson has the
following additional orthographic variants: (First
Catechism) nusun, nusan, nusen, (Enchiridion)
noūsan, noūsen. Although spellings with -on seem
to predominate in this (apparent genitive plural)
ending, they are insufficient to allow us to
establish an /o/. If indeed there were an /o/ in
Old Prussian, presumably it would have been
restricted to word-final position, the initial
element of tautosyllabic diphthongs, and loan
words. It seems easier to suppose that if /o/
ever existed in Old Prussian, it was limited to
loanwords. The orthographic -on of the genitive
plural ending is surely to be phonemicized as
/an/."[47]
5.406 In his remarks on palatalization in Old
Prussian Stang, 1966, 103, says that OP peuse
(EV - 597) 'pine' retains Indo-European eu, cf.
Gk. peúkē 'id.' Furthermore Stang says that one
cannot decide whether the eu in peuse reflects a
pronunciation eu or whether it represents a
pronunciation 'au ('ău). cf. Lith. iau, Latv. 'au,
Slavic 'u), cf. OP driāudai 'forbade' (IIIrd
catechism). See also 5.505.

5.500 Karaliūnas, 1968, 73-76, uses as one of his arguments against the hypothesis of Balto-Slavic unity the assumption that Proto-Indo-European *eu did not become jau in Old Prussian as it did in the other Baltic languages and as we can assume it might have in Proto-Slavic. As Karaliūnas, 73, points out, such a graphemic sequence as OP bleusky (EV - 286) 'sedge' is ambiguous. Some investigators would say that the eu merely denotes the diphthong au after a softened consonant, whereas others believe that OP eu really denotes the diphthong eu and that it never passed to jau in Old Prussian. An argument in favor of the passage of *eu to jau, according to Karaliūnas, 74, is the existence of OP iaukint 'to train,' cf. Lith. jaukinti 'to domesticate.' This argument, however, is not reliable because the root of this word may be *ouk- (not *euk-), cf. Slavic učiti (with u- < *au-) and Skt. okaḥ 'house.' The initial j- of the Baltic words may then be prothetic.

5.501 Karaliūnas, 1968, 74, quotes the following words from the Elbing vocabulary: bleusky (286) 'sedge,' geauris (757) 'cormorant' (cf. Lith. giaurỹs 'Rallus aquaticus') gleuptene (247) 'smoothing board on a plough,' keutaris (762) 'ring-dove,' keuto (156, 497) 'skin, hide' (cf. Lith. kiáutas 'shell'), peuse (597) 'pine,' skewre (685) 'sow' (cf. Lith. kiaŭlė 'pig'). Karaliūnas says that before the digraph eu we never find the letters i, y or g which we could interpret as a marker denoting palatalization and which we might expect if Old Prussian had retained the sequence iau. The grapheme i does appear from time to time before front vowels, cf. plieynis (38) 'powdery ash,' pleynis (75) 'membrane.' In Karaliūnas' opinion this seems to show that in the Elbing vocabulary there existed the diphthong eu.

5.502 Since OP *sj became š (cf. OP schuwikis [EV - 496] 'shoemaker,' schumeno [EV - 507] 'shoemaker's thread,' schutuan [EV - 471] 'thread'), it is usually thought that j disappeared after other consonants also (after softening these latter). (See 5.506.) But in Karaliūnas' opinion some written forms, especially

117

when the grapheme g is used, seem to show that the
sound j is denoted, cf., e.g., angurgis (EV - 565)
'eel,' ansalgis (EV - 506) 'narrow strip of shoe
leather,' kargis (EV - 410) 'army' (although
Karaliūnas does not mention it at this point, it
must be noted that *kargis is a correction for
kragis), saligan (EV - 468) 'green,' wargien
(EV - 525) 'copper,' (cf. cugis [EV - 518] = Lith.
kujis 'hammer'). Karaliūnas thinks that in these
latter words it is doubtful that g denoted
softness. As Lithuanian and Latvian show, it is
not necessary that j have disappeared in all
positions. Possibly in some positions it
disappeared earlier, in other positions later.
Thus the passage of *sj to š does not necessarily
mean that other consonant sequences with a
following *j would have changed. (But see 5.506.)
Karaliūnas, 1968, 74, writes further that when
trying to decide whether the OP diphthong eu still
existed or not, it is not so important to know
exactly what the writings bia, bio, piu, pio, pya,
mya, mye and wio denote. It is, however,
important that the graphic representation is
different from the graphic representation of the
analogical word peu-se. Karaliūnas maintains that
if the diphthong eu had become iau in Old Prussian,
we would expect the same graphic representation of
the labial consonant (palatalized or with following
j) before the back vowels, viz., *piau, *pyau,
*pyeu. Karaliūnas, 1968, 74 asks then: Doesn't a
different graphemic representation reflect a
different phonetic sequence? and adds that
Endzelīns, 1935, 96, proposed that the IInd
catechism form pyienkts 'fifth' showed that after
a labial consonant a j may have appeared.
Karaliūnas does not mention, however, that
Endzelīns, 1943, 18, had suggested that the forms
pyienkts, piēncts, piencktā, might show that in
Old Prussian as in the neighboring Polish language
consonants before i and e were palatalized. In
addition I don't know why the German scribe must
live up to our requirements or expectations of him.
(See also 5.918 and 5.921.)
5.503 Karaliūnas, 1968, 75, says that before back
vowels we do find graphemic sequences which seem
to indicate either palatalization or the

presence of a j in the Elbing vocabulary: maldian
(438) 'foal,' median (586) 'forest,' medione (699)
'hunt,' brunyos (419) 'armor,' dragios (386)
'yeast,' etc. Karaliūnas then says that such
palatalization should have been shown in the words
keutaris, keuto, skewre, geauris if the initial
consonant of these words had occurred before a back
vowel. In addition it should be noted, according
to Karaliūnas, that before front vowels the letters
i and y are not written except for a few cases
such as plieynis (38) beside pleynis (75), geytye
(339) 'bread,' etc. Karaliūnas concludes then
that there are no data showing that the change of
eu to jau is even a Common Baltic phenomenon.
5.504 I would have the following comments
concerning the words keuto, keutaris, skewre and
geauris. If indeed there ever was a front vowel
following the velar we should certainly expect
there to have been palatalization of the preceding
velar consonant. If not, then Old Prussian would
stand alone in the entire group of families of
languages, Baltic, Slavic and Indo-Iranian. In
other words, velar consonants are palatalized by
following front vowels in all of the above
languages except, supposedly, Old Prussian. It
would appear to me quite surprising if velars were
not palatalized by following front vowels in Old
Prussian. In the dialect of the catechisms we
find evidence of the palatalization of velars
before front vowels in such variant spellings as
gieidi vs. geide 'waits,' see Schmalstieg, 1974,
8.
5.505 The fundamental question is, however, not
to show whether *eu passed to jau or not, but to
show whether Old Prussian maintained a phonemic
contrast between etymological *eu and *jau, a
contrast which was lost in Slavic and East Baltic.
The real pronunciation of the Old Prussian
graphemic sequence eu hardly matters. Since the
examples with eu following a velar are probably to
be excluded from consideration immediately, the
Old Prussian evidence is skimpy indeed. One
might suspect also that the word geauris is to be
interpreted as [ǵauris]. For the word pannean
(EV - 288) 'mossy fen' I reconstruct a

phonemicization /paɲan/ in which the -ea- denotes
[a] with palatalization of the preceding consonant,
cf. Lith. pania[b̓ùdė] 'kind of mushroom.' We do
not really know what the graphemic sequence eu may
have meant to a German scribe. Since there was no
chance of contrast between /e/ and /a/ after a
palatalized consonant or /j/, the graphemic
sequence eu may merely have been a kind of
abbreviation for eau written out in full in the
word geauris. In conclusion I would say that the
evidence of the Elbing vocabulary is not sufficient
to allow us to draw any far-reaching conclusions
about Balto-Slavic relationships. Certainly it
does not prove that Proto-Indo-European *eu was
retained as eu rather than passing to Baltic jau.
5.506 Perhaps it would be appropriate here to
comment on the initial sequence sch- of the words
schuwikis, schumeno, schutuan. Since German never
had a contrast of the type */ś/ or */sj/ vs. /š/,
there seems to be no way of knowing whether sch-
denoted OP /ś/, /sj/, /š/ or /š̌/. It must be kept
constantly in mind that the German scribe must
have heard the sounds of Old Prussian through the
phonological filter of his native language.
5.600 For determining the pronunciation of Old
Prussian Marchand, 1970, 110-111, discounts
immediately the evidence from etymology and loan
words. He writes, 110: "The evidence of loan words
has always been seen as quite strong, but it is
just as obviously weak as that of etymology. One
has but to inspect the German loans in the Elbing
Vocabulary and place them beside their German
counterparts to see the unreliability of loan words:
e.g., 292 klette, OP clattoy 'weed'; 359 leffel,
OP lapinis 'spoon'; 428 stechmess' OP stakamecczer
'butcher-knife'; 473 Schroter, OP scrutele
'tailor'; 429 ros, OP russis 'horse.' Marchand
continues, 111, saying that names must be treated
with the same caution as loan words, of which the
former are but a subclass.
5.601 Internal alternations, according to
Marchand, 1970, 111, can indeed be important, but
one must keep in mind that these offer information
about the time when the alternation arose. The
alternation a/o in OP kinship terms, e.g., pomatre

(EV - 180) 'stepmother' vs. passons (EV - 181)
'stepson' may indicate an earlier type of
accentuation, if it isn't just a graphic
alternation.
5.602 Marchand, 1970, 111-112, has little faith
in linguistic universals. He writes (111): "Thus,
Jakobson once affirmed that length and stress
could not be phonemic in the same language, only
to be contradicted by later evidence." On the
extreme end I would object, however, that there
must be at least some universals which we can use
to define the concept 'language.' It is just in
the nature of human beings to find recurrent
phenomena more credible than rare or non-recurrent
phenomena.
5.603 Marchand, 1970, 113, notes that the Elbing
vocabulary has the usual suspensions and
abbreviations of 15th century hybrida texts. It
is difficult to tell the difference between t and
c; commonly Middle German e is written above or
within the line to denote length; y and i are used
interchangeably; z presumably indicated /s/.
5.604 The dialect of the Elbing vocabulary is
Ordensdeutsch, i.e., according to Marchand, 1970,
113, "the mixture of East Middle German as a basis
with Upper and Low German which became common in
the Ordensland and which we would expect of a
document written in Marienburg at this time."
5.605 Of particular importance is Marchand's
demonstration of the confusion of various letters
denoting vowels. Thus i and e of whatever
provenience are confused: (3) hemel (Himmel)
'sky,' (246) schene (Middle High German schine)
'plow iron,' (307) slete (Schlitten) 'sled.'[48]
Similarly a and o of whatever provenience are
confused: (12) jor (Jahr) 'year'; (23) sonnobent
(Sonnabend) 'Sunday'; (69) hoer (Haar) 'hair';
(82) wimpro (Middle High German wintbrâ) 'eyebrow';
(161) blo (Middle High German blâ) 'bruise'; (146)
vüssale (Fussohle) 'sole'; (182) stiftacht'
(Stieftochter) 'stepdaughter'; (482) sacken
(Socken) 'socks.' As Marchand comments, 1970, 114,
".... it would seem impossible to use the evidence
of this document in the question of Proto-Baltic a
and o." Likewise u and o are not well distinguished,
particularly in the neighborhood of nasals or

liquids: (9) wulken (Wolken) 'clouds'; (205) suller
(dial. söller) 'attic'; (220) stobe (Stube) 'heated
room'; (240) vorch (Furche) 'furrow'; (274)
stuppel (Stoppel) 'stubble'; (284) gromot (dial.)
Grummet 'second haying'; (312) commot (Kummet)
'yoke.'
5.610 Fraenkel, 1952b, 131, explains the
retention of the guttural (I prefer the term
velar) in OP pecku, peckan and Lith. pẽkus, pẽkas
'cattle' (beside Sanskrit paśú-, Avestan pasu-) as
being the result of the mixture of a native form
with š or s respectively with Gothic faíhu. The
regular sibilant, according to Fraenkel, 132, is
retained in Lith. pèšti 'to pluck' = Gk. pékein
'to comb,' pékos 'plucked fleece,' Latin pecus,
pecoris 'cattle, livestock.'
5.611 Fraenkel, 1952b, 132, proposes that the
initial velar of Lith. klausýti, Latv. klàusît,
OP klausīton 'to listen to' (as opposed to the
expected š, s respectively on the basis of Slavic
slyšati 'to hear,' etc.) is the result of the
influence of the related word represented by Lith.
glusnùs, which, like Lith. (pa)klusnùs, paklùsnas,
etc., means obedient. Fraenkel may be right here,
but one might also consider the possibility that
the distribution of the pure velars and the
palato-velars was different in different lexical
items in Indo-European already.
5.620 Kiparsky, 1970b, 260-261, suggests that the
vacillation between the spellings in OP clokis
(EV - 655) 'bear' and (caltestis-)klokis (EV -
656) 'common bear' with an initial kl- vs. forms
such as Tlokun-pelk, a place name, 'bear's swamp'
with an initial tl- are originally allophonic
variations. Kiparsky, 261, quotes Hill, 1967, 205,
who in turn quotes Bloch, 1948, 25: "In some
varieties of American English the segments [k] and
[t] are in free variation with each other when
they occur initially before voiceless [L], e.g.,in clear,
clean, class, etc., all pronounced by speakers of
these dialects indifferently with [kL-] and with
[tL-]." I would agree with Kiparsky that the
difference could have been minimal, the type of
lateral release determining whether the velar or
the dental closure is heard predominantly.

It is possible that in the Old Prussian language
there was really only one kind of lateral release,
but that various German scribes heard this lateral
release in various ways.
5.700 Grinaveckis, 1965, 194, says that Lithuanian
dialects bordering on the old territory of the
Jatvingians and Old Prussians can give us some
information about these latter languages. Thus
the narrowing (or raising) of the vowels ā and ē
began earliest in the western territory of
Lithuania, where the Lithuanians were the neighbors
of the Old Prussians. In Old Prussian (but perhaps
only in some of its dialects) already in the 14th
century ā and ē were narrow, if one judges by the
data of the Elbing vocabulary, cf. brote (EV -
173)'brother' beside Lith. broterėlis, moazo (EV -
178) 'aunt' beside Lith. móša 'husband's sister,'
Latv. māsa 'sister,' plieynis (EV - 38) 'powdery
ash,' cf. Lith. plenys 'membrane, film,' Latv.
plēnes 'white ash on burning coals.' In western
Lithuanian dialects the narrowing of ā and ē may
have taken place in the 14th century after the
shortening of the old long acuted endings. Otherwise the -ā of the acuted endings would have
changed into -o just as in OP galwo (EV - 504)
< *galvā. This word is defined in German as vorvūs^e
'upper part of the shoe.' Cf. also glawo (EV -
68) 'head.'
5.701 In the Elbing vocabulary old *ā and *ō have
the same reflex, according to Grinaveckis, 1965,
195, cf. podalis (351) 'worthless pot,' beside
Lith. puodẽlis 'cup,' Latv. puods 'bowl,' and OP
woasis (EV - 627) beside Lith. úosis, Latv. uosis
'ash tree.' The examples, OP brote, moazo of the
preceding paragraph show the reflex of etymological
*ā, whereas the examples of this paragraph show
the reflex of etymological *ō, which apparently
merged in the dialect of the Elbing vocabulary,
i.e., both are reflected by graphic o and oa.
5.702 Grinaveckis, 1965, 195, then notes a
parallelism in western Lithuanian dialects, i.e., the
south-western part of northwestern High Lithuanian
[aukštaičių] and in the dialect of the Samogitian
donininkai where the etymological ā and ō have also
merged (just as have ē and ẹ < ei), cf., e.g., kóje

123

(beside standard Lith. kója 'leg') and dóna (beside
standard Lith. dúona 'bread'). Examples of the
merger of ē and ę̄ (< *ei) are furnished by dẹt
(beside standard Lith. dė́ti 'to put') and pẹns
(beside standard Lith. píenas 'milk' [with -ie-
from *ei]).[49]
5.703 Grinaveckis, 195, also notes the lowering
of OP i and u, but adds that perhaps it took place
in only a part of the dialects and perhaps not in
all circumstances. He gives the examples dessempts
'ten' beside dessimpts, prosnan 'face' beside
prusnan (acc.). In the westernmost High Lithuanian
(aukštaičių) dialects i and u have been lowered to
ę and ǫ respectively: vẹsas, bǫva beside standard
Lith. vīsas 'all,' bùvo 'was.' I would comment
that if the Old Prussian forms quoted in this
paragraph are not merely orthographic variants,
then the lowering of i to e and u to o is a
reflection of the adoption of an innovating system
as opposed to an older conservative system, see
paragraph 5.002.
5.704 Grinaveckis, 1965, 195, says that in Old
Prussian tautosyllabic n was retained in all
circumstances. In western Lithuanian dialects as
well as in the standard language tautosyllabic n
disappeared before j, v, l, m, n, č, s, š, z, ž
and in word-final position, but the loss of
tautosyllabic n in these dialects took place
relatively recently and was still not completed
until the 17th century. This means that when Old
Prussian was still a living language the tautosyllabic n still existed in those western
Lithuanian dialects which bordered on Old Prussian.
I certainly would not dispute the existence of
Old Prussian tautosyllabic n, but I wonder if we
can know definitely whether it still did exist in
Old Prussian. One could just as well imagine that
a German scribe hearing a nasal vowel would have
rendered it as vowel plus n because there was no
other way to render this in his alphabet. Thus,
for example, if we didn't know how French was
pronounced, but judged purely from the orthography,
what would we imagine for the pronunciation of
rendre, bon, prononcer, etc.? Would this be
evidence that tautosyllabic n was retained in

modern French? See also ⊥1.201.

5.705 Grinaveckis, 1965, 196, notes that in the
Elbing vocabulary in many cases short a̲ in word-
final position is dropped and he points to the
parallelism in development in the Old Prussian and
the neighboring western Lithuanian dialects. He
says further that it is characteristic that the
laws of the reduction of final vowels in Old
Prussian and in the neighboring Lithuanian dialects
are almost identical. In certain cases short a̲, e̲
and i̲ are lost and unstressed vowels are shortened.
Grinaveckis is surely right here, but the
phenomenon of the loss of short vowels and the
concomitant shortening of unstressed final vowels
is so common in the languages of the world that it
is reasonable to doubt its significance.

5.706 Grinaveckis, 1965, 198, also ties in the
Zietela dialect pronunciation of standard u̲o̲, i̲e̲
as ū and Ī with the pronunciation of OP pūton 'to
drink'< *pōton. This seems most unlikely to me. In
the first place even according to the traditional
explanations the passage of Proto-Baltic *ō to OP
ū took place only after velars and labials, see
Endzelīns, 1943, 27, or Trautmann, 1910, 129. In
the second place this particular phonological
feature of the Zietela dialect must be studied in
connection with the entire system of that dialect,
not as a fragment. In any case the letter u̲ after
labials and velars is probably merely a mark of
Old Prussian labialization, see paragraph 5.200.

5.707 Grinaveckis, 1965, 199, notes that in
Zietela we encounter the loss of vowels in word-
final position: vaĩks<vaĩkas 'child,' stóu
'stands' (cf. standard Lith. stóvi), aĩt<eĩti
'goes,' dẽst< desti 'puts,' gíest<gíesti 'sings.'
Again Grinaveckis connects this with the reduction
of word final in Old Prussian and again I would
counter that such phenomena are too common in the
languages of the world to have much significance
in relating two languages.

5.708 Grinaveckis also connects the pronominal
forms of the Zietela dialect: sajim 'with oneself
[reflexive],' tajim 'with you,' with such forms as
OP māim 'with me,' etc.

5.800 Milewski, 1966, 120, writes that of all the

Balto-Slavic language family only Old Prussian has retained the original accentual state of Balto-Slavic, viz., an acute rising accent and a circumflex falling accent. These are distinguished in the diphthongal sequences by a macron over the second element (for the acute) and a macron over the initial element (for the circumflex), cf., e. g., OP pertraúki 'closed up,' Lith. tráuke 'dragged, drew'; OP pogaūt 'to receive,' Lith. pagáuti 'to catch, to seize'; OP toūlan 'much,' Lith. tūlas 'many a one'; OP soūns 'son,' acc. sg. soūnon, Old Lith. (Daukša) súnus (= sūnus) on the one hand vs. OP kaīma-luke 'visits,' Lith. kiẽmas 'courtyard'; OP prakaīsnan 'perspiration,' Lith. kaīsti 'to heat'; OP laīku 'holds fast,' Lith. laīko 'holds'; OP acc. sg. swaīgstan 'appearance,' Lith. acc. sg. žvaĩgždę 'star'; OP eīt 'goes,' Lith. eĩt, etc.

5.801 Milewski, 1966, 122-124, finds that Old Prussian has essentially the same four nominal accent classes as does Lithuanian. The first class is the acute barytone paradigm which is made up in turn of four subcategories: 1a. Proto-Indo-European barytones with a long root vowel, e.g., OP brāti 'brother' beside Serbo-Croatian bràt, brāta, Vedic bhrātā, Gk. phrātēr, Gothic broþar; 1b. Proto-Indo-European oxytones with the accent shifted to a long acuted vowel in accordance with Hirt's law in the Proto-Balto-Slavic epoch, e.g., OP acc. pl. wīrans 'men,' Lith. výras, but Vedic vīráḥ; OP soūns, acc. sg. soūnon, Old Lith. súnus but Vedic sūnúḥ; OP mūti 'mother,' Old Lith. mótė, Serbo-Croatian màti but Vedic mātā, Old Frisian moder from Proto-Germanic *mōdér; 1c. Baltic innovations such as the OP acc. sg. kaimīnan, Lith. kaimýnas 'neighbor'; 1d. Forms created according to old patterns, but only within Old Prussian, e.g., biāsnan 'fear' and other derivatives in -snā.

5.802 The second class is the Proto-Balto-Slavic circumflex barytone paradigm, cf. OP acc. pl. preī-pīrstans 'rings,' Lith. pir̃štas 'finger,' OP acc. sg. rānkan, inst. sg. rankān. Milewski, 122, says that the OP instrumental singular form, like the Lithuanian instrumental singular form shows the results of de Saussure's law according to which the stress was shifted from a preceding circumflex syllable to a following acute. Milewski says also that deverbative nouns in -*snā* retained the accent of the infinitive stem from which they were created, cf., e.g., *biāsnan* 'fear' from *biātwei* 'to fear' (cf. Lith. *bijóti* 'id.') If the infinitive stem was short or circumflex, one would expect the stress on the final syllable in the nominative singular according to de Saussure's law, cf., e.g., OP *etwerpsnā* 'forgiveness' from the infinitive *etwiērpt* 'to forgive' (cf. Lith. *ver̃pti* 'to spin.') Milewski, 1966, 123, suggests that the difference between the stress of the accusatives plural OP *prēi-pīrstans*, *rānkans* on the one hand and the Lithuanian cognates *pirštùs* 'fingers,' *rankàs* 'hands' on the other hand is the result of the different origin of the accusative plural endings in Old Prussian and in Lithuanian. In Lithuanian the endings -*ùs*, -*às* continue long acuted *-*ṓs* and *-*ā́s* respectively which attracted the stress according to de Saussure's law, but the Old Prussian ending -*ans* continues *-*ons*, *-*ans* which do not attract the stress.

5.803 Only three Old Prussian forms represent the third accent class, i.e., the acute mobile paradigm: the nom. sg. *mensā* 'flesh' (an old *-*o*-stem noun, cf. Russian *mjáso*, nom. pl. *mjasá*, Vedic *māṃsám*, pl. *māṃsā*); the nom. sg. *gallū* 'head,' cf. Lith. *galvà*; Lith. *žvėrìs* 'wild animal,' acc. pl. *žvė́ris* like the OP acc. pl. *swīrins*.[50]

5.804 The fourth accent class is the circumflex mobile paradigm and is represented by such words as OP *lāiskas* 'booklet,' Lith. *laĩškas* 'leaf, letter,'[51] OP *kāima-(luke)*, a loan translation of German *heimsucht* 'visits,' Lith. *kiẽmas* 'courtyard,' OP *mergu*, acc. sg. *mērgan*, dat. pl. *mergūmans*, cf. Lith. *mergà* 'maid,' gen. sg. *mergõs* (or *mer̃gos*), acc. sg. *mer̃gą*, dat. pl. *mergóms*.

Milewski, 1966, 125, concludes then that both Lithuanian and Old Prussian continue the four nominal and adjectival accentual paradigms which were created in the Proto-Balto-Slavic epoch as a result of a remodeling of the Proto-Indo-European system. Any differences between Lithuanian and

Old Prussian arise from the more archaic nature of
the latter.
5.805 Kazlauskas, 1967, 243, objects that Milewski
has not proved that the action of de Saussure's law
is to be observed in Old Prussian. In the first
place the fact that deverbative nouns in -snā might
have an end-stress in the nominative singular does
not prove the action of de Saussure's law, because
derivatives in -snā in Old Prussian may have had
an acute root syllable and have been declined
according to the third accent class (cf., e.g.,
Lith. nom. sg. galvà 'head' [acc. sg. gálvą]) and
perhaps metatony from circumflex to acute root
syllable was a derivational process for deverbative
nouns in -snā. Cognate verbal and nominal bases
do not necessarily have the same intonation. In
addition Kazlauskas doubts Milewski's statement,
1966, 123, that OP semmē 'earth' occurs in an
instrumental singular equivalent to the Lith.
inst. sg. žemè 'id.' According to Kazlauskas
there is a Lithuanian dialect form with the stress
on the final syllable, viz., žemẽ. And that leaves
then only the difference in stress between the OP
gen. sg. ālgas vs. Lith. algõs 'salary,' certainly
an insufficient amount of evidence to prove the
existence of the action of de Saussure's law in
Old Prussian.
5.900 Levin, 1972, discusses the Old Prussian
adaptation of Slavic /a, o, ě, e/ as attested in
the Elbing vocabulary transcriptions of words
borrowed from Slavic. He says his approach to be
'pragmatically generative' and establishes the
following distinctive feature system for the
Elbing vocabulary:

	ī	i	ū	u	$\bar{\epsilon}$	ϵ	$\bar{\jmath}$	$\jmath$
High	+	+	+	+	−	−	−	−
Back	−	−	+	+	−	−	+	+
Long	+	−	+	−	+	−	+	−

In order, however, to account for the vowel
spellings found in the Elbing vocabulary in the
surface realization Levin assumes the lowering of
short vowels with respect to their long correlates,
thus: /i/ > [I], /u/ > [ʊ], /e/ > [æ], /ɔ/ > [a].
Examples of the Pomesanian (Elbing vocabulary)
replacements of Slavic /a/: Cristionisto, Common
Slavic *krьstьjan-; Slavic /o/: abasus, Russian

128

oboz 'string of carts'; Slavic /e/ nadele,
Common Slavic *nedělja; Slavic /ě/: mestan,
Common Slavic *město. According to Levin, 1972,
151, "The analysis of Slavic borrowings in Elb
containing Slavic [ě e] encounters two difficulties
not met with in analyzing Slavic [a o]. The first
is the smaller corpus of borrowings with Slavic
[ě e] – there are only eleven, if we consider
ponadele and nadele as separate borrowings..., and
if we count the two occurrences of ratinsis as a
single borrowing. These borrowings contain a
total of fourteen instances of Slavic [ě e].
5.901 "The second problem is the orthographic
underdifferentiation of Prussian /ɛ̄ ɛ/ in Elb.
/ɛ̄/ is written e + C, while /ɛ/ may be spelled
e/a + C(C). Thus, a spelling e + C in a borrowing
is inherently ambiguous – it may be read as
Prussian /ɛ̄/, /ɛ/ (or even /i/). However, the other
spelling variants of /ɛ/ are unambiguous with
respect to the /ɛ ɛ̄/ contrast, although spellings
with a may be read as /ɔ/ as well as /ɛ/."
5.902 Levin, 1972, 152, rejects the assumption
that the Slavic length distribution is somehow
directly reflected in the borrowings found in the
Elbing vocabulary, and says: "Our underlying
assumption is that a synchronically valid phonological explanation for the replacement of foreign
sounds in borrowings is preferable to one based on
historical relationships, tradition, etc." He
proposes then that rather than length, the features
of tenseness and rounding were the most important
elements in borrowings from Slavic into Old
Prussian. Levin, 1972, 153, establishes the
following phonetic realization of the pre-Elbing
vocalic system:

ī   ū

  i   u

     ɛ   ɔ

        ǣ   ā

and then proposes the following substitution rule:

$$\text{Slavic} \begin{bmatrix} -\text{Cons} \\ -\text{High} \\ \alpha\text{Round} \\ \beta\text{Back} \end{bmatrix} \text{ is replaced by Prussian } \begin{bmatrix} -\text{Cons} \\ -\text{High} \\ \alpha\text{Round} \\ \beta\text{Back} \end{bmatrix}$$

5.903 Levin writes, 1972, 153: "Thus a Slavic segment perceived as [-High, -Round], i.e., [ě, a], regardless of its phonetic length, was replaced by a Prussian segment which was [-High, -Round, +Long], since in Prussian the concomitant feature [-Round] perceptually signaled the feature [+Long] in [-High] vocalic segments. Since Slavic [e o] were [-High, +Round], they were perceived as [-High, +Round, -Long], because rounding was a concomitant feature of [-Long, -High] vocalic segments in Pomesanian Prussian."

One thing that slightly puzzles me is the motivation for perceiving Slavic [e] as rounded.[52]
5.904 It must be kept in mind now that we have the following correspondences of the pre-Elbing vocalic system given above with the underlying Elbing vocalic system:

1. pre-Elbing	2. Elbing underlying system	3. with lowering of short vowels
ī	ī (+High, -Back, +Long)	ī
i	i (+High, -Back, -Long)	ɪ
ū	ū (+High, +Back, +Long)	ū
u	u (+High, +Back, -Long)	ʊ
ǣ	ɛ̄ (-High, -Back, +Long)	ɛ̄
e	ɛ (-High, -Back, -Long)	æ
ā	ɔ̄ (-High, +Back, +Long)	ɔ̄
ɔ	ɔ (-High, +Back, -Long)	a

5.905 Levin, 1974, 25-44, repeats essentially the same explanation, but here, 29, he gives explicitly the vocalic system which results from his vowel lowering rule:

```
    ī                                        ū
       ɪ                              ʊ
          ɛ̄                    ɔ̄
              æ        a
```

5.906 Now the chief gain in Levin's analysis is that it purports to explain the reversal of the renderings of a and o in their transition from Slavic into the Old Prussian Elbing vocabulary. For me the difficulty is the rule which lowers underlying short vowels. For somebody who has not grown up with TG grammar an explanation which involves rule change is not an explanation but a

description. The matter has been discussed in
Anttila, 1974, 128-189, so there is no need for me
to repeat what Anttila has already said so well.
In the final analysis the solution to the problem
depends upon what human beings find credible and
what is credible seems to be more of a matter of
the predominant social movement than anything else.
5.907 Here I should like to paraphrase Levin's
theory in terms which are easier for a non-
generative linguist to understand. At an early
stage in Pomesanian Old Prussian the long vowels
ǣ and ā were lower than their short counterparts
ɛ and ɔ. At this time the Slavic low vowels ǣ(ě)
and ā were perceived as OP ǣ and ā respectively
and the Slavic vowels e and o were perceived as OP
ɛ and ɔ. The length distinction had been
retained in Pomesanian Old Prussian, but not in
Slavic. After the Slavic words had been borrowed
into Old Prussian, there was a rule change such
that the Old Prussian long and short non-high
vowels reversed their position as regards height.
The long vowels were raised and the short vowels
were lowered. (The raising of the long vowels is
obscured by the intercalation of the underlying
vocalic system which has only two degrees of
vocalic height.)
5.908 I personally prefer to see gradual changes
in vocalic systems in somewhat Labovian or Prague
school terms 53 Such sudden shifts from one system
to another do not seem likely to me, but, of
course, this is my personal preference. I suspect,
however, that the theories of language change which
see sudden shifts as a result of the application
of rules are rather a function of the desire of
the linguist to find a rigorous theory to match
his intellectual tastes rather than the result of
any profound study of sound change in progress. All
of the rigorous scientific theories of language
from de Saussure on have put blinders on linguists
and these blinders have directed research and
impeded empirical observation or data gathering.
Levin's vowel lowering rule appears to me to be
a description of what might have happened rather
than an explanation of what did happen. But
apparently just as one man's meat is another man's

poison, one man's explanation is another man's
description. Much of linguistics depends upon
what you can get people to believe. A charismatic
personality and an unrelenting condescension to
opposing views seem to be just as effective in the
missionary process as an appeal to direct
observation.[54]

5.909 It does seem to me that Levin is correct in
assuming that distinctions in vocalic length were
retained in Old Prussian. But if it can be
assumed that the length correlates existed in Old
Prussian at the time of the borrowings, one could
perhaps assume that the same length correlates
existed in Slavic. Thus nothing would be easier
than to set up side by side:

$\breve{\imath}$	Proto-Slavic $\breve{u}$		Proto-Old Prussian $\breve{u}$
$\overline{\imath}$	$\overline{y}$	$\overline{u}$	$\overline{\imath}$	$\overline{u}$
$\breve{e}$		$\breve{a}$	$\breve{e}$	$\breve{a}$

For the development of the Slavic vocalism see
Schmalstieg, 1971c. If borrowings were made at
this stage, then one could assume a following step
in which, at least, in some positions, the length
distinctions were neutralized in both languages.
In Proto-Slavic the long low vowels were lowered,
whereas in Old Prussian the short low vowels
were lowered, creating respectively:[55]

Proto-Slavic		Proto-Old Prussian	
i (< *ī) y (< *ȳ) u (< *ū)		i (< *ī)	u (< *ū)
ь (< *i)	ъ (< *u)	I (< *i)	ʊ (< *u)
e (< *e)	o (< *a)	e (< *ē)	o (< *ā)
ě (< *ē)	a (< *ā)	æ (< *e)	a (< *a)

But I would prefer at the moment at least not to
insist on such an evolution since, like Levin, I
would prefer to see a solution which did not
involve Slavic length correlates. Essentially I
have no answer to the problem which Levin has
taken up and within the framework of generative
grammar Levin's solution seems quite acceptable to
me.

5.910 I assumed, 1959a, chiefly on the basis of an
analysis of the Old Prussian catechisms that there

had been in Old Prussian a merger of */Cja/ and
*/Ce/ (<**/Ce/ and **/Cje/) similar to the one
observed in standard Lithuanian. (See also 5.000.)
The assumed merger of */Ce/ and */Cja/ would have
passed to /C'a/ (or /C'e/) and would have rendered
the etymological contrast /e/ vs. /a/ without
function in position after consonant, the /e/
following a palatalized consonant and the /a/
following an unpalatalized consonant.
5.911 But Levin argues, 1974, 9: "The evidence of
Elb, however, controverts this supposed identity.
In that monument we find unmistakable differentiation in the spelling of etymological /Cja/ and
/Ce/. Examples of the former are: median - Lith.
mẽdžias, wargien - Lith. vãrias, garian - Lith.
girià, and kargis - Lith. kãrias. Examples of the
latter are: mettan - Lith. mẽtas, pleske - Lith.
plẽškẽ, kraclan - Lith. krẽklas, melato - Lith.
meletà, semme - Lith. žẽmė." (To the best of my
knowledge there is no form semme in the Elbing
vocabulary. We find there only samyen [237]
'field,' and same [24] 'earth' and in the IIIrd
catechism we find [Trautmann, 1910, 65, line 33]
semmē.) See also 11.010.
5.912 But in standard Lithuanian /e/ can be
written as -ia- or e, the difference in graphemic
representation being morphophonemic rather than
phonemic. Thus Lith. mẽdžias = /m'eˑdž'es/,
vãrias = /vaˑr'es/, girià = /gir'èˑ/, kãrias =
/kaˑr'es/, mẽtas = /m'eˑtas/, krẽklas = /kr'eˑklas/,
meletà = /m'el'età/, žẽmė = /ž'eˑm'ėˑ/, etc. Now
one could argue that one would not expect
morphophonemic orthography on the part of the
German scribe, i.e., that morphophonemic
orthography demands native competence in a
language. Levin may be right, if he were to argue
thus, but a comparison with Lithuanian is hardly
very important. In other words we find in
standard Lithuanian the orthographic principle
that e or ia denotes [e] after a soft consonant and
a denotes [a] after a hard consonant with contrast
between /e/ and /a/ in word-initial position only.
Why couldn't the same principle hold for Old
Prussian as well?
5.913 Levin's evidence could be used to support

the thesis that there was a contrast between /Cj/
or /C'/ vs. a plain consonant /C/, but the examples
do not say much about the nature of the following
vowel. In both <u>wargien</u> and <u>garian</u> I would assume
the final syllable to be /-r'an/ or /-rjan/ or
/-r'en/ or /-rjen/, but I do not see the vowels as
contrasting in spite of the graphemic evidence.
Levin, **1974**, 10, writes: "The loss of /j/ after the
liquids is most unlikely. It is difficult to
imagine a German scribe consistently marking a
palatalized /l'/ from original /lj/, as he would
seem to in <u>kelian</u>, <u>saligan</u>, L <u>žãlias</u>. One would
expect him to identify a sequence /l'a/ with his
own /la/." If Levin is right, then the example,
<u>melato</u> could show /l'a/ (from */le/ **or** */lja/)
as I might have proposed. Of course, this example
is a kind of trick which I have quoted in order to
show Levin's inconsistency.[56] But I do not wish to
be tricky, but to get at the truth of the matter.
I would be willing to concede that there might not
have been palatalization of consonants before front
vowels in the Pomesanian dialect, but I would not
be willing to concede that /e/ and /a/ contrasted
after an etymological */Cj/ or */C'/. My thesis
rests, of course, on the generally held assumption
that the Common Baltic contrast between */Cje/ and
*/Ce/ was abolished in all of the Baltic languages,
cf., e.g., the Lith. voc. sg. <u>svetè</u> from <u>svẽčias</u>
'guest.' Once this latter contrast was abolished
there could be no contrast between /e/ and /a/
after */Cj/ because the sequence */Cje/ would no
longer exist.
5.914 Levin writes, 1974, 10: "Not only do I
interpret the spelling to show a surface /j/
(perhaps with phonetic palatalization of the
preceding consonant), but I consider it probable
that /j/ was preserved or restored after liquids
even before a front vowel, at least across a stem
boundary. Examples are: <u>kargis</u>, and <u>angurgis</u>,
Lith. <u>ungurỹs</u>."[57]
5.915 The problem of <u>angurgis</u> is particularly
complex. If the final syllable is identified with
that of Lith. <u>ungurỹs</u> 'eel,' then we must assume
one of the following phonemicizations: 1. */-rīs/,
2. */-r'īs/, 3. */-rjīs/. If the first is assumed,

then we may ask why the -g- is written after the
r-. Perhaps it is just a whim of the German
scribe.
5.916 If the second is assumed, then we might
make the following proposals: A. This is merely
evidence that consonants before front vowels were
palatalized and were haphazardly noted as such by
the German scribe. B. Perhaps the palatalized
-r'- derives from positions where -r'- originally
occurred before a non-front vowel and was
substituted analogically back into position before
a front vowel, cf., e.g., Lith. gen. sg. ùngurio.
C. The second situation derives directly from
situation three.
5.917 If the third situation is assumed, then we
may presuppose one of the following developments:
A. The phonemic sequence */-rjīs/ was inherited
directly from Common Baltic. If this is the case,
then we must give up the generally held opinion
that in the sequence of consonant plus *j plus
front vowel the *j was lost. We must also ask how
*j came to be there in the first place, because
from the Indo-European point of view the *j is a
kind of automatic variant of *i and as such will be
ordinarily replaced by i between consonants. Thus
a sequence like */Cjī/ is really impossible for
Indo-European. A Sievers-law variant could be
*/-Cijī/, but this is not to be expected since the
preceding syllable (i.e. /-gu-/ is light). B. Now
another posibility is that post-consonantal */j/
retained in position before non-front vowels was
again substituted into position before front vowel,
i.e., before the sequence */īs/.
        Levin, 1974, 47, says further that spellings
such as angurgis (and *kargis, corrected from
kragis) show the introduction of /j/ before a front
vowel as a result of the analogical influence of
the other cases. He comments in footnote 3: "The
change is also a strong argument against the
existence of palatalization in Pomesanian, at
least as traditionally formulated. If Pomesanian
had had phonetic palatalization before front vowels,
as well as palatalized consonants from original
C + j before back vowels, the first stage indicated
above would have been realized as

Stem *[kɔr'ɔ-]
Nom. *[kɔr'is].

There would have been no grounds for the
introduction of an 'analogical' /j/, attested in
angurgis and kragis, since the realization would
have been identical." Levin's argument assumes
what is to be proved, viz., that the grapheme -g-
must denote /j/ rather than palatalization of the
preceding /r/. In addition, if we accept the
traditional statement that post-consonantal *j was
lost in Common Baltic before a front vowel, then
we must assume the analogical restoration of a
phonemic sequence which had been abolished for
phonological reasons. Such a solution is not, of
course, impossible, but one would prefer some other
solution. Would one assume, for example, that
final consonants could have been restored
analogically in Common Slavic after the action of
the so-called 'law of open syllables.' Would one
assume a new nominative singular *slovos could have
been created on the basis of a gen. sg. slovese,
etc.? C. The sequence */-rjis/ could have come
directly from */-rjas/ since in the Elbing
vocabulary all final */-as/ seem to be represented
by orthographic -is at least, although it is not
certain whether the final */-as/ passed to /-is/
or whether final -is is merely a graphemic
representation of /-as/. It seems likely that at
least some Baltic language probably had final
*/-rjas/ in this word, cf. Finnish ankerias 'eel.'
There are probably other possibilities which have
not occurred to me, but the preceding shows at
least the theoretical complexity of the situation.
5.918 Levin states, 1974, 10: "In fact, the
existence of even phonetic palatalization in Elb
cannot be maintained with certainty, except for /sj-/.
The sole spelling interpreted this way in Elb -
plieynis for *pleynis... - involves a phonetic
environment where palatalization is acoustically
less noticeable to a foreigner than in many other
environments. There are no examples with an
indication of phonetic palatalization after
labials, where it is much easier to hear."
Although it isn't specifically mentioned here I
assume that Levin is considering palatalization of

consonants by following front vowels since the
examples from the Elbing vocabulary piuclan (547)
'sickle,' wupyan (9) 'cloud,' wormyan (463) 'red,'
knapios 'hemp,' etc. are well known, see Endzelīns,
1943, 33. Of course, if one is unwilling to
accept writings with y, i, g as denoting palatalization, then indeed it is impossible to show
palatalization, since the German scribes did not
have a set of phonetic symbols at their disposal
for this purpose. I would only note that at least
the letter i is used to denote palatalization
under some circumstances in Polish and Lithuanian.
If one is willing to accept the possibility that
these letters may have denoted palatalization since
the scribe had no other means of denoting
palatalization at his disposal, then I believe that
my argument is stronger. In any case I believe
that there is an example which may show palatalization of a labial before a front vowel, viz.,
samyen (237) 'field' which both Endzelīns, 1943,
241 and Trautmann, 1910, 418, connect with same
(EV - 24), semmey, etc. from the catechisms and
Lith. žẽmė, Latv. zeme 'earth.' Endzelīns writes
samyen with -yen< *-jan, but it would seem much
more plausible to me to consider samyen an
accusative singular form equivalent to Lith. acc.
sg. žẽmę. If this latter example is interpreted
then in the way which I propose, it would
indeed constitute evidence of palatalization of a
labial by a following front vowel. In fact I would
suggest that even if samyen were to be analyzed as
a neuter with a stem in -en, the -y- would seem to
denote palatalization of the preceding m-.
5.919 I would grant that we don't actually know
what the scribe may have meant by the orthographic
sequence -ea-, but we do find a word pannean 'mossy
fen' (EV - 288) which is commonly compared with
Lith. pania-bùdė 'kind of mushroom,' Latv. paṇa,
pane 'puddle, liquid manure.' If the etymology is
correct, and it would seem to be quite good to me,
then we can see that either /nja/, /n'a/, /nje/ or
/n'e/ is rendered by -(n)nea-. Extrapolating from
this then, we may guess that in peadey 'socks'
(EV - 482), cf. Lith. pedẽ 'sandal,' the p- is
palatalized.[58]
5.920 I think that it is clearly established that

the evidence from one dialect should not be used to
establish the phonemic system of a second dialect.
On the other hand, I think it should be pointed out
here that the evidence of phonetic palatalization
of labial consonants before front vowels is fairly
strong in the orthography of the dialect of the
catechisms, cf. OP penckts, pyienkts, piēncts,
fem. piencktā beside Lith. peñktas 'fifth.' See
Endzelīns, 1943, 18.
5.921 Levin, 1974, 17, writes: "There is one
clear example of a Prussian /C + j/ sequence for
a Slavic [r' + back vowel], and one other example,
which is, however, questionable. First, the
sounder example is Prussian sweriapis, Elb 431,
'jousting horse,' as the source of which an Old
Polish *s'v'er'op...is reconstructed, cf. świerzop,
'wild trefoil,' świerzopa, 'young mare.' This
example is a stronger argument against phonetic
palatalization before front vowels than any of the
examples given above. If Prussian possessed a
[r'æ] - [ra] or /r'a/ - /ra/ contrast, as
Schmalstieg believes, in addition to /r + j/
sequences, we would expect a Prussian *[r'æ]
(spelled re or ra) for Slavic [r'o]. Instead,
Slavic [r'o] is replaced by Pomesanian /rja/.
A presumably nonpalatalizing language replaces
/C' + back vowel/ with /C + j + back vowel/
sequence."
    I believe that the fatal flaws in Levin's
argument center on the words 'we would expect'
and 'one would expect him [a German scribe] to'
(see 5.913). A German scribe is free to write Old
Prussian in any way he sees fit and is not required
to conform to our theoretical expectations. If he
wishes to write palatalized /r'/ as -ri- (as is
done in contemporary Lithuanian) he may. If he
wishes to disregard this palatalization in his
transcription he is free to choose this option
also. I might point out here that if one judges by
the way an English speaker hears Lithuanian, one
can easily understand why the palatalization of
consonants before front vowels which is much less
clear to the non-native might go unmarked, whereas
the palatalization of consonants before non-front
vowels would be more frequently marked.

The important point is, however, that other people do not have to live up to our expectations, whether it be in choosing the correct way of writing another language or in choosing the correct doctrine of linguistics. Thus, for example, it may be perfectly obvious to one person that generative grammar is the only way to handle linguistic phenomena, but it may be just as obvious to another person that generative grammar has nothing to do with the way people actually use language. In other words people do not have to conform to our preconceived notions of logical and consistent behaviour patterns.

5.922 Levin also says, 1974, 10, that a lowering of front vowels might imply phonetic palatalization, but that vowels can be lowered for reasons other than for palatalization. I would definitely agree with Levin on this point and I would see palatalization as neutralizing the front/back contrast rather than the contrast in height. I feel that the Lithuanian lowering of */ĕ/ and */ă/ is definitely connected with the creation of a vocalic length contrast when */ĕNs/ and */ăNs/ passed to /ęs, ąs/ and /ēs, ās/ respectively. Likewise the lowering of Slavic ě and a is to be connected with the loss of the length contrast in certain environments, see Schmalstieg, 1971c and 1972b.

5.923 Levin, 1974, 33-44, discusses the rendering of Slavic /u, i,ъ,ь, y) in the borrowings of the Elbing vocabulary, but here we find no real surprises. Examples are: OP dusi (EV - 153)'soul,' Polish dusza; OP garkity (EV - 269) 'mustard,' Polish gorczyca; OP tuckoris (EV - 454) 'weaver,' from Common Slavic *tъkarь; sticlo (EV - 401) 'glass,' from Common Slavic *stьklo.

In terms of distinctive feature analysis the Old Prussian rendering of Slavic y by Baltic ui presents a few problems so that we end up with a kind of monster rule: (Levin, 1974, 40)

$$\text{Slavic} \begin{bmatrix} +\text{High} \\ +\text{Back} \\ -\text{Round} \end{bmatrix} \rightarrow \text{Prussian} \begin{bmatrix} +\text{High} \\ +\text{Back} \\ +\text{Round} \end{bmatrix} + \begin{bmatrix} -\text{Round} \\ -\text{Back} \end{bmatrix}$$

I must confess to seeing nothing unusual in the rendering of Slavic /y/ by Baltic /ui/. American

students of the Russian language frequently render
Russian /y/ by English /ui/, /uj/ or the like. I
believe that they hear a slight labialization of
the preceding consonant, a labialization which
fades quickly, but which is sufficient to cause
the American to hear a /u/.
5.924. I would not be surprised at the rendering
of Slavic ǫ by Old Prussian un. We encounter, for
example OP dumpbis (EV - 512) 'tanbark,' Polish
dąb; OP *cunclis (EV - 272) 'corn-cockle,' Polish
kąkol; OP wumbaris (EV-556) 'pail, bucket,' Polish
węborek; OP weloblundis (EV-437) 'mule,' Polish
wielbłąd, see Levin, 1974, 41-42. I assume that
prior to the creation of nasal vowels in Proto-
Slavic the sequence *-aNC (from *-oNC and *-aNC)
passed to *-uNC. Evidence of the early Common
Slavic merger of *-aNC with *-uNC is furnished by
the development of the *ā-stem accusative plural
ending *-āNs which passed to *-aNs and the *o-stem
accusative plural ending *-oNs which also passed to
*-aNs. The merged *o- and *ā-stem accusative
plural ending *-aNs then passed to *-uNs (as in
eastern Lithuanian dialects) and with denasaliza-
tion to *-ūs and then to *-ū (with loss of final
*-s) and then to -y, see Schmalstieg, 1971c.
5.930 In her 1974 article I. Steponavičienė notes
that there were about 130 Old Prussians serving the
Knights of the Cross as spies who helped to prepare
the famous Wegeberichte or intelligence reports.
For the majority of them even their place of origin
is shown, so that it can be established that they
are not all from the same tribe. Most are from
Samland (Sambia), but the territories of Scalovia,
Nattangia, Nadrovia, Varmia, Pogesania and Barthia
(this last by one only) are also represented. On
the basis of this Steponavičienė, 165, suggests that
the Lithuanian names may have been somewhat
Prussianized before being written down for the
Germans.
5.931 She writes, 1974, 166, that in the Wegeberichte Lith. s may be rendered by s(ss), cf.
e.g., Lith. Saũslaukis = Sawlawken, Lith.
Stãkliškės = Stakelisken, Lith. Skrandénai =
Skrunden, Lith. Strévà = Strewe, Lith. Sasnà =
Sassene, Lith. Semelìškės = Symyliskin. Lith. š

may also be rendered by s (ss), cf., e.g., Lith.
Satìjai = Setin, Lith. Bìrštonas = Birsten, Lith.
Ašvijà = Aswee, Asswe, Asswee, Lith. Pãšilė =
Passeel, Lith. Máišiagala = Maysegaln, Meysegaln,
Lith. Šlynà = Isslene, Lith. Širvintà = Sirwinte,
Lith. Šventupỹs = Swintoppe, Lith. Šalčinykai =
Salseniken.
5.932 Steponavičienė points out also that the
writing of the s is not uniform at all. It is
frequently written with the letters sz, cz, z, ssz,
scz, which could also, by the way, denote the
consonant š. She lists also, 166: Rawsze, Rawse,
Rause = Lith. Raũsvė; Werszaka, Wersaka,
Wersszaka = Lith. Versekà, Versakà; Thobesze,
Dobyse = Lith. Dubỹsa; Zele. Sele = Lith.
Selos, all of which show various renderings of
Lithuanian s. As examples of the rendering of
Lithuanian š she gives: Parzepil, Parssenpil,
Parsepil = Lith. Paršo pilis; Sczeszuwa, Sessow =
Lith. Šešuvìs; Szyse, Czyse, Syse = Lith. Sỹšà;
Szalltona, Saltone = Lith. Šaltuonà.
5.933 According to Steponavičienė the orthographic
s(ss), cz, sz, z, scz instead of the expected sch
to denote Lith. š is the fault of the Old Prussian
agents who, when they heard a place name with
Lithuanian š, changed it to s on the basis of the
corresponding word in their own language, cf. Lith.
šuõ = OP sunis 'dog.' The German author of the
Wegebericht, himself pronouncing the Lithuanian
place name according to the pronunciation of the
agent, wrote letters corresponding to the consonant
s rather than š.
5.934 On the other hand Steponavičienė, 166-167,
says that cases are encountered where the letters
sch denote š: Karschowin, Karsov = Lith. Karšuvà;
Schawden = Lith. Šiaũduva; Lakawsche = Lith.
Lókauša; Eikschisken, Eiksischken = Lith. Eĩšiškės.
These place names are from the Wegeberichte in
which the Old Prussian agents were from Scalovia
and Samland, i.e., from those areas which were
closest to Lithuanian territories and therefore we
can assume that they had a better knowledge of the
Lithuanian language.
5.935 Steponavičienė, 1974, 167, writes that we
find the ž replaced by z and written with the

letters s or z: Seymen, Zeymen = Lith. Žeĩmiai,
Žeĩmis; Sillyn = Lith. Žilinaĩ; Drabose = Lith.
Drabùžis; Gresen = Lith. Greižénai; Weywirse =
Lith. Veivìržas; Esenen = Lith. Ýžnė; Crasien =
Lith. Krãžiai; Sysmare = Lith. Žiežmãriai;
Semegallen = Lith. Žemýgala, etc.; Zereens = Lith.
Ežerỹnas. We do find in several cases an sch
denoting a ž, cf. Naweschen = Lith. Nevėžis,
Graschyn = Lith. Krãžiai.

5.936 It seems to me that for a study like
Steponavičienė's one might ask exactly what
contrastive possibilities there were in German.
In the dialects of the German order did /s/, /z/,
/š/ and /ž/ contrast and how could they be written
in order to show this contrast? If there was no
*/ž/, for example, as there well might not have
been, why would we expect the German scribe to
write sch rather than s?[59]Neither writing would
render exactly the Lithuanian /ž/. Did /s/
contrast with /š/ and if so under what
circumstances? Steponavičienė quotes Karschowin
and Karsov = Lith. Karšuvà, but could a German
contrast the phonemic sequences /rs/ and /rš/ and
indeed as long as he could understand what place
was meant did it really make any difference to him
how it was pronounced? Different speakers within
the very same dialect area may be capable of
assimilating a non-native sequence or manner of
pronunciation with varying degrees of ability. As
an American I note all kinds of pronunciations of
non-native names. I notice that some Americans are
incapable of the consonant cluster /šm/, whereas
others seem to have no trouble, so I hear my own
name, for example, pronounced variously sometimes
with an initial /šm-/ and sometimes with an initial
/sm-/.[60]

5.937 Steponavičienė, 167, writes that the
Lithuanian place name Ẽžeruona = dial. Ẽžerūna is
written as Asarune and that here we find Asar-
instead of the expected Eser- with the vocalism
remodeled on the basis of OP assar-an (EV - 60)
'lake.' But Lithuanian e is very open and perhaps
a German scribe heard the e as being closer to his
a. Steponavičienė herself gives the form Naweschen
for Lith. Nevėžis in which an a is used to render

a Lithuanian e.

Steponavičienė, 167, also suggests that the rendering of Lith. Šventója (river name) by Swintove was influenced by the existence of the Old Prussian morpheme swint- 'holy.' She also finds one case in which Lithuanian -ie- is rendered by Old Prussian -ai-, -ay-, viz., Wayswille, Waiswilgen = Lith. Viesvilė.

Old Prussian Nominal Morphology

6.000 In my discussion of the nominal inflection
I shall concentrate on those cases concerning the
origin of which there is some dispute in the recent
literature.
6.010 According to Stang, 1966, 10, in the genitive
singular of the etymological *o-stem nouns we find
a trace of the old ending *-s(ī)o: deiwas '[of]
god.' The fact that the -a- is retained in deiwas
shows that originally there was some vowel after
the final -s. Traces of the ending in a vowel are
preserved in the masc. gen. sg. form stessei. See 11.202.
6.011 Schmitt-Brandt, 1971, 226, says that in the
Old Prussian genitive singular deiwas < *deiuoso
we see the retention of an ending which has a
correspondent in Proto-Norse godagas where -as
<*-oso follows   the pattern of the other cases
which have a and thereby replaces *-eso which
comes from the pronoun (cf. Old Norse þess, OP
stesse, Old Church Slavic česo). Schmitt-Brandt
remarks further that an Indo-European *-os such as
represented in the Hittite genitive singular ending
-aš would have given a form such as *deiws similar
to what we find in the nominative singular. If
there had been an original *-as after the pattern
of the a-stems (replacing earlier *-ā < *-ad/t) one
would expect in the IIIrd catechism after labials
and gutturals *-us or *-os instead of *-as. I
would suggest that whatever the origin of the
genitive singular may be, there is no particular
reason to assume that /as/ would always be rendered
by *-os or *-us after labials or 'gutturals.'
The graphemic o or u after labials and velars is
merely the sporadic rendering of the labialization,
see para. 5.201.[61]
6.012 Kazlauskas, 1968, 173-174, derives the OP
*o-stem genitive singular ending -as from *-asja.
He assumes that in the phonemic sequence *-sja the
short a became e and then the j before the front
vowel e disappeared, in other words, *-sja> *-sje>
*se. Later the short vowel -e disappeared for
systemic reasons according to which the disyllabic
ending became monosyllabic. In the genitive
singular of the pronouns such an -e (cf. stesse

144

'of that') could have remained longer since in the pronominal paradigm there were more cases having a disyllabic form (cf. the dat. sg. stesmu).

6.013 Mažiulis, 1970, 94, proposes that the OP *o-stem genitive singular ending was -as < Indo-European *-os and that there never was any second element *-ja. Essentially Mažiulis, 1970a, 97, assumes that the nominative singular and the genitive singular were originally the same and that later they were distinguished by place of stress or perhaps for morphological reasons, in other words, OP nom. sg. *(deiu-as) > (deiw)-s, gen. sg. *(deiu-as) > (deiw)-as.

6.014 Schmid, 1963, 103, has argued that the genitive singular ending -as cannot derive from Indo-European *-os since final -as either passed to -is (as in the Elbing vocabulary) or to -s as in the IIIrd catechism. Mažiulis, 1966c, 109, says, however, that although the forms are the same phonetically, they are quite different from the structural morphological point of view. He compares then the various treatments of Indo-European *-ōn, which, in his opinion developed to Lith. nom. sg. (akm-)uõ 'stone' and gen. pl. (vilk-) ų̃ '[of] wolves.' Schmid, 1963, 103, writes further that the OP gen. sg. in deiwas is to be compared with the Goth. gen. sg. dagis, Anglo-Saxon dagas with -is, -as < *-eso, *-oso. Mažiulis, 1966c, 109-110, says, however, that there is no need to derive the Germanic forms from *-oso. According to Mažiulis, 1966c, 111, the Proto-Indo-European form of the ergative could be expressed not only by the ending *-o + s, but also by the ending *-e + s, i. e., *-o/es. Thus OP (deiw)-as < *-os, Hittite (ish)-as < *-os, Anglo-Saxon (dóm)-aes < *-os-, but Gothic (wulf)-is = (þ)-is < *-es- < *-es, OCS (č)-eso < *-es, etc. After the loss of the ergative construction the original Indo-European inflectional ending *-o/es was split into the ending *-os (generalized as the nominative singular) and the ending *-o/es, retained as the genitive singular, and later extended in some of the Indo-European dialects with the suffix *(i)e/o, cf. Skt. tas-ya, OP stess-e, Old Church Slavic čes-o, etc.

6.015 Already in 1876 Leskien, 32-33, suggested that the OP *o̦-stem genitive singular ending *-as had been borrowed from the etymological *ā-stem endings. Leskien defends his view by pointing out the various parallels between the *o̦- and *ā-stem endings, e.g., nom. pl. *o̦-stem *deiv-ai, *ā-stem gen-ai, gen. pl. *o̦-stem *deiv-an, *ā-stem *gen-an, acc. pl. *o̦-stem deiv-ans, *ā-stem gen-ans, etc. I would prefer Leskien's view, but rather than assume that the change had taken place within the Old Prussian language, I suspect that the German pastors (Abel␣Will and others) had discovered that the ending *-as of the *ā-stem nouns was a good ending for the genitive case (and one which was reinforced by their German speech habits) and they used it indiscriminately with nouns of whatever stem. Note, for example, that the attested genitive singular forms of the word for 'son' are sunos, soūnas, saūnas and sounons (which Trautmann, 1910, 433, corrects to sounous). I am reminded of the situation of some of the elementary students of Russian who, having found that the ending -u is a good ending for the accusative of *ā-stem nouns, use the ending with great abandon for the accusative of all Russian nouns. Fortunately I am in a position to correct their mistakes, but it is difficult to imagine that an Old Prussian serf would correct the mistakes of a German pastor. It seems far more plausible to me that the original *o̦-stem genitive singular ending was *-ā just as it is in the other Baltic and Slavic languages and indeed as it is attested in the two fragments discussed in 4.503 and 4.601 which probably reflect the real Old Prussian language without the outside influence of the German pastors.

6.020 According to Stang, 1966, 181, in the *o̦-stem nouns the dative singular ending *-ōi passed to *-ūi after guttural (I prefer the term velar) and labial and then developed into -u, e.g., grīku 'sin,' schismu malnīku '[to] this child.' Since we also find the apparent dative singular in such expressions as enstesmu wirdai 'in the word' and stesmn (n for -u) kērmeneniskan īstai 'the bodily food' Stang, 1966, 181, suggests that the phonetic successor of *-ōi is -ai and that the -u of such

dative singular forms as <u>Steismu</u> <u>Piru</u> '[to the]
parish,' <u>prei</u> <u>sīru</u> '[to] heart' comes from a
transfer of the post-velar and post-labial -<u>u</u> to
other positions.[62]
6.021 Schmid, 1963, 9, suggests that the dative
in -<u>ui</u> > -<u>u</u> derives from the dative singular ending
-<u>ai</u> in position after a guttural or labial. Schmid
notes that in other morphological categories the
existence of the vacillation between -<u>ui</u>/-<u>u</u>
chiefly after guttural and labial on the one hand
and -<u>ai</u> after other consonants on the other hand,
e.g., the adverbs <u>skīstai</u> 'modestly,' <u>laimisku</u>
'amply,' the nom. pl. <u>malnijkai</u> 'children' and
<u>malnijkiku</u> 'id.' In Schmid's opinion, 1963, 11,
both the -<u>ai</u> and -<u>u</u> were spread outside of their
original boundaries, but we do not know how much
is due to Abel Will's poor control of Old Prussian
morphology and how much is the result of analogical
leveling.
6.022 Kazlauskas, 1965, 88, objects that if -<u>ai</u>
became -<u>ui</u> after labials and velars (gutturals)
and after <u>r</u>[?], why did the -<u>ui</u> then pass to -<u>u</u>?
In Lithuanian, according to Kazlauskas, the
passage of -<u>ui</u> to -<u>u</u> took place for reasons other
than phonetic reasons. Kazlauskas objects also
that in the verbal ending we almost always find
-<u>mai</u>, hardly ever -<u>u</u>. Kazlauskas presents some
further findings based on the orthography, but I
personally find both Schmid's and Kazlauskas'
traditional heavy reliance on the evidence of Old
Prussian orthography very implausible. I would
only say that Schmid has indeed noted the same
phenomena which I attribute to the German rendering
of the vowel after a labialized consonant. See
paragraph 5.200.
6.023 Mažiulis, 1970, 116, says that the Old
Prussian dative singular of the type (<u>sīr</u>)-<u>u</u>
'heart' is to be derived from Indo-European *-<u>ō</u>.
In 1968, 24, he said that the *<u>o</u>-stem dative
singular ending *-<u>ō</u> functioned in Baltic with
dative and instrumental meaning and this is why we
find such forms as <u>sen</u> <u>stesm-u</u> 'with the' and <u>sen-
ku</u> 'damit, so that.' In East Baltic the acute
ending is retained in the new paradigmatic
instrumental, cf. Lith. (<u>vilk-</u>)<u>ù</u> 'wolf' (< *-<u>ō</u>),

whereas a new intonation (the circumflex) is introduced into the dative singular (vilk-)uo.
6.030 The Old Prussian *o-stem acc. sg. (deiw-) an is just what is to be expected phonologically from *-oN (N = m or n) and all seem to be agreed on its origin, see Stang, 1966, 182.
6.040 As far as I can see, Stang, 1966, makes no mention of any Old Prussian *o-stem instrumental singular and Kazlauskas, 1968, 174, states flatly that Old Prussian had no instrumental. Mažiulis, 1970, 163, says that Old Prussian had no paradigmatic instrumental, but he finds a reliquary instrumental in the OP pronouns stu (ste) and ku, although he calls this a non-paradigmatic dative singular. The words are found in such expressions as stu ilgimi 'until' and sēnku 'so that,' kuilgimai giwassi 'as long as you live.' Stang, 1966, 177, suggests that the preceding forms reflect the instrumental case, but the fact that the instrumental case is attested in the pronoun is not necessarily proof that it existed in the noun. Stang notes the example of English which has the cases he:him, she:her and we:us in the pronoun, but no corresponding formal distinction in the noun. Stang finds a clear example of the instrumental case in such expressions as sen māim, sen maim 'with me.' On the other hand the same form does function as a dative in the expression: As N. imma tin N. māim prei ainan Salubin 'I N. take thee to myself as wife.'
6.050 Stang, 1966, 182, writes that OP bītai 'in the evening' seems to be an old adverbialized locative singular. Mažiulis, 1970, 127-129, says that the Indo-European locative and dative singular were originally the same case and that in Old Prussian the locative is expressed by en plus the dative or the accusative, e.g., en wissai nautei 'in all need' (dat. sg.) and en wissans nautins 'in all needs' (acc. pl.). Originally according to Mažiulis, 1970, 129, there was probably a distinction of dative/locative of location with en vs. an accusative as object of motion with en, but later this distinction was completely lost.
6.051 Toporov, 1961b, 283, however, writes that in Old Prussian in general there is no locative

case if one does not take into consideration the
lone example: bhe stallēti pērdin en schisman
ackewijstin Krixtiāniskan astin 'and represents
him in this evident Christian affair.' The word
schisman 'this' supposedly in the locative case
has no formal correspondent in other languages.
6.052 For the vocative singular, Stang, 1966, 183,
lists deiwa (2X) beside deiwe (2X) and tāwa
'father' (6X) vs. tāwe (7X). Mažiulis, 1970, 82,
notes the forms in -a and quotes Endzelīns, 1943,
59, to the effect that it cannot be ascertained
whether this -a replaces an earlier -e or whether
it is derived from Indo-European *-o. I assume
that the -a in place of the expected -e is merely
a scribal error. See also 11.007.
6.060 As Stang, 1966, 184, says, the *o-stem
nominative plural ending is attested by such forms
as wijr-ai 'men,' grīk-ai 'sins,' bratrīk-ai
'brothers,' waik-ai 'children,' etc. He also says
that the nom. pl. malnijkiku 'little children'
could go back to *-kūi < *-kāi and therefore serve
as support for the theory that Lith. -ai goes back
to *-āi, cf. wiss-ai smūnenisk-u 'to all human...'
as opposed to sen reddisku perdāsai 'with false
ware.' Stang states, however, that when one takes
into consideration the fact that -u occurs in the
nominative plural only twice and only in this
particular word, it seems more likely that the
ending in malnijkik-u reflects an old nom.-acc.
neuter plural. Stang quotes van Wijk, 1918, 105-
106, who in turn relies on Trautmann, 1910, 219
and Berneker, 1896, 192, disputing Bezzenberger,
1897, 303, who had suggested that the ending was
an old dual form. See Schmalstieg, 1974, 10.
6.061 Kazlauskas, 1968, 175, wrote that the Old
Prussian ending -ai which had its origin in the
noun was transferred to the pronouns and adjectives,
cf. OP nom. pl. mald-ai 'young.' The adjectival
nominative plural ending -ei is attested in OP
wert-ei 'worth, worthy,' kanxt-ei 'proper,' etc.
Mažiulis, 1970, 171, following the hypotheses of
van Wijk, 1918, 62 and Endzelīns, 1943, 69,
says that the most plausible theory of the origin
of the -ei in the adjective is that it comes from
the pronominal forms, cf. the nom. pl. masc.

tennei 'they.' Concerning the *o-stem nominative
plural ending of the adjective Stang, 1966, 258,
wrote that he considered the few forms in -ei to
be errors. I am inclined to follow Stang in this.
Mažiulis may well be right that there existed an
ending *-ei along with the ending *-oi, but the
Old Prussian evidence is not very good for this
assumption. It would appear to me that such forms
as Slavic vlьc-i 'wolves,' dobr-i 'good,' t-i 'the,
these' and Lith. ger-ì (<*-ei) 'good,' t-iẽ
'these' are better evidence for this assumption,
see Mažiulis, 1970, 172. Mažiulis, 174, also
quotes such Latin forms as nom. pl. (SERV)-EI,
(FOIDERAT)-EI and (QV-)EI to support his
assumption.
6.070 Old Prussian has a variety of forms which
seem to express the *o-stem genitive plural:
grecon, grekun, griquan 'sins' and the frequent
pronominal forms: stēison, steison, noūson
(noūsan 1X), schiēison (1X), iouson (2X), vs.
ioūsan (1X), iousan (1X). On the other hand
according to Stang, 185, we also find swintan in
which the final -an can hardly reflect the
pronunciation -ōn or the -on which derived from
it. Thus Stang proposes two genitive plural
endings, viz., *-ōn and *-an. In his opinion the
ending *-ōn passed to -on and is to be read that
way in such words as stēison, noūson, etc.
Kazlauskas, 1968, 176, says that the OP ending
-an (as in grīkan) may have derived from *-ōm
since *ō in unstressed position may have become ā.
Mažiulis, 1970, 27, says that the genitive plural
ending represented in OP grīk-an, grec-on and
grek-un all derive from Indo-European *-ōm. I do
not see any evidence in Old Prussian for deriving
the genitive plural ending from *-ōn or *-ōm. If
the *-ō- in other positions passed to -ā- one
wonders why it didn't pass to -ā- in this position.
Or if the *-ō- was shortened to -o-, then why
didn't it pass to -a-? I personally assume an Old
Prussian gen. pl. ending -an deriving directly from
Indo-European *-oN. Spellings with -on, -un, -uan
are not to be taken into consideration.
6.080 Stang, 1966, 185, writes that the Old
Prussian dative plural ending was -mans: waik-ammans
'children,' auschautenīk-amans 'debtors,' etc.

Corresponding forms are not to be found in any
other languages, but traces of the old ending -mas
are retained in the personal pronoun: nūmas (1X),
noūmas (6X) 'us,' ioūmas (3X), ioumas (6X) 'you,'
beside noūmans, ioūmans. Stang says that the form
in -mans seems to have been influenced by the
accusative plural.[63] Mažiulis, 1966d, 51-52,
derives the ending -mans from *-mons and the
ending -mas from the dual ending *-mo strengthened
by the addition of the plural marker -s, see also
Mažiulis, 1970, 209-210. Kazlauskas, 1970, 89,
assumes an etymological dative plural ending -mas
(< *-mos) in which the a was somewhat rounded so
that the ending passed to Lith. -mus but to OP
-mas. Kazlauskas also assumes an OP dative dual
formant *-man (cf. Skt. -bhyām) under the
influence of which the dative plural ending -mas
passed to -mans. Mažiulis, 1971, 103, writes that
the fundamental idea of Kazlauskas' article is
based on the following assumption: If, e.g., in
Latin and the Indo-Iranian languages after the
dative plural formant *-bh(i̯)- there follows a
vowel *-o-, then in the Balto-Slavic languages
after the dative plural formant *-m- one should
reconstruct the same *-o-. Mažiulis then objects
that this assumption is not necessarily valid at
all, because if the formants *-m- and *-bh- do not
agree, then why should the vocalic elements
agree? Likewise one may note that the short vowel
of the Sanskrit inst. pl. ending *-bhis does not
agree with the long vowel posited for the Lith.
inst. pl. ending -mis (< *-mīs). Mažiulis says
that Kazlauskas considers as the strongest
argument allowing him to derive Lith. -mus from
*-mas is his assumption that at a rather early
date the *-a- in the formant *-mas was reduced to
*-ẕ- and thus Baltic *-mas developed into Lith.
-mẕs which was reflected in early Lithuanian as
written -mus. Kazlauskas assumes also that this
Lith. -mẕs, losing the reduced vowel -ẕ- gave
Lith. -ms found in old writings and in contemporary dialects. But Mažiulis, 1971, 104, objects
that nobody has shown that the vowel written as
-u- in the sequence -mus was indeed a reduced
vowel. In Daukša's Postilė (16th century) the

formant -mus occurs 3,471 times whereas the formant
-ms occurs only 68 times. One might expect that if
such a reduced vowel had existed in the dialect of
Daukša's Postilė, the ending -ms would have been
written everywhere, but this is not the case.
Mažiulis, 1971, 104, also finds that Kazlauskas'
hypothesis concerning the prior existence of an Old
Prussian dative dual formant *-man < *-mān is not on
firm ground either. Such a form is not indicated
by the evidence of the other Baltic or Slavic
languages. It is true that Kazlauskas cites the
Skt. dative dual ending -bhyām, thinking that the
addition of the final nasal is a common Indic and
West Baltic feature. But this is doubtful since
the addition of the nasal in Indic is not old, but
an Indic innovation as one can see by the Old
Persian cognate ending -biyā which lacks the
nasal. See also 11.201.
6.090 Stang, 1966, 186, proposes that a common
Baltic accusative plural ending *-ōns passed to
*-uons in West Baltic where it furnished the basis
for the Lith.-Latv. ending -us. The ending *-ōns
passed to *-ons and eventually to the attested
ending -ans in Old Prussian. Mažiulis, 1970, 188,
suggests that the ending *-ōns gave the East Baltic
accusative plural ending, whereas its unstressed
allomorph *-ans gave the Old Prussian ending. I
have suggested, 1973a, 151, that Proto-Indo-
European had an original undifferentiated nom.-
acc. plural ending *-ōs (derived from *-ō + s)
which was in competition with a newer accusative
plural ending *-ons (derived from the accusative
singular *-on + s). I assume the East Baltic
accusative plural ending to reflect the old *-ōs
(with nasalization in dialects from other stems or
else from contamination with the innovation *-ons).
The Old Prussian ending *-ans comes directly from
the Indo-European *-on + s.
6.100 Stang, 1966, 187, says that the Elbing
vocabulary retained the neuter gender better than
the catechisms. In the former we find such
examples as assaran 'lake,' lunkan 'bast,' etc.,
but in the catechisms we find only a few scattered
examples, e.g., testamentan, testamenten in the Ist
and IInd catechisms respectively, but testaments

in the IIIrd catechism. Mažiulis, 1970, 84-87,
suggests that in Proto-Old Prussian there were
originally two variants of the neuter nominative-
accusative singular ending, viz. -an and -a (this
latter attested in two adjectives from GrG salta
[47] 'cold,' debica [48] 'great,' and wissa 'all'
from the IIIrd catechism). In Old Prussian for the
most part the ending -an was generalized in the
nouns and adjectives. The ending -a is still to be
found in the pronoun sta 'this' and in the three
adjectives mentioned above. This latter ending is
cognate with the ending of Russian mal-o, Lith.
mãž-a 'little.'
6.200 There are apparently some -(i)i̯o-stem nouns
in Old Prussian. Stang, 1966, 191, compares OP
cuylis (EV - 683) with Lithuanian kuilỹs 'stud
boar' and OP insuwis (EV - 94) with Lith. liežùvis
'tongue,' etc., but notes that in Pomesanian (i.e.,
the dialect of the Elbing vocabulary) -as passed
partially to -is. Here also -i̯as and -ii̯as are
also represented by -is; in the IIIrd catechism we
encounter, e.g., poūis 'drink,' Īdis = Lith. ědis
'food.' The IIIrd catechism word rikijs and the
noun medies (EV - 696) 'hunter' belong, according
to Stang, 1966, 192,to the category of -Īi̯o-stem
nouns. Stang, 192, suggests that the -ie- in
medies = Ī. I am inclined, however, to accept what
Trautmann, 1910, 376, says, viz., that medies =
Lith. medijas.
6.210 Stang, 1966, 195, lists the genitive
singular forms of the word for 'neighbor':
tawischas (3X), tauwyschies (1X), tawischis (2X)
and tauwyschis (1X). According to Stang the word
must be a i̯o-stem, because we encounter sch, i.e.,
š < sj. The genitive singular in -as (-'es) can be
compared to the gen. sg. deiwas beside the nom. sg.
deiws. In Stang's opinion the ending -is of
noseilis 'spirit,' powaisennis 'conscience' and
tawischis is probably a remodeling of *-'as under
the influence of the nominative in -is. In my own
view, if the word noseilis is an i-stem noun, the
genitive singular should be read as /naseil-eis/,
see Schmalstieg, 1974, 75.
6.300 Stang, 1966, 197, lists the typical ā-stem
nominative singular endings found in OP mens-ā

153

'flesh,' genn-a 'woman,' and mens-o (EV - 154, 374)
'flesh, meat.' Since he believes that after
guttural (I prefer the term velar) and labial
Sambian -a̅ (i.e., the dialect of the catechisms)
passed to -u̅, he gives the examples OP merg-u
'maid' = Lith. mergà, OP gall-u̅ (cf. EV 504 galwo)=
Lith. galvà 'head.' In my opinion there is also
the possibility that the orthographic u denoted
[ua], see 5.323. Stang says that in the IIIrd
catechism the ending -a̅ is frequently extended with
the particle (a)i, e.g., crixtisnai (2X) beside
crixtisna (4X) 'Christianity,' mensai (1X) beside
mensa̅ (1X). The same phenomenon is found in the
pronoun, cf., e.g., the nom. sg. fem. stai 'this.'⁶⁴
Although the final -i in these forms may bear
evidence of an etymological particle, there is also
the possibility that it just denotes the length of
the preceding vowel according to the orthographic
habit of Middle Low German, cf. Lasch, 1914, 25,
who gives such examples as raid 'wheel' and jair
'year' for standard German Rad and Jahr respectively.
6.310 Stang, 1966, 197, quotes van Wijk, 1918,
67ff. to the effect that the genitive singular
ending -as has a short vowel. Stang says that the
shortening seems to be older than the supposed
passage of a̅ to u̅ after labial and guttural (velar),
cf. OP a̅lgas 'wage, salary' beside Lith. algõs
'id.,' OP galwas-delli̅ks 'chief article' beside
Lith. galvõs, OP menses in the genitive singular
beside the nom. sg. mensa̅. Van Wijk, 1918, 71,
suggested that a̅lgas and menses had short vowels in
the genitive singular by analogy with the
accusative singular, the ending for which was
always unstressed, and which was rendered by -an
already in Proto-Baltic. Likewise in van Wijk's
opinion there must have been stem-stressed classes
in which the vowel of the genitive singular was
automatically shortened. The short vowel from
these classes was then generalized throughout the
paradigm. Stang, 1966, 198, thinks, however, that
such accusative singular forms as are attested in
the IInd catechism, e.g., mergwan 'maid,'
perronisquan 'parish' are etymologically
the expected result. Thus the shortening in the

vowel of the accusative singular must have taken
place after the change of ā after the velar. If
the shortening in the genitive had taken place
before the change of ā to ū, then the shortening in
the genitive could not be explained by the
shortening in the accusative where we find clear
traces of the vowel change in question. One
could, however, suppose that a form *mergũs
changed to mer̃guas following *mer̃guan and finally
to *mērgas following the newly created mērgan in
the dialect of the IIIrd catechism. Supposedly
there would have existed the type *mergwas in the
Ist and IInd catechisms, but there are no genitive
singular ā-stem forms attested in these catechisms.
I personally do think that it is a real problem
as to whether the long vowels were shortened in
word-final position in Old Prussian, but the
spellings with -qu- and -gw- merely denote the
labialization of the preceding consonant, see
paragraph 5.200.
6.320 Stang, 1966, 198, lists three kinds of ā-
stem dative singular endings after a guttural
(velar): 1. pack-ai 'peace,' schlaītisk-ai
'particular,' 2. empijreisk-u 'in sum,' kanxtisk-u
'discipline,' spartisk-u 'strength,' 3.
alkīnisquai 'sorrow, trouble.' Stang agrees
with Endzelīns, 1943, 62, that it is unsatisfactory
to explain the second group as old instrumentals as
does van Wijk, 1918, 85. According to Stang, 1966,
199, these are pure dative forms and he assumes
that *-kāi > *-kūi > *-ku. Stang says that the
form alkīnisquai stands isolated in the IIIrd
catechism and that it was modeled after an
accusative singular *alkīnisquan which must have
existed at one time in that dialect. Perhaps
*-kuai was the phonological successor of *-kāi in
certâin dialects; then the form in question would
have been lent from a dialect other than that
which is common for the IIIrd catechism. Stang
considers the form in -kai to be analogical and
to have been remodeled after -kan (which in turn
replaced an earlier -quan). Again I find all such
explanations as strained and incredible and assume
merely scribal variation depending upon the German
rendering of a vowel after a labialized consonant.

6.330 Stang, 1966, 199, writes that for the accusative singular of the ā-stems Old Prussian has the following forms in post-velar position: Ist catechism -quan, -kun, -con, -gwan; IInd catechism -quan, -gwan; IIIrd catechism -kan, -gan. Stang believes that -quan -gwan reflect the regular phonological developments (lautgesetzlich) from *-kān, *-gān, etc. The forms peroniskan, mergan are the result of later analogical generalizations. I am, of course, highly dubious of this assumption. Again we have to do merely with the rendering of non-phonemic labialization by the German scribe, see 5.200.

6.331 Mažiulis, 1968, 25, suggests that in East Baltic an accusative singular *-ān split into the accusative singular ending *-añ and an instrumental singular ending *-án. In Old Prussian, however, a more archaic situation is to be observed, i.e., the accusative singular of the *ā-stems is used with the function of the instrumental singular. This explains such Old Prussian forms as sen madl-an 'with prayer' on the one hand and by extension other forms where we find the accusative instead of the expected instrumental, cf., e.g., sen sendit-ans rank-ans 'with folded hands.' In Mažiulis' opinion the inflection with the acuted ending *-án retained its original form in the East Baltic instrumental singular, cf. Lith. rankà vs. the new intonation with the circumflex *-añ reflected in the Lith. acc. sg. rank-ą. Mažiulis, 1968, 28, proposes that finally in Old Prussian the contrast between the *o-stem acc. sg. *(deiv)-añ and the *ā-stem acc. sg. *(rank)-án was neutralized. The instrumental singular (sen madl) -an came to be equivalent to the acc. sg. (madl) -an, so that for the *o-stem nouns also one could use the accusative singular for the instrumental giving (sen wird)-an beside the older (sen stesm) -u. Thus it became possible to have constructions with sen governing either the dative or the accusative. As a result we encounter such mixed constructions as sen stesm-u (dat.) wird-an (acc.) 'with the word' and sen wissa-mans (dat.) christian-ans (acc.) 'with all the faithful.' Mažiulis concludes that the lack of congruence

between the adjective and noun is not to be
ascribed to the translators, but to the practice
of Old Prussian of the 16th century.
6.340 The *ā-stem nominative plural is represented
as one would expect by Sambian (madl)-as 'prayers'
and Pomesanian (lauxn)-os (EV - 4) 'stars,'
crausios (EV - 618) 'pears.' There exist also
such forms as genn-ai, gann-ai 'wives' which
Bezzenberger, 1897, 303, saw as duals. Berneker,
1896, 193-194 and Trautmann, 1910, 227-228, see
these as new formations which were influenced by
the etymological *o-stems. This would, in their
opinion be similar in origin to the Gk. khorai
'peoples' and Latin equae 'mares.' I am more
inclined to see in the endings *-ai and *-ās
competing endings. The *-ās became consistently a
plural marker, but the *-ai became a plural marker
in some languages and a dual marker in others. We
find it as a marker of the dual in OCS rǫc-ě,
Lith. rank-ì (< *ronk-ai). Bezzenberger, 1897,
303, suggested that the use of the etymological
dual for the plural could be a feature of the Old
Prussian language or perhaps just derive from Abel
Will's usage.
6.350 For the genitive plural of the *ā-stem
nouns Stang, 1966, 200, merely says that in Old
Prussian one encounters menschon with unclear
consonantism. Mažiulis, 1970, 312, says that the
ending in menschon is to be derived from *-ōn
< *ōm. [65]
6.360 The *ā-stem dative plural ending consists
of the stem vowel ā (sometimes written as ū) after
labials and velars) plus the ending -mans, already
discussed above with the *o-stem nouns. Stang,
1966, 200, lists the forms gennāmans 'women,'
mergūmans 'girls,' widdewūmans 'widows.'
6.370 According to Stang, 1966, 200, the Old
Prussian accusative plural ending of rank-ans
'hands,' genn-ans 'wives' derives from *-āns just
as does the ending of Lith. žiem-às 'winters' and
the definite adjective ger-ás-ias 'good.'[66]
6.400 At one time I had proposed that the Baltic
*ē-stem nouns had their origin in some kind of
remodeling of the *jā-stem nouns, see Schmalstieg,
1960. Stang, 1966, 203-204, says that the Baltic

157

ē-stems at least partially go back to ii̯ā-stems,
but that nothing stands in the way of the theory
that they represent in part old ii̯ē-stems.
Although this class of nouns is poorly represented
in Indo-European I now propose that the *ē of this
stem is to be traced back to an earlier *oi (which
was monophthongized within Indo-European, see
Schmalstieg, 1973a, 139-140). Since I believe that
this monophthongization did not take place in
Hittite I would connect such Hittite nouns as
hurt-ai-š 'curse' and zahh-ai-š 'battle.' In
Latin and Lithuanian one can observe the following
stem doublets: Latin volpēs/volpis 'fox,' vatēs/
vatis 'seer,' rupēs/rupis 'rock,' Lith. bìtė/bitìs
'bee,' mùsė/musìs 'fly,' kùmštė/kùmštis 'fist.'
Note that Latin volpēs and Lith. lãpė 'fox' both
have the same stem. Nagy, 1970, 96, suggests that
*-Ci̯æ passes to *-C'ǣ, whereas *-Cii̯æ passes to
*-Cǣ in Proto-Baltic. I have objected, 1970a,
196, to Nagy's suggestion of the phonemic
identification of *-ǣ after palatalized consonant
(traditional *Cj̄ā) with *-ǣ after an unpalatalized consonant (traditional *Cē from *Cii̯ā). If
such an identification had indeed existed it must
have been lost in Lithuanian where the ō (< *ā) in
the sequence Cō (< *Cā) is phonemically the same ō
as in the sequence C'ō (< *Cj̄ā), cf. the genitive
singular of the word žõdžio '(of the) word' the
initial syllable of which reflects etymological
/žã-/ and the second syllable of which reflects
etymological */-dj̄ā/. In other words, if Nagy is
correct then the */ā/ of the sequence */Cj̄ā/ must
have been phonemically identified with Proto-Baltic
*/ē/ at first and then later re-identified with
Proto-Baltic */ā/. Such shifts back and forth of
phonemic identification are, of course, possible,
but here it seems ad hoc just to explain this
nominal class. A complete review of the literature
on the origin of the Baltic *ē-stem nouns is not
possible in a short space, but suffice it to say
that neither Kuryłowicz, 1966, nor Kazlauskas,
1967, 241, accepts the suggestion (most fully set
forth by Sommer, 1914) that *-ii̯ā passes to Proto-
Baltic *-ē.
6.401 According to Stang, 1966, 204, in the
Sambian dialect of the catechisms the -ē is

retained only in stressed position, otherwise it
is represented by -i̅: semmē 'land,' kurpi 'shoe,'
perōni 'parish, community.' In the Elbing
vocabulary we find -e even in unstressed syllables,
but we also find -i: addle (EV - 596) 'fir tree'
(cf. Lith. ēglė 'spruce'), alne (EV - 647) 'hind'
(cf. Lith. élnė 'id.'), bitte (EV - 787) 'bee' (cf.
Lith. bìtė 'id.'), gerwe (EV - 715) 'crane' (cf.
Lith. gérvė 'id.'), kurpe (EV - 500) 'shoe' (cf.
Lith. kùrpė 'id.' but also asy (EV - 241) 'ridge,
border,' (cf. Lith. ežė̃ 'id.'), cosy (EV - 96)
'throat,' pelky (EV - 287) 'swampy meadow' (cf.
Lith. pélkė 'swamp'), crausy (EV - 617) 'pear
tree' (cf. Lith. kriáušė 'pear'). Kazlauskas,
1968, 190, writes that in Old Prussian there are
some i-stem nouns which have transferred into the
ē-stem declension, cf. OP nozy (EV - 85) with Lith.
nósis 'nose' and OP wolti (EV - 276) with Lith.
váltis 'oats panicle, ear.'
6.402 Stang, 1966, 204, says that the etymological
*ē-stems occasionally end in -ei: giwei (1X)
'life,' peisālei 'writing' and suggests a
comparison with the ending -ai of the ā-stem nouns.
I would definitely agree with such a comparison,
but I would only remark that ei may have been
way of writing /ē/ just as -ai may have been an
alternative way of writing /ā/.
6.410 The genitive singular of the ē-stems is
represented in Old Prussian by the ending -is:
gijwis 'life,' kīrkis 'church,' pergimnis
'nature,' teisis 'honor.' Stang, 1966, 204, says
that the ending -is is best explained as being from
*-ēs since ē, except in absolute stressed final
position, passed to ī. I would agree that the
the derivation is correct, but I would suggest that
either this shows the innovating system of Old
Prussian phonemics, i.e., [1] ē > [2] ī (see
paragraph 5.002) or else it is just the misinterpretation by Abel Will. The dative singular of
the ē-stems is represented by semmey, semmiey
'land.'
6.420 Stang, 1966, 39, agrees with van Wijk,
1918, 24-41, who proposed that *-ēn passed to -ien
rather than to *-īn. Stang, 1966, 205, says,
however, that although the pronunciation cannot be
established for certain, he considers a

pronunciation -ien likely in the following
accusative singular forms: geywien 'life,'
mutien, mutien 'mother,' peronien 'parish,
community,' sem(m)ien 'land,' warrien 'power,
might.' In addition to the ending -ien one also
finds -in in such words as dusin 'soul,' gijwin
'life,' mutin 'mother,' etc. Stang, 1966, 205,
says that these forms could have come from old i-
stems (in the language itself or in the imperfect
speech of the translator), or in the inexact
perception of -ien on the part of the translator.
I assume the ending -en on the basis of the
evidence from the other Baltic languages, cf.
Lith. acc. sg. žẽm-ę 'earth.' If the -i- in the
forms with -ien means anything, it denotes palatalization of the preceding consonant. The various
renditions depend merely on the whim of the German
scribe.
6.430 The nominative plural ending *-ēs seems to
be attested in the Elbing vocabulary words (255)
aketes 'harrow,' and (111) peles 'muscle,' see
Stang, 1966, 205. Stang, 1966, 206, says that the
acc. pl. kurpins 'shoes' is built analogically on
the nom. pl. *kurpis. I assume merely a German
rendering of the expected accusative plural ending
/-ens/.
6.500 An example of an *i-stem nominative singular
is furnished by the Elbing vocabulary word (298)
assis 'axle.'
6.501 Although there do not seem to be many well
attested forms of the i-stem genitive singular in
Old Prussian, I have suggested, 1974, 74-75, that
nierties 'anger' might be phonemicized as /nerteis/
and that amsis 'people' might be phonemicized as
/amzeis/ in which case we would have an example of
a genitive singular ending /-eis/. Mažiulis,
1970, 271, assumes that the genitive singular
ending (etnīst)-is 'grace' reflects an etymological
Indo-European genitive singular ending of the
neuter gender, viz., -is.67
6.502 The most usually quoted i-stem Old Prussian
dative singular ending is in the noun naut-ei
'need,' see Stang, 1966, 207 and Kazlauskas, 1968,
192.
6.503 For the accusative singular usually the form
naut-in 'need,' is quoted, see Stang, 1966, 209,

and Kazlauskas, 1968, 192.

6.504 The nominative plural ending in ack-is 'eyes' is thought to be derived from *-iies according to Stang, 1966, 212 and Kazlauskas, 1968, 198. Stang also suggests the possibility of an analogical creation: ackis: acc. ackins = -as: -ans. I assume that the i-stem nominative plural ending -īs has its origin in an old dual ending *-ī (< **-iN) plus a plural marker *-s, see Schmalstieg, 1973a, 154.

6.505 The Old Prussian accusative plural ending in ack-ins is usually compared with the ending of Gothic gast-ins 'guests,' Cretan Gk. pól-ins 'cities,' see Stang, 1966, 213, and Kazlauskas, 1968, 199.

6.600 Eckert, 1959, tries to show that there were probably originally more u-stem nouns in Indo-European than is commonly thought and he gives many examples of such with good evidence that they were originally u-stem nouns. Evidence of a *u-stem origin is to be found in the following Old Prussian words: bebrus (EV - 668) 'beaver'; the word for 'wood,' *dru is represented in OP drawine (EV - 393) 'wooden beehive'; OP ladis (EV - 56) 'ice' just like Lith. lẽdas was an old *u-stem transferred into another category, cf. Lith. dialect ledus (Eckert, 1959, 118). Eckert, 1959, 118-120, says that Old Russian olŭ and modern Slovene ôl are the old Slavic words for 'beer' now replaced by pivo. Good evidence for the belief that this is an old u-stem word is furnished by Old English ealu, Old High German alu, Lith. alùs 'ale, beer,' OP alu (EV - 392) 'mead.' Eckert, 1959, 120-122, suggests that Slavic *pьs-u 'dog' shows the etymological reduced grade of the Indo-European root *pek'-us 'cattle.' The meaning of *pьs-u was originally 'the sheared, shorn (one)' and we find evidence of the fact that it was originally a u-stem noun in Latin pecu 'cattle,' Gothic faíhu, Lith. pẽkus, OP pecku. 68

6.601 The u-stem nominative singular masculine is represented by OP dangus 'heaven,' see Stang, 1966, 213. Kazlauskas, 1968, 227-228, assumes a passage of many *u-stem nouns to the *o-stem category, e. g., OP souns 'son.' As was noted in the previous paragraph Old Prussian also has a fair number of

neuter u-stem nouns, e.g., meddo (EV - 391)
'honey.'
6.602 Kazlauskas, 1968, 228, and Stang, 1966, 214,
agree that the ending -as of soun-as is from the
*o-stem nouns. The ending -as is to be compared to
the ending of deiw-as. In my opinion this could
well be an *o-stem ending, but rather in the sense
that the Germans had found the ending -as as a
viable ending for the genitive case of all the
stems and used it indiscriminately, see 6.015 and
paragraphs 4.503 and 4.601. Mažiulis, 1970, 270-
271, quotes van Wijk, 1918, 74, who corrects sounons to sun-os and reads it as *(sūn)-us, a genitive
singular created on the following model: gen.
deiwas, acc. deiwan: gen. gennas, acc. gennan:
gen. etnīstis, acc. etnīstin: gen. kermenes, acc.
kermenen. Hence gen. sun-us on the basis of the
acc. sun-un. Mažiulis finds van Wijk's interpretation of the reading correct, viz., sūn-ŭs, but
Mažiulis interprets the form sūn-ŭs as representing a new Old Prussian genitive singular derived
from the Indo-European neuter u-stem genitive
singular *-ŭs (originally non-ablauting).
6.603 Mažiulis, 1970, 268, assumes an Old
Prussian *u-stem dative singular ending in -u, the
only attested example of which would be in the
expression (Trautmann, 1910, 53): kas stesmu Pecku
swaian perdin dāst 'who gives the cattle his
fodder.' This dative singular ending would have
had its origin in the old neuter non-ablauting
*u-stem nouns.
6.604 Stang, 1966, 215, suggests that the Old
Prussian infinitive ending -twei is an old *u-stem
dative singular derived from *-tuu̯ei.
6.605 Stang, 1966, 215, finds the etymological
u-stem accusative singular ending reflected in sun-
un 'son' and in the supine represented
orthographically in Old Prussian by -ton, -tun.
Kazlauskas, 1968, 228, assumes that the Old
Prussian accusative singular forms sounan 'son,'
dangan 'heaven,' peckan 'cattle' show the transfer
of the original u-stem noun into the *o-stem
category. If I understand Mažiulis, 1970, 270,
correctly, he posits a merger of the OP *o-stem
dative singular ending *(deiw)-u (< *-ō) with the

162

u-stem dative singular *(sūn)-u leading to a merger
of the *o-stem nominative singular (deiw)-s with
the u-stem nominative singular *(sūn)-s. This
merger led to the creation of the new *o-stem
accusative singular soūn-an for the u-stem nouns.
I would assume here, rather, that either it is
merely a question of scribal inaccuracy which led
to the introduction of the ending -an for the u-
stem nouns, or else, that the Germans having found
-an a good accusative ending elsewhere, used it
here also, unless specifically corrected by the
Old Prussian informant.
6.606 Mikalauskaitė, 1938, 105, suggested that in
the Old Prussian form andangonsvᵉn 'in heaven' in
the fragment discussed in para. 4.701 we find the
trace of an Old Prussian directive or illative
case, used here in the sense of a locative.
Mikalauskaitė, 106, says that this Old Prussian
locative dangonsvᵉn has arisen from the genitive
plural plus the postposition un. This illative or
locative was strengthened by the use of the
preposition an-. Endzelīns, 1948, 143, apparently
accepts Mikalauskaitė's theory, but Stang, 1966,
231, says that the photograph published in
Mikalauskaitė's article is too difficult to make
out in order to establish a certain conclusion.
6.700 Stang, 1966, 219-220, notes the following
Old Prussian consonant stem nouns (nom. sg.):
brote (EV - 173) 'brother,' duckti 'daughter,'
mothe (EV - 170), mūti 'mother,' smoy (EV - 187)
'man'; (neuters) seyr (with -r < *-rd-, EV - 124)
'heart,' semen (EV - 256) 'seed.' Old neuters
remodeled as masculines are emmens 'name' (cf.
Slavic imę 'id.'), kērmens 'body.'
6.701 Those forms ending in a vowel represent the
Indo-European forms without a final sonant such as
we encounter in Skt. matā 'mother,' rajā 'king,'
Latin homō 'man,' which contrast with nouns which
seem to have retained the final sonant such as Gk.
patér 'father,' ákmōn 'anvil,' Latin pater
'father,' etc.
6.702 I have proposed, 1973a, 104, that Indo-
European word-final *-oN, *-eN, *-or, *-er either
remained as such in case the following word began
with a vowel, or else passed to *-ō, *-ē, *-ō, *-ē

respectively if the following word began with a consonant. This established sandhi doublets of the type *-oN/-ō, *-eN/-ē, *-or/-ō, *-er/-ē, etc. For the most part a generalization took place such that in the consonant stem nouns the new form, i.e. the form with the long final vowel took over the primary function, the function of the nominative case, whereas the old form with the short vowel plus sonant was relegated to the secondary function of vocative. For Sanskrit compare the nom. sg. rājā 'king' vs. the voc. sg. rājan, the nom. sg. svásā 'sister,' vs. the voc. sg. svásar. Sometimes, however, the new form with the long final was lost completely and the older form with the short vowel plus final sonant was retained in the nominative singular, cf. Latin pater, Gothic fadar 'father,' Latin frater, Old Irish brathir, Gothic broþar 'brother.' In the Greek nominative singular we find a contamination of the two etymological forms, viz. the nom. sg. *patē (= Skt. pitā 'father') and the actually attested Gk. voc. sg. páter (= Skt. pítar) which combine to give the attested Gk. nom. sg. patér.

I would assume then that such words as OP duckti (= Lith. duktḗ 'daughter') and mothe, mūti 'mother' (= Lith. mótė 'woman') reflect etymological word-final *-ē < *-er.

Kazlauskas, 1968, 247, quotes the Lithuanian dialect vocative forms sẽser 'sister' and dùkter 'daughter.' Zinkevičius, 1966, 259, mentions also the voc. sg. píemen 'shepherd,' but notes the eastern Lithuanian forms píemen' and dùkter' with a soft final consonant which would seem to indicate that at one time there had been a following front vowel.

6.703 Mažiulis, 1970, 241, corrects the word seyr (EV - 124) to *sēr which he compares with Gk. kēr 'heart.' Szemerényi, 1970b, 528 writes: "'Heart' was described in Early IE as the 'jumper, springer, leaper' with a root *(s)ker-d-. Its IE inflexion was nom.-acc. *kēr, gen. *kr̥d-ós, loc. *kérd-i. Although this noun is one of the best preserved elements of the IE lexicon, no language (except Hittite?) preserves the old inflexion in its entirety and especially with all ablaut

164

variants. Some have generalized one ablaut-grade,
cf. Greek kêr (and OPr sīr-) on the one hand, Lat.
cor, cordis, on the other..."

In 1973b, 154, I wrote: "The Old Prussian
word for 'heart' is given as seyr (word no. 124)
in the Elbing vocabulary and we find the forms
(gen. sg.) sīras, (dat. sg.) sīru, (acc. sg.)
sijran, sīran and (acc. pl.) sirans in the
catechisms. Trautmann (1910, 424) suggests that
an Old Prussian form *sīr is derived from Indo-
European *kērd- = Gk. kêr, Armenian sirt. The
cognate forms in other Indo-European languages,
viz. Lithuanian šerdìs 'pith, core,' Russian
sereda 'middle,' etc., would seem to indicate the
original presence of a root-final -d.

"There is not a single case of a long diphthong
surviving as such from Indo-European into any
Baltic or Slavic language. I suggest then that
there must have been some kind of analogical
development leading to the creation of /sēr/ which
I propose as the correct phonemicization for the
form seyr... One might assume a situation similar
to that of Lithuanian (nom. sg.) duktė̃ 'daughter,'
gen. sg. dukter̃s ‹dukter̃es as the starting point.
Thus the following paradigm might be reconstructed:
(nom. sg.) *sē, (gen. sg.) *ser-es, (dat. sg.)
*ser-ei, (acc. sg.) *ser-in, etc. The word-final
-r may have been substituted in the nominative
case giving sēr, the oblique cases then adopted the
*o-stem endings. Since the nominative case is from
the Elbing vocabulary and the oblique cases are
from the catechisms it may well be a mistake to
establish a paradigm with a nom. sg. sēr and a gen.
sg. sēr-as, etc. The word may have had a different
declension in the Pomesanian dialect of the Elbing
vocabulary than in the Sambian dialect of the
catechisms."

6.704 Mažiulis, 1970a, 241, says that in OP sem-en
(EV - 256) 'seed' the final -en may replace an
earlier *-in, the -en in the nominative having
arisen on the basis of the other cases. In Latin
sēm-en the final -en may derive directly from Indo-
European *-n̥. Mažiulis' assumption seems to stem
from the fact that in the Sanskrit nom. sg. neut.
(nām-)a 'name' the final -a derives from Indo-

165

European *-ŋ.
6.705 The genitive singular of the consonant stem
nouns is rendered by -es in Old Prussian kermen-es
'(of the) body,' see Stang, 1966, 220 and Mažiulis,
1970, 246.
6.706 Stang, 1966, 220 and Mažiulis, 1970, 248,
both give the Old Prussian participial form
giwāntei 'living' as an example of the dative
singular of a consonant stem, in this case, of
course, a present active participle. The form
giwāntei occurs once in the expression (Trautmann,
1910, 61, line 23): sta ast giwāntei aulause
(literally) 'she is living dead' (where it is a
question of a widow living for pleasure). In this
expression one might wonder whether the form is
not the nom. sg. fem. pres. act. participle, cf.
the Lith. nom. sg. fem. pres. act. participle
nešanti. Maybe the OP word is to be phonemicized
as /gīvantī/. On the other hand Stang, 1966, 220,
also gives the example of stānintei, which occurs
in the expression (Trautmann, 1910, 51, line 14):
Nostan poquelbton adder stānintei stan Druwien bhe
Tawa Noson Iquoitu - Darauff kniendt oder stehendt
den Glauben und Vater unser Wiltu 'So that kneeling
or standing you will (say) the creed and the Lord's
Prayer.' The same word occurs again with the
spelling stāninti 'standing' in a similar
expression, see Trautmann, 1910, 51, line 32. The
analysis is most unclear.[69]
6.707 The consonant stem accusative singular seems
to be represented in the word smunent-in 'man.'
The accusatives singular of kermens 'body' and
emmens 'name' are kermenen and emnen respectively,
see Stang, 1966, 225. Kazlauskas, 1968, 284, says
that the noun mūti 'mother' (originally a consonant-
stem noun) apparently passed into the Old Prussian
*ē-stem class, cf. the acc. sg. mūtin, mūtien. I
assume that Kazlauskas is right and I would
phonemicize these words as /māten/. As Kazlauskas
points out, such a form would be equivalent to the
Old Lithuanian form motę.
6.708 According to Stang, 1966, 226, OP smoy
(EV - 187) 'man' must be connected with Lith. žmuo
'id.' Stang lists the following additional forms:
smūni (1X) 'person,' nom. sg. smunents (4X),

'man,' smūnets (for -ents, 1X), acc. sg. smunentin
(2X), smunentien (1X), acc. pl. smunentins (4X),
acc. sg. smunentinan (1X) 'man,' acc. pl.
smunentinans. For the explanation of these last
two forms see para. 6.709. In addition we also
find smonenawis (EV - 67) 'man.' Stang says that
the Sambian ū after m can stand for ā (or perhaps
ō), but that the o in smonenawis points to ā. One
is therefore inclined to identify the ū in OP
smūni with the *ā of Lith. žmónės 'people' rather
than with the u of Lith. žmūni̯ (encountered in the
writings of Daukša). Since Lith. žmónės is a
feminine noun in many Old Lithuanian texts, one
supposes that the fundamental meaning is 'human
being' rather than 'human male.' Possibly there
was originally some kind of abstract or collective
meaning to this word. OP smūni translates the
word 'person' in the expression endirisna steison
smūni 'respect of persons.' Furthermore Stang,
1966, 227, says that the word *smūnents was
created by adding an individualizing suffix to
smūni. This suffix was equivalent to the Slavic
suffix -ęt- which finally got a diminutive meaning.
An expanded stem from smūnent- was created giving
smunentina-, cf. the acc. sg. smunentinan, pl.
smunentiuaus to be read as smunentinans.

In connecting OP smoy with Lith. žmuo the -y[70]
causes some difficulty. Stang, 1966, 227, quotes
the East Lithuanian dialect forms in -uoi, cf., e.
g., in the Lazūnai district the forms žmuŏi 'man,'
piemuõi 'shepherd,' unduõi 'water,' šuõi 'dog,'
etc. In the catechisms I would be tempted merely
to see in all of these forms of the word for 'man'
the writing of /ā/ after a labial consonant,
although the existence of the Old Lithuanian acc.
sg. žmūni̯ and the nom.-acc. dual žmūne in Daukša
lead one to suspect the possibility of the
existence of an original ū in this word.
6.709 In the spring of 1973 when I was in Moscow
for a brief period Prof. V.N. Toporov was kind
enough to share with me some of his thoughts on the
Old Prussian language. At this time he pointed out
to me that there may well have been grammatical
forms existing in Old Prussian, but which had just
not been recorded by the German scribes or were

167

just not used by the Germans. He drew a parallel
with the case of those non-native speakers of
Russian who have perhaps learned a few case
endings, and have found that they can make themselves understood quite well without bothering to
learn any more. I am, of course, quite familiar
with this phenomenon in English, but it probably
does not strike the speaker of English, which has
a sparse morphology, as much as it does the speaker
of the Slavic languages, which have a rich
inflectional system. The implications of Toporov's
thought are clear, however, and I regret now that
I did not have the foresight to include them in
my 1974 work.

The two fragments discussed in 4.503 and 4.601,
and Leskien's (1876, 33-34) interpretation of OP kas
arrientlāku as being equivalent to Lith. kas ãria
añt laũko 'which plows on the field' seem to be
sufficient to ensure that the Old Prussian *o-stem
genitive singular ending was really -a and that it
corresponds quite nicely with the *o-stem genitive
singular ending of the other Baltic languages, cf.
Latv. -a and Lith. -o (< *-ā). The same ending is,
of course, attested in Slavic -a also. The ending
-as, perfectly correct in the *ā-stems was transferred to all other categories. In addition the
ending -as was reinforced by the German genitive
singular ending -s. Above all any speaker of Old
Prussian would understand the meaning of a German
who used the ending -as. One may then assume that
the Germans speaking Old Prussian had developed an
idealized or generalized Old Prussian on the basis
of various etymological stems and that the Germans
didn't worry too much about whether they were
using the right ending with the right etymological
stem. In the catechisms then we find a varied
picture. Sometimes the German scribes copied down
exactly (or as close to that ideal as possible)
what they heard from the informant, but at other
times they suggested forms from their own
generalized paradigms, forms which the Old Prussian
informant, in view of his lower social status, was
either afraid or unwilling to contradict,
particularly when he understood the intended
meaning.

As mentioned above the Germans had an active

command of a single genitive singular ending in Old
Prussian, viz. -as, and they used this ending with
abandon, applying it to all stems. We then find
the explanation for the following genitive singular
forms: sou̅nas, sau̅nas, sunos (if this latter stands
for *sunas) 'son' (for which we would expect a *u-
stem genitive singular ending, cf. Lith. sūn-aũs
'[of the] son'); sīr-as 'heart' (for which we
would expect a consonant-stem ending, cf. Lith.
dukteřs ‹ dukterès '[of the] daughter').
    We find, for example, the expected correct
nominative plural for the a̅-stem nouns in madlas
'prayers' (cf. Lith. nom. pl. maĩdos 'id.'‹ *-a̅s)
and perhaps in the adjective wissas 'all' which
modifies ackis 'eyes' (cf. Lith. vĩsos ãkys 'all
eyes'), but we find the generalized ending -ai,
undoubtedly the work of the German scribes, in OP
gennai, gannai 'wives' and preibillīsnai
'promises.'
    There would be good evidence for the
accusative singular ending -an and the accusative
plural ending -ans for both the *o- and *a̅-stem
nouns in Baltic, so it is impossible to decide
which is original here. Perhaps they had indeed
coincided in the Old Prussian language. At least
in East Baltic we have definite evidence that the
*o- and *a̅-stem accusatives singular were the
same, cf. Lith. nãm-ą 'house' and rañk-ą 'hand,
arm.' On the other hand the apparent consonant-
stem noun which denotes 'heart' has an acc. sg.
sīr-an, sijr-an and an acc. pl. sir-ans with case
endings which may reflect just the generalized
paradigm used by the Germans. Likewise the
apparent *u-stem noun denoting 'son' has the
accusative singular forms sou̅nan, sau̅nan, saunan,
sounan in which the final -an may a Germanism or
else merely a scribal error. The same is to be
said for the acc. sg. dangan, dengan 'heaven,'
peckan 'cattle,' etc., all of which one would
expect to be u-stem nouns. Cf. Lith. sūn-ùs 'son,'
dang-ùs 'heaven,' pḛk-us 'cattle.'71
    One may note also the particularly curious
forms smunentinan 'man' and *smunentinans corrected
from smunentiuaus. These forms show the correct
OP acc. sg. smunentin, see para. 6.708, attested
as such elsewhere in the catechisms and to which

the Germans added their own acc. sg. ending -an
and acc. pl. ending -ans. Each of the preceding
forms occurs once in the IIIrd catechism and
probably Abel Will asked his informant how to say
'man' or 'men' in order to check his memory.
Somehow the informant gave an answer in the
accusative case *smunentin and Will, understanding
this as an accusative case added the ending -an in
one place, see Trautmann, 1910, 63, line 20: Stwi
dai Deiws ainan gillin maiggun krūt nostan
smunentinan - Da liess Gott der HERR einen tieffen
Schlaff fallen auff den Menschen 'So God caused a
deep sleep to fall upon the man.' In the other
example (Trautmann, 1910, 61, line 27): sen madlan
prei wissans smunentiuaus - mit Beten für alle
Menschen 'with prayers for all men' the word
is broken at the end of the line as smunentiuaus and one might in general suspect a misprint
involving more than the two -u-'s in place of the
expected *-n-'s. On the other hand the explanation
might be similar to the one proposed for
smunentinan above.

The theory proposed above might also explain
such a curious dative singular as wirdai
(presumably an *o-stem form) in the expression
enstesmu wirdai - in dem wort 'in the word.' If
the preposition en did indeed take the dative case,
then perhaps the form stesmu is the correct dative
from the Old Prussian point of view, whereas
wirdai reflects the German idealized dative.[72]
6.800 In general the adjective declension is not
significantly different from the noun declension.
For the *o-stem nominative plurals Stang, 1966,
258, says that the ending -ei is a mistake for -ai.
I assume that Stang's view here is in principle
correct, but not so much that -ei is a mistake as
it is just an alternative spelling.
6.801 Stang, 1966, 268, quotes the Old Prussian
expression (Trautmann, 1910, 45, line 30): sen
stawīdsmu adder muisieson grīkans 'with such or
greater sins,' and asks whether we have here a case
of a reduplicated comparative suffix *mu-is-ies-
< *mā-is-ies-. OP *muis- would correspond then
with Gothic mais, Oscan mais (= magis). I have
suggested, 1968a, 191 and 1974, 20, 121, that

muisieson is to be phonemicized as /maiśesan/ and
that the -u- following the m- is merely a spelling
which shows the labialization of the preceding
consonant.
6.802 Stang, 1966, 268, notes that in Old Prussian
there is a series of comparative degree forms with
the element -ais-: acc. sg. masc. uraisin, acc. pl.
uraisins from urs 'old,' cf. Lith. võras 'old';
nom. pl. masc. maldaisei 'the disciples,' acc. pl.
maldaisins, dat. pl. maldaisimans; acc. pl. ucka
kuslaisin weakest.' According to Stang the
element -is- represents the zero grade of the Indo-
European suffix *-i̯es-. The element -a- in the
suffix -ais- is then just as unclear as the Slavic
-ě- in the Slavic comparative suffix -ěj ь š- and the
-o- of the Gothic suffix -ozan. Endzelīns, 1943,
72, assumes that the -ais- comes from *-ōis < *-ō-is.

     André Vaillant, 1958, 568, assumes that the
Old Prussian type maldais- consists of the stem
malda- plus the suffix *-yos- which is found in the
Slavic type bol-jĭš. In Old Prussian the ending
-ais- instead of the expected *-ēis is based on the
stem in -a of the positive degree.

     I have proposed, 1972c, 7, that: "the suffix
-ais- is actually a fossilized form of the stem in
-a plus the nominative singular masculine form of
the definite adjective -is. That the nominative
singular masculine form of the definite article
was indeed -ais seems to be supported by the OP
nom. sg. masc. ordinal pirmois 'the first' which
probably represents a phonemic /pirmais/."
Further on I have written: "... a form such as
maldaisin is to be divided into the stem malda
plus the nominative singular masculine of the
pronoun -is- plus the accusative singular masculine
of the same pronoun, i.e., -in." Parallels for the
doubling of the pronoun in the definite adjective
are to be found in such Old Lithuanian forms as
krikszaniszkas-is-is 'Christian,' geras-ys-is 'the
good,' from gẽras 'good.' We also find examples of
the nominative case of the adjective used as a stem
with the addition of the pronoun in the accusative
case, e.g., acc. sg. masc. pirmàs-į 'the first'
(pirmas is nom. sg. masc. and -į is acc. sg.
masc.), mẽlynàs-į 'the blue,' mãrgàs-į 'vari-

colored.' Semantic parallels for the use of the
definite adjective in Lithuanian to denote a
superlative degree are also to be found, e.g., the
Samogitian dialect example: Stasis buvo visu
gražias-is 'Stasis was the most handsome.'

The form massais stems from a misunderstanding. In 1972c, 10, I wrote: "It is interesting to
note that Endzelīns, 1943, 208, suggests a
pronunciation mazais for the Old Prussian word
massais which is usually translated as 'less.'
This Old Prussian word occurs once in the following
phrase: Teinu adder Deiws Taws wissas etnīstis bhe
engraudīsnas swaian Sounon Christon stēismu gantsan
switan bhe tīt dijgi steimans malnijkikamans ni
massais kai steimans uremmans potaukinnons bhe
pertengginnons ast... = Unnd aber Gott der Vater
aller Genaden und Barmhertzigkeyt seinen Sohn
Christum der gantzen Welt unnd also auch den
Kindlein nicht weniger denn den Alten verheisen
unnd gesandt hat 'And, however, God the Father of
all mercies and compassion has promised and sent
His Son to the whole world and therefore also to
the children not less than to the adults.'

"The word wenig apparently originally meant
'little, small,' cf. the Middle High German daz
wenege kint 'the small child.' (See Curme, 1952,
176 and Paul, 1956, 735.) I propose then that
when Abel Will used the word weniger, the Old
Prussian informant became confused at the
complicated syntactic construction with the meaning
'to the children not less than to the parents' and
thought that the word weniger had something to do
with the children. He therefore translated it with
the definite form of the adjective, the word which
for him meant 'the small one' or perhaps 'the
child.' Thus massais has nothing to do with the
comparative degree and Endzelīns' proposed
pronunciation of the word, mazais corresponds very
nicely to Latvian mazais '(the) small.'"
6.900 Levin, 1973, examines the 137 words ending in
-e and the 25 words ending in -y/i in the Elbing
vocabulary and suggests that (190):"...nouns in -y
represented the nominative singular of a Pomesanian
-ja stem declension, probably the only nominative
singular ending (in contrast with Lithuanian, which

preserves vestigially $-\grave{\imath} < \acute{\imath}$, as well as $-j\bar{a}$). On
the other hand, nouns in -e represented an -ē stem
declension, whatever the latter's origin."
6.901 Not all of the 25 words in -y/i necessarily
represent -jā stem nouns in Levin's opinion (191),
e.g., nozy 'nose' could well be a nominative dual
of the i-stem declension. Other OP words which are
possible candidates for this category are plauti
(EV - 126) 'lungs,' noseproly (EV - 86) 'nostril,'
scaydy (EV - 311) 'shaft(s) for a horse collar,'
kexti (EV - 70) 'plaited hair [i.e., 'braids'],'
and perhaps less likely wubri (EV - 82) 'eyelash,'
and culczi (EV - 138) 'hip.'
6.902 Levin, 1973, 190, does not believe that
there was any change of *-ē to -i because there is
little, if any, evidence of a phonetic reduction in
Pomesanian desinences. He finds that the spelling
-is/s for the -o stem endings reflects the
replacement of the historic -o stem by a -jo or -i
stem ending. Likewise he finds no evidence for a
reduction of the -ā stem ending either in the free
-o of the nominative singular nor in the checked
-os of the nominative plural. The spelling e in
the -ē stems could well reflect /ē/, since the
variant a for the short [æ] does not occur.73
6.903 Levin compared the words in -e and the words
in -y/i with those in East Baltic and found that
34 nouns in -e had exact equivalents in East
Baltic, whereas of the 25 nouns in -y/i only two
correspond unambiguously to -ē stems in East
Baltic (191).

To support his hypothesis further Levin,
192, notes that the -ē stem category seems to be
productive in the Elbing vocabulary words, just as
the corresponding -ė stems are productive in
Lithuanian. Levin, 192, writes further: "Another
argument supporting the interpretation of -y/i as
the nominative singular of an -jā stem declension
is that such an assumption would fill the
distributional gap caused by the apparent absence
of -jā stems in the singular, as attested by Elb.
There are 137 words in -o in Elb (including a
handful of neuter plurals), seven words with
nominative plural -os; 136 words in -e, some ten
words with nominative plural -es. On the other

hand, there are four words ending in -io, three
with doubtful etymologies, including one probable
misspelling (Prio for ?*piro). The fourth word,
*carbio, is a Slavic borrowing; the reading /ijɔ̄/
for Slavic *-ьja is most likely. The other two -
claywio and sutristio - can also be read with
final /ijɔ/. In contrast with this apparent poor
attestation of singular -ja stems, we find six
nominative plural words ending in -ios, some of
which may represent nouns in /-ijɔ̄/, but which
also must include some -jā stems. The most
probable candidates are Elb 386, dragios, 'dregs,
lees,' Lithuanian dragės, and knapios, 'hemp,'
Polish konopia. Another one of these plurals, Elb
618, crausios, 'pears,' probably is the plural to
the singular krausy [read crausy - WRS], Elb 617,
'pear tree.' Regarding all or most of the twenty-
five words in i/y as -jā stems with nominative
singular in -ī would eliminate this distributional
anomaly." See paragraph 11.008.
6.904 In his study of the Slavic borrowings in the
Elbing vocabulary, Levin, 1974, 46, gives the
following table of stem-classes plus their
renderings in the Pomesanian dialect:

Stem   Spellings in Elb (Nom. sg.)
classes

-o	is, s, (rarely) es [masc.]; an [neuter]
-io	is [masc.]; ian, ien, ean [neuter]
-ī	is
-u	us [masc.]; u, o [neuter]
-ā	o
-e	e, i
-ī/jā	i, io

Original consonant stems in various degrees of
preservation (not important for Slavic borrowings).
        On the basis of medies (EV - 696) which
Trautmann, 1910, 376, compares with Lith.
medijas 'hunter' (attested now in the Lithuanian
Academy Dictionary, Vol. 7, 985), I would put
this noun in the jo-stem (= Levin's -io) category
also. It would seem to me that the Polish
borrowing tisties (EV - 184) 'father-in-law' which
Levin, 1974, 107, phonemicizes as /tistijɔs/
would also belong in this category. I would see
no motive for ascribing rounding to the vowel

following the /j/. The spellings would seem to me
to show also the neutralization of the /e/ vs. /a/
contrast following /j/.

Levin, 1974, 47, also emphasizes the important
fact that although in word-final position the -o,
-i̯o and -i stem nouns are all represented by the
ending -is, there is evidence from the compounds
that they were separate stem classes, cf. the -i̯o
stems karya-woytis (EV- 416) 'martial parade,'
karya-go (EV - 411) 'military expedition,' beside
*kargis (corrected from kragis; EV- 410) 'army,'
cf. Lith. kãrias. One can compare also malunakelan (EV - 321) 'mill wheel' with malunis (EV -
316) 'mill' and daga-gaydis (EV - 260) 'summer
wheat' with dagis (EV - 13) 'summer.' [74]
6.905 Levin, 1974, 48, writes: "There is little
evidence of any phonetic reduction in Pomesanian
desinences. The only evidence for the reduction
is the spelling is/s for the -o stem Nom. sg. masc.
I regard this as morphophonemic, not phonetic. It
is the replacement of the historic -o stem Nom.
ending by the -i stem ending, or the use of the
otherwise unused zero marker as a vocalic allomorph in the desinential system." Levin's
explanation smacks of academic sophistication
and I suspect that it does not have too much to do
with the real situation. The German scribe found
that -is was a good way to denote some kind of
obscure vowel in word-final position before -s. In
a few cases he used just -s and in a few -es.
It would seem surprising to me that a scribe who
seemed to confuse, e.g., i and e spellings in his
native language (see 5.605), would keep them
separate in a foreign language.
6.910 Eckert, 1963, shows that the Indo-European
heteroclitic r-/n-stem nouns are well represented
in Old Prussian where we find such forms as
OP wundan (EV - 59), a neuter form, and unds
'water' (masculine in the catechisms), cf. Lith.
vanduõ, Latv. ûdens 'id.' I personally would wonder whether the form wundan attested in the
Elbing vocabulary is not just an accusative
singular form. It would then be a good match for
the accusative singular undan attested in the IIIrd
catechism. In any case Eckert is right, in my

opinion, in classing this as an n-stem noun, at
least from the East Baltic point of view. Another
n-stem form is OP panno (EV - 33) 'fire,' cf.
Gothic fōn, gen. funins, Iranian panu (Eckert,
1963, 882). Formations in *-sn (884-885) are
represented by Lith. širšuõ, -eñs, Latv. siȓsenis,
siȓsins 'hornet,' Lith. šišlȳs 'wasp,' OP
sirsilis 'hornet,' cf. Old High German hornūz,
hornaz; OP lauxnos (EV - 4) 'stars,' Russian luná
Latin lūna 'moon,' Avestan raōxšna- 'light.' are
then derived from Indo-European *louksnā 'moon,
weak light.' Formations in *-men are represented
by OP semen (EV - 256), Latin sēmen 'seed,' Lith.
sémens, sémenys 'linseed.' An example of an l/n-
stem is furnished by Lith. ą́žuolas vs. OP ansonis
(EV - 590) 'oak.' (887) Old l-stems are represented by OP arelis (EV - 709), Lith. erẽlis, Latv.
ẽrglis 'eagle,' OP saule (EV - 7), Lith. sáulė,
Latv. saũle 'sun.'75 Several examples show an i-stem
beside a generalized n-stem: OP wagnis (EV - 244),
Greek óphnís, Old High German waganso 'plowshare'
are contrasted with Lith. vãgis 'hook,' Old High
German wecki 'edge.' In addition Old Prussian has
retained a word for 'milk' that was originally
dithematic, viz., dadan (EV - 687), cf. Sanskrit
dádhi, gen. sg. dadhnás 'id.' (889) Note also the
-n- in Old Lithuanian viešpatni, fem. of viešpats
'master' and in the OP acc. sg. waispattin 'wife.'
It would appear to me, however, that waispattin
could be merely the accusative singular of an
i-stem noun, see Schmalstieg, 1974, 75, cf. the
i-stem forms of Sanskrit páti, Greek pósis, Latin
potis.
6.911 Eckert also shows, 1963, 890, that compound
suffixes in which the element -n- was the sign of
an original heteroclitic stem have become somewhat
productive. The suffix -sn- has come to form
abstract verbs from nouns: OP waisnan 'report,
information'< *wait-sn-ā, werpsnā [sic!] 'forgiveness,' au-mūsnan 'washing, ablution,' minisnan
'remembrance,' pogirschnan 'praise,' ausaudīsnan
'faith, hope.'
6.920 Bammesberger, 1973, gives a careful analysis
of the abstract formations in the Baltic languages.
The work is organized according to the various

suffixes and contains a certain amount of Old
Prussian material, although the discussion centers
chiefly on Lithuanian and Latvian. In general one
could only applaud Bammesberger's analysis, but I
would comment on some of the spelling problems
which have been raised to phonological status. E.
g., Bammesberger, 1973, 40, fn. 2, says that the
OP acc. sg. maiggun 'sleep' supposes a nom. sg.
*maigū. This is completely unnecessary. One may
well consider the word a masc. acc. sg. form which
should be phonemicized /maigan/, see Schmalstieg,
1974, 58. The u after the velar is just the way
of showing labialization. Bammesberger, 46, fn. 3,
says that in giwei the -ei is remodeled according
to the a-stems, cf. Endzelīns, 1944, paragraph
124. The gen. sg. gijwis does not have to be
compared with Lith. gȳvis, gývis; it can be
phonemicized /gīvēs/ and the acc. sg. gijwin,
geiwin, geywien can be phonemicized as /gīven/,
see Schmalstieg, 1974, 71. Bammesberger, 54,
lists (EV - 415) wackis 'war cry' as an i-stem
noun. This could be the case, but it is not
necessary to assume this since etymological *o-
stem nouns also appear with final -is in the Elbing
vocabulary. OP gorme (EV - 41) 'heat' seems to
present a problem if one insists that the grapheme
-o- in the Elbing vocabulary could represent only
Indo-European *ā. In the first place I consider
it highly doubtful that long diphthongs ever
existed in Balto-Slavic, much less Indo-European.
In the second place as Marchand, 1970, 114, has
pointed out, it is typical of Middle German
dialects to confuse a and o of whatever origin,
see paragraphs 5.317 and 5.605. It would seem to
me most likely that gorme is to be phonemicized as
/garmē/. [76]
6.930 Arumaa, 1970, 23, writes that with the
exception of words for young animals it is only
inanimate objects which are denoted by neuter
nouns in Old Prussian. This latter usage is of
Indo-European origin and the Old Prussian suffix
-stian (of the type eristian (EV - 681) 'lamb' as
opposed to Lith. éras) is a feature shared with
Thraco-Illyrian. For comments on the phonology of
the type eristian, see para. 2.105. Arumaa says
that k has diminutive meaning in the nouns wijrikan

'man' and <u>madlikan</u> 'little prayer,' although I cannot make out whether he wants to say that these two
nouns are indeed neuters or not. He seems to
suggest they are, although Trautmann, 1910, 463,
says that <u>wijrikan</u> is acc. sg. masc. and that
<u>madlikan</u>, 373, is acc. sg. fem. Endzelīns, 1943,
275, 206, is a little more careful and labels both
of the aforementioned words as accusatives without
specifying the gender. Since both words occur as
direct objects of verbs only, we would expect an
accusative, but of what gender could not be told
since they do not occur in any case but the
accusative. Arumaa, 1970, 23, suggests that the
noun <u>paustocaican</u> (EV - 654) 'wild horse' must also
have some kind of hypocoristic meaning.
6.940 Fraenkel, 1950b, 44, says that OP <u>nauns</u>
'new' derives from a contamination of *<u>naujas</u> (cf.
Lith. <u>naũjas</u> 'new') and *<u>jaunas</u> (cf. Lith. <u>jáunas</u>
'young'), cf. also the OP family name <u>Naunyn</u> and
the place name <u>Naunesede</u>. In addition, Old
Prussian has the form *<u>nawan</u> 'new' which
corresponds exactly to Skt. <u>náva-</u>, Gk. <u>né(F)os</u>,
Lat. <u>novus</u>, Old Church Slavic <u>novъ</u>. Fraenkel
says that the form <u>neuwenen</u> is the
definite adjective form; cf. also the Lith. place
name <u>Navikaĩ</u>, the personal name <u>Navìkas</u>, OP
<u>Nawekeyn</u>, <u>Naweke</u>. Otrębski, 1950b, 275, objects
that OP <u>neuwenen</u> is not a definite adjective, but
rather that it reflects a stem *<u>nave-na</u> encountered
also in the place names <u>Nawenynen</u>, <u>Nawensede</u>. The
stems *<u>navena</u> and *<u>nauna</u> represent, in his opinion,
a reduplicated formation as in the cognate adverb:
Lith. <u>nūnaĩ</u>, Old Church Slavic <u>nyně</u>, Sanskrit
<u>nūnám</u> 'now.' I would rather dispute Otrębski's
theory and would assume rather that either
Fraenkel is right in suggesting a definite
adjective formation which I would phonemicize as
/navan-an/ or else that <u>neuwenen</u> is the indefinite
accusative singular /naun-an/. I believe that the
orthography does not allow us to make a clear
decision here.
6.950 Jēgers, 1970, would explain many of the
Baltic nouns of instrument (<u>nomina instrumenti</u>)
in -<u>tas</u> (Lithuanian) and -<u>ts</u> (Latvian) as having
originally been past passive participles which

took on the function of instrument. According to
Jēgers, 82, the past passive participles originally
implied that by an action something acquired a
certain state and finally these past passive
participles lost their verbal character and became
either adjectives or nouns. See 11.009.

He writes, 83:"...Li. káltas and Latv. kaĩts
'chisel' was originally the same as Li. káltas and
Latv. kaĩts 'forged, hammered.' In other words,
this Baltic name for 'chisel' originally might have
meant '(that which was) hewn (off),'...e.g., a chip
of flint or bone later used as a chisel because of
its form. This explanation is in conformity with
archaelogical finds where chips of flint or bone
are often called 'chisels'...Similarly also Russ.
mólot 'hammer' and its cognates acquired their
present meaning, having originally meant '(that
which was) ground (crushed).' If a piece, e.g.,
of stone, thus obtained was ground still more...it
could be used as a hammer." Russian dolotó
'chisel' and OP dalptan (EV - 536) 'a pointed
instrument of iron and steel for making holes' are
to be explained the same way. Other words which
have a similar explanation are: OP -saytan in
largasaytan (EV - 446) 'leather strap' which was
originally '(that which was) bound (together),' cf.
also OCS sětь 'net'; OP warto (EV - 210) 'house
door,' Lith. vartai, Latv. vãrti 'gate,'
originally '(that which was) opened and shut.'

To illustrate a somewhat different change of
meaning Jēgers, 1970, 84, mentions OP deicton,
deicktan 'place,' deickton 'something,' Lith.
dáiktas 'thing, object; place,' Latv. daikts
'thing; tool.' Jēgers suggests that an older
meaning was 'dot, spot, place' derived in turn from
the meaning 'that which is pricked, a prick, a
dot.' This latter meaning is to be expected of a
derivative of Lith. díegti 'to prick, pierce' and
Latv. diêgt 'to prick, to sew.' Jēgers concludes,
85, that one can assume that the oldest meaning was
preserved by OP deicton 'spot, place,' whereas Lith.
dáiktas and Latv. daikts in the meaning 'thing,
object' might be a later development from the
meaning 'a pointed (sharp) tool (for pricking).'
6.960 In his 1973 article Marvan pursued

his contention that research into Lithuanian solves among other things (181) "...the principal problems of the typology and chronologic stratification of the IE cases, proving that the oldest case system was nominative-vocative-genitive (No-Vo-Ge); i.e., a system in which not an objective (Ac*) but only an ergative (Ge*) structure was possible."

After proposing a theory as to how the ergative state of Indo-European passed to the attested nominative-accusative state he lists five features which, in his opinion, give evidence of earlier ergative stages in various Baltic and Slavic languages. (Marvan separates Old Prussian from the East Baltic languages and classifies the latter with Slavic, thereby creating a dichotomy between Old Prussian on the one hand and what he calls East Balto-Slavic on the other hand.)

6.961 The original predicate is unmarked, thus, for example, the Lith. third person present dìrb-a 'works' formally has the same ending as the old neuter singular gẽr-a 'good.' Marvan finds that there never was a third person plural in Baltic.

6.962 The usage of the participles in finite constructions developed into the Baltic modus relativus. This development prevented the merging of the participle with the indicative paradigm and explains why there is no third person plural form in East Baltic.

6.963 In the neuter forms the morpheme -n has replaced the zero ending characteristic of the neuter nominative-accusative and the masculine accusative singular in all of the Indo-European languages except East Balto-Slavic (and a few residues in Hittite).

6.964 In Old Prussian the neuter is retained and the genitive (deiwas < devasia) opposes the nominative/vocative, whereas in Lithuanian the genitive/vocative oppose the nominative.

6.965 The Indo-European barytone neuters pass to masculine oxytones in Slavic since the barytone genitive of the neuters (*'dvar-as) was identical with the barytone nominative of the masculines (*'rag-as). The main distinctive feature of the nominative (oxytony) was neutralized in the

barytone paradigm and the form *'dvar-as was
identified as nominative and neutralized with the
masculines.
6.966 In East Baltic the neuter could not serve as
the subject and was normally replaced by the
genitive, from which the barytony of the nominative
is derived (cf. the noun vilkas 'wolf' vs. the
adjective basàs-is 'the barefoot.') The neuter was
eliminated completely from the nouns and survives
only in such special adjective forms as gĕr-a
'good.'
6.967 The genitive of the o-stems used the
ablative form since the original genitive form
appeared in the nominative. This process, caused
by the existence of the ergative, is an innovation
of East Balto-Slavic. Finally Marvan comes to the
conclusion (186) that: "Old Prussian is originally
a Baltic language which did not participate in the
East-Balto-Slavic development." Marvan maintains
that further study will show that there are
paradigmatic isoglosses denoting two areas: East-
Balto-Slavic and Old Prussian + Germanic.
6.970 Eckert, 1974, studies the i-stem nouns in
Old Prussian.
6.971 In part I, 220-223, he analyzes those words
which occur only in the nominative singular with the
ending -is. Eckert quotes Stang, 1966, 191-192, who
wrote that in the Pomesanian dialect the ending -is
may represent etymological -as, -ias and -iias.
Eckert establishes then two groups of words in this
category, those which can be established as i-stem
nouns on the basis of evidence from Baltic and
other Indo-European languages and those which can
be established as i-stem nouns only on the basis of
evidence from other Baltic languages. In the former
group we find, e.g., such words as OP angis (EV -
774), Lith. angìs, Old Latv. uodzis, Proto-Slavic
*ǫžь, Latin anguis, Armenian ōj, auj, gen. sg. auji
'snake'; OP nowis (EV - 151) 'body,' Lith. novis,
-ies 'pain, death,' Latv. dialect nâvs 'death,'
Proto-Slavic *navь 'death spirit, death,' Celtic
*nŏvis, Gothic nawis 'dead'; OP *grandis (corrected
from graudis; EV - 251) 'ring,' Lith. grandìs, -iẽs
'link (of a chain),' Skt. granthí-ḥ 'knot, tie,
bunch or protuberance of any kind'; OP antis
(EV - 720), Lith. ántis, -ies, Proto-Slavic *ǫtь

'duck,' Skt. āti-ḥ 'an aquatic bird'; OP slaunis
(EV - 139) 'upper part of the thigh,' Lith. šlaunìs,
-iẽs 'hip,' Skt. śróṇi-ḥ 'the hip and loins,
buttocks,' Avestan sraoniš 'id.,' Latin clūnis
'buttock,' Gk. klónis 'coccyx,' modern Welsh clûn
'hip,' Old Icelandic hlaun 'buttock.'

Since Baltic alone furnishes the evidence for
the assignment of the latter group of nouns to the
i-stem category, we can be less certain of the
original stem class for these nouns. Some examples
are: OP doalgis (EV - 546), Lith. dal̃gis 'scythe';
OP dantis (EV - 92), Lith. dantìs, -iẽs 'tooth'
-support for its classification as an i-stem noun
also comes from the OP compound danti-max (EV - 93)
'gum'; OP kulnis (EV - 143) 'anklebone,' Lith.
kulnìs, -iẽs 'heel'; OP pettis (EV - 106) 'shoulder
blade,' Lith. petỹs, -iẽs (as given by Eckert, 223)
'shoulder'; OP winnis (EV - 398) 'peg or pin for
closing a vat,' Lith. vinìs, -iẽs 'nail.'
6.972 In part II Eckert, 1974, 223-224, discusses
those Old Prussian nouns with the nominative
singular in -y or -i. Quoting Endzelīns, 1944, 91,
94, Eckert, 223, says that the etymological ē-stem
nouns may have the nominative singular in -i when
unstressed and compares OP kurpi with Lith. kùrpė,
Latv. kur̃pe 'shoe.' Eckert, 224, writes further
that OP sansy (EV - 719) 'goose' may be from
*zansē, cf. Latv. dial. zuose, dzùose. This ē-stem
noun attested in Old Prussian and Latvian could
have existed along with the i-stem forms attested
by Lith. žąsìs, -iẽs, Latv. dzùoss, -s. Eckert
also quotes Fraenkel's, 1955, 1292, opinion that
OP sansy could stand in some kind of relationship
to Skt. haṃsī 'female goose' just as Lith. deivẽ
'fairy' is to Skt. devī 'goddess' and Lith. vìlkė
is to Skt. vr̥kī 'she-wolf.' One may also propose
that sansy could be derived from *zansī and thus
belong to the same class of nouns as Lith. martì
'bride.' For a similar view see paragraph 6.900.
According to Eckert, 224, essentially the same
things which have been said about sansy above
could be said about other nouns of this category:
OP culczi (EV - 138) Lith. kùlšė 'hip'; OP nozy
(EV - 85) 'nose.' Support for the assumption that
this may be an ē-stem noun is found in the existence

of the compound nose-proly (EV - 86) 'nostril';
OP wolti (EV - 276) 'ear of corn' apparently has
no e̅-stem cognate in the other Baltic languages; in
Lithuanian we find váltis 'oats pannicle, ear.'
6.973 In part III Eckert, 1974, 224, lists two
nouns which correspond to i- and e̅-stems in other
Baltic languages. OP greanste (standing probably
for *grẹnste in Eckert's opinion; EV - 305) 'rope
made from twisted branches,' Lith. grĩžtis, -ies
(beside grìžtė) and Latv. grĩzts, -s (beside
griezte)'bundle of flax.' OP blusne (EV - 127),
Lith. blužnìs, -iẽs and blužnė 'milt, spleen.'
Eckert says that these examples along with the
examples given in the previous sections support the
notion that in Baltic there are particularly close
relationships between the i- and the e̅-stem nouns.
I am, of course, convinced that this is correct and
in 1973a, 139-140, I have tried to suggest that
this derives from an old ablaut alternation.
Etymological *-e̅ comes from the monophthongization
of *-oi in pre-consonantal position, whereas *-i
shows merely the zero grade of the suffix.
6.974 In part IV Eckert, 1974, 225, examines Old
Prussian substantives with the accusative singular
in -in and the accusative plural in -ins. He states
first that although there is no doubt that in Old
Prussian the i-stem accusative singular ended in
-in and the accusative plural in -ins, it is also
clear that this ending was transferred into other
declensions as well. Thus we find the accusative
ending in -in (beside those in -ien, -ian) in the
(i)i̯o-stem nouns as well (noseilin 'soul,'
etwerpsennin 'forgiveness') and in the e̅-stem
nouns, cf., e.g., OP dusin 'soul,' gijwin 'life,'
mu̅tin 'mother' beside the forms in -ien which are
said to derive from *-en (geywien, mu̅tien). In
addition the consonant stem accusative singular
*-m̥ passed to Baltic -in and the accusative plural
*-n̥s became -ins. Eckert sees only the following
nouns as surely i-stems: OP acc. sg. naktin
'night,' acc. pl. ackins 'eyes,' acc. pl. ausins
'ears,' dat. sg. nautei, acc. sg. nautin, acc. pl.
nautins 'needs,' dat. sg. mattei 'measure.' Eckert
establishes these on the basis of evidence from
Baltic and other Indo-European languages. Other

examples which are less certain include OP īdin
'meal,' which might be a io-stem form, cf. Lith.
ė̃dis, gen. ė̃džio,' food,' but also the Lithuanian
i-stem word ìrmė̃dis, -ies 'grip, influenza.' In
all of the Old Prussian words for 'food' with
different stems Eckert finds parallels in Slavic,
227:

a̅-stem OP īdai : Proto-Slavic *(j)ĕda
o̅-stem OP īstai : Proto-Slavic *(j)ĕsto
 < *ē̅d-to, cf. Middle Bulgarian jasto
i-stem OP īdis : Proto-Slavic *(j)ĕdь < *ē̅dis

6.975 In part V Eckert, 1974, 227-229, discusses
Old Prussian verbal abstracts in -tis and -stis.
In this category he lists OP astin 'thing,'
auschautins 'sins,' pagaptis (EV - 362) 'spit,'
dijlapagaptin 'instrument,' gen. sg. etnīstis,
'grace.' In this section Eckert discusses the
tendency of Baltic initial e- to pass to a- in
connection with the word astin. As I have pointed
out elsewhere, this could be orthographic
vacillation or it may be a reflection of the loss
of contrast between /e/ and /a/ in Old Prussian,
see paragraph 5.001 and Schmalstieg, 1959.
6.976 In part VI, Eckert, 1974, 229-231, discusses
the stem class of those nouns which have a final
-i when they function as the initial member of a
compound. This -i- then functions as a composition
vowel, e.g., dantīmax (EV - 93) 'gum' beside dantis
(EV - 92) 'tooth.' The situation, according to
Eckert, 231, is not without problems. We find some
words in which -i- functions as composition vowel
for e̅-stem nouns, e.g., OP lapiwarto (EV - 212)
'small pedestrian gate or door next to the
vehicular gate in the courtyard wall,' literally:
'fox's gate' beside lape (EV - 658) 'fox,'
wosigrabis (EV - 611) 'spindle-tree,' the first
element of which Eckert equates with wosee (EV -
676) 'goat.' Eckert quotes Gerullis, 1922, 241,
to the effect that i- appears in all compounds the
initial element of which is an etymological e̅-stem
noun. Cf. the place names OP Laumygarbis beside
Lith. Laumė̃, OP Warnikaym beside OP warne (EV -
722) 'crow,' OP Woblikaym beside OP woble (EV -
616) 'apple.' Among personal names there is a
fairly widespread vacillation between -e- and -i-

in the composition vowel. Eckert quotes Trautmann, 1925, 187, who gives the example Awste-gaude beside Austi-gawdis.

The Lithuanian noun ùpė, Latv. upe 'river' have by-forms Lith. upìs, -ies (Samogitian dialect), Latv. ups, -s, i.e., i-stem forms. Therefore we may assume it is possible that the api- in apisorx 'kingfisher' reflects an i-stem, even though we find OP ape (EV - 62) 'brook' which is apparently an ē-stem noun.

According to Eckert, 231, as far as the place names OP Woblicayn and Woblikaym are concerned, it is not necessary to establish an etymological ē-stem on the basis of OP woble 'apple,' Lith. obelẽ, Latv. âbele 'apple tree.' One may compare also Lith. obelìs, -iẽs 'apple tree,' óbuolis, -ies, Latv. ābels 'apple' (also an i-stem). The i-stem is probably older than the ē-stem since in this word the i-stem category ousted the old l-stem (i.e., a variety of consonant stem). OP possi- ssawaite (EV - 20) 'Wednesday' could well have retained the i-stem form of the initial element which has an i-stem cognate in Old Lithuanian and the Lith. dialect gen. sg. pusies 'half.' On the other hand the more common ē-stem form is attested in Lith. pùsė, Latv. puse 'half.' OP pauson, pausan, however, may indicate another stem. Only in the case of the place names OP Wagi-pelki 'thieves' swamp' beside Waygis-pelkis, Waykis-pelkis and Waygi-kaymen which can be compared with Lith. vagìs, -iẽs 'thief' do we find that there is no by-form with an ē-stem.

I should like to comment here that occasionally we find a similar phenomenon in Lithuanian. Thus the Lithuanian Academy Grammar, Vol. 1, 446, lists some compounds with the composition vowel -i- the first element of which is an ė-stem noun in the standard language: eglìšakė 'spruce branch' beside ẽglė 'spruce'; mentìkaulis 'shoulder-blade' beside meñtė 'id.'; meškerìkotis 'fishing-rod' beside meškerẽ 'id.'; žvakìgalis 'candle-end' beside žvãkė 'candle.' One might suspect that in these cases the initial element of the compound was derived from an old *jo-stem noun, because we find, e.g., in the Academy Dictionary, Vol. 2, page 1052, eglìs 'spruce,' Vol. 8, 18, mentìs = meñtė 'oar,' Vol. 8, 90, meškerìs 'fishing-rod.' The Academy Dictionary has not yet reached the letter ž, and neither Senn-Salys, 1932ff., Vol. 5, nor Kurschat, 1968ff., Vol. 4, gives a form *žvakis. In any case it is a reasonable assumption that the *jo-stem category comes from the thematicization of the *i-stem category, so one may speculate that in view of the largely derivative character of the *ē-stem nouns, an original *i- or *jo-stem noun lay at the base of the compounds which have the linking vowel -i-. The direction of the derivation would be *i-stem > *jo-stem > *ē-stem.

6.977 In part VII Eckert, 231, discusses Old Prussian nouns with the suffix -ix, -ico which were derived from i-stem nouns. Examples include the following: OP instixs (EV - 114) 'thumb' may point to an earlier i-stem noun, since we find the Latv. dial. form iksts, -s and Samogitian Lithuanian nìnkstis, -ies 'thumb'; OP gunsix (EV - 162) 'boil' corresponds to standard Lith. gūžis, -ies 'crop, caw, ovary'; OP grandico (EV - 632) 'plank, thick board,' cf. Lith. grindìs, -iēs 'flooring board'; OP debica 'big,' cf. Proto-Slavic udobь 'convenient'; OP dellijks 'article,' cf. Lith. dalỹkas 'affair,' dalìs, -iēs 'part' (it is unclear to me why dalis seems to be dubbed specifically Old Lithuanian as does Eckert here - the word is quite common in modern Lithuanian as well), Old Russian dolь 'id.' and Skt. dalí-ḥ 'a clod of earth.' Eckert, 233, also notes the co-existence of Old Prussian derivatives and East Baltic i-stems even in some words borrowed from Slavic. Thus OP kuliks (EV - 487) 'bag, pouch, sack' can be compared with Lith. kulìs, -iēs 'scrotum' (Acad. Dict. Vol. 6, 835-836) and Lith. kulìkas 'wallet, money bag' (Acad. Dict., Vol. 6, 831). Both the Lithuanian and Old Prussian words are borrowed from Belorussian. Likewise OP lonix (EV - 671) 'bull, steer' can be compared with Lith. lónė 'hind' both of which words are borrowed either from East Slavic lanь or Old Polish łani, according to Žulys, 1966, 157.

Eckert concludes this section by saying that

he does not intend to dispute the existence of the
suffix -ik(a)s, -iko for Old Prussian. The
comparisons with the i-stems as the fundamental
noun should only help to explain certain relationships which exist between these categories and
perhaps contribute to the clarification of the
origin of these suffixes. We find a similar
phenomenon in Slavic so that the whole type could
be considered a Slavic imposition on Old Prussian.
Eckert is, however, more inclined to see in this
phenomenon evidence of closer relationships between
Old Prussian and Slavic.
6.978 In part VIII Eckert, 233, notes two
Lithuanian i-stem words which, in his opinion, are
borrowed from Old Prussian: Old Lith. dimstis,
-ies 'courtyard, farmstead; antechamber,
vestibule.' Beside the more usual Lith. malūnas
'mill' we find also Lith. malūnis (fem.) which
probably stems from OP malunis (EV - 316).
Fraenkel, 1955, 404, thinks that even Lith.
malūnas, which occurs first in the writings of
Bretkūnas, is also borrowed from Old Prussian.
6.979 It seems to me that Eckert is in general
right in finding that the i- and u-stem and the
consonant-stem categories were as important in
Proto-Indo-European as the much better attested
*o-stem category. On the other hand, Old Prussian
orthography is so misleading that it is dangerous
to establish morphological categories on the
evidence of Old Prussian. Thus spellings such as
wosigrabis beside wosee and Warnikaym beside warne
and Woblikaym beside woble don't prove very much.
6.980 Górnowicz, 1974, discusses the problem of
the Old Prussian suffix -īt- and the Polish
suffix -īc- in place names of Prussian Pomesania.
He writes, 235, that the German scribes were able
to distinguish between the phoneme /c/ adopted in
Polish names and the phoneme /t/ adopted in Old
Prussian place names. The first was identified
with German /ts/ which was written with z, tz, cz
and the second was identified with German /t/ which
was written as t or th, cf., e.g., Pol. Laskowice,
German Lescowiz; Pol. *Zaliwice, German Saluitz;
Pol. Lasowice, German Lesewicz; OP Katpanean,
German Katpanye; OP Kariot-, German Cariothen .

In Polish the suffixes -icy (later -ice) and
-owicy (later -owice) could either form patronymic
names of the type Wojsławicy from the personal
name Wojsław, Mirowicy from the personal name Mir
or ethnic names of the type *Zaliwicy 'people who
live on the other side of the river Liwa,'
Karczewicy 'people who come from the village
Karcze Miedzickie.' In Old Prussian, on the other
hand, the suffix -īt- had chiefly a diminutive
function, both in the formation of place and
personal names. Thus Górnowicz concludes that the
cause of the identification of names in -ic- with
OP names in -īt- is the appearance of this suffix
in the toponymy independently of the actual and
etymological function in each of the toponymic
systems. The phonetic similarity made the mutual
substitution easier, but it was not the cause,
since the substitution has a morphological
character. One cannot talk of the confusion of the
Polish phoneme /c/ with the Old Prussian /t/, but
rather of the confusion of the Polish toponymic
suffix -ic- with the Old Prussian suffix -īt-.
6.981 Górnowicz, 1974, 236, writes further that
in Pomesania there were 11 Old Prussian place
names with the suffix -īt- of which four were
Polonized: a. *Parsavīte attested as Parsowite
(OP form) around 1399, but as Polish Pierschowicze
(1565) and Pierzchovice (1570)(according to
Gerullis, 1922, 115, the place name is to be
compared with Lith. prã-paršas 'ditch, trench,'
prapersà 'unfrozen patch of water on an ice-covered
surface'); b. *Trankoīten, known in the OP form as
Trankoiten (1303), Trankoten (1321) and in the
Polish form as de Trankwitz (1402) and Trankwicz
(1440). c. *Tulekoīte, known in the OP form
Tulekoyte (1354) and in the Polish form ze wsi
Telkwic 'from the village Telkwic' (1624); d.
*Vusīt, which in German documents appears from the
beginning in its Polish form, although its Old
Prussian character is immediately manifest,
Wuschycz (1391), Wossicz (1399), Wusitcz (1422)
etc. The OP place name *Gorovīten attested in the
OP form as Gorowyten, Gorowythen (1300) is
Polonized as Gorowychen (1300). The other six
place names are not Polonized in German sources.

I would comment here that the reconstructions
*Trankoīten and *Tulekoīte are highly unlikely.
In all probability we have to do here with either
the Common Baltic suffix -eit- or -ait- both of
which show origin or possession, cf., e.g., Lith.
vókietis, Latv. vãciẽtis 'German,,' Lith.
gimináitis 'relative,' see Endzelīns, 1948, 107.
A syllable with a long second element would be a
canonical oddity in any of the Baltic languages.
Thus in Lithuanian, for example, there is no
*-aī- as opposed to *-aĭ- (except perhaps if one
would wish to analyze a circumflex -aĩ- as /aī/
as opposed to an acute -ái- as /ai/, but in any
case the second element would not reflect an
etymological */ī/).
6.982 Górnowicz, 238, writes that in Pomesania
there were 19 Old Polish place names with the
suffix -ic- of which three appear with the Old
Prussian suffix -īt- in German sources: a.
*Połkowicy known as Polkewicz (1360), Polkewyce
(1399) and in the OP form as Polkuiten (1295).
b. *Strzeszewicy known in the OP form as
Stiessewite (for Stressewite in 1242, but in
Polish without the suffix -ic- in the forms
Strasewo (1565) and Straszevo (1570). c.
Wojszewice, known in the OP form as Woysewite
(1366), Wusewithen (end of the 14th century).
Górnowicz, 239, writes that this is surely the
Polish personal name *Wojsz (of the type Wojciech)
plus the suffix -'ewice. Górnowicz draws the
general conclusion that in borrowings the phonetic
similarity of the suffixes simplifies the
morphological adaptation, but it does not determine
it.
6.983 Ivanov, 1974, 200, writes that OP smuni
'person' just like the corresponding Old Lith. žmů
'man,' acc. sg. žmûnį, nom.-acc. dual žmûne from
the semantic point of view corresponds with those
meanings of 'human being' derived from the name of
the earth such as Latin homō 'man,' nemo 'no-one'
(<ne-hemō), Umbrian homonus, Oscan humuns, Old
English and Gothic guma 'man.' Both from the
point of view of semantics and word formation a
closer analogy is presented by Old Irish duine
'man' (cf. dú, gen.-acc. don 'earth').

The transfer into the n-stem noun category coincides with the process which took place in Old Prussian and Old Lithuanian. Although Indo-European dialect forms in which the final nasal was reflected by -n (from the archiphoneme *-N) should be considered the starting point, nevertheless the resemblance between the Irish and Baltic phenomena is striking and should be taken into consideration in works on Indo-European linguistic geography.

7.000 Stang, 1966, 232, says that OP <u>stas</u> 'the, this' might be identified with Lith. <u>šĩtas</u> 'this,' but that it is possible that the form contains a garbled prefixed particle which is no longer recognizable. Stang does not think, however, that the form derives from a contamination of the stems <u>so-</u> and <u>to-</u> as did van Wijk, 1918, 110, because he, Stang, considers a contaminatory process of this kind psychologically unlikely. Furthermore the older form *<u>tas</u> is retained in the third person singular of the verbs as an enclitic element, cf. <u>astits</u> beside <u>ast</u> 'is,' etc. [77]
7.010 The other cases of this pronoun are written with an initial syllable <u>stes-</u>, <u>steis-</u> or <u>stei͞s-</u> and furnish numerous orthographic vacillations, cf., e.g., the gen. sg. masc. <u>stesse</u>, <u>stessei</u>, <u>stei͞si</u>, <u>stei͞se</u>, <u>steisei</u>, see Schmalstieg, 1974, 134. Stang, 1966, 240, suggests an etymological *<u>-e-</u> in the stem and compares Old Church Slavic <u>česo</u> 'of what' and Gothic <u>þizos</u>, <u>þizai</u> as far as the root vocalism is concerned. See 11.202.
7.011 In 1971a, 134-135, I have shown some uncertainty myself concerning the rendering of the vowel of the initial syllable of this pronoun. Thus, I assume that <u>stas</u>, <u>stes</u> render /stas/, but the welter of forms representing, e.g., the gen. sg. masc., see above, could really denote anything and I have suggested the following four alternatives: /steśa, stesa, staiśa or staisa/.[78] Perhaps a stem /stais-/ was generalized on the basis of the nom. pl. /staɪ/, cf. the Old Church Slavic nom. pl. <u>ti</u> (< *<u>toi</u>) 'these,' gen. pl. <u>těxъ</u> (< *<u>toi-s-on</u>), etc. See 6.300 and 11.202.
7.200 Stang, 1966, 234, quotes Meillet to the effect that the Old Prussian enclitic anaphoric pronoun <u>din</u> has its origin in a third person singular verbal ending <u>-d</u> plus the appropriate form of the pronominal stem *<u>i-</u>, thus, e.g., <u>proweladin</u> 'they betrayed him' is a result of the reinterpretation of *<u>prowelad-in</u> as *<u>prowela-din</u>. One might be perhaps somewhat surprised at the voicing of the secondary ending *<u>-t</u>, which might, however, seem plausible if one accepts Szemerényi's

1973, 72, explanation that perhaps the voiced
member of the stop was the unmarked member for an
early stage of Indo-European.[79]
7.300 Stang, 1966, 235, notes that the nom. sg.
masc. tāns, third person anaphoric pronoun, occurs
only in Old Prussian. In the IIIrd catechism one
finds the following forms: nom. sg. masc. tāns
(very frequent), fem. tennā (2X), tenna (3X),
tannā (1X); gen. sg. masc. tennessei (1X); dat.
sg. masc. ten(n)esmu (3X); dat. sg. fem. tennēi
(1X); acc. sg. masc. tennan (4X), tennen (2X); acc.
sg. fem. tennan (4X); nom. pl. masc. tennei (7X);
gen. pl. tennēison, tenneison; dat. pl. tennēimans,
acc. pl. masc. tennans (9X), tannans (1X); acc.
pl. fem. tennans (1X).[80]Stang wonders whether the
alternative stem ten- is a result of the
assimilation of the a to the e of the following
syllable. He notes the sporadic orthographic
variants tanna, tannans and the forms tanassen
from the Ist catechism and tanaessen from the IInd
catechism and also the vacillation in the word for
'heaven': nom. sg. dangus, acc. sg. dangon, but
also dengenennis, dengniskas, etc.
7.310 In 1971a, 132 and 1974, 125-126, I have
assumed that the stem of tāns is indeed tan- and
that the spellings with ten- have no significance,
just as I assume that the Old Prussian preposition
sen 'with' is really /san/ and is to be compared
directly with the Lithuanian prefix san- (as in
sántaka 'confluence'). I do not believe that
statistical frequency of a spelling·is any
guarantee of the accuracy of graphemic representation. I assume, for example, that the nom. sg.
fem. tannā, although it occurs only once, is a
better orthographic representation of this pronoun
than the more frequent spellings tennā and tenna.
Thus a nom. pl. masc. tennei should probably be
phonemicized as /tanai/, and the acc. sg. masc.
tennan, tennen, acc. sg. fem. tennan should all be
phonemicized as /tanan/.
7.400 Stang, 1966, 243, lists the following forms
of the interrogative pronoun: nom. sg. masc. kas,
nom. sg. neut. ka, dat. sg. masc./neut. kasmu, acc.
pl. masc. kans. As a nom. pl. masc. we find quai,
of which quoi is said to be an unstressed variant.

Stang says that the expected forms of the nominative
plural are masc. *$\underline{kai}$, neut. *$\underline{k\bar{u}}$ or a form expanded
with the particle -$\underline{ai}$, *$\underline{ku̯ai}$. Stang considers it
likely that in the Sambian dialect of the catechisms
in which there are few traces of the neuter in the
singular, in the plural the two forms *$\underline{kai}$ and
*$\underline{qu̯ai}$ were not kept apart and the form $\underline{qu̯ai}$ won
out. In the case of $\underline{qu̯ai}$ and $\underline{qu̯oi}$ in the nom. pl.
I have assumed, 1971a, 135, a phonemicization
/kai/, the orthographic difference between the
-$\underline{o}$- **an**d -$\underline{a}$- being meaningless and the $\underline{qu}$- perhaps
expressing a labialization of the preceding
consonant as heard by the German speaking scribe.
Stang, 1966, 243, suggests that the nom. sg. fem.
$\underline{qu̯ai}$ (4X) could derive from *$\underline{k\bar{u}}$ (< *$\underline{k\bar{a}}$) plus the
particle -$\underline{ai}$ (*$\underline{k\bar{u}}$-$\underline{ai}$ > ku̯ai). I have assumed,
1971a, 135, and 1974, 135, for the nom. sg. fem.
forms $\underline{qu̯ai}$ (4X) and $\underline{qu̯oi}$ (1X) a phonemicization
/k$\bar{a}$/. One might assume that the form is
phonemicized as /kai/ if one assumes a feminine
/k$\bar{a}$/ plus a particle /-i/.
7.500 In 1971a, 134, and 1974, 132-133, I have
suggested a declension of OP $\underline{schis}$, $\underline{sis}$ somewhat
parallel to that of Lith. $\underline{šìs}$ 'this,' although
there are many clear differences: nom. sg. masc.
$\underline{schis}$, $\underline{sis}$ /šis/; gen. sg. masc. $\underline{schie\bar{i}se}$ /šeiśa/
or /šeisa/; dat. sg. masc. $\underline{schismu}$ /šism$\bar{a}$/, acc.
sg. masc. $\underline{schan}$, $\underline{schian}$, $\underline{schien}$ /šan/; loc. sg.
masc. (?) $\underline{schisman}$ /šisman/ (See 6.051); nom. pl.
masc. $\underline{scha\bar{i}}$ /šai/; gen. pl. masc. $\underline{schie\bar{i}son}$
/šesan/ or /šeisan/, cf. Slavic $\underline{sixъ}$; acc. pl.
masc. $\underline{schans}$, $\underline{schins}$ /šans/; gen. sg. fem.
$\underline{schisses}$ /šis$\bar{a}$s/ or /šiśas/; dat. sg. fem. $\underline{schissai}$
/šisai/; acc. sg. fem. $\underline{schan}$, $\underline{schin}$, $\underline{schen}$, $\underline{schian}$,
$\underline{schien}$ /šan/; acc. pl. fem. $\underline{schiens}$ /šans/; dat. sg.
neut. $\underline{schismu}$ /šism$\bar{a}$/; acc. sg., gender
undetermined $\underline{sien}$ /šan/.[81]
7.600 Stang, 1966, 238, analyzes the Old Prussian
reflexive pronoun $\underline{sups}$ (5X), $\underline{subs}$ (1X), etc. as
being derived from a stem *$\underline{su-bho}$ and compares it
with a reconstructed stem *$\underline{su̯o-bho}$- encountered in
Old Church Slavic $\underline{svobodь}$ 'free,' $\underline{sobь}$ 'trait,
characteristic,' etc. I have proposed, 1973a, 107,
that the earliest etymological form of the word
'to be' in Indo-European is *$\underline{bhe}$-/$\underline{o}$- attested, in

such Sanskrit forms as vṛṣa-bhá 'bull,' garda-bhá
and rā́sa-bha 'ass,' and in sa-bha 'assembly.' One
might easily assume that the element su/suo-
denotes 'self' and the element *-bho denotes
'being,' the form *su-bho- denoting then 'self-
being.'
7.700 Stang, 1966, 238-239, assumes a connection
between Latv. viņš 'he' (nom. sg. masc.) and OP
winna 'outside' and says that the fundamental
word is a Baltic substantive *vina- for which he
finds a cognate in OP wins 'air' (EV - 45),
following Endzelīns, 1951, 517. Likewise the form
winnen (acc. sg.) attested in the IIIrd catechism
is also said to be related. I am of the opinion
that wins, as suggested to me in a personal
communication from James Marchand is, nevertheless,
borrowed from German Wind. I have written, 1974,
323-324, "One can imagine, however, that a German
Wind, phonemic /vint/ was supplied with a Baltic
ending */as/ giving phonemic */vint[a]s/ or
probably phonetic [vints]. The [-t-] was
interpreted as an automatic epenthetic consonant
between the [n-] and the [-s] so that it was
eventually understood as /vins/... The form /vins/
was reinterpreted as underlying /vin[a]s/ and an
acc. sg. masc. /vinan/ was created with a short
initial vowel denoted by the spelling with the
double n." The form winnen represents, of course,
/vinan/.
7.701 Grinaveckis, 1972, 73, notes a previously
unrecorded Lithuanian personal pronoun (3rd sg.
nom.) jeĩnis 'he,' jeĩnė 'she' in the Samogitian
dunininkai dialect. This pronoun, according to
Grinaveckis, 74, could be connected with OP ains
'one,' and could have changed its meaning in this
dialect just as did Latv. viņš, viņa 'he, she.'
A connection with the Old Prussian form seems
likely in view of the fact that the pronoun is
found in the region bordering on Prussia.82
7.800 Stang, 1966, 247, says that the personal
pronoun as (46X), es (2X) 'I' along with Lith. àš
(eš in certain older texts), Latv. es derives from
an etymological *ež. Ordinarily, in Stang's
opinion, a following syllable would not have disappeared, but Stang thinks that because of the

special psychological position of this word, such
might have been the case here and that the
possibility is not to be excluded, cf. Skt. ahám,
OCS azъ, Lat. egō, Gk. ȇgō. I would rather see
a root *eĝ(h)- plus a particle *-om, which, of
course, also had the sandhi alternant *-ō, from
etymological pre-consonantal position, see
Schmalstieg, 1973a, 104. In Baltic, and perhaps
in Germanic, this final particle was just never
added.
7.801 Stang, 1966, 247, says that OP tu
(frequent), tū (1X), toū (6X), tou (frequent) all
are derived from a form with an etymological long
vowel, *tū 'thou, you [sg.].'[83]
7.802 We also encounter, according to Stang,
1966, 248, such dat. sg. forms as mennei (9X)
'(to) me,' tebbei (frequent) '(to) thee,' tebbe
(4X), sebbei (3X), reflexive. Stang suggests that
the stem men- comes from the gen. sg. stem attested
in the OCS gen. sg. mene, Avestan mana.
7.803 Stang, 1966, 248, cites the forms for the
accusative singular of the personal pronouns: mien
(frequent) 'me,' tien (frequent), tin (enclitic,
1X) 'you (sg.)', sien (frequent), -sin (enclitic,
9X), -si (4X), reflexive pronoun. In Stang's
opinion the forms mien, tien, sien reflect a
pronunciation mi̯en, ti̯en, si̯en and derive from an
etymological *mēn, *tēn, *sēn, cf. Skt. mā́m, tvā́m
and OCS mę, tę, sę. I have suggested in 1971a, 137
and 1974, 137-139, for these three pronouns either
the phonemicization /men, ten, sen/ respectively or
/min, tin, sin/ with automatic palatalization of
the initial consonant. I see no more evidence here
for an etymological long vowel plus nasal than I do
elsewhere in any of the Baltic or Slavic languages.
7.804 Stang, 1966, 254, equates the OP 1st pl.
pronoun, nom. mes with Lith. mẽs, as would most
scholars. He does not mention the form mas (1X)
which is either a scribal error, or else an
indication of the very open pronunciation of the
-e- in this word.
7.805 For the genitive plural Stang, 255, gives the
form noūson '(of) us' and adds the comment that it
is found with variations. See also 7.807 below.
7.806 Stang, 255, says that Lith. jũs, Latv. jũs

and OP io͞us 'you (pl.)' all correspond with Avestan
yū̃s (enclitic), yūžəm, Gothic jus, etc.
7.807 For the second person gen. pl. Stang, 1966,
255, lists iouson (with variations). He claims that
the first and second person genitive plural forms
are to be derived from *nús͞on and *jús͞on
respectively. He says that for the first plural
one would have expected *nōs͞on on the basis of
Slavic nasъ, but that the form has been remodeled
under the influence of the second plural, for
which one might have expected *u̯ōs͞on on the basis
of Slavic vasъ. This latter form, however, was
also remodeled on the basis of the nom. pl. *jū͞s.
7.808 Stang, 1966, 255, says that the -u̅- vowel
of the first person dat. pl. pronoun nou̅ma(n)s and
the corresponding second person form iou̅ma(n)s
comes from the other cases. See 6.080 for more on
the ending -ma(n)s. See also 11.201.
7.809 For the accusative plural of the first
person we find mans and for the second plural
wans. Stang, 1966, 255, says that the form wans is
a remodeling of *vō͞s or *vas (< *u̯ōs) according to
the usual nominal and pronominal accusative forms,
cf. Avestan vā̇, Skt. vah̤. Slavic vy could be
identical with the Old Prussian form or else it
could go back to *u̯ōs. In the first person we
might expect an initial n-, but the form has been
remodeled after the nom. pl. mes.
7.820 Stang, 1966, 239, says that the Old Prussian
possessive pronouns mais 'my, mine,' twais 'your,
yours (sg.),' swais (reflexive possessive) are to
be traced back to the stems *maja-, *tvaja-,
*svaja-, etc. and correspond exactly to Slavic
mojь, tvojь and svojь respectively. I do not
believe that anybody would argue against that.
For a complete discusssion see Schmalstieg, 1971a,
132-134 and 1974, 126-130.
7.900 Stang, 1970 (=1957), 69-72, draws a
parallel between Slavic prepositions in -dъ, cf.
nadъ 'over, above,' podъ 'under,' *perdъ, which,
in his opinion derive respectively from na 'on,'
po 'after, according to' and *per 'through' with a
suffix -dъ and the Old Prussian prepositions in
-dau, viz. pirsdau (pirschdau) 'before,' sirsdau
'among,' pansdau 'thereafter.' According to Stang,
1970, 71, the formation in Slavic -dъ and OP -dau

is not clear, but Slavic -dъ could go back to *-du.
*-dus, *-dun or *-dos, *-don. OP -dau appears to
be the locative singular of a *u-stem. The fact
that Russian zad and pered 'front' belong to a type
of noun with the nom.-acc. pl. ending with accented
-ý could indicate that these are old u-stems, cf.
also the old instrumental singulars zadómъ and
peredómъ.

7.910 Shopay, 1970, carefully analyzes the
occurrences of the Old Prussian adverbs in -n and
concludes that many of these are merely accusative
case forms of an Old Prussian adjective. She
assumes that Abel Will's informant was frequently
unsure of what form exactly Will wanted, since it
seems quite likely that Will asked his informant
for the Old Prussian equivalent for each word as he
went along. Shopay writes, 1970, 161, "Since Will
used a word-for-word translation, and since all of
the German words cited can function either as
adverbs or adjectives, it is reasonable to assume
that his Old Prussian informant was uncertain as to
the use of these forms." Thus, for example, such
presumed adverbs as OP enwāngiskan = German
entlich 'finally'; ginnewīngiskan = German
freundtlich 'friendly, in a friendly manner';
isspresennien = German Nemlich 'namely';
kērmeneniskan = German Leiblich 'bodily' are all
adjective accusative singular forms.[84] The assumpt-
tion that the adverbs in -an are really adjectives
makes the phonetic correspondence of Baltic
neuters in -a (e.g., Lith. gẽr-a 'good') and Slavic
neuters in -o (e.g., Russ. mal-o 'little') easier,
because ordinarily one would expect an Indo-
European or Balto-Slavic *-om to pass to Slavic -ъ.
One can assume then that the Balto-Slavic neuter
singular nominative ending was -o, not *-om.[85]

Old Prussian Verb Morphology

8.000 Since my own analysis of the Old Prussian verb is presented in Schmalstieg, 1970 and 1974, 309-382, I will present here other views along with my criticism of these views.

8.001 Stang creates the following system of classification for the Baltic verb according to the present stem (1966, 309):
1) Athematic verbs
2) Half-thematic verbs
   a) i-verbs
   b) ā-verbs
3) Thematic verbs
   a) e/o-verbs
   b) i̯e/o-verbs

8.010 Stang, 313, says that Old Prussian has such old athematic verbs as 1st sg. asmai 'I am,' 2nd sg. assei, essei, 3rd person ast, 1st pl. asmai, 2nd pl. astai, estei, asti; 2nd sg. ēisei 'you go,' 3rd person ēit, 1st pl. -ēimai; 2nd sg. dāse 'you give,' 3rd person dāst. A new athematic present deriving from the old perfect present is 2nd sg. waisei 'you know,' 1st pl. waidimai, 2nd pl. waiditi with a secondary transfer to the i-inflection.

8.011 Apparent traces of the athematic inflection are to be found (Stang, 1966, 313) in the OP 3rd person quoi 'will' beside quoitē, 1st pl. quoitāmai, 2nd pl. quoitēti; 2nd sg. etskīsai 'you arise,' 1st pl. etskīmai. In 1974, 174, I have suggested for quoitē and quoitā a phonemicization /kaitá/ and an etymological connection with Lith. káitēti 'to lack; to worry,' Latv. kaitēt 'to be harmful.' The form quoi /kai/ is merely an abbreviated form used as a modal auxiliary. See 10.088 and 11.003.

8.012 Stang, 1970, 202, explains the growth of the athematic verbal class in the following manner. First, it is clear that the old athematic verbs which denoted a state (even though this may not have been the inherent function of this type) could have taken on an infinitive stem with a stative suffix. For example, Lith. rausti 'cries' (cf. Skt. roditi) could have taken on the infinitive stem with a stative suffix *-āti, just

198

as Lith. veizdmi (athematic, cf. the OCS
imperative vižde 'see') has an infinitive veizdéti
'to see, to look' (cf. the OCS infinitive vidéti
'to see') in order to mark the stative meaning of
the non-present forms. Second, many of the
innovating athematic presents arose when certain
perfects took on present meaning and inflection.
These perfect-presents had by nature stative
meaning and once they had taken on the present
meaning they adopted the infinitive suffix, thus,
e.g., Lith. gelbti, sergti, miegti which now have
the infinitives gélbéti 'to help,' sérgéti 'to
watch over,' miegóti 'to sleep.' One can find a
parallel to this development in Slavic where we
note the infinitive vědéti 'to know' beside the
athematic 1st sg. věmь (beside the older vědě).
8.013 Stang, 1970, 201-202, says that in his 1942
work, 133f., he suggested the possibility that the
3rd pres. wīrst, which translates German wird, 1st
pl. wīrstmai, 2nd pl. wīrstai, could be athematic.
On the other hand Stang suggests now that
Endzelīns, 1937, 429, is correct in proposing that
the 3rd person *wīrsta could have been shortened to
wīrst as a result of its being used as an
auxiliary verb. The forms wīrstmai, wīrstai could
then have been remodeled according to the 3rd
person. Stang believes that Endzelīns' theory is
further supported by the existence of Lith. virsta
'becomes.' Stang concludes finally that little
can be decided on the basis of the Old Prussian
material. See also Stang, 1966, 314.
8.020 Stang, 1966, 320, gives as an example of a
half-thematic verb with a stem in -i the OP verb
turri (inf. turīt 'to have') and as an example of
a half-thematic verb with a stem in -ā OP bia
(inf. biātwei), cf. Lith. bijóti 'to be afraid of,'
see Stang, 324.
8.030 As an example of a thematic e/o-verb Stang,
1966, 336, gives OP 2nd sg. giwassi (2X), gīwasi
'you (sg.) live,' 1st pl. giwammai. Stang, 339,
gives OP polīnka 'remains' as an example of a
thematic verb with an -n- infix and, 345,
poprestemmai 'we feel' as an example of a thematic
verb with the -sta- suffix. Stang finds, 363, that
the 3rd person verbal ending -ē derives from *-ēja
in such verbs as seggē 'does,' pallaipsē 'covets,'

milē 'loves,' etc.[86]For this class of verbs I
would suggest that the final -ē could stand for
/-ei/ which would show the diphthongization of an
original /-ī/. The parallel forms are gijwans =
/gīvans/ and geiwans = /geivans/; the second
phonemicization shows the innovating system, see
paragraph 5.002. This would bring these verbs
into line with the corresponding verbal class in
Lithuanian, cf., e.g., Lith. mýli 'loves.'
8.040 Stang, 1966, 375, says that we find the same
two preterit endings *-ā and *-ē as in the other
Baltic languages, e.g., 3rd preterit kūra 'created,'
prowela-din 'betrayed (him),' and weddē-din 'led.'
Furthermore Stang says that there is a series of
preterits in -āi, -ā, -ū, in which the ā (ū) is
identical with the final vowel of the infinitive
or the present stem. Following the stem was -i̯-
plus another vowel which later must have disappeared. I list below a few of Stang's examples:
dai 'gave,' postai 'became,' perpīdai 'brought,'
billai 'spoke,' widdai 'saw,' driāudai 'forbade,'
etc. In my own analysis of the Old Prussian verb
I see the orthographic -ai as denoting only /-ā/.
In Middle Low German one of the ways to denote a
long vowel was to add another grapheme denoting a
vowel. For example, Lasch, 1914, 25, gives the
examples raid = Rad 'wheel,' jair = Jahr 'year,'
etc. Within Old Prussian one also finds final -ai
and -ā apparently to denote the same sound, cf., e.
g., mensai and mensā 'flesh, meat,' signai and
ebsgnā 'he blessed,' etc. I have thus analyzed
such forms as dai, postai, etc. as root aorists,
/dā, pa-stā/, cf. Old Church Slavic 3rd sg. aor.
da, sta. Forms such as widdai denote either
/vid-ā/ (cf. Slavic vidati) or /vid-ē/. See
Schmalstieg, 1974, 157-158.
8.050 Stang, 1966, 437-438, gives six different
categories of Old Prussian imperative endings.
8.051 The first set of endings (2nd sg.) -ais/
(2nd pl.) -aiti derive from Proto-Baltic *-ais/
*-aitē < *-ois/*-oitē and is to be found in such
thematic verbs as immais 'take,' klumstinaitai
'knock,' and in one athematic verb idaiti 'eat.'
8.052 The second set of endings (2nd sg.) -ais,
-āis/(2nd pl.) -āiti (-aiti) is to be found in the

optatives which are derived from verbs with an
infinitive stem in -ā-, e.g., (2nd sg.) dais,
(2nd pl.) dāiti, daiti 'give,' etc.
8.053 The third set of endings (2nd sg.) -eis/
(2nd pl.) -eiti is to be found in the athematic
verbs, e.g., īdeiti, edeitte 'eat,' in thematic
verbs with a monosyllabic infinitive stem, e.g.,
(2nd sg.) wedeys 'lead,' in i̯e/o-verbs, e.g.,
draudieiti 'forbid,' cf. Lith. draũdžia 'forbids,'
and verbs with the infinitive in -īt, e.g., (2nd
pl.) crixteiti 'christen.'
8.054 The fourth set of endings (2nd sg.) -īs/
(2nd pl.) -īt(e)i is found in verbs with the
infinitive in -īt, e.g., seggītei 'do,' billītei
'speak, say.'
8.055 The fifth set of endings (2nd sg.) -aus/
(2nd pl.) -auti is limited to verbs with the
infinitive in -aut, e.g. gerdaus 'speak,'
dīnkauti 'thank.'
8.056 The sixth set of endings (2nd sg.) -s/
(2nd pl.) -tei is found respectively in the verbs
teīks 'put forth, produce,' powiērptei 'leave.'
8.060 For Old Prussian I would certainly not
distinguish between the following forms:
wedais and weddeis 'lead'; idaiti and edeitte
'eat.' (The orthographic variation here is similar
to that observed in the *o-stem nom. pl. adjective
forms mald-ai 'disciples' and wert-ei 'worth,
worthy.') In the form draudieiti the graphemic
sequence -di- may denote a palatalized /d/ of the
present stem. There may also have been a set of
endings (2nd sg.) -īs/ (2nd pl.) -īte represented
in endirīs 'look at' and crixtity 'baptize' and
with the diphthongization characteristic of the
innovating vocalic system dereis and crixteiti
respectively.
8.061 Stang notes, 1966, 439, that he has given up
his theory published in Symbolae Osloenses, XX, p.
45ff., according to which he compared the Old
Prussian endings -eis, -eīti with the Aeolian
optative aorists lúseia, lúseias, lúseie.
8.062 Stang says, 1966, 440, that the imperatives
in -aus, -auti and the forms teīks, powiērptei are
formed on analogy with verbs with the infinitive
in -īt and the imperatives in -īs, -īti,
respectively.

The verb form teīks occurs once in the following
expression (Trautmann, 1910, 45, line 3): Mijls
Brāti Teīks mennei ainan īnsan isspressennen prei
Grikaut - Lieber stelle mir ein kurtze weise zu
Beychten 'Dear brother provide a short method of
confessing for me.' In this expression the form
teīks could be a misprint for *teīkais or perhaps
a 2nd sg. future *teīks(i) or a 3rd future as I
have suggested, 1974, 182. The verb form
powiērptei occurs once in the following expression
(Trautmann, 1910, 61, line 8): powiērptei iouson
trēnien - lasset ewer drewen 'leave off your
threatening, menacing.' I have assumed, 1974,
183, a simple misprint and have phonemicized the
word as /pa-vérpaite/. In any case I would not
draw far-reaching conclusions about these two words
each of which occurs only once.
8.063 Stang, 1966, 440, remarks that the form
eykete 'come here' found in Simon Grunau's
vocabulary shows that imperative forms in -k- were
not lacking in Old Prussian either. I am rather
inclined, however, to accept Trautmann's, 1910,
326, explanation that the expression is just Lith.
eīki teñ 'go there.' Or even better one might
equate it exactly with Lith. eīkite (2nd pl.
imperative) 'come.'
8.064 Stang, 1966, 440, also remarks that the
forms in -sei, -sai which appear only in the 3rd
person are used chiefly in main clauses and
express a wish or a request. These forms can be
understood as a 3rd person imperative and can be
compared with the Lithuanian permissive. An
example is from Trautmann, 1910, 51, line 23:
twais swints Engels baūsei sen maīm 'thy holy
angel be with me.'
8.065 According to Stang, 1966, 442, the optative
endings occur in the following forms and with the
following frequencies: -sei (14X), -se (9X), -sai
(3X), -si (2x). Here Stang writes that -se and -si
are only a way of writing -sei and that the ending
-sai is only a mistake connected with the athematic
2nd sg. -sai and 2nd pl. -tai). He connects the
-s- with the future tense and the element -ei with
the old optative suffix. This view is also
represented in Schmid, 1963, 50. In 1974, 153,

202

I have followed Specht, 1928, in proposing that
the Old Prussian imperative in -sai is only the
particle -ai added to the 3rd sg. future, i.e.,
the same as the future stem.
8.066 Stang, 1966, 443, says that Old Prussian
-lai- is an innovation formed from the infinitive
stem by means of the inflected suffix -lai-.
Stang lists the following forms: 3rd pr. -lai;
2nd sg. -laisi < *-laisei (quoitīlaisi 5X); 2nd pl.
-limai < *-laimai (by dissimilation?); 1st. pl.
-laiti (quoitijlaiti). Furthermore Stang says
that the element -lai- has nothing to do with
Lith. laĩ, Latv. laî 'let, may,' because the
latter forms can be derived from laid-, the
imperative of Latv. laîst, Lith. léisti 'to let,
to allow.' Stang suggests rather that -lai could
be connected with the particle -le which is found
in Old Lith. esle 'may it be thus' and in eĩkeĺ
'come, go,' dúokeĺ 'give.' Stang compares further
the Slavic particle *-le, cf. Pol. byle 'any' and
the -li in Russian esli 'if.' Perhaps in Old
Prussian -lai the final element has been remodeled
according to the optative of the thematic verbs,
cf., imai- 'take,' etc. I personally see no reason,
however, why the OP -lai- might not have been taken
from a verb cognate with Lith. léisti or Latv.
laîst and then incorporated into the verbal
paradigm as a marker of the optative.
8.100 The verb as-mai 'I am' occurs in Old Prussian
ten times. Zabrocki, 1947, 306 and Stang, 1966,
406, following many others before them have assumed
that the ending -mai is an etymological middle
ending. Stang says that although the ending
corresponds well with the Greek ending -mai, one
must keep in mind the fact that the ending may have
arisen as a result of an analogical remodeling of
the ending -ai, cf. Skt. dviṣé. Furthermore Stang
remarks that it is remarkable that in Baltic the
first person singular of the athematic inflection
has a middle ending. If one accepts the notion
that old perfect tense forms frequently received a
present meaning, one might suppose that Endzelīns,
1948, 176 (paragraph 328), is right in thinking
that Baltic *-mái (> Lith./Latv. -mi, OP -mai) is
a result of a contamination of the perfect ending

-ai (cf. Old Church Slavic vĕdĕ 'I know') and the
athematic present ending *-mi (cf. Old Church
Slavic damь 'I give').

I am of the opinion that the middle ending
for the present tense was originally something
like *-oi and the subject of the verb was in the
ergative case (which later became the genitive).
At this point there was no concord between subject
noun and verb. At a later date when concord was
introduced into the middle voice (under the
influence of the active voice) the middle endings
resulted from a contamination of the active endings
plus the old middle ending *-oi. Thus a form such
as Greek phéromai is to be analyzed etymologically
as phér-om-ai (root = pher, etymological 1st sg.
secondary ending = -om-, old ending deriving from
pre-concord middle voice *-ai replacing earlier
*-oi). The usual morphemic division phér-o-mai
is then incorrect and the Greek form itself is the
result of a contamination and cannot be compared
directly with the Baltic form.

8.101 I do not accept the usual assumption that a
Proto-Baltic ending *-mai plus the reflexive
particle *-s(i) stands at the origin of such forms
as Lith. (duo)-mies. In the East Baltic diphthongs
/ie/ and /uo/ the second elements do not contrast,
and if we denote the non-contrastive second
element by /A/ we find that /ie/ = /iA/ and /uo/ =
/uA/. Thus the thematic 1st sg. ending /-u/ has a
reflexive counterpart /-uAs/, usually written as
-uos. By analogy with the thematic 1st sg.
reflexive we find the athematic 1st sg. reflexive
/-miAs/, usually written as -mies. In other words
-u:-uAs :: -mi:x and x = -miAs (or -mies). See
Schmalstieg, 1961 and 1974, 149-150; Kazlauskas,
1968, 294-295. See also paragraph 5.322.

8.102 Kazlauskas, 1968, 294, says that in OP the
first singular and plural ending is -mai. Originally Old Prussian had the same thematic first
singular ending as the other Baltic languages and
this is reflected in the form asmu 'I am.'
Kazlauskas writes further that there is no need to
connect the OP 1st pl. ending -mai with the Gk.
1st sg. middle ending -mai, since the latter
ending is an innovation of the Greek language.
Neither does Kazlauskas accept the contamination

theory proposed above for the origin of the Old
Prussian ending -mai. Kazlauskas proposes that
since in the 3rd person the distinction between
the singular and the plural does not exist
this could have influenced the other persons.
Now there is in Lithuanian a Samogitian 1st plural
ending -ma (and Slavic has a common 1st pl.
ending -mo) so we may assume that there existed
also in Old Prussian an ending *-ma. Since the
1st singular ending was -mi, the 1st plural ending
was *-ma and the difference between the singular
and plural was not well marked, the Old Prussian
ending -mai developed as the result of a contamination of the two endings in question, ousting both
the old ending *-mi and the *-ma. I assume rather
that final -ai stands for /-ā/ and that the -u in
asmu was a way of writing /-ua/ as it was in Old
Lithuanian and Latvian texts.[87]
8.103 Kazlauskas, 1968, 294, likewise does not
accept the derivation of the Lithuanian ending
-mies from an earlier *-mei, but assumes an
analogical development on the basis of such forms
as prausì vs. the reflexive prausíesi 'you (sg.)
wash,' prausdamì 'washing' vs. the reflexive
prausdamíes.
8.104 According to Mažiulis, 1972a, 95-96, in
unstressed position the Indo-European 1st singular
ending *-ō (of the *[i̯]o-stem verbs) passed to
*-ā̄ > *-ă̄ in Old Prussian and thus merged with the
3rd person present form in -ā̆. The ending *-ā̄ was
either shortened to -ă̄ before the passage of OP
*ā̄ > *ū̄ in post-velar position, or else the -ă̄ was
restored analogically. Mažiulis suggests that
both the root-stressed (barytone) and mobile
stressed verbs had an unstressed first person
singular. This phonological merger explains why
so frequently the Old Prussian 1st singular and
sometimes even the 2nd singular endings are the
same as those of the 3rd person.
    Mažiulis, 1972a, 96-97, assumes that in
the OP 1st sg. pres. asm-u 'I am' the final -ŭ
developed after *ā̄ had passed to *ū̄ in post-labial
and post-velar position and then *ū̄ was shortened
to -ŭ. This latter development took place in some
dialects, whereas in other dialects *esm-ā̄ > *esm-ă̄

205

and the element -i was added giving the attested
asmai 'I am.' Another possibility is that *esm-ā+
i > *esm-ai, thereby leading to the attested asmai.
8.105 Schmid, 1968, 358, points out that the
difference between thematic and athematic verbs is
without function in Old Prussian. He assumes then
a gradual shift of athematic personal endings to
thematic verbs and a leveling of the endings within
the paradigm. He establishes then, 1968, 359, the
following pattern for the singular of the Old
Prussian verbal paradigm:

	Athematic	Thematic
1st sg.	-mai	-a < *-ā
2nd sg.	-sai	-ei < *-ei
3rd sg.	-t(i)	-∅ < *-t

The athematic endings then are nothing but the
result of a contamination of the inherited *-mi,
*-si, *-ti and the thematic endings *-ā, *-ei,
*-t. In the third person there was no change, in
the second person *-si and *-ei gave *-sei and in
the first person *-mā, the expected form, was
remodeled to -mai. The form asmai is the earliest
form and the other forms, asmu and asmau come from
a period after which -ai in position following
gutturals (velars), labials and r became -u.
Sometimes the -ai and sometimes the -u form was
generalized. The form asmau is to be explained as
a contamination of *-mu plus the thematic ending.
I would assume nothing in principle wrong with an
explanation based on contamination. In fact I
believe that in the past linguists have ignored
this possibility to their peril and only as a result of the fact that it did not fit neatly into
any preconceived notions of structure. On the
other hand in this case I would assume, as
mentioned before, that the endings -mai, -mau, -mu
are nothing more than graphemic variants. Most
likely, however, Schmid is right in assuming that
the 1st person singular ending does derive from a
contamination of the thematic and athematic forms.
8.106 Zabrocki, 1947, 308-309, formalizes this
contamination in the following way: *esmō > *esmū
*esmau. Although I accept the principle of con-
tamination I assume that the variant spellings
asmai, asmau and asmu are all to be phonemicized

as /esmā/ and I assume that the final -i of asmai
may have denoted what appeared to the Old Prussian
informant as a long vowel. The forms asmau and
asmu merely show the labialization of the preceding
consonant as it was sporadically noted by the
German scribe, see 5.200.
8.107 The Old Prussian 2nd person singular ending
is rendered by -sei (10X), -sai (8X), -si (8X),
-se (7X) according to Stang, 1966, 407. He says,
408, that the ending -sai is not a way of writing
-sei and since one finds further certain examples
of -e, -i < -ei whereas no sure examples of -i < -ai,
perhaps one should derive -se, -si from -sei
rather than -sai. As far as the thematic form
giwassi 'you (sg.) live' (2X), gīwasi (1X) is
concerned, one could be tempted to identify the
ending with the Indo-European primary active
ending -si, cf. Skt. 2nd sg. pres. jīvasi 'you
(sg.) live.' But, according to Stang, since the
-i in the third person of the athematic verbs is
lost (cf. ast 'is,' eit 'goes,' dāst 'gives'), it
seems rather unlikely that the -i in polysyllabic
verbs in *-asi would be retained. Therefore Stang
interprets the forms as *gīvasei and he concludes
further that the type seggēsei 'you (sg.) do' is
modeled on the 3rd person sege, following the
pattern *gīvasei:*gīva (3rd person giwa).
Similarly Stang would read quoitīlaisi 'you (sg.)
would, will' as -laisei and would ascribe the
orthographic variants gīwasi, giwassi, quoitīlaisi
to the inexact aperception of unstressed final -ei
on the part of the translator. Stang then says
that he considers the 2nd person singular thematic
ending to have been *-asei and to be similar to the
ending attested in Old Church Slavic živeši 'you
(sg.) live,' and veliši 'you (sg.) order,' etc.
The ending -sai he takes for an Indo-European
middle ending and compares it with Skt. bhárase
'you (sg.) carry' and Gk. dídosai 'you (sg.) give.'
8.108 Like Stang, Zabrocki, 1947, 309-311,
considers the ending -sai to reflect an old middle
ending, but he considers the ending -sei to be the
result of a contamination of the ending -ĕi with
either the old middle ending -sai or else the
thematic ending -si. Zabrocki supposes that the

form -si is characteristic of the thematic verbs,
but that the athematic verbs end in -sai, -sei or
-se. He assumes that in stressed position the -ei
was perceived as -ei or -e, but in unstressed
position as -i. Likewise Zabrocki, 1947, 312,
denies the existence of the sigmatic future in Old
Prussian. He says that from the point of view of
the content a form such as postāsei 'you (sg.) will
be, become' is future, but from the point of view
of form it is a 2nd singular present. Forms such
as dasai 'may he give,' bousei 'may he be' and
ebsignāsi 'may he bless' are old voluntatives which
derive from optatives in a fashion similar to the
Latv. 1st plural optative iêsiẽm 'let us go'
⟨*ei-sei-me. Zabrocki, 1947, 316-317, concludes
that Old Prussian only shows a trace of the
sigmatic future in the -s- of the 3rd singular
optative, the ending of which is from the present
optative. The new form of the Old Prussian future
is formed chiefly under the influence of Polish.
8.109 Of all the varied Old Prussian endings for
the second person singular Mažiulis, 1972a, 97,
says that the ending -e may stand for -ei or -i
and that the ending -ai is probably remodeled on
the basis of the 1st sg. asm-ai. Mažiulis states
that the morpheme -ei is represented either
directly or indirectly 25 times and the morpheme
-i eight times. If this ending -si was not a form
of -sei remodeled by the translator himself, then
the -si could be an old dialect feature. In fact
Mažiulis suggests that Balto-Slavic -sei could
derive from a contamination of the ending -si and
the o-stem ending *-ei.
8.110 Kazlauskas, 1968, 297, points out, however,
that those who believe that the Old Prussian 2nd
singular ending -sei is a result of the influence
of the thematic verbs have not taken into consideration the fact that in Old Prussian there are no
thematic verbal forms in -ei such as we find in
Lithuanian. Old Prussian forms such as tulninai
'increase,' sātuinei 'satisfy,' and turei 'have'
are probably 3rd singular forms used with the
meaning of the 2nd singular. Kazlauskas also
assumes, as do I, that the forms giwassi, gīwasi
do indeed show an original ending -si. As we have

208

seen above, most linguists deny that the -si could
represent an original Indo-European ending because
Old Prussian lost the final -i in such third person
forms as ast 'is,' dāst 'gives,' eit 'goes,' etc.
and the infinitive forms. Kazlauskas, 1968, 297-
298, objects that the infinitive forms in -t, if
they are derived from -ti, do not show at all that
final -i had to disappear in Old Prussian, because
infinitive forms are not necessarily shortened
according to phonetic laws, cf. Lith. bégt 'to
run,' and eĩt 'to go' in those dialects in which
final vowels are not necessarily shortened.
Likewise a loss of -i may have begun with the
third person form ast 'is,' which was an auxiliary
verb and then spread to other verbs. I personally
believe that the final -i may well have been
optional just as is the final -e in such Lithuanian
forms as eĩnam(e) 'we go; let's go,' and eĩnat(e)
'you go,' etc.
8.111 Stang, 1966, 409-411, points out that the
third person athematic ending is -ti represented in
the form astits 'is.' In bi- and polysyllabic
stems, according to Stang, 1966, 410, we find the
same endingless forms that we do in West Baltic,
cf. OP imma 'takes,' turri 'has,' perbānda
'tempts,' pertraūki 'covered, closed up,' weddē
'led, brought.' Both in the thematic as well as in
the athematic verbs beside the aforementioned type
we also find verbs with an ending in -ts. Stang
believes that this -ts is etymologically the Baltic
anaphoric pronoun -tas in the nominative singular.
Stang lists all the forms encountered and then
says that such forms are apparently archaisms since
most of the words occur in the institutional words
of the communion service. Stang assumes that
these institutional words must have had a certain
fixed form even before the time of the reformation
and that these words are otherwise rare in the
catechisms.
8.112 Kazlauskas, 1968, 303, notes that in Slavic
we also find cases where the pure stem is used
without any ending, cf. Serbian nese, Czech nese,
Polish niesie 'carries,' etc. On the other hand
OP -ts could formally be identical with Slavic -t
according to Kazlauskas, who also thinks that the

ending -t̲s̲ was just beginning to spread in Old
Prussian.
8.113 Taking up the problem of the third singular
verbal ending in Old Prussian, Zabrocki, 1947, 317,
writes that it is only the verbal form a̲s̲t̲i̲t̲s̲
which shows the continuation of the old ending -t̲i̲.
All the other verbs show the continuation of the
old ending -t̲. The retention of -t̲ < -t̲i̲ in the
athematic verbs is explained by the fact that if
the -t̲ had been lost, then only the verbal stem
itself would have remained.
8.114 Zabrocki, 1947, 318, thinks that in general
the middle endings may have had some influence on
the creation of the 1st plural ending -m̲a̲i̲ of Old
Prussian. He notes the same straightening out in
the 1st and 2nd singular endings. Thus all the
final sequences would be the same, viz., -a̲i̲. And
the ending of the 1st person plural was assimilated
to the ending of the 1st person singular.
Zabrocki cites a parallel from the Poznań and
other dialects in which we find a Polish 1st plural
mogẹ̄my 'we can' patterned after the 1st singular
mogẹ 'I can' and replacing the etymological moẓemy
'we can.' Stang, 1966, 417, writes that the Old
Prussian first plural ending is very common, and
is unknown in any other Indo-European language.
Apparently assessing the situation very differently
from Kazlauskas, 1968, 294, who minimizes the
importance of number, Stang says that it is
difficult to believe that two forms which express
such a necessary distinction in the language system
as the distinction between the 1st person singular
and plural should become so similar even if there
was an original difference in position of stress.
Stang would rather find in -m̲a̲i̲ the same particle
-i̲ which he sees in the 2nd plural ending -t̲e̲i̲,
-t̲a̲i̲. The form which was basic to Old Prussian
would have then been *-m̲a̲ (< *-m̲o̲) or *-m̲ā̲. I
have assumed, 1974, 152, that the Old Prussian
1st plural ending is indeed /-ma/ and that the
orthographic -m̲a̲i̲ is meaningless. For Kazlauskas'
view on this see paragraph 8.102.
8.115 Both Zabrocki, 1947, 320 and Stang, 1966,
418, say that the usual Old Prussian 2nd singular
ending -t̲i̲ derives from *-t̲ē̲ which is historically

identical with Lith. -te (lengthened form in the
reflexive -tėsi). Stang, 1966, 418, quotes
Endzelīns, 1943, 105, to the effect that the
Old Prussian ending -ti (-ty) occurs about 80
times and the other forms with the following
distribution: -tei (9X), -tai (8X), -te (4X),
-ta (1X). The circumstance that -tei is found
chiefly in the imperative and optative forms leads
him to suppose that this form of the ending had a
particle with an original affective or emphatic
meaning and is therefore to be derived from *-tē +
-i. Perhaps -tei was originally used with
imperative meaning and later spread to forms used
as optatives. Stang, 1966, 419, assumes that the
ending -te is a mistake for -ti. He notes also
that the ending -tai is not only imperative.
Except for the single occurrence of the verb
klumstinaitai 'knock' the ending is limited to
the verb astai 'are,' wīrstai 'will.' Stang
considers it likely that the ending -tai arose
through the double influence of the 2nd singular
ending -sai and the 1st plural ending -mai.[88]
Zabrocki, 1947, 320, derives the endings -tei and
-tai from a form which correspnds to the endings
-tie(s), -ti of Lithuanian and Latvian. According
to Zabrocki, van Wijk's, 1918, 61, assertion that
the ending -tai arose under the influence of the
1st singular ending -mai is not acceptable. In
Zabrocki's opinion the influence of the 1st person
on the 2nd person would be a rather unusual
phenomenon. On the other hand one may anticipate
the influence of the 2nd person on the 1st person.
In the 1st person, however, we find only
-mai, which excludes the assimilation between the
two persons. The form -ta found once is either
a misprint or else perhaps the continuation of an
old dual ending.

I personally assume that all of these varied
graphemic sequences are merely different orthographic representations of the ending -te which is
well attested in other Indo-European languages.
For Baltic in general there is no need to reconstruct
a 2nd plural ending *-tē. See Schmalstieg, 1961,
1974, 150. The Lithuanian reflexive in -tės
merely reflects /-teAs/, i.e., the allomorph /-As/
of the reflexive particle. Kuryłowicz, 1958, 208,

suggests that the relationship of -u: -uos = -i:
-ies (reflexive) and perhaps -va:-vos (reflexive)
are responsible for the Lithuanian reflexive
endings -mės, -tės, -tos as opposed to the non-
reflexive -me, -te, -ta. According to Kuryłowicz,
nowhere else do we find in the historically
attested languages endings of the type *-me, *-te
*-ta. The Vedic lengthening in the endings -ma,
-tha is secondary.

8.200 Zabrocki, 1947, 305, writes that the
conjugation of the Old Prussian verb shows two
special characteristics: 1) confusion of persons in
the present and the preterit and 2) confusion of
present tense forms with preterit tense forms.
According to Zabrocki such phenomena are
encountered in other Indo-European languages, e.g.,
we find the use of the 3rd singular form in
singular and plural function in many Rheto-Romance
dialects and we note the disappearance of the
personal forms in northern Latvian dialects. In
many languages, however, the cause of these
mergers is to be found in the result of the action
of sound laws connected with the word-final
position. Zabrocki asks then if this might not
also be a factor in the mergers observed in Old
Prussian also.

8.201 Zabrocki's classification of the Old Prussian
verb is too long and complicated to be given here
in toto, but his general conclusion, 1947, 378-381,
that the present conjugation of the Old Prussian
verb is essentially similar to that of the Latvian
and Lithuanian verb is quite acceptable in my
opinion. He notes in principle the influence of
the thematic conjugation on the athematic
conjugation, cf., e.g., the forms asmu, asmau
'I am' discussed in 8.106. Zabrocki, 379, lists
the following endings for the Old Prussian verb
in the thematic conjugation: 1st sg. -ō, 2nd sg.
-ei, 3rd sg. -ă. As a result of specific
developments of word-final syllable laws we find
the following forms of these endings: 1. -ă, -ō,
(-u, -au); 2. -ei, -e, -i, 3. -ă; (i̯o-stems) -i̯ă,
-i̯e, -i̯. Zabrocki writes further that the 2nd
singular ending -sei, -si, -se was transferred
from the athematic to the thematic verbs.

212

The lack of the sigmatic future in Old Prussian was also an important factor in this substitution according to Zabrocki.

8.202 Zabrocki, 1947, 319, writes that the stress of the 3rd person also had an effect on that of the other persons. Thus a form like the OP 1st plural perēimai 'we come,' has its stress from the 3rd person perēit, whereas we might expect the ending -mai would be stressed according to the action of de Saussure's law. I personally would not assume de Saussure's law to have taken place here anyway (cf. Lith. eĩname 'we go'), since I do not believe the Old Prussian ending would have been acuted.

8.203 The merger of the 1st singular and the 3rd singular under certain conditions, e.g., -ă < *-ō led to the identification of these forms and the use of the 3rd person elsewhere in the function of the 1st singular, e.g., as quoi 'I will, I shall.' Other possibilities suggested by Zabrocki, 1947, 324-325 are that *quoi-ō, *quoi-ei, *quoi-ă passed to *quoi-ō, *quoi, *quoi or that perhaps the 1st singular had a middle ending *quoi-ai which passed by haplology to *quoi or even one might suggest that *quoi̯-ai > *quoi̯ei > *quoi̯i > *quoi.

I have proposed, 1974, 174, that quoi is to be phonemicized as /kai/ and is merely a shortened form of /kaitá/ the 3rd person of a verb which I would reconstruct as /kaitēt/ (infinitive) and would connect with Lith. káitėti in the meaning 'to lack, to be wanting; to worry' and Latv. kaitēt 'to be harmful.' See also Schmalstieg, 1969, 164-165.

8.204 Zabrocki, 1947, 338, also says that the form of the infinitive was very important for the remodeling of the present tense. As an example he gives the form dīnkaumai 'we thank,' which is remodeled on the basis of the infinitive. As in the work of most other scholars in the field, in Zabrocki's work also I find too great a reliance on the spelling and not enough skepticism of the written word.

8.300 According to Toporov, 1961a, 55, the Baltic languages preserve a state of affairs which for Proto-Slavic can only be attained by lengthy reconstruction.

8.301 But the various Baltic dialects differ from
each other in the distribution of preterit forms
with -ā and -ē. Old Prussian texts contain a few
examples of these preterits, but according to
Toporov, 1961a, 56, they translate the German forms
so inconsistently that one gets the impression that
the translator in a number of cases was unable to
distinguish the present and the past tenses.
Toporov writes further that frequently there is a
difference between the Old Prussian preterit and
the more authoritative Lithuanian forms, cf., e.g.,
OP kūra 'created' vs. Lith. kùrė 'heated;
established,' OP prowela 'betrayed' vs. Lith. výlė
'deluded.'

8.302 Toporov, 1961a, 62, writes that the East
Baltic ending *-ēi (2nd singular) could be
supported by the existence of such an ending in
other Indo-European languages, cf., e.g., Old
Irish beri < *berēi. Toporov supports the
contamination theory to explain the endings -sei,
and -sai in Old Prussian. See paragraphs 8.107-9.

8.303 Toporov, 1961a, 62, assumes that in the
oldest periods of the Indo-European dialects known
to us the 3rd person singular existed in the form
of the pure stem. Old Prussian which was in a
stage of transition presented both the form with
the pure stem and the forms with the optional -ts,
a good example of which, according to Toporov, 63,
is the sentence (Trautmann, 1910, 49, lines 6-7):
imma tans stan geitin dīnkauts bhe līmauts bhe dai
'he took the bread, gave thanks and broke (it) and
gave...' in which imma 'took' and dai 'gave' have
no ending, but dīnkauts 'thanked' and līmauts
'broke' have the optional -ts.

8.304 Toporov, 1961a, 67, concludes then that
perhaps an analysis of Baltic and Slavic suggests
two types of paradigms for the present conjugation,
viz. -mi, -si, -ti and -ō, -i and zero.

8.400 Schmid, 1963, 97, proposes that for Germanic,
Baltic and Slavic there was a verbal class with
a present tense conjugation as follows: (1st sg.)
*-i̯ō, (2nd sg.) *-ēi̯(e)si, (3rd sg.) *-ēi̯(e)ti.
He continues further, 101, that the languages which
have this type of inflection, i. e., Germanic,

Baltic, Slavic, Latin and Celtic belong to that
group of languages which Hans Krahe had included
under his concept of 'old European' on the basis of
his investigations of river names.
8.401 I believe that Schmid is correct in assuming
that such a verbal type did indeed exist, but I
would simplify matters a great deal. Briefly put,
I suggest that there was a morphophonemic
alternation such that the 1st singular does have
the *-jō, but that the 2nd and 3rd singular have
*-oi-, i.e., (1st sg.) *-jō, (2nd sg.)
*-oi(e)-s(i), (3rd sg.) *-oi(e)-t(i). The
diphthong *-oi- was monophthongized to *-ē- in
Indo-European in pre-consonantal position (i.e.,
in this case if the verb was athematic). As a
result I would assume the following chronological
stages for each person of the verb: (1st sg.)
***-ojóm > **-jóm > *-jō; (2nd sg.) ***-ój-e-s- >
-óis > *-ēs; (3rd sg.) *-ój-e-t- > **-óit > *-ēt.
Once the verbal type in *-jō, *-ēs, *-ēt had been
created it was subject to rethematicization and
analogical substitution of *-ē- in the 1st
singular creating a new verbal paradigm *-ējō,
*-ējes, *-ējet, etc. The monophthongization also
took place in the infinitive giving us forms of
the type of Latin sed-ē-re, Lithuanian séd-é-ti,
Old Church Slavic sěd-ě-ti 'to sit' (here, of
course, an Indo-European monophthongization, not a
Slavic monophthongization is envisioned). Thus we
see a morphophonemic reason connecting the
infinitive in -ē- with the verbs in *-(ē)-jō,
*-ē-(je)-s, *-ē-(je)-t. For further details see
Schmalstieg 1972a and 1973a.
8.402 Schmid, 1964, 125, suggests that Old Prussian
verbs of the type endyrītwei 'to look at, to see'
and billīt 'to say, to speak' reflect an etymological type of verb with an infinitive suffix in *-ē
and a preterit suffix in *-ā. The ā of the preterit
endeirā and billā goes back to *-āiāt and the Old
Prussian forms are to be compared with Lith. dýrojo
'looked' and bylójo 'spoke, said.' This shows that
Old Prussian had not only an old present tense
inflection of some ē-verbs, but that it also shows
in the preterit formation an archaism which consists
of the distribution of ē(i̯) in the present stem

215

and $\bar{a}(\underset{\wedge}{i})$ in the preterit stem. Different generalizations led to the creation of such Lithuanian
doublets as klūpéti, klūpoti 'to kneel' and dyréti
dýroti 'to look at,' etc.
8.403 Schmid compares this Old Prussian verbal type
with the Tokharian B third verbal class
e.g., lipetär 'is left over' (3rd sg.). The
Tokharian verbs of this class usually have a zero-
grade root vocalism, for the most part a durative-
stative meaning and are almost exclusively middle
voice. This class is cognate with the Balto-Slavic
*ē-verbs with zero-grade roots and generally
correspond with the Sankrit -ya-verbs. In both
Old Prussian and Tokharian we find a preterit in
-ā- for such verbs, cf., e.g., the Tokharian 3rd
singular preterit (with a suffixed personal pronoun) lyukā-me. The following comparison is also
instructive: OP billā < *billajat is to Tokharian
lipa <*lipāt as Lith. stójo is to OCS sta, Skt.
asthāt. In Old Prussian verbs with the infinitive
in *-ēti have an imperative in -ī, cf., e.g.,
endirīs 'look at,' mijlis 'love.' In Tokharian B
an imperfect in -ī- is derived from the present
stem and this imperfect in -ī- may come from an
earlier optative construction, e.g., 3rd singular
present lipetär vs. the imperfect līpitär -ne .
8.500 Hamp, 1973, 47, equates the participles in
-m- in Balto-Slavic, Luvian and Albanian, but says
(49): "Yet, while the incorporation of the *-m-
participle into the central paradigm is to be
viewed as an innovation supporting Balto-Slavic and
Albanian dialect unity, I agree with Benveniste
that the formation is, especially now on the Luwian
testimony an old one; and I feel that his identification of the 'quasi-participial' adjectives
represented by gharma-/warm/ thermós/ zjarm is
correct. In light of this, we are not then
compelled to see the sharing of this old formation
by Luwian and Balto-Slavic and Albanian as pointing
to a common dialect basis in contrast to the *-meno-
dialects." Thus Hamp concludes that OP poklausīmanas
'heard' represents a correspondence to Skt. -māna-,
Gk.-meno-, Tokharian A -mām.
8.510 A. Jakulienė, 1969, shows that there are two
kinds of reflexive verbs in Old Prussian, those

216

which are clear loan translations from the German
(using as reflexive object <u>mien</u> 'me,' <u>tien</u> 'you
(sg.),' <u>sien</u> 'oneself' (i.e. German <u>sich</u>), <u>mans</u>
'us,' <u>wans</u> 'you') and those which seem to be of
native Baltic origin which use the native morpheme
-<u>si(n)</u> for all persons. Examples of the first type
are (Trautmann, 1910, 45, line 20): <u>as quoi mien</u>
<u>walnennint</u> - <u>ich will mich bessern</u> 'I will improve
myself'; (Trautmann, 1910, 67, line 7) <u>seiti</u>
<u>weijsewingi bhæ tūlninaiti wans</u> - <u>Seid fruchtbar</u>
<u>un mehret euch</u> 'be fruitful and multiply (your-
selves).' According Jakulienė, 1969, 42, the
native Old Prussian reflexive particle -<u>si(n)</u>
is encountered only as a suffix for both prefixed
and unprefixed verbs, cf., e.g., the unprefixed
forms <u>wartinna sin</u> - <u>wende er sich</u> 'may he turn,'
<u>maitātunsin</u> - <u>sich neeren</u> 'nourish themselves,'
vs. the **prefixed** forms <u>au-dasseisin</u> - <u>geschee</u>
'(may it) come to pass,' <u>et-lāikusin</u> - <u>enthalt</u>
<u>sich</u> 'refrain,' etc. I am convinced that
Jakulienė's conclusion is correct.
8.520 Stang, 1961, 72-73, writes that in Proto-
Indo-European the perfect tense had a non-resultative
meaning related to that of the middle voice. The
circumstance that the Baltic nasal verbs are in
part derived from or remodeled after old perfects
may help explain the middle-intransitive character
of the Baltic nasal verbs, since nasal verbs did
not have this meaning in Indo-European. Thus
Lithuanian <u>kàkti</u> 'to be sufficient' (3rd present
<u>kañka</u>) continues an old perfect form and the Old
Prussian cognate <u>kackint</u>, <u>kakīnt</u> 'to attain' has
the causative suffix -<u>in</u>-. An Old Prussian verb
with the vocalism of the perfect is <u>polaikt</u> 'to
remain' and it seems likely to Stang, 1961,72, that
<u>polīnka</u> 'remains' is a present form derived from an
old perfect by means of the nasal infix.
8.530. Specht, 1954, 249, compares the Old Prussian
infinitives of the type <u>biātwei</u>, <u>biātwi</u> 'to fear'
with the exceptional infinitive formation <u>regêtuve</u>
found in Daukša's Postille 164, 29. Specht says
that both are derivatives from an old <u>tu</u>-stem.
8.540 Vaillant, 1962b, 449, suggests that Old
Prussian <u>et-winūt</u> 'to pardon, to excuse' is a
borrowing from Polish <u>winować</u> and that Old Prussian
<u>ni-winūton</u> 'innocent' is from Old Polish <u>nie-</u>

winowaty. The Slavic stem vinova- gave OP *winawū
(with the treatment of ā to ū after labial) and
*wina(w)ū was reduced to winū. In pronunciation the
ū vacillated between au and ou, but the case of
-winūt is, in Vaillant's opinion, special since the
other borrowed verbs are adapted to the type with
the infinitive -aut, 3rd present -awie, corresponding to Polish -ować, -uje-, e.g., OP dīnkaut 'to
thank' from Polish dziękować. But here the
borrowing was made principally from the Polish
adjective winowaty which gave winūt-. I have
assumed, 1974, 196, that the graphemic -ū- is
merely a scribal error for /au/, but if it is
indeed a /ū/, I prefer Endzelīns', 1943, 174,
explanation that the ū in the Old Prussian word
merely shows that the word was borrowed from the
Slavic present stem vinuje-.

Miscellanea
9.000 Areal Linguistics
9.100 The Old Prussian Pantheon

9.000 A special section must be devoted to A. P.
Nepokupnyj's studies of areal linguistics in
connection with Old Prussian. Frequently
Nepokupnyj finds that linguistic phenomena
observed in Old Prussian are found in other
languages spoken on former Old Prussian territories
or in areas neighboring on former Old Prussian
territories.

9.010 Nepokupnyj, 1972, gives some examples of
prefixed formations which are common to Old
Prussian and Belorussian or Lithuanian: a. OP
etwiērpt 'to forgive' to be compared with Lith.
atverpti for which Skardžius, 1932, 52, gives the
sample sentence atverpk velėną which he explains as
meaning 'push in with a shovel and lift (the sod or
turf) from the ground.' b. OP epkieckan 'vice'
according to Nepokupnyj, 1972, 12-13, is to be
connected with Lith. ap-kéikti 'to curse out'
known in western High Lithuanian dialects (vakarų
aukštaičių). c. OP preigērbt 'to teach'
corresponds to western High Lithuanian prigerbti
identical in form to the Old Prussian word and
close in meaning, i.e., 'to have in view, to suspect.' d. sengidaut 'to attain' corresponds to
Lith. sugeidáuti 'to wish for, to want' known in
Samogitia. e. Sometimes the prefixes will be
cognate and the roots will be formally different
but semantically the same, e.g., OP ep-war(r)īsnan
'victory' is to be compared with Lith. apgalė
'id.,' a word found in the writings of the
Samogitian authoress Šatrijos Ragana (Marija
Pečkauskaitė), although standard Lithuanian uses
the word pérgalė for 'victory.' This prefix would
correspond to the existing form in Belorussian
peramoha and Ukrainian peremoha 'victory.' Still
Nepokupnyj, 1972, 14, quotes an excerpt from a
1489 Čet'ja Mineja in which we find the word
obmagati and says that contemporary dialects of
Belorussian attest to a verb abmahac' in the
meaning 'to conquer.'

Nepokupnyj, 1972, 17, concludes this article
by saying that the geography of Lithuanian

correspondences to the Old Prussian prefixal formations is the territory of the Samogitian and
western High Lithuanian dialects. As Nepokupnyj
shows on his map, 18, the Lithuanian and Belorussian
forms are found precisely on the edges of the
former Old Prussian territory. He seems to leave
open the possibility for speculation that Old
Prussian might have been spoken here also, although
as far as I can understand him he does not state
this explicitly.
9.020 Nepokupnyj, 1973a, 77, notes that Endzelīns,
1943, 157, in his commentary on OP dauris (EV - 211)
says the form should be corrected to duaris =
dwaris, cf. Latv. dvars or dvaŗš, OCS dvorě, etc.
Nepokupnyj points out, however, that the Latvian
word stems from the northern Curonian dialect area.
Nevertheless, he has found the form duors 'gate'
in the Curonian Nėringa (Nehrung) in a folklore
study dating from 1931 by M. Miezone (Kuršu kāpu
folklora [Latviešu folkloras krātuves materiali,
B.2]). Nepokupnyj assumes then that Latv. dvars,
(dvaŗš, dvari), duors in the attested meaning
represent a relic of the Curonian language. The
forms in question then bear witness to an Old
Prussian-Curonian isogloss relating OP dauris =
dwaris 'large door, gate' with Curonian dvars,
etc. He writes further that in the reconstruction
of the Old Prussian-Curonian lexico-semantic
isogloss one must take into consideration the fact
that in the dialect of the Lithuanian fishermen of
the southeastern coast of the Curonian Bay Lith.
durys does not mean 'door in a house,' but rather
'small gate within a large gate, gate in a fence.'
9.021 Nepokupnyj, 1973a, 78, says that on the
other hand Lith. vartas means 'door' in the dialect
of the Lithuanian fishermen of the village of Tave
(now Zalivino of the Slavskij region, Kaliningrad
district). Interestingly enough OP warto (EV -
210) denotes 'door.' Thus, according to Nepokupnyj,
the relationship of OP dauris 'gate' to OP warto
is a clear example of a lexico-semantic feature of
Old Prussian confirmation for which is found in a
series of contemporary premaritime dialects of
the Baltic languages.
9.030 Trautmann, 1910, 456 and Endzelīns, 1943,

270, connect OP waitiāt 'to speak' with Old Church
Slavic věštati 'id.' Vaillant, 1947a, 153, wrote
that the identity of the Old Prussian and the Old
Church Slavic verbs is too complicated to be
explained otherwise than by borrowing. Safarewicz,
1967, 254, suggests that the Old Prussian verb
does not correspond to OCS věštati. Both verbs,
in his opinion, were innovations formed independently of each other.
9.031 Nepokupnyj, 1973a, 79, calls attention to
the existence of Ukrainian vajtjati, Belorussian
vajcjac', the fundamental meaning of which is 'to
scold, to reprimand.' The verb is well known in
Belorussia along the Nemunas and also in the
Ukraine in neighboring dialects. The word is also
found in the form vojtjati in Old Russian.
9.032 Several other words given by Nepokupnyj,
1973a, 80-83, which belong to the Old Prussian-
Belorussian-Ukrainian linguistic area include the
following:

Old Prussian		Belorussian	Ukrainian
winsus (EV - 102)	'neck'	vjazy	v'jazy
			'cervicle vertebrae'
neikaut	'to enter into'	nikac' (dial.)	nykaty 'to wander about'

Nepokupnyj, 81, says that according to the
logic of the situation the number of Belorussian
correspondences to the Old Prussian lexicon should
exceed significantly the number of those common to
Belorussian and Ukrainian. In addition one must
pay special attention to those dialects which are
closest to the Old Prussian area of the Grodno
district in Belorussia. Thus, for example, just
here one meets the words burvalak 'piece of a log;
stocky person,' and pasta 'pasturage' which can be
compared with OP burwalkan 'courtyard' and posty
(EV - 801) 'pasture.'
One also finds in the Nemunas area such
Belorussian words as artaj 'plowman,' bryzgul'
'wooden button,' naŭda 'use,' pasojta 'handle of a
bucket,' with which one can compare OP artoys
(EV - 236) 'farmer,' brusgis (EV - 315) 'lash,
whip,' Nauden (place name), (linga-)saytan

(EV - 446) 'stirrup.'
9.040 Nepokupnyj's 1973b article suggests a
further study of Old Prussian personal names in
various recently published books and articles on
German family names, chiefly the works of W.
Fleischer, 1968, and J.K. Brechenmacher, 1957-
1963. Nepokupnyj notes, 85, that in the lists of
students at the University of Königsberg in 1642
there was mentioned a certain Matthias Rosteck,
Prussus and in 1648, Joh. Fried. von der Schleuse,
Prussus. In addition to these names we find in
the student lists names which reflect directly the
ethnonyms and ethnic territories of the Old
Prussians, e.g., Caspar Samland (1634), Cornel.
Sahm (1644), Jac. Samius (1651); Joh. Nadrovius
(1636), reflecting the name Nadrowia. In the
recently published Wer ist wer Nepokupnyj found
the name Skalweit in which one can easily recognize
the Old Prussian ethnic name Skalva plus the suffix -ait-, cf., e.g., Lith. kalvaĩtis 'inhabitant
of a hill.'
9.050 In a 1974a article Nepokupnyj shows that
the Polish dialect word pedy 'trough' is derived
from Old Prussian. Nepokupnyj quotes Nesselmann,
1873, 122, who noted that the German dialect word
pēde was a provincialism meaning 'water bucket,
pail' and was used in the dialects of East Prussia.
Nesselmann derived this German word from the OP
root *pīd attested in OP pīst, pyst (inf.),
pīdimai 'we bring,' etc. Nepokupnyj quotes a
number of other sources which support in a satis-
factory way in my opinion his assumption that the
word is a borrowing from Old Prussian into the
Polish and German dialects in question. Nepokupnyj
finally concludes that the material examined by
him shows that the German pēde and Polish pedy
in the meaning 'trough' were (and in part are)
used in adjacent territories in the lowlands
between the Vistula and the Nemunas in former East
Prussia and contemporary Poland.
9.060 In a similar vein Sabaliauskas, 1974, writes
that standard Lith. palˇvė 'low land between fixed
and mobile sand dunes' is known in the special
literature which has to do with the Curonian
Nehrung (Nėringa, strip of land extending into the
Baltic sea) and in the work of the authoress Ieva

222

Simonaitytė. In a certain dialect area in the
neighborhood of former East Prussia (around
Eržvilkas, Jurbarkas) the word denotes a variety
of thorn bushes (Rubus chamaemorus). The name of
the plant shows a connection with the aforementioned geographical designation. For the
semantic aspect one can compare Lith. lùkštas,
lùkšta 'marsh marigold (Caltha palustris)' with
Latv. luksts 'a damp, low-lying meadow.' The
root palv- is widely attested in Old Prussian
toponymy, cf. OP Palwe, Palweniken (< Palwe- +
suffix -enik-), Popalwen (< prefix pa- 'under' +
palwe-), Sorpalwe (< sur- 'around, about' +
palwe). Likewise the word is found in German
dialects of that area, cf. Palwe 'heath with mossy
grass and frequently low scraggly bushes, for the
most part juniper, used only in case of necessity
for pasture land.' Sabaliauskas says that the word
geography shows that the Lithuanian word is of
Old Prussian origin. Old Prussian Palwe is to be
connected with Lith. pal̃vas 'pale, pallid' and
shows a semantic procedure of forming geographical
terms from color designations, a procedure which
is typical for the Baltic languages.
9.070 In his 1973c article Nepokupnyj examines the
Old Prussian Slavic borrowings cognates of which
have been retained in the Cassubian (Kashubian)
and Masurian dialects of Polish. In a convenient
map at the end of the article (181) he shows the
limits of occurrence (isoglosses) of seven Cassubian
and Pomeranian words which had been borrowed into
Old Prussian and which currently exist in Polish
dialects of this area. He concludes that the
isoglosses established for the Polish equivalents
of the Old Prussian Slavisms run from the north-east
to the south-west becoming denser in Pomerania, in
the territory of the Cassubian dialects. This
refers particularly to such lexemes as Polish
węborek 'pail,' korzkiew 'ladle,' etc. Nepokupnyj,
180, says that the linguistic value of these isoglosses is varied and, obviously, the greater the
territorial extent of the word, the weaker is its
value for the establishment of a picture of the
former dialect relationships between the Polish
and the Old Prussian languages.

9.100 Toporov, 1972, gives us an interesting analysis of the Old Prussian pantheon.

9.101 The name of the Old Prussian god Okopirms can clearly be etymologized as meaning 'the very first,' i.e., oko- (also known in the catechisms in the variants ucka-, uckce-) means 'very' and pirms means 'first.' In this god we find a mixture of two traditions. On the one hand he is the almighty and everything that exists in the world is subject to him (deum coeli et terrae,... den Gott himels und der erde). On the other hand in the descriptions of the Old Prussian pantheon in connection with the vertical structure of the world Okopirms is the god of the highest of the spheres (...der erste Gott Himmels vnd Gestirnes,... ein Got des himels vnd gestirns). Inasmuch as Okopirms is always in the first place in the lists, but never figures in texts of any other character (in distinction from the great majority of the other gods), one can with considerable certainty assume that Okopirms had exactly the same function as Diēvas-Dìevs in the East Baltic tradition. The latter, functioning as the fundamental representative of the entire mythological system as a whole, becomes so abstract and passive that he (it?) loses some of his reality (aktual'nost') and as a compensation for this, gives more reality to the lower gods. Okopirms is glossed as Saturnus.

9.102 Svaixtix glossed as Sol and defined as 'god of light' is, after Okopirms, also a representative of all the gods and corresponds perfectly to the position of the sun among the objects worshipped by the Old Prussians. (Toporov, 295)

9.103 Autrimps is the god of the sea and Potrimps the god of rivers and springs (297). Bardoits is the god of boats and, according to Toporov, 297, it is quite possible that he was created quite late or owes his existence to the kabinetnaja mifologija 'armchair mythology' of the 16th and 17th centuries. There is also a form of this name Gardo(a)eten. The form with the initial G-, if not just a misprint, could have been created under the influence of the word gardas 'ship, boat.' Originally Bardoits may have denoted

'bearded' (cf. Lith. barzdótas 'id.') and have
been an epithet of Patols 'an old man with a long
green beard.' (Toporov, 1972, 301)
9.104 Aušauts is called the god of healing and
curing of sicknesses (Toporov, 305). The name
could be connected with Lith. aušrà, Latv. àustra
'dawn.' Toporov, 303, notes that in De Diis
Samagitarum we find: "Ausca dea est radiorum
solis." (Ausca is the goddess of the rays of the
sun).
9.105 Pilvits and Pergrubrius are 'earth gods'
connected with the prosperity of men, harvest,
cattle and wealth. (Toporov, 1972, 304)
Pergrubrius is connected with the vernal awakening
of nature, and promises a good harvest from the
fields, an increase in livestock, whereas Pilvits
is more or less the embodiment of wealth in its
abstract form and is not connected directly with
plant and animal life.
9.106 Toporov, 1972, 299, explains the relationship between Patols, Pekols and Pokols in the
following way. Pekols (also in the catechisms
pickūls 'devil') is connected with Lith. peĩkti
'to blame, to rebuke,' pу̃kti 'to get angry,'
pìktas 'angry,' paĩkas 'stupid, foolish,' etc.
Patuls is to be analyzed as Old Prussian po-, pa-
'under' and tula- 'ground,' cf. Old Church Slavic
tьlo, tьlo 'bottom,' Russian dotla 'to the
bottom.' Thus the OP Patuls denotes 'under the
ground.' The third word, Pokols, is a blend of
the two preceding words Pekols and Patols.
     Puškaits is a nature god similar to
Pergrubrius, a god of the forest who protects the
sacred groves (306). He is served by the
Barstucke and Marcopole (307).
9.107 Toporov, 1972, 308, then establishes the
following two possibilities for the Old Prussian
pantheon:

M

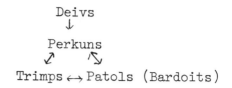

Deivs
↓
Perkuns
↗   ↘
Trimps ↔ Patols (Bardoits)

Puškaits → Pergrubrius → Pilvits → Aušauts
↙   ↘
(Barstukas)   (Markopole)

N

Deivs
↓
Perkuns
↗ │ ↘
Trimps ↔ Patols (Bardoits)
│
Pergrubrius → Pilvits
↑   │   ↙
Puškaits — Aušauts
↙   │ ↘
(Barstukas)   (Markopole)

9.108 Some of the obvious oppositions expressed
here are the following: Deivs (chief, not present,
master, lack of description of his appearance,
lack of motifs) as opposed to Perkuns (subordinate,
present, doer, description of outward appearance,
existence of motifs); Trimps (young, spring, life,
green) as opposed to Patols (old, autumn, death,
white); Puškaits, Pergrubrius (wild, nature) as
opposed to Pilvits, Aušauts (cultivated, human);
Puškaits (forest) as opposed to Pergrubrius
(field); Pilvits (riches) as opposed to Aušauts
(health, moral norm).
9.109 In the following evolution Deivs received
the epithet Okopirms which finally became the
fundamental form of the name. Trimps was divided
into Potrimps and Autrimps. Bardoits as an
epithet of Patols became separated and independent.
Patols received the name of Pekols which in turn
was divided into Pekols and Pokols. Svaixtix

226

was included in the pantheon. Two principles were
most popular, the cosmological principle and a
mixed principle in which cosmological elements were
combined with socio-economic elements.
9.110 Toporov, 1970, 535, derives the name of the
Old Prussian god Diviriks from a sequence equivalent to Lith. Diẽvo rýkštė 'God's whip,' an
epithet of Perkūnas. The gods Nᵻnadej and Andaj
are the same or very close in function and the
final element may include the word for 'god.'
Thus Nᵻnadej may be derived from *Nō-(an)-deiv-
(*Nu-/an/-deiv-?) and Andaj from *An(t)-deiv-.
The relationship of Diviriks, Nᵻnadej, Andaj to
Perkūnas may be that of servant to master. In
general, Toporov says, 536, that for the northern
peoples the idea of god is too abstract and
passive and therefore a servant must fulfill his
functions. The god Teljavel' is then seen as a
helper of Perkūnas and the former appears in the
role of a smith. Teljavel' the smith corresponds
then to the Old Norse god Thjálfi, the servant
and helper of the thunder god Thor. The role of
Teljavel' as helper to Perkūnas is exactly the
same as the role of Thjálfi as helper of Thor.
In view of the formal and functional similarity
undoubtedly we have to do here with a borrowing,
according to Toporov, 1970, 537. It is important
to note also that the name of Thor's mother Fjǫrgyn
can be formally compared with Perkūnas.
9.120 Ivanov and Toporov, 1974, 145, write that
in many respects Common Baltic mythology continues
more faithfully the tradition of Indo-European
mythology than do some of the better developed
mythological traditions. This latter statement is
particularly clearly confirmed by an analysis of
the fundamental myth about the duel between the
thunder god and his opponent, a myth which is
reflected on all levels of the Baltic mythological
system. According to Ivanov and Toporov, 145-146,
in no other tradition (even including the Vedic)
is this myth reflected so accurately as in the
Baltic data, which relate not only to the **myth**
itself, but to the ritual which is at its base.
Only in Baltic (and the closely related Slavic)
tradition are the names of the main characters of

the myth *Perkūn- and *Vel-.

9.121 For example, Ivanov and Toporov, 1974, 151,
note that in ancient Baltic rites the cult of fire
is connected with the basic myth about the thunder
god. In particular in sources on old Lithuanian
religion the creation of fire by rubbing together
two pieces of oak or stones of a certain color
(other than red) is associated with Perkūnas. The
making of fire with two stones is known in the
Belorussian tradition and the Vedic hymns where the
stones are related with the male and female
principle respectively and the production of fire
is considered analogous to the creation of a living
being. The most archaic representation of this
seems to be the Old Prussian formula: Oho moy myle
Schwente Panicke 'Oh, my dear, holy fire.'
Another example is furnished by the deep entrenchment of the Old Prussian god Puš(k)aits in the
Indo-European mythological system. His fundamental
traits are a connection with the earth and his
location under an elder tree. The ritual in honor
of Puš(k)aits consists in particular of bringing
grain and beer under the tree during the celebration
and an injunction to the gathered assemblage to
increase the harvest. One may assume, perhaps,
according to Ivanov and Toporov, 1974, 152, that
the Old Prussians might have called the elder tree
by a name which was from this same root. The
root of the name Puš(k)aits may be connected with
Latv. puškuôt, puškuôt 'to adorn, to decorate,'
Lith. puškúoti 'to break out in pimples.' The
semantics of the Lithuanian verb and a series of
other words with this root shows a more archaic
level than the related Latvian verb and allows one
to   establish a trustworthy connection between
the Balto-Slavic and Sanskrit facts. Cf., e.g.,
Slavic pux- (from *pous-, *pus-), reflected in
Russian puxnut' 'to swell up, to become large' and
on the other hand Sanskrit púṣyati 'blooms,' púṣpa-
'flower,' etc. It is then possible to establish a
connection between Puš(k)aits and Sanskrit Pūṣán-.
This latter name belongs to a god among the
characteristics of which are particularly
important the motifs of blossoming, fruitfulness,
riches, a connection with nature, vegetation,

livestock, etc. Ivanov and Toporov, 153, also connect the name of the Greek god Pán with this root.

9.122 They conclude, 1974, 157, that as a result of its archaism the Baltic mythological system gives a much earlier picture of Indo-European mythology and its individual elements (in particular, the personages of the pantheon) than that which is reflected in the richer and more highly developed mythologies. In addition it is easier to see the linguistic motivation behind the names of the Baltic gods.

9.130 Puhvel, 1973, discusses in detail the authenticity of the accounts of the Baltic pantheon and in general comes to the conclusion that such a source as Simon Grunau is not to be discounted at all. According to Puhvel, 102-103, "Grunau's Preussische Chronik (1517-1521) tells of the Cimbrian Witowudi and his brother Bruteno, who came from Sweden and settled on the Vistula in the early 6th century; Witowudi was made king by the local population, and Bruteno became high priest with the title Crywo Cyrwaito, in the service of the three gods Patollo, Patrimpo, and Perkuno, whose idols stood in a thick oak-tree in a place called Rickoyto, which became the habitat of Bruteno and his priesthood, the waidolotten." On Witowudi's banner Potrimppo's depiction is said to be that of a young man without a beard, crowned with ears of corn and of joyful appearance, the god of grain. The second face was that of an angry middle-aged man, his face like that of fire and crowned with flames, his beard curly and black. The third face, that of Patollo, showed an old man with a long green beard and a wholly deathlike complexion. Crowned with a white cloth he looked up at the others from below. Puhvel writes further, 103, "Three other gods are then mentioned by Grunau. Wurschayto or Borsskayto was worshipped generally in villages, wherever there was an oak tree; a young fish was sacrificed to him, and he conferred luck in fishing and good health. Fowl were sacrificed to Szwaybrotto, and first-fruits to Curcho. These three are obvious rustic deities..."

Puhvel continues, 105, "Grunau may thus be regarded
as the transitional figure between the eyewitness
era and the antiquarian one. However distortedly,
he transmitted a piece of the pagan establishment
which by the 16th century was irretrievably lost.
His contemporary and later sources were reduced to
repetition or to amassing whatever folk-religion
remained, and it is not surprising that they
record a confused and multiplex crew of divinities."
Finally Puhvel, 107, comes to the conclusion that
we do indeed find the ancient tripartite Indo-
European structure in the Baltic pantheon in terms
of the magical sovereign, the warlike thunderer,
and the god of peace and fertility. Thus Puhvel
says, "Grunau did not have to lie about Patollo,
Perkuno, and Potrimpo; they or their typological
peers were all too real to the ideology of the
ancient Balts."
9.140 Toporov, 1974, expands upon the similarities
uniting OP Puš(k)aits, Sanskrit Pūṣán and Greek
Pán. Toporov notes that Pūṣán is attested from
the end of the second to the first half of the
first millenium B.C. whereas OP Puš(k)aits is
attested from the middle of the 16th century A.D.
According to Toporov the only reliable means of
relating the various elements are linguistic data
connected with the corresponding mythological
motivation for the process of naming the gods.
Thus Pūṣán (morphemically Pūṣ-án, cf. OP
Puš(k)aits = Pūš[k]) presupposes a root pūṣ-,
usually connected with the same root in the verb
puṣ- (púṣyati, but also puṣṇáti in epic and
classical Sanskrit) with the meanings 'to blossom,
to bloom; to feed, to nourish; to strengthen' and
the suffix -an. Thus Pūṣán can be understood as
denoting the one who is connected with blossoming,
blooming, growth, the one who causes something to
grow, the one who nourishes, etc. In other words
the basis of the name is to be found in the
concepts of broadening, swelling up, augmentation
of size, the denotation of riches, the possession
of these qualities in a direct or indirect
fashion. Thus the connection of the name of the
god with Vedic pūṣaryá- 'well fed' is better
motivated and allows the establishment of a

heteroclitic stem pūṣ-an : *pūṣ-ar-, forms which
can be compared with the Greek forms Pán and pûar
(*pāus-on : *pus-ar).
9.141 Toporov, 1974, 19, writes further that the
aspect of fruitfulness, harvest, riches noted in
connection with Puš(k)aits is very well documented
in Vedic texts which relate to Pūṣán. He also
quotes from the Rig Veda in which we find evidence
that Pūṣán multiplies riches, increases or gives
property and strength, brings happiness, discovers
treasures, donates food and is somehow connected
with the kakambīra tree which is known as the
master of the forest. People pray to Pūṣán for
riches and treasures. He is connected with horses.
The same motifs are found in the other Vedas.
In connection with Pūṣán they talk of the growth
of plants. One encounters particularly frequently
the theme of cattle, food and their multiplication.
But there are between Pūṣán and Puš(k)aits even
more specific coincidences according to Toporov,
1974, 20. First of all, one of the fundamental
characteristics of Pūṣán which sharply
distinguishes him from other Vedic gods is that
he travels not with the aid of horses, but rather
with the aid of goats. In the horse sacrifice
Pūṣán received a goat as his share. Now the
connection of Puš(k)aits with the goat is just as
certain. In the book about the goat sanctification
ceremonies of the heathen Sudovians (Der
vnglaubigen Sudauen ihrer bockheiligung mit sambt
anderen Ceremonien) the chapter on the goat
sanctification (Wie sie den Bock heiligen)
immediately precedes the chapter on the god of
the earth Puschkaytus (Der erden gott Puschkaytus).
And the ritual of the slaughter of the goat
possesses all the characteristics of a rite
for the evocation of fruitfulness analogical to
that which is connected with Puš(k)aits.
Toporov adds, 21, that the account of the ritual
slaughter of the goat is supported by the report
of Meletius in De sacrificiis Et Idolatria
Borvssorum.
9.142. Toporov, 1974, 21-22, remarks that the
connection of the elder tree with the goat and the
oak with other animals is to be found in the

traditions of both the Baltic and the Slavic
peoples. As the basis of this subject we find
an archaic scheme: The thunderer, vanquishing
his opponent (the victim) and the murder of the
opponent (the victim) as a hostage to harvest,
health and well-being. In the light of this
scheme the appeal to the god of heaven (Okopirms)
or to his substitute, the god of thunder (Perkuns),
on the one hand and to the god of earth
(Puš[k]aits), on the other hand is a request for
two blessings, the blessing from heaven and the
blessing from below (blagoslovenie bezdny),
which regulate the life of man in the mytho-
poetical cosmos.
9.143 This mythological theme (mifologema)
explains to a significant degree other similarities
as well. One may note the motif of the tangled
and disheveled hair and beard of Pūṣan, rather
exceptional for Vedic gods (with the exception
of Rudra), according to Toporov, 1974, 22-23.
Now it may be recalled that in Old Prussian
mythology certain deified earth people, about as
tall as a human finger is long, live in the
ground under elder trees and serve the earth god
Puš(k)aits. These tiny beings are called
Bezdukkai or Barsedukkai and undoubtedly have
their name from their beards which reach to their
knees (cf. Lith. barzdà, OP bordus [EV - 101]
'beard'), see Toporov, 1974, 9, fn. 10.
9.144 Likewise Pūṣán has a direct connection
with the two most important links in the cycle of
fruitfulness, viz., marriage and death, which are
characteristic of gods which unite in themselves
the heavenly aspect with the earthly. Thus Pūṣán
delivers the bride to the bridegroom at the wedding, he marries the daughter of the sun, he
becomes the lover of his sister and claims to be
the bridegroom of his own mother. In addition to
this he accompanies the dead on the long journey
to their forefathers and from this, of course, stems
the fairly common union of Pūṣán with Yama. It
is not excluded that the same functions may have
been characteristic of Puš(k)aits as well. Such
a conclusion is warranted not only by typological
parallels, but from the holidays dedicated to

Puš(k)aits, in the spring (when there is freer
contact between youths and maidens) and in the
fall (when the dead parents are remembered).
Likewise Pūṣán is the son of the heavenly twins,
the Ashvins. In the Old Prussian hierarchy of
gods Puš(k)aits is preceded by Potrimps and
Bardoits (the latter of whom may be considered
the 'bearded' one). Potrimps and Bardoits may
be considered the parents of Puš(k)aits.
9.145 In support of the connection established
years ago by Schulze, 1908, 81 and 374, between
Pūṣán and the Greek god Pán, Toporov, 1974, 28,
writes that Pán is connected with the principle of
the goat, as one can judge from the artistic
representations in which we note the goat's beard,
the goat's legs, two horns, the curly, dirty hide,
the thick beard; he is dreadful and his glance
inspires horror. One may note also, according
to Toporov, 30, Pán's relationship to music and
the fact that Pūṣán encourages poetic creation
and helps singers. When one takes into consideration the fact that the Balts and the Slavs made
flutes and musical pipes from the branches of
elder trees, one might suppose that Puš(k)aits
also had some connection with music.
9.200 Nepokupnyj, 1974b, studies the lexical
relationships between the names Lith. Dainava
and Belorussian Jatvez' and quotes Otrębski,
1963b, to the effect that Dainava is the old
name of the Jatvingian area. In his article he
reproduces a small map, 1974b, 147, on which he
shows a number of isoglosses. Among these is an
isogloss showing the southern extension of the
various places bearing forms of the name Dainava
and an isogloss showing the northern extension
of the various places bearing forms of the name
Jatvez'. One can see from these isoglosses,
according to Nepokupnyj, 1974b, 147, that they
run parallel to each other for a rather long
distance along the plain formed by the Narew
river. Nepokupnyj draws the conclusion then that
these isoglosses are not accidental, but rather
that they show fragments of the common border, the
name Jatvez' in the south being the Slavic term for
these peoples and Dainava in the north being the

Lithuanian name. Nepokupnyj also points out that
it is just exactly on the left bank of the area
along the Nemunas that in Belorussian as a derivative
of the ethnonym we find the word jatvez' with the
meaning 'river anchor.'
9.300 Kiparsky, 1949, 502, writes that in the Old
Prussian catechisms there are eleven words containing the prefix er- and which have a resultative or
perfective meaning. In these words the meaning of
the prefix seems to correspond perfectly to the
meaning of the German prefix er-, but the roots of
these eleven words are surely not Germanic: OP erderkts 'poisoned' (cf. Lith. derkti 'to dirty, to
soil'); er-kīnina 'sets free' (etymology uncertain,
but surely not Germanic); er-laikūt 'to preserve'
(cf. Lith. laikýti 'to hold'); er-lāngi 'may he lift
up' (cf. Lith. langóti 'to fly back and forth' or
leñgvas 'light'); er-mīrit 'to imagine, to invent'
(Kiparsky believes the root to be borrowed from
Slavic měr-iti 'to measure'); er-naunīsnan
'renewal' (for attested ernaunīsan according to
Trautmann, 1910, 331) to which Kiparsky compares
Lith. naũjinimas 'id.'; er-nertiuns 'angered' (cf.
Lith. nértingas 'stubborn, obstinate'); erpilninaiti 'fill' (cf. Lith. pìlnas 'full'); erschwāigstinai 'enlightens' (a derivative of Old
Prussian swāigstan 'appearance' which translates
German Schein and which corresponds etymologically
to Latv. zvàigzne, Lith. žvaigždẽ 'star'); ersinnat 'to recognize' (cf. Lith. žinóti, Latv.
zināt 'to know'); er-treppa 'transgress' (cf.
Lith. trepséti, trepinéti 'to stamp with the feet,'
Russian tropá 'path'). Kiparsky maintains that
for the most part these translate a German model
with er-: erhalten 'to preserve,' erhebe 'may he
raise,' erdichten 'to invent,' Erneuerung 'renewal,' erzürnt 'angers,' erfüllet 'fill!,' erleuchtet
'enlightens,' erkennen 'to recognize.' The extant
Old Prussian texts have, indeed, a preposition or
a particle er which translates German bis 'up to,
as far as' and which corresponds with Latv. ar
'with,' ir 'also,' Lith. ar, Old Lith. er, an
interrogative particle, according to Kiparsky, 503.
There is also even an Old Prussian compound er-ains
'each one' formed exactly like Latv. arvien 'always.'

But, according to Kiparsky, it is difficult to
imagine that this preposition would have assumed
in Old Prussian the role of a verbal prefix, since
we do not find either in Lithuanian or Latvian the
slightest tendency for a parallel development.
9.301 Kiparsky proposes then two possibilities:
1) None of the German borrowings with the prefix
er- happens to have been preserved in any of the
extant Old Prussian texts or 2) the German prefix
has entered Old Prussian even though the latter
language borrowed no German models. Since the
borrowing of derivational and inflectional
elements takes place only with the introduction of
large numbers of vocabulary items which contain
these derivational and inflectional elements, the
majority of specialists in Baltic linguistics have
accepted the first possibility, even though it may
seem less probable, because such foreign vocabulary
items are no less numerous nor infrequent than
derivatives with native stems.
9.302 Kiparsky says, however, 1949, 503, that a
lucky find enables him to prove that under certain
conditions a prefix can be borrowed into a
language even if there are no such native items
with a borrowed prefix. Kiparsky notes that in
spite of the strong German influence in Latvian
(even in the 16th and 17th century texts written
by German pastors) nobody has found any verbs of
German origin with the prefix er- and this prefix
is completely unknown in contemporary Latvian.
Nevertheless in a parish register of Pilten in
Curonia (Kurland), copied down, but not edited, by
a former professor of Baltic history in Riga,
Kiparsky found among some notes made by a German
pastor in 1663 the following phrase: Ottilia, no
Siszen Schwanna meita... sawu bāhrnu erkawusz
'Ottilia, daughter of Zvans of Sissen... killed
her child.' Apparently the German pastor created
the past participle erkawusz on the model of
German erschlagen 'killed,' because the correct
Latvian form, current today, would have been nuo-
kāvus(i). We know that the Old Prussian catechisms
were also written by a German pastor with the aid
of a native interpreter. Given the fact that a
German pastor was able, at least once, to intro-

235

duce the prefix er-- into a Latvian sentence, it
seems probable that the editor of the Old Prussian
catechisms proceded in the same way. Since these
catechisms are the only Old Prussian texts of any
consequence, it is impossible to say whether this
prefix had really become a living prefix in Old
Prussian or not. In any case, Kiparsky concludes,
1949, 503-504, that it seems in case of a total
cultural domination, the subjects who speak a very
evolved language can impose the use of a foreign
suffix on a less evolved language, at least in
writing. I find Kiparsky's reasoning quite
acceptable in this regard.
9.350 According to Kortlandt, 1974, 299: "It can
be demonstrated that Old Prussian shared the common
Balto-Slavic accentual innovations and that its
accentual system differs from the Balto-Slavic base
mainly by a single progressive accent shift, which
is comparable to Dybo's law in Slavic rather than
to de Saussure's law in Lithuanian."

Kortlandt objects to the customary view that
a stressed short vowel is followed by a double
consonant. He points to the numerous examples
which seem to show that double consonants
frequently appear before stressed long vowels:
semmē 'land,' weddē 'led,' billīt 'to speak,'
skellānts 'owing,' dessīmts 'ten,' seggīt 'to do,'
epwarrīsnan 'victory.'
9.351 He then writes, 1974, 300, "...it is a
priori more probable that double consonants occur
under the same conditions in word forms without a
macron as they do in word forms where we can derive
the place of the stress from the macron, we can
formulate the following HYPOTHESIS: a double
consonant indicates that the next vowel was
stressed."

Kortlandt supports this hypothesis by suggesting that the vacillation between e and a before
the double consonant in such forms as wirdemmans,
waikammans; giwemmai, giwammai; tennā, tannā is
the result of a pretonic neutralization of vowel
quality in unstressed syllables. Kortlandt also
says that thus one does not need to posit an ad
hoc rule for the retraction of stress in the
isolated words kadden 'when,' dabber 'still,'

which are identical with Lith. kadà 'when,' dabar̃
'now, still.' He also maintains that this hypothesis facilitates the derivation of Old Prussian
accentuation from the Balto-Slavic base.
9.352 Although in Kortlandt's view, 1974, 301-
302, both Lithuanian and Old Prussian underwent a
progressive accent shift, this accent shift did not
operate under the same conditions in Old Prussian
and Lithuanian. One can compare on the one hand
Lith. žẽmė 'earth,' vẽdė 'led' with OP semmē and
weddē and on the other hand the Lith. (acc. pl.)
ausìs 'ears,' rankàs 'hands' with OP (acc. pl.)
ausins, rānkans. Kortlandt says that this latter
comparison is not surprising, because de Saussure's
law did not operate in Latvian or Slavic and is
rather recent in Lithuanian. He then proposes for
Old Prussian the following law: 'a stressed short
vowel lost the ictus to the following syllable.'
This law explains such forms as semmē, weddē.

Next he states, 303, that the forms widdewū
'widow,' (dat. pl.) widdewūmans (which correspond
accentually with Russian vdová 'id.,' acc. sg.
vdovú, Sanskrit vidhávā) present a problem because
the double consonant does not stand immediately
before a stressed vowel. He proposes, 303: "...
the solution is to be found in the strongly
reducing effect of the w on the pretonic vowel,
which must have resulted in some kind of schwa."

In my own view Kortlandt is probably right
in assuming that the doubled consonant may not
have denoted a preceding stressed vowel. If the
doubled consonant had any meaning at all, it
merely showed that the preceding vowel was short.
On the other hand it seems improbable to me that
the doubled consonant denoted that the following
vowel was stressed. The following vowel may have
been stressed, and quite probably was in the cases
where a macron follows the doubled consonant. I
do not, however, see the stress of the following
vowel as a necessary correlate of a graphemic
doubled consonant. It is merely an accidental one.
One may note, for example, that the earliest Latvian
texts also make use of the device of the doubled
consonant to denote a short preceding vowel, but
here, obviously, this device does not show that
the following vowel was stressed. See Ozols, 1965,

Likewise I am quite doubtful that the
vacillation in writing between e and a is similar
to the Russian type of neutralization of vocalic
contrasts in unstressed syllables. I would
guess that if the vocalic contrast between /e/ and
/a/ was neutralized in Old Prussian the
neutralization was in favor of the /e/ after
palatalized consonants and in favor of the /a/
after unpalatalized consonants as in Lithuanian,
see paragraph 5.000. Probably the orthographic
vacillation between e and a had more to do with
the German perception of Old Prussian than with
the language itself. In unstressed position it
seems quite possible that the German scribe did
not distinguish well between /e/ and /a/.

I do not assume any particular logical
consistency on the part of the scribe, but if one
did, as Kortlandt seems to, then one would have to
ask why it was necessary to write a macron at all
in such cases as semmē, weddē, dessīmts, etc. The
doubled consonant would have been sufficient to
show that the following vowel was stressed, if one
were to accept Kortlandt's hypothesis.

9.400 Levin, 1975a, argues strongly for the
accuracy of the transcription of the Old Prussian
texts. He says that spelling systems may have
differing principles for roots and desinences and
that for non-linguistic cultural reasons the same
phoneme may be spelled in different ways in
different lexemes. His first principle then is to
narrow his scope of study to a single manuscript.,
viz., the Enchiridion (IIIrd catechism) in order
to study high-frequency vocabulary items, con-
sistencies in the spelling of which, Levin believes,
reveal important linguistic information. Levin
opts for a strong reliance on the orthography of
the Old Prussian texts as opposed to accepting
the evidence of the related Baltic languages, a
procedure which he terms as 'frivolous' since it
does not reveal how Old Prussian differed from
Lithuanian and Latvian. His use of the word
frivolous with its pejorative connotation is, of
course, very helpful for his argument. It adds a
little heat to what might be a calm exchange of

views otherwise. I understand the feeling, however, because I also am inclined to feel that linguistic analyses which do not reveal that which I consider necessary are 'frivolous.' In a field such as linguistics, where so little depends on the facts and so much depends on the interpretation one needs every weapon one can muster in order to bring the doubters to the true faith.

Levin writes: "The distortions caused by abandoning the task of normative text reconstruction in favor of 'etymologizing' reconstruction can be seen in recent treatments of the active verb desinences and of the third person personal pronouns. In the case of the verbs, the 1st person plural ending has been reconstructed as */-ma/ on the basis of the "comparative method", even though the only 1st person plural desinence attested in the Enchiridion, occurring in fifty-five different verbs, is -mai."

Now, according to Trautmann, 1910, 304, the 1st sg. pres. tense of the verb 'to be' is attested as asmai nine times. It is attested as asmau once and as asmu two times. The 1st pl. pres. tense of the verb 'to be' is attested as asmai three times. Trautmann gives no other forms for the first person plural. Now if the majority of orthographic attestations is the decisive factor in text reconstruction, we are forced to admit that Old Prussian did not distinguish between the first person singular and the first person plural of the verb 'to be.' I admit that I am not overly impressed by arguments from language typology, because anything is possible in this world of surprises. On the other hand humans are more impressed by the possibility of the occurrence of common rather than rare phenomena. It seems likely to me that Old Prussian was like Greek, Latin, Sanskrit, French, Bulgarian, Lithuanian, Slovene, German, Finnish, Gothic, Arabic, etc. in that it probably did distinguish between the first singular and first plural of the verb 'to be.'

Furthermore Levin says that a text can be 'structured, systematic, and linguistically informative' and offers the spelling of English as a good parallel, although he finds that the

spelling system of the Enchiridion is better than
that of English. Levin says, "...there is much in
the Enchiridion which is absolutely consistent with
the model of a language being set down by scribes
entirely familiar with it, using a unique,
developed spelling tradition. Many of the con-
sistencies found in the text are difficult to
account for except as learned scribal behaviour;
i.e., they represent conventions unknown in contemporary German scribal practice, which must
have been learned by the scribe(s) before starting
to record the Enchiridion."
   It would be interesting to know the historical
sources which show that in addition to the German
pastors and the Old Prussian informants there were
scribes transcribing the Old Prussian speech.
As Levin himself points out there can be written
consistency which has nothing to do with
pronunciation. Thus English their and there are
certainly distributed according to function in the
majority of written English texts. Certainly few,
if any, speakers of modern English distinguish
the two words in pronunciation. On the other hand
read could have two different pronunciations in
a sentence such as: they read the book.
   Levin writes though: "The spelling system of
the Enchiridion does not represent phonemic or
morphophonemic consistency, but it does represent
a spelling system which was striving towards word-
level consistency." He then cites words which
occur in only one variant, e.g., as 'I,' the
verb stem mukin- 'to teach,' deiw- 'god,' etc.
Next he notes some striking differences between
German habits of spelling and the evidence of the
Enchiridion, -h is used in the German text as an
allograph for length, but this is not found in the
Old Prussian version of the Enchiridion, th is an
allograph of t- in the German text, but not in the
Old Prussian version. I should like to point out
here, however, that apparently other German texts
than those bound with the Old Prussian catechisms
were used in the preparation of the translations,
see Trautmann, 1910, xxviii-xxix.
   Levin says: "One of the strongest proofs that
the Enchiridion text was not set down by a German

scribe ignorant of Old Prussian is the morphophonemic spelling of stem-final consonants..."
Thus we find unds 'water' (cf. also undan),
gerbt 'to say' (cf. also gerbaiti), adj. suffix
-ingan vs. -ings. Now Levin has said
elsewhere that the spelling system of the
Enchiridion does not represent morphophonemic
consistency. Yet here he uses the morphophonemic
principle to support his point that the German
scribes did know some Old Prussian. It seems to
me, however, that a rudimentary knowledge of the
morphophonemics of a language does not imply a
perfect knowledge of that language. I have a
rather good knowledge of the morphophonemics of
both Russian and Lithuanian, but I still make
mistakes when I speak and write these languages.
The use of -ings could, of course, be the result
of Low German influence, cf. Middle Low German
Henning as quoted by Lasch, 1914, 90. According
to Levin the rarity of examples which contradict
the morphophonemic principle underscores the
accuracy of that principle. To me this seems to
contradict his statement that the Enchiridion does
not represent morphophonemic consistency. Levin
claims to have found only one exception to the
morphophonemic principle, viz. lubnigs (once)
vs. lubeniks (2 X). He writes: "I suppose there
are other exceptions, but I have not been able to
find them." In order to help with Levin's research
I should like to quote the word for 'self' which
occurs five times in the form sups, once in the
morphophonemic form subs, as gen. sg. masc.
supsas, supsei, subsai, dat. sg. masc. subbsmu
and supsmu, etc., see Trautmann, 1910, 442.
    Surely to some extent there must be a scribal
tradition. The very shapes of the letters imply
to me that they derive from the Latin-German
tradition of writing. But if there are differences
from the Latin-German tradition it is surely
necessary to show how and why such differences
arose.
    Levin writes: "As for the claim of a
developed spelling tradition, it might be argued
that there is not enough evidence to support such
an assumption. But a "tradition" need not be a

a long development; it could be the product of a
single "school", a handful of scribes, developing
an orthography over the time spanned by the three
monuments (i.e., sixteen years). In these monuments
we do have concrete evidence of a developing
orthographic tradition and an interest in "correct"
language, contrary to some opinions." Levin then
gives some examples in which he shows the evolution
of the scribal system in the three catechisms and
writes further, "Of course, if we recognize these
changes as manifestations of an evolving spelling
tradition, we cannot dismiss the motivation of the
scribes. Will and his helper(s) were interested
in setting down the language "properly", as well
as transmitting the message. This is clearly proven
in the introduction to the Enchiridion, where the
reader is warned to pronounce correctly the vowels
marked with a long sign. We cannot deny them this
motivation merely because they lacked our definition
of "correct" spelling."

According to Levin, "Arguments based on the
spelling abilities of American college students
are no more relevant than their architectural
abilities are relevant to the question whether
the cathedrals of 16th century Koenigsberg were
well-built." I am particularly puzzled by this
statement which does not seem to me to be an apt
analogy at all. If it were a question of American
architects vs. German architects, I could indeed
see some relevance in the comparison. The American
and the German architect faced with certain common
problems presumably hit upon similarities in the
solution of these problems.

One would think that it is sufficiently clear
that even specialists cannot always be trusted to
come to the right conclusion concerning their
specialty. A firm reliance on the scribes'
professionalism seems to me somewhat surprising.
Thus Sever Pop, 1950, 261, quotes Abbé Rousselot
to the effect that in dialect study the human ear
is, of course, the most rapid and efficient means
of experimentation, but that the human ear does
not hear everything and we cannot assign a value
to everything which it does hear. Pop writes that
L. Gauchat emphasizes the psychological process of

242

interpretation which takes place in the brain of
two observers from the moment of perception of
the sounds pronounced by the informants to the
transcription with a certain number of conventional
signs. The transcription is not performed
mechanically and the perceptions of the different
dialect specialists is reflected in different
manners of interpreting what they hear. Sever
Pop continues, saying that the experience of three
Swiss dialectologists (Louis Gauchat, Jules
Jeanjaquet and Ernest Tappolet) proves irrefutably
the existence of a large number of divergences of
notation among them when they observed the speech
of the same individual, although all three
dialectologists were natives of the country, came
from the same school of linguistics, were pupils
of the same teacher, had the same system of
phonetic transcription and also had several years
of experience in working with informants in their
native place. Levin's faith in the ability of the
scribe to give an adequate rendition of what he
heard seems unfounded when we note that trained
dialectologists frequently hear things incorrectly.
Thus the fact that the IInd catecism was 'ge-
corrigiret' and that there were warnings to the
reader to read the macrons in the Enchiridion do
not mean that any special care was taken for the
language. It probably meant that the German
pastors were completely incomprehensible to the
Old Prussian peasants. I am reminded here of
Sabaliauskas, 1967, 142, who relates that
German pastors who preached in Latvian knew the
Latvian language very poorly. There is a saying
from the 17th century that a Latvian peasant, when
asked what the contents of a pastor's sermon was,
shrugged his shoulders and said, "Who knows what
that German cat is saying?"

It is useful here to draw some parallels with
the early Latvian texts which were created under
roughly the same cultural conditions as the Old
Prussian texts, i.e., they were German religious
texts prepared for native Baltic populations.

As far as the orthography is concerned, Ozols,
1965, 75, writes: "The first written language
is based on the Middle Low German manner of

writing. It does not indicate vocalic length
(one can intuit many indications, of course, but
there is no system, such that exceptions would be
mistakes), the diphthong ie is not distinguished
from e (short, long, open, close), there is no
indication of soft consonants (occasionally they
are written with i, y and g), voiced and unvoiced
sibilants and shibilants are not distinguished,
there is no order in the indication of affricates;
in general in the denotation of consonants one may
find a sequence of letters (doubled consonants;
sequences of several letters to denote one sound
especially for sibilants and affricates; for the
decoration of the text the letter h)..."

According to Ozols, 1965, 76, in the phonetics
we find the following phenomena: "e in place of
the short vowels of the endings, in place of the
-u we also encounter -o (only from the point of
view of the early written language is this
phenomenon included in the phonetics; the rare
examples of the correct endings show that in
reality the incorrect orthography is a result of
the lack of knowledge of the language), sometimes
the vowel is completely lost, sometimes on the
other hand there is an extra vowel letter, i.e.,
e; in place of au we find ou; in place of i we
find u, ue; in place of šk we find sk."

In the morphology, according to Ozols, 1965,
76, many endings are hidden by the letter e,
mistakes, ignorance, fumblings. As the most
characteristic common feature for the first texts
A. Augstkalns mentions the use of the letter e
in all of the endings with a short vowel. If one
were to follow Levin's line of reasoning one would
reconstruct all of these endings as -e for early
Latvian, because reconstruction of other endings
on the basis of what we know about modern Latvian
would be 'frivolous.' A preponderant statistical
majority with the ending -e must mean something!!!
I assume that indeed it did mean something, viz.,
that the scribe did not know the Baltic languages
very well.

Augstkalns, 1934, 13, wrote: "Many of these
texts are rather full of errors and are rather
confused, in others we see a high degree of

linguistic unity, such that it surely had its own grammar. For example, the translator or the final editor of the 1586-87 Enchiridion, the Non-German Psalms, the Gospels and the Epistles knew rather well the words and forms of the Latvian language. The chief deficiencies are only 1) poor orthography which can be read correctly only by a person who already knows the Latvian language and 2) a slavish transfer of sentences word by word from the German language." Augstkalns wrote, 1930, 104: "Concerning the first written language one must frequently say: absurd."

Obviously linguists who have built part of their academic careers on a belief that the Old Prussian texts are a faithful record of Old Prussian speech are not going to be happy with my conclusions. Lack of faith in the reliability of the Old Prussian texts for an Indo-Europeanist is tantamount to a confession of agnosticism for a clergyman. One can well understand the cries of rage and antagonism which such a lack of faith will generate. One expects, however, the words not convincing, a loan translation from the common and trite German phrase es überzeugt nicht. To judge by the literature, one must conclude that this latter phrase has served as a club for generations of linguists as a verbal weapon.

10.000 The following paragraphs contain the most important etymologies of Old Prussian words proposed since 1945.

10.001 Aboros. Mažiulis, 1964a, 66, notes that Endzelīns, 1943, 135, has suggested that OP aboros (EV - 228) 'hay rack' might be a word of native Old Prussian origin rather than a borrowing from Polish obora 'cow barn' < *ob-vora. The initial ab- could be the prefix, cf. OP eb-immai 'includes' and the Lith.-Latv. prefix ap- 'about.' Endzelīns compares further Lith. apý-voras 'field work, entrenchment' and Latv. sa-vari 'cross bar on a harrow,' supposing that OP aboros is to be derived from *ab-vōros. While accepting the etymological connections proposed by Endzelīns, Mažiulis suggests that there is no need to assume a long vowel in the second syllable of the reconstruction and Mažiulis would rather reconstruct an etymological *ab-vŏrōs with a short vowel in the second syllable. Such a reconstruction can be justified by the existence of OP wo-bse (EV - 789) 'wasp,' cf. Lith. vapsà 'id.' The Samogitian Lithuanian ãparos 'strings for tying (bast shoes)' would give an exact 'phonomorphological' correspondence, cf. standard Lith. ãp-varos, apì-varos, apý-varos 'id.' Mažiulis, 67, calling attention to Lith. vãras 'pole, stake' and noting that the Baltic root *ver- also had the meaning 'to stick into; to shut a door,' suggests that the Old Prussian word may have originally meant 'fence (possibly made of stakes) around an enclosure.' Thus OP aboros (< *ab-vŏrōs) may be cognate with (but not borrowed from Slavic) Russian obora, Upper Lusatian wobora 'fence,' Polish, Czech obora 'cattle barn,' Serbo-Croatian òbor 'pen, enclosure.'

10.002 Abskande. Mažiulis, 1964a, 67, agrees with the usual correction of OP Abskande (EV - 602) 'alder' to Alskande or Aliskande. In Mažiulis' opinion, 68, al(i)skande should be corrected to al(i)skands (cf. EV 709 arelie 'eagle' to be corrected to arelis, EV 339 geytye 'bread' to be corrected to geytys, EV 664 naricie 'skunk' to be corrected to naricis). The -d- stands for an

epenthetic -t- and the form was originally
al(i)skans which in turn is derived from *al(i)skn̥s
< *al(i)ksnas. As far as *-na-> -an- is concerned
one can compare OP tickars 'right' < *tikr̥s
< *tikras = Lith. tìkras 'sure, certain.' As far
as *-ks-> -sk- is concerned, cf. the Lith.
infinitive tvyksti 'to flash,' vs. 3rd tvysko. The
Lithuanian cognates alksnis, alìksnis and Latvian
àlksnis 'alder' are i̯o-stem nouns, whereas OP
*al(i)ksnas is apparently an o-stem, but Lith.
alksnà 'alder grove' and Latv. àlksna 'alder
forest' probably bear witness to the existence of
an earlier o-stem form, as do the toponyms Lith.
Al̃ksnas (name of a few lakes), Alksnà (name of a
few rivers). In Lithuanian we find the following
variants of the word for 'willow': glúoksnis,
glúosnis and glúosis. On the basis of the analogy
with the word for 'willow' one could propose for
the word for 'alder' a Proto-Baltic *ŏlisŏ which
could eventually be compared with Old Church Slavic
jelьxa, Russian ol'xa, Polish olsza 'alder,' etc.
10.003 In 1969, 166, I proposed that OP accodis
(EV - 214) 'hole in the wall for the elimination
of smoke' is to be phonemicized as /akutis/ and is
to be analyzed as a diminutive of ackis /akis/
'eye.' The fundamental meaning of accodis /akutis/
is then 'little eye,' hence 'window.' The
semantic development is similar to that of Slavic
okьno 'window' (cf. oko 'eye') or English window
from Old Norse vindauga < vindr 'wind' + auga 'eye.'
10.004 Aclocordo. Mažiulis, 1974, 218, writes
that OP aclocordo (EV - 313) is a compound made up
of the elements aclo- and -cordo. It is not quite
clear, however, what the German translation
leitseyl may have meant, although it is customary
to assume a meaning 'bridle' or 'driving rein.'
Mažiulis suggests that OP aclocordo = aklakarda̅
comes from an earlier *arklakarda̅ or *artlakarda
in which the first *-r- was lost by dissimilation.
Parallels are found in Lith. aklãvirvė < arklãvirvė
'a rope to fasten the plowshare fork to the plow'
and kim̃grauža < kirm̃grauža 'worm-eaten spot' where
the first -r- has been lost by dissimilation. The
first element (*artla-) > *arkla (> *akla- = aclo-)
is apparently the same as in Lith. árklas = Latv.

ârkls (< Baltic *artla[n]), Old Church Slavic
ralo (< Proto-Slavic *ordlo) 'plow.' One might
suppose that OP aclocordo = *aklakardā
(< *arklakardā) could be corrected immediately to
atlocordo = *atlakardā (< *artlakardā), cf. OP
addle (EV - 596) = Lith. ĕ-gl-ĕ 'spruce.'
Mažiulis remarks that perhaps at the time of the
preparation of the Elbing vocabulary the old
sequences *tl and *dl had passed to *kl and *gl
respectively. (But see paragraph 5.620). In any
case we would derive OP aclo-, Lith. árklas, Latv.
ârkls all from Baltic *artla[n] 'plow.' The
second element of the word *-kardā (= -cordo),
can be identified with Lith. kardà 'strips of
bark from any kind of tree for braiding, plaiting;
willow bast,' cf. also Lith. karnà which has the
same meaning. Mažiulis proposes then that OP
*aklakardā < *arklakardā (< *artlakardā) original-
ly meant 'rope of bast on a plow.' It is
difficult to say today exactly how this was used
on the plow and whether the rope was plaited or
whether it was merely a broad strip of bast. It
is clear, however, that one can make from bast a
strong and cheap line or rope. Although OP
*arklakardā originally meant only 'bast rope of
a plow = bast rope or strap which was used on a
plow'; later the term became generalized to mean
any rope or strap used on a plow or wagon.[89]
10.005 Aglo. Mažiulis, 1974, 212, writes that
one would be inclined to read OP aglo (EV - 47)
'reyn (= rain)' as *aglu and to connect the word
with Gk. akhlús 'darkness, cloud,' etc. On the
other hand, as Mažiulis notes, the word is indeed
a hapax legomenon not only in Old Prussian, but in
the Baltic languages as a whole. It would then be
quite reasonable to suppose that the -g- might be
a mistake for a voiceless velar stop and that
perhaps the word should be read as aclo (aklo) =
*aklā, i.e., a root ak- plus a suffix -lā. The
ak- could be connected with Hittite eku-,
Tokharian yok- 'to drink' or Latin aquā 'water,'
Gothic ahv-a. Such an etymology would assume a
semantic development 'clouds which have taken up
(drunk) water' > 'rain clouds' > 'rain.' If,
however, this OP *aklā is a substantivized

adjective of the type of Lith. ãklas, aklà (Latv.
akls) 'blind' (??) then one could assume a semantic development such as the following: 'blindness,
darkness' > 'dark cloud' > 'rain cloud' > 'rain.'
Another possibility is to assume a scribal error
in which the -g- and the -l- are metathesized to
give *algo = *algā and to assume a root *al- plus
a suffix *-ga and to connect the root with Lith.
aĩ-mės 'liquid which comes from the mouth of a
dying person or corpse.' If we do not correct the
orthography of the word we can assume a root *ag-
(which may be retained in the Lithuanian hydronyms
Ãg-umas, Ag-iõnė). This OP *ag- (= Lith. Ag-)
can be considered a descendant of the Proto-Indo-
European root *ag- 'to drive' and one may suppose
that OP *aglā = aglo denotes not only 'rain' =
'pouring rain' (for that there existed suge [EV -
49] 'rain'), but 'rain' in the sense of 'driving
rain, forward movement, rain arising.' One may
note also that this word is found in the Elbing
vocabulary among words denoting such concepts as
thunder, lightning, wind, hail, etc.
10.006 Čop, 1971, 31-32, connects OP algas, Lith.
algà 'wages,' Gk. alphḗ 'earnings' with Hittite
halkueššar (gen. halkuešnaš) 'harvest.' Čop says
that the latter word may be a derivative of an
Indo-European primary verb *Halg^whe-ti or perhaps
it is based on a secondary verb derived from a
substantive *Halg^whā.
10.007 Anctan. Mažiulis, 1966b, 102-103, examines
OP anctan (EV - 689) 'butter' (Simon Grunau's
*ancte = aucte) from the point of view of 1. the
form of the root (= Sanskrit anak-ti 'anoints,
greases,' añj-as 'grease, ointment'), 2. word-
formation, a. suffix -ta (< *IE -to-), b. *o-stem,
and c. neuter, and 3. the meaning. The Old
Prussian word agrees with Lith. svíestas, Latv.
sviêsts 'butter' in 2a. and 2b., i.e., the suffix
and the *o-stem, and, of course, it is possible
that the Lithuanian and Latvian words were neuter
originally also; the meanings agree. One can say
then that OP anctan agrees with its Old High
German cognate ancho in two characteristics, viz.,
root and meaning; it shares one characteristic
with Slavic maslo, viz., meaning; it shares two

249

characteristics with Lith. svíestas, Latv.
sviêsts, viz., word formation and meaning.
10.008 Arrien. In Trautmann, 1910, 55, line 34,
we encounter the sentence: tu turei stesmu kurwan
kas arrien tlāku ni stan āustin perrēist - Du
solt dem Ochsen der da dreschet nicht das maul
verbinden 'thou shalt not tie up the mouth of the
ox which threshes.' Many suggestions have been
brought forward to explain the collocation kas
arrien tlāku 'which threshes.' Most recently
Toporov, 1958, 113, suggests that arrien derives
from a root *ār- and denotes 'there,' cf. Lith.
orañ 'on the outside, there,' Latv. aran 'on the
outside; without' and also 'out of' in 16th and
17th century texts. Toporov, 1958, 113-114, notes
that OP arrien in this case would correspond in
position exactly to da in the German text. There
would be nothing surprising in the fact that
arrien (with a final -n) expressed not only
direction but location. We note such a situation
in regard to OP stwen 'there,' schien 'here,'
Lith. teñ 'there.' Written arrien could reflect
*ārin and perhaps be compared with Lith. šaliñ
'away, off.'
10.009 Arwis. Fraenkel, 1952a, 138-140, suggests
that Lith. arvas 'free' is to be connected with
OP arwis 'certain, sure,' arwiskai 'surely,
certainly,' isarwiskas 'true,' perarwi 'for
sure,' perarwiskai, perarwisku 'certainly, truly.'
All these words are to be united in a broad group
of words including Lith. ìrti 'to be separated, to
come apart,' ardýti 'to separate, to destroy.'
The relationship between Lith. arvas and OP arwis,
etc., can be explained by a comparison with
Middle High German vrîliche 'free, unhindered,
candid, frank, without restraint, to be sure,
certain.' Cf. Modern High German freilich 'to be
sure.' Thus originally Lith. arvas, OP arwis
meant 'let loose, untied,' and the semantic
development can be compared with that of Lith.
laĩsvas 'free,' láisvė 'freedom' which are
related to Lith. léisti, Latv. laĩst 'to let go,
to let loose.'
10.010 Attolis. Gāters, 1954, proposes that OP
attolis, Lith. atólas, Latv. atāls 'second

haying' derive from *at-volis or *at-volas
respectively. The initial element at- is, of
course, the Baltic prefix at- 'again, back' and
the second element can be connected with Latv.
vals 'swath of mown hay' (a meaning which
developed from the notion 'to mow' rather than
the notion 'round'). Lith. võlas 'cylinder,'
Slavic valъ 'wave' have developed from the basic
meaning 'round,' but we also find words with the
meaning 'to mow,' cf. Lith. valýti 'to harvest,
to clean,' válymas 'harvest; cleaning.' In
early times, according to Gāters, 1954, 114, the
loss of -v- between -t- and -uo- was widespread.
Thus the spread of forms without the v in the
root in the Baltic area. The semantic development can be compared with that of German Nachmahd
'aftermath' (literally: 'after mowing.').
10.011 Attratwei. Endzelīns, 1943, 146, compares
OP attratwei 'to answer' with Latv. rāt 'to
scold, to chide,' and Russian rájat' which he
translates as 'to resound.' Jēgers, 1966, 68,
adds Lith. rojóti 'to crow (at the wrong time),'
Old Icelandic rōmr 'voice, call,' Old High German
ruod 'roaring.'
10.012 Audāst sien. Mažiulis, 1966b, 103, shows
that the OP prefix au- has approximately the same
meaning as Lith. nu- (cf. OP au-skandints = Lith.
nu-skandintas 'drowned'). Mažiulis then
demonstrates that Lith. nu-si-dúoti and OP audāst
sien share the meaning 'to take place, to happen.'
In the Old Prussian and Lithuanian (Willent's)
translations of the Enchiridion (= IIIrd catechism
in OP) the use of OP audāst sien and Lith.
nùssidùst are parallel. Thus the Old Prussian
expression has native Baltic parallels and is not
only to be compared with Czech udáti se 'to take
place.'
10.013 Augus. Mažiulis, 1966b, 104, would
correct the reading of OP augus 'miserly' to
*angus and then compare it etymologically with
Lith. éngti (eñgti) 'to oppress, to torment.'
This suggestion seems excellent to me.
10.014 Aulis. Čop, 1971, 32, connects OP aulis
(EV - 141) 'shin bone,' Lith. aũlas 'leg of a
boot,' Old Church Slavic ulica 'street,' Greek

aulṓn 'valley, ditch,' Lith. aulỹs 'bee-hive' with
Hittite hallu- 'deep,' halluwa-nu- 'to deepen.'
10.015 Auwirpis. The town Alt Warp is on the
west bank of the channel which drains the Warper
lake into the small lagoon of the mouth of the
Oder. Schall, 1964, 155-156, notes cognate names
in Lith. Var̃pė, Varpénka, but says that the key to
the etymology lies in the fact that the Old
Prussian root varp- : verp- : virp- has a special
meaning of 'release, let go' which has not figured
importantly in previous etymologies, but cf. OP
auwirpis (EV - 320) 'mill-race, channel,'
kraujawirps (EV - 551) 'leech,' literally krauja-
'blood' and wirps 'one who lets, one who
releases,' and Lith. krauja-leidỹs (krauja-
'blood,' leidỹs 'one who lets, releases.') See 11.000.
10.016 Ayculo. Mažiulis, 1966b, 101, disputes
the traditional explanation of OP ayculo (EV -
470) 'needle' which connects it with Greek aíkloi
'javelin ends' and says that it is more important
to note that the -c- may be a mistake for -g-
which is actually attested in GrA angle, perhaps
a mistake for *aygle. A form *aygulo 'needle'
(= *aigulō or *eigulō) would be a close relative
of Slavic *jьgъla 'needle' and then the Old
Prussian word could be compared with Lith. aĩgara or aĩg-aras 'end of straw, small bit.'
10.017 Aytegenis. Mažiulis, 1974, 215, writes
that it is to be accepted that OP aytegenis (EV -
745) 'small woodpecker' is a compound word, the
second element of which, -genis is to be connected with OP gen-ix (EV - 742), Lith. gen-ўs, Latv.
dzen-is 'woodpecker.' This second element is to
be derived from the Indo-European root *gʷhen-
'to strike, to beat,' an obvious reference to the
activity of the woodpecker and the original
meaning may have been 'the hammerer' or 'the
beater.' Mažiulis rejects those etymologies of
the initial element ayte- which connect the word
with Sanskrit eta- 'of a variegated color,
shining, brilliant' and proposes rather that ayte-
= *aita is a derivative of the Baltic root *ei-
'to go' with the suffix -ta. He compares the
Lithuanian adjectives ei-kl-ùs (< *ei-tl-), ei-
gl-ùs, ei-n-ùs 'fast, nimble, fleet' and

especially the Lithuanian substantive ái-tas
'vagabond; mischief-maker; impatient person,'
eî-tena 'fast person.' In Old Prussian e- in
initial position usually passes to a- (cf. also
Lith. áitas). Thus, according to Mažiulis,
1974, 218, aytegenis = *aita-genīs has its name
from the fact that it is the smallest and fastest
woodpecker, i.e., aytegenis is the 'quick
hammerer, the fast knocker.' Mažiulis thinks that
the form *aita-genīs is, in many respects,
similar to Lith. áit(i)-varas, áič-varas, éit(i)-
varas 'house-demon; hob-goblin.'
10.018 Vaillant, 1947b, 151, connects the
Lithuanian particle be- which marks the duration
of a verbal action with the preterits OP bēi, bhe
and Old Church Slavic bě. According to Vaillant,
the Lithuanian particle be- is the successor of
the old preterit *bē, cf. the OCS examples bě učę
'was teaching' (= Greek en didáskon), bě bo
umiraję 'for he was dying' and the Lithuanian
examples beválgant lìjo 'while eating, it rained,'
radaũ močùtę beveřpiančią 'I found (my) mother 90
still spinning (thread or something).' Vaillant
quotes the Lithuanian example: kolei be diena
'while the day(light) lasts.' In Lithuanian this
old preterit was replaced by bùvo 'was,' whereas
in Old Church Slavic and Old Prussian the old
preterit was retained.
10.019 Bītai. Mažiulis, 1966b, 105, suggests
that OP bīta- 'evening' derives from the Indo-
European root *bhi- 'to fear,' cf. Latv. bī-ties,
Lith. bij-óti, OP biātwei (i.e., *bij-ātvei) 'to
fear, to be afraid,' Sanskrit bhītíṣ 'fear.'
Mažiulis then gives some examples which show that
the Baltic peoples in general seemed to fear the
evening hours more than the night.
10.020 Vasmer, 1957, 351-352 suggests that in
Russian Church Slavic abrědь (jabrědь) 'grasshopper' the initial element is the Indo-European
prefix ē-:ō- which has an approximative function,
cf., e.g., Sanskrit anīlas 'darkish, slightly
dark or blue' beside nīlas 'of a dark color, dark
blue, green or black,' adīrghas 'longish,' beside
dīrghas 'long,' alōhitas 'reddish' beside rōhitas
'red,' Serbian Church Slavic jagugnivъ beside OCS

gọgnivъ 'dumb, mute,' Greek ē-réma 'quiet, calm'
beside Gothic rimis 'calm.' The second element
-brědь is to be compared with OP braydis (EV -
650) 'elk,' Latv. briêdis 'deer, stag; hart,'
Lith. bríedis 'stag, hart; elk.' It is frequently
the case that insects with long feelers are compared to animals with horns, cf., e.g., Russian
olë̈nka 'dung beetle' which is related to Russian
olen' 'deer.' 91

10.021 Cawx. Toporov, 1963a, 255, notes a parallel between OP cawx (EV - 11) 'devil,' Lith.
kaũkas 'goblin, gnome' and Bulgarian kuk, kuker
'person with an odd appearance,' kukir. In this
place Toporov gives further reference to an
article entitled Fragment slavjanskoj mifologii,
Kratkie soobščenija instituta slavjanovedenija,
30, 1961, pp. 14-32, but this article was un-
available to me.

10.022 Curtis. Schmid, 1958b, disputes the
usual etymology which derives Lith. kùrtas, Latv.
kurts, OP curtis (EV - 700) 'greyhound (dog)'
as a Slavic loanword *xъrtъ. The word is attested
in the OP place name Curtoyen, in Lithuania there
is a river Kùrtuva and in Latvia a lake called
Kurtavas ęzęrs. These names seem to indicate
first of all a common Baltic meaning for kurtas
and in the second place they show a suffix
alternation known elsewhere: -oy-/-uva-/-ava-,
cf. OP Randoin, Lith. Rándavos. The root kur-
denotes 'to be born, to generate' and can be
connected with an existing root in Iranian, viz.,
*kur-na which stands at the basis of Modern
Persian kurrah 'young of horse, ass and camel,'
Zor. Pehlevi kwlg, kwlk 'colt, mare' and Greek
kúrnoi· oí nóthoi (Hesychius) 'bastards, baseborn
sons'; I would point out here that Frisk, 1970, 54,
says that this word is not explained yet.92

10.023 Curwis. Sabaliauskas, 1968b, 133, notes
that OP curwis (EV - 672) 'ox,' is probably not
borrowed from Polish karw which in the oldest
texts means 'old, sluggish ox' but is rather a
native Old Prussian word, since we find such Old
Prussian place names as Corwedompne < curwis +
dompne, Korwelaucken < curwis + laucks 'field,'
etc.

10.024 Dagis. Eckert, 1966, 147-148, writes that OP dagis 'summer' (EV - 13) is the old Baltic word for the concept of summer, cf. also OP dago-augis (EV - 638) 'a shoot of a plant as it grows in one summer.' Eckert supports his assumption with two arguments: 1) Lith. atúodogiai, atúoda(u)giai 'summer rye' belongs to the same group of words as Lith. dãgas 'summer heat,' dègti 'to burn.' It is quite likely that the second component of the Lith. atúodagiai < *dog has retained the original meaning 'summer'; 2) the Lithuanian word degèsis (as given by Fraenkel, 1955, 85) denotes 'month of August.' Since the word denotes one of the months of the summer, Eckert, 1966, 148, says that it seems to him that it might reflect an older meaning 'summer.'

10.025 Dēigiskan. Toporov, 1958, 116, suggests that OP dēigiskan 'kind, gentle' is a borrowing from some Germanic language, cf. German teig, teigig, teigicht which is found with the meaning 'soft' in East Prussia according to Frischbier, 1883, 397.

10.026 Dereis. Jēgers, 1969, 81, compares OP dereis 'see,' endyrītwei 'to see, to look at,' 3rd pres. endeirā, inf. endeirīt, etc. finally with Lith. dirti 'to flay, to skin.' The fundamental root is *der- 'to tear.' Jēgers notes the Russian expression prodirat' glaza 'to tear open the eyes' (after sleep).

10.027 Dīlas. For the noun dīlas 'work,' acc. pl. dīlnikans 'workers' Jēgers, 1966, 84, suggests a proto-form with a root *dī- and connects all of the cognate forms in Old Prussian with Lith. dailé 'work, creation; handwork; art,' dáilyti 'to divide' and OCS dĕliti 'id.'

10.028 Dragios. Fowkes, 1957, 102, connects OP dragios (EV - 386) 'yeast' with Welsh drewi 'to stink' (formerly 'rot'), drewedig 'stinking, fetid,' drewgi (drew + ci 'dog') 'stinkard, skunk,' Albanian drā (Gheg drą-ni) 'oil sediment from rancid butter,' Latin fracesco, fracēre (with f- from dh-) 'become rancid, stinking,' fracēs 'oil sediment,' Lith. dérgti 'to dirty, to soil.'

10.029 Druwi. Marstrander, 1945, 344, says that

OP druwi, druwis 'faith,' and the verb druwīt 'to
believe' correspond in form and meaning exactly
to the Germanic *trūwō- and the verb *trūwēn
Druwīt is an ē-verb of the same old type as
Germanic trūwēn. Marstrander then quotes a
personal communication from Chr. S. Stang in
which the latter has suggested that one must
reckon with the possibility that the root vowel of
druwīt may have been long, although he does not
insist on this.

Marstrander, 344, continues, saying that the
complete agreement in the Christian terminology
between the two languages of different families
suggests that there is reason to ask whether the
term has not entered into Baltic at a later date.
The term is isolated in Baltic where it includes
only the substantive druwis and the denominative
verb druwīt and regular derivatives, but in
Germanic it is spread over the whole language
family and without doubt it is old in this latter
group.

Marstrander, 345, then suggests that the word
penetrated into Old Prussian when the German order
invaded Prussia in the 13th century. OP druwis :
druwīt is then nothing but Middle German drûwe :
drûwen in Baltic inflectional forms. The
Christianization of Prussia was simultaneous with
the Germanization of Prussia. The process began
in the first half of the 13th century when Duke
Conrad of Mazovia invited the Teutonic Knights to
fight against the heathen Old Prussians. The Old
Prussian territory was devastated and opened for
German colonists especially from Low German and
Middle German language areas as the place and
personal names, all kinds of writing and speech
characteristics show.

Marstrander, 346-347, writes that the development of Germanic tr- to dr- is typical for a whole
series of Middle German dialects, especially
Rhine Franconian and Middle Franconian. In the
second half of the 9th century Ottfrid spells
drûên, driuua, gidriuui, drôst. Likewise in East
Franconian there is a tendency to replace tr- with
dr-.

From these historical, cultural and linguistic

facts one is led to conclude that OP druwis, druwīt is a German loan from the 13th century. Marstrander, 347, says that such conclusions could not be avoided if in the German speech area trûwen had ever been used as a Christian term. But this is not the case, since glauben 'to believe' has been used with this significance from the earliest times until today. Wherever trûwen is used in a Christian text it has the meaning 'to rely on, to depend on,' cf. Notker Ps. 117, 8: an got ze trûenne (just as in Old English trúwian on Crist, Old Norse trúa á goð, Gothic trauan du guda). But trûwen can still occur in German as well as in Old and Middle English in many expressions where the meaning comes close to that of Latin credere, since the difference in meaning between 'confidence' and 'belief' is rather tenuous.

The Baltic word may have been borrowed either before or after the first sound shift in Germanic. If it was borrowed after the first sound shift, it stems from the time of the Gothic kingdom on the Vistula. If it was borrowed at this time, according to Marstrander, it must come from an East Germanic dialect in which the initial cluster tr- had become dr- as in Middle or High German. But neither Ulfilas' Gothic nor the East Germanic names in Latin and Greek authors show any trace of such a development.

One could conclude that a Germanic *drūwen (*trūwen) was borrowed into Baltic before the original Germanic voiced consonants were devoiced and that with the Christianization of Prussia the old heathen term took on a new meaning here as in Scandinavia. One may doubt, however, that any Germanic loanwords in Old Prussian really do precede the Germanic sound shift. On the other hand, there are Old Prussian words which do seem to show traces of early borrowing from Germanic, e.g., OP kelmis (EV - 474) 'hat,' seems to have been borrowed before the Gothic passage of e to i, i. e., evidently before the establishment of the Gothic kingdom on the Vistula.

I personally tend to doubt the great age of the word druwīt in Old Prussian and am inclined

more to Marstrander's first hypothesis that the
word comes from Middle or Low German. 93
10.030 <u>Enkopts</u>. André Vaillant, 1968a, connects
OP <u>enkopts</u> 'buried' with Latv. <u>kàmpt</u> 'to seize, to
grasp,' Gk. <u>káptō</u> 'I gulp down' and suggests an
Indo-European root *<u>kap-</u> possibly of expressive
origin. Vaillant says that the OP <u>enkopts</u> is to
be dissociated from Slavic <u>kopati</u> 'to dig,' Lith.
<u>kapóti</u>, Latv. <u>kapât</u> 'to chop,' denominative verbs
the stem of which is represented by such nouns as
Lith. <u>kãpas</u>, Latv. <u>kaps</u> 'grave,' because OP
<u>enkopts</u> is from *<u>-kaptas</u>. I would express my
agreement with Vaillant that the second element
<u>-kopts</u> could be from *<u>-kaptas</u>, but I would go
farther and suggest that <u>-kopts</u> is to be
phonemicized as /-kapt[a]s/ or /-kāpt[a]s/ and
that the graphemic -<u>o</u>- denotes merely the labialization of the preceding consonant. In 1974,
180, I have compared Lith. <u>kõpti</u>, the fourth
meaning of which, according to the Acad. Dict.,
Vol. VI, 352, is 'to bury.'
    I would also point out that Otkupščikov,
1971, 120, says that Lith. <u>kaplỹs</u>, Latv. <u>kaplis</u>
'hoe, mattock,' Lith. <u>kãpas</u> 'grave' and OP <u>en-
kopts</u> can be connected with Lith. <u>kapóti</u> in a
meaning 'to dig' rather than 'to chop, to cut.'
10.031 <u>Enterpon</u>. Jēgers, 1966, 53-54, compares
Latv. <u>tẽrpt</u> 'to dress, to adorn,' <u>tẽrpa</u>
'strength,' <u>tãrpa</u> 'capacity, ability,' Lith. <u>tarpà</u>
'growth, prospering' with OP <u>enterpon</u>, <u>enterpen</u>
'useful.'
10.032 <u>Epkieckan</u>. Schwentner, 1952b, 152,
suggests that Lith. <u>kikìlis</u> 'chaffinch' is
derived from onomatopoetic <u>kik</u>, <u>kiki</u> and is then
to be connected with OP <u>epkieckan</u> 'vice.' But
Nepokupnyj's 1972a etymology is much more convincing for me, see paragraph 9.010.
10.033 <u>Eristian</u>. Fraenkel, 1949, 307, wrote
that Lith. <u>éras</u> and OP <u>eristian</u> 'lamb' belong to
a group of words which includes Gk. <u>ériphos</u>,
Umbrian <u>erietu</u> 'arietem,' and Armenian <u>oroǰ</u>.
Lith. <u>jéras</u>, Latv. <u>jẽrs</u>, on the other hand are
connected with Avestan <u>yar-</u>, Greek <u>hóra</u>, Gothic
<u>jer</u>, Russian Church Slavic <u>jara</u> 'spring,' Old
Russian and Ukrainian <u>jarka</u> 'young sheep, lamb.'

Sabaliauskas, 1968b, 117, disputes Fraenkel's 1955, 121, hypothesis that Lith. vèras 'lamb' is to be separated from éras and connected rather with Skt. úraṇaḥ 'sheep, lamb' and Armenian gaṙn 'lamb.' The Lithuanian word is certainly to be connected with OP eristian (EV - 681) 'lamb' and the place names Eren, Iragarbis < OP er-istian + garbis 'hill.'

10.034 Etbaudints. Jēgers, 1966, 130, notes that although OP etbaudints and budē denote 'awakened' and 'watch over' respectively, there is good reason to give an additional meaning of 'to strike, to hit' (and hence presumably 'to awaken'), cf. Lith. baũsti 'to punish,' Old Icelandic bauta, Old English beatan, Old High German bōz(z)an 'to beat.'

10.035 Etnīstis. Toporov, 1958, 116-118, suggests that OP etnīstis 'grace' contains the Indo-European root *nē(i̯)- 'to tie' and is a deverbative noun implying the verb *etnīt (inf.), *etnija (3rd present). The prefix is et- and the fundamental meaning is something like 'to untie, to remove the bonds.' Further cognates would include Lith. nýtis 'heddle,' Slavic nitъ 'thread.'

10.036 Etskīuns. Toporov, 1958, 118-119, derives OP etskīuns, etskīans, etskyuns, attskiwuns 'resurrected' and other forms of the same verb from a root *skei̯ the reduced grade of which is *skī- and the fundamental meaning of which is 'to divide, to separate,' cf. Lith. atskíesti 'to divide, to separate,' skiẽtas, Latv. šķiẽts 'weaver's rod, comb,' Skt. chinátti 'splits,' OP staytan (to be read scaytan; EV - 421) 'shield,' German Abschied 'leave.' We also find the Old Prussian 2nd sg. future etskīsai 'you will get up (out of bed)' so it would be a mistake to restrict the meaning of this word to the religious meaning of Russian voskresat' 'to be resurrected,' but we should also note that it had the meaning of Russian vstavat' and podnimat'sja 'to get up.' I would add that the English word 'to rise' covers both meanings quite easily and serves as an added proof that Toporov is right. As far as the verb is concerned I feel little semantic difference between the phrases he rose from bed and he rose

from the dead.   In any case Toporov would want to
add the meaning of 'to be separated from' to the
Old Prussian word in question in order to take
into account the etymologies he proposes above.
10.037 Etwerreis. Toporov, 1963b, 189, suggests
that Hittite uauarkima 'door hinge' is to be
connected with the Indo-European root *uer- 'to
turn' and then further with Latv. vārsti 'door
hinges,' vārstīt 'to open and close (the door)'
and OP etwerreis 'open,' Lith. várstymas 'opening
and closing of a door.'
10.038 Geits and guntwei. Vaillant, 1962a, 60,
assumes that the infinitive stem gun- of OP
guntwei 'to drive, to make' has furnished the stem
for the 1st pl. pres. gunnimai. He would separate
this root which is also found in Lith. giñti 'to
chase,' gìnti 'to defend' from Slavic žęti 'to
harvest.'   In Old Russian we find the present stem
krĭnje-, infinitive stem kriti 'to buy' corresponding to Skt. *kriṇāti (Vedic krīṇāti, pl.
krīṇánti), past participle krītáḥ, with the usual
adaptation of the athematic present to the presents
in -je-. This is the only clear example in Slavic
of the Indo-European type represented by Sanskrit
verbs in -nāmi, but this present with nasal infix
was regular with disyllabic roots, i.e., roots having an acute intonation in Slavic. The retention
of the two stems krĭnje-, kriti is unusual in
Slavic, but we may suppose that it existed for
other verbs as well. Thus, for the verb denoting
'to harvest' we may presuppose an etymological
stem *gin- for the present, but *gī- in the verbal
adjective. The stem *gin- was generalized from
the present to the infinitive giving žęti 'to
harvest,' but the stem *gī- was retained in such
derivatives as Slavic žito 'grain,' OP geits
'bread.'   I find Vaillant's argument quite
attractive, but I would suggest that the alternation *gin- vs. *gī- is merely a reflection of
the Indo-European development of *-in> *-ī under
certain conditions, see Schmalstieg, 1973a, 103.
10.039 Jēgers, 1966, 62, connects OP gīrbin
'number' and gerbt 'to speak' and from the
semantic point of view points to the parallels in
Old Norse where we find tal 'number,' and telja

260

'to count; to speak' and Slavic čislo 'number,'
čьtǫ 'I count; I honor,' čьstь 'honor.' Although
the contemporary languages seem to show the
meaning 'number' as secondary and the meaning 'to
praise' as primary, probably the etymological
situation was just the reverse. Jēgers, 1966, 66,
derives the Old Prussian words eventually from a
root *gerbh- 'to scratch.' The development of the
meaning followed this path: 'nick, groove, notch'>
'number' (OP gīrbin)> 'to count'> 'to honor' (Lith.
ger̃bti 'to honor'; from 'to count' also 'to speak'
in OP gērbt)>'to take care of, to treat well'
(Latv. gḗrbt, gārbêt, gãrbît²)> 'to dress, to put
on, to adorn, to clean' (Latv. gḗrbt, Lith.
ger̃bti).
10.040 Gewineis. In 1969, 163, I proposed that
Nesselmann, 1873, 46, was correct in seeing
perhaps -lb- rather than -w- in the word which is
usually transcribed as gewīneis (EV - 191)
'servant.' The word could therefore be
transcribed as gelbineis and would be phonemicized
as /gelbinējas/ or /gelbinējis/ and connected with
Lith. gelbinéti 'to help.'
10.041 Gudde. Ekblom, 1959, 94, wrote that OP
gudde, Lith. gùdas and Latv. guds derive from
Swedish and Gotlandish gute and gotländning
'Gotländer.' In the 8th century and even earlier
there was contact between the continental Swedes
in battles against the Curonians in the neighborhood of Liepāja and Apuolė in what is now the
northwestern corner of contemporary Lithuania. At
this time there was apparently contact between the
Gotlandish settlers and Old Prussians in
neighborhood of Elbing. As the Swedes began to
withdraw, however, the name gudas, guds remained
to denote any foreigner; the names gudde, gudas
and guds then came to denote 'worthless, of little
value.' Baltic gud- replaced gut- because in
Baltic the phonetic sequence gut- is rare. Finally we find such a name as Lith. gùdobelė 'apple
bush or apple tree; wild apple tree with rather
useless fruit.' One can imagine that there
had existed a German *buschappelbom which was
translated by OP *gud(de)wobalne and that somebody
with a poor knowledge of Old Prussian would have

abstracted gudde as Pusch 'bush.'

Fraenkel, 1950b, 64, writes that in Lith.
gùdkarklis 'swamp willow,' gùdobelė 'wild apple'
the initial element is to be connected with OP
gudde 'bush,' not with Lith. gùdas 'White
Russian, Belorussian.' Fraenkel disputes Ekblom's
etymology (which had already been published
previously) and suggests rather that OP *gudān-
'inhabitant of a forest' supplied with the Slavic
suffix -ĭsk- gives the Polish city name Gdańsk(o).
Otrębski, 1950b, 276, connects OP gudde with
Slavic *gvozdъ, Serbo-Croatian gvozd, Polish
gwozd (gozd) 'woods.' The divergence among the
Slavic forms is a result of a contamination of the
root in question, i.e., *gŭd- with that of the
old word for 'peg, nail': OCS gvozdъ, etc.

10.042 Insuwis. Pisani, 1954, 141, says that a
proto-form *dṇĝhua stands at the base of the
following words for 'tongue' in the various Indo-
European languages: Old Latin dingua, Old Irish
tenge, Gothic tuggo, OCS językъ, OP insuwis (EV -
94), Lith. liežùvis, Skt. jihvā, Avestan hizvā
and probably Armenian lezu, Tokharian A kăntu,
B kantwa (Krause-Thomas, 1960, 143, give kantwa
as the oblique case, kantwo as the nominative).
Pisani discusses in detail the changes which took
place in the various languages to lead to the
attested forms. According to Pisani, 1954, 142-
143, OCS języ-kъ, OP insuw-is and Lith. liežùvis
all show a final -ū, a -ū which stands in the same
relationship to -ua (cf. Latin dingua) as does -ī
to -ia, cf. Skt. váhant-ī, OCS vezǫšt-i, Lith.
vežant-ì vs. Gk. phérousa from *-ont-jā.

André Martinet, 1955, 54, supposes that the
Indo-European phonological sequence */uH₂/ yielded
/uw/ before vowel, /ŭk/ before /s/ and /ū/ before
other consonants. We can imagine then a paradigm
with a nom. sg. ending in *-ŭks (< *uH₂s), an
acc. pl. ending in -ūm (< *-uH₂m). When the
inflection became thematic the -ū was transferred
to the nominative singular giving thereby -ūk-.
This is the result which we find in Slavic językъ,
whereas in OP insuwis we find the -uw- reflecting
*/uH₂/ in prevocalic position.

10.043 Kăaubri. Čop, 1959/60, 177, discusses the

Indo-European root *qeub which is known in Old
Saxon as hiopo, Old High German hiufo, English
hip, Norwegian hjūpa and OP kaaubri 'thorn.'
These are to be connected with Latin vepres 'thorn
bush' deriving from a stem *queprē- with a loss of
*q- before the -u- as in Latin vapor 'steam' from
quəpōs beside Gk. kapnós 'smoke' from *quəpnós.
10.044 Kadegis. Rūķe-Draviņa, 1955., 406, writes
that it is no chance that the following words for
'juniper' are so similar in so many neighboring
languages: OP kadegis (EV - 608), Lith. kadagỹs
(with variants), Latv. kadiķis (with variants);
East German names Kaddik, Kaddeck, Kaddegbusch,
etc.; Polish dialect kadyk; Estonian kadakas,
Livonian kadà'g or gadà'g, Veps kadag, Votic
kataga, Finnish katajas, etc. It is interesting
to note also that the contemporary Baltic languages
have such words only in the western dialects, viz.
Old Prussian, West Lithuanian and West Latvian
dialects. Rūķe-Draviņa, 407, says that the
question as to whether these Baltic names are
native or Finno-Ugric then remains. It is
important to note that Lith. kadagỹs, Latv.
kadiķis, etc. are by no means the only names for
this plant in Lithuanian and Latvian, cf., e.g.,
Latv. paeglis 'juniper.' Rūķe-Draviņa, 409, concludes that both ethnographic and linguistic data
show that the word kadak- is more firmly ensconced
in the Finno-Ugric languages than in the Baltic
linguistic area. Thus OP kadegis, Lith. kadagỹs
and Latv. kadiķis are more likely to be old borrowings from Finno-Ugric rather than an Indo-European
inheritance connected with Slavic kaditi 'to
smoke,' etc.
10.045 Kalis. Sabaliauskas, 1968b, 108, disputes
Būga's 1958, 524-525, comparison of Lith. kalẽ
'bitch' with the name of the Old Prussian village
Kalis and the personal name Kalioth. Sabaliauskas
would rather compare OP Kalis, Calyen, Kalcz, a
name of a lake with kalis (EV - 569) 'sheat-fish.'
10.046 Kalpus. Fowkes, 1957, 97, connects OP
kalpus (EV - 302) 'Rungenstock, supporting cross
block on wagon,' with Welsh coliant (masc.),
colsaid (fem.) 'part of the scythe and similar
tools that is let into the handle; tang.' In

colsaid the element -said is an independent word meaning 'haft.'

10.047 Kaywe. According to Sabaliauskas, 1968b, 158, OP kaywe (EV - 433) 'mare' may have been a mistake in transcription for *kieywe or *keywe in which the -y- may have denoted that the preceding vowel was long. Thus kaywe could have come from Lith. kévė 'poor thin animal; nag.' Cf. also Lith. kíevė 'bad mare,' kẽvinas, kėvis, keĩvis 'poor horse, nag,' Latv. ķève, ķève, ķèva 'mare.'

10.048 Keckers, Lituckekers. Sabaliauskas, 1957, 351, notes that the Old Prussian words for 'pea,' viz. keckers (EV - 264), lituckekers (EV - 271) 'lentils,' keckirs (Simon Grunau's vocabulary) are probably not to be connected with Lith. kẽkė 'bunch, cluster,' Latv. ķekars 'id.,' Armenian sisern 'pea,' Latin cicer 'chickpea.' Trautmann, 1910, 355, thought that the word came from Polish, but Sabaliauskas, 1957, 352 agrees rather with Endzelīns, 1943, 191, that the word came into Old Prussian from German Kicher 'pea.'

10.049 Kērdan. The root *ger- with the extension -d by *gerd- is attested in such varied words as OP kērdan 'time,' Lith. keřdžius 'shepherd,' Russian čereda 'turn, time,' according to Jēgers, 1966, 46. The Russian čereda also denotes 'herd,' and also a 'herd consisting of two cows or a horse or two calves or two sheep.' A Russian would say of a person who owned this amount of livestock u nego četyre čeredy 'he has four čereda's.' Thus čereda changed its meaning from 'series' to 'herd.' The derivation of Lith. keřdžius 'shepherd' thus becomes evident.

In 1971b I proposed a connection between OP kērdan and Lith. kar̃tas 'time' and I assumed a phonemicization /kártan/. The late Prof. Jonas Kazlauskas wrote to me then and said that in reality the Old Prussian word did not correspond in meaning to the Lith. kar̃tas. Prof. Kazlauskas convinced me that my etymology was wrong, but my letter to him in which I asked to withdraw this article apparently did not reach him before his untimely death.

10.050 Keutaris. Schwentner, 1955, proposes that OP keutaris (EV - 762) 'ring dove' along with

early modern High German kūto 'dove,' Swiss chūt,
chuter, chutter, Alsacian kütter, Swabian kauter,
kⁱuter is a borrowing from the orient where the
dove was raised in many varieties and then imported into Europe. One can compare modern Persian
kautar, Pushto kautar (kewter), Kurdish kotir
'dove' with loss of the medial p from Persian
kapūtar, kabūtar (kebūter) = Sanskrit kapóta-
'dove.'

10.051 Kīsman. Eckert, 1963, 890, says that OP
kīsman ⟨ *kēs-man 'time' and is to be connected
with Albanian kohε 'time, weather,' korε ⟨ *kēsrā
'harvest, summer.' The words all belong to the
group *kes- 'to cut,' a group which is also
represented in Slavic *časъ 'time,' *sěnokosъ
'hay mowing,' kos-iti 'to mow,' etc.

Hamp, 1972, 268, writes that in Albanian
kohⁱ the initial consonant could not derive from
Indo-Eurpean *ḱ which would give Albanian th-.
In the Slavic cognate časъ there may have been an
initial *kʷ palatalized before the front vowel,
but before an original front vowel it would have
given Albanian s-. Therefore the only possible
initial is the Brugmannian pure velar *k. The
most likely origin of Albanian -h- is *sk' or
*k's, either of which could give Slavic s.
Therefore the most sensible reconstruction for the
Slavic and the Albanian words is *kēsk'- or
*kēk's-. Such a reconstruction would also fit
OP kīsman.

10.052 Klente. Sabaliauskas, 1968b, 137-138,
notes that the previous etymologies of OP klente
(EV - 673), GrG (7) klint 'cow' are probably
unsatisfactory. He proposes a connection with a
root which is not attested in the Old Prussian
texts, but which corresponds with Lith. klénkti
'to move with difficulty,' Latv. klencêt 'to go
clumsily, to limp along,' Russian kljakat' 'to
stumble, to trip,' Slovene klékati 'id.'

10.053 Kragis. Jēgers, 1966, 15-48, derives a
vast number of words from the Indo-European root
forms *ǵer-, *ǵr-, etc. and from the ablaut grade
*ǵor-, 48, he derives Lith. kãras, Latv. karš
'war,' OP kragis (for kargis; EV - 410) 'army,'
Russian korá '(tree) bark,' kóren' 'root,' ukór

'reproach'; Lith. kárti, Latv. kãrt 'to hang.'
Lith. kĩrna 'a branch or a stump washed by water
on the bank of a river,' Lith. karnà 'the lower
bark of a willow or linden tree,' OP kirno (EV -
637) 'shrub, bush,' Lith. kẽras 'stump,' OP
kerberse (EV - 614) 'kind of plant, betula
fructicosa Pall.,' and a host of other words are
introduced into this etymological group.
10.054 Kurpe. In his analysis of the Lithuanian
influence in German vocabulary as illustrated by
the words in Frischbier, 1882/3, Sabaliauskas, 1966,
98, includes some words which are possibly of
Old Prussian origin. For example, German Kurp
'bast-shoe' could be from Lith. kùrpė 'shoe,' OP
kurpe (EV - 500) 'id.' or from Polish kurp (which
in turn was probably borrowed from Old Prussian
anyway, see Milewski, 1947, 80).
10.055 Lasto, loase, lasinna. Schmid, 1958, 221,
suggests a relationship between OP lasto (EV - 209,
492) 'bed' and lasinna 'put.' Schmid notes the
numerous examples of the suffix -to, -tā in the
Baltic languages, e.g., OP dalptan (EV - 536)
'chisel,' Lith. dálba 'lever; crowbar,' Lith.
báltas 'white.' Schmid then proposes that the
root common to OP lasto and lasinna is to be reconstructed as *leĝh- (with a palatal *-ĝh- rather
than the pure velar which one assumes for Slavic
lešti, lęgǫ 'I lie down'). The co-existence in
Baltic of roots with palatals and pure velars is
well known, cf., e.g., OP saligan (EV - 468)
'green' beside gelatynan (EV - 464) 'yellow,'
Lith. žolẽ 'grass' beside gèlẽ 'flower.'
    Schmid then gives five conclusions (1958,
225-226): 1. The archaic method of word formation
of lasto 'bed' shows the earlier existence of the
root *leĝh- for Baltic. 2. Lith. lažà 'corvée,' Latv.
laža 'camp' (= Tokharian A lake 'id.') is to OP
lasto just as Lith. dálba is to OP dalptan. 3.
OP lasinna is the regularly formed Baltic
causative from the root *leĝh-. 4. lasinna is not
a loanword. 5. Since Lith. pãlažas 'lying down
being bed-ridden; stamped down surface in a grain
field' and Lith. palėgỹs 'difficult, incurable
illness' co-exist this means that there existed
in Baltic the well known alternation between the

palatal and velar in the root *legh-. Schmid,
1958, 226, also suggests the OP loase (EV - 493)
'cover' is cognate.[94]

10.056 Licuts. Fowkes, 1957, 109, connects OP
licuts 'small' with Middle Welsh llyth (masc.),
lleth (fem.) 'soft, tender, weak,' Armenian aɫk'at
'poor, needy, scant,' Lith. ligà 'illness,
disease,' etc.

10.057 Landan. Jēgers, 1966, 52, fn. 2, notes
that Latv. lìst 'to crawl' also has the meaning
'to push into, to taste, to please' and he quotes
the Latvian expression pēc darba maize lien
'after work bread tastes good.' Jēgers then asks
whether OP landan 'food' might not be connected
with such words as Dutch slinderen 'to glide, to
crawl,' Gothic fraslindan 'to swallow,' etc.

10.058 Laxde. Čop, 1971, 30-31, connects OP
laxde (EV - 607) 'hazel-bush,' Latv. lazda, Lith.
lazdà 'stick' with Hittite alkišta(n)- 'branch'
the root of which is alk-.

10.059 Laydis. From the Indo-European root *lei-
'slimy, slippery' Jēgers, 1966, 88, derives (with
a -t extension) such words as Latv. làitît 'to
massage, to stroke,' Lith. liẽsti 'to touch,'
etc. To the same root one can ascribe Lith.
laistýti 'to plaster, to putty,' OP laydis (EV -
25) 'loam, clay.'

Fowkes, 1957, 108, connects OP laydis with
Welsh llys 'slime,' Latin līmus 'slime, mud,
mire,' Old High German leim, leimo 'glue,' Old
English lām, modern English loam, Lith.
laistýti 'to plaster, to putty.'

10.060 Lindan. Jēgers, 1966, 50, connects OP
lindan 'valley' with the Lithuanian meadow name
Léndimai, Gothic, Old Icelandic, Old Saxon, etc.
land 'land, earth,' Old Russian ljadina 'weed,'
Belorussian l'ádo 'new land, land cleared of
forest growth,' Old Irish land 'free space,'
Breton lann 'heath,' etc.

10.061 Līse. Jēgers, 1966, 53, says that OP
līse 'crawls' is related to Latv. lēzêtiês 'to
come down a mountain in a sled,' lēzêt 'to move
slowly, to lurk.'

10.062 Ludini. Levir, 1973, 194, explains the
form ludini (EV - 186) 'mistress of the house' as

being derived from Common Slavic *ljudinъ 'free-
man,' attested in Old Church Slavic with this
meaning. According to Levin, 194, "Originally
Prussian must have had *ludinis > ludini, forming
an animate feminine according to the -ja stem
declension."

10.063 Maldian. Mažiulis, 1963b, notes that
Slavic *moldъ (OCS mladъ, Russian mólod, Serbo-
Croatian mlâd) has an exact parallel in OP maldai
'young (persons)' (cf. OP maldian [EV - 438]
'foal,' the personal names Malde, Maldenne, Lith.
Maldẽniai, Maldūniai, Maldučiai, Latv. Mald-uone,
a personal name from Vidzeme). According to
Mažiulis, it is quite plausible to posit an
original meaning 'soft, tender' for East Baltic
*maldas. From this meaning the Old Prussian and
the Slavic meaning 'young' developed.[95]

10.064 Megato. Otrębski, 1950a, 74-79, says that
the name of the first Christian prince of Poland
was Měžько or Měžька, i.e., the name we know today
as Mieszko. Two difficulties, however, arise.
In the first place the root *měg- is not found in
Polish and in the second place the suffix -ька is
used only to form sobriquets and feminine nouns.
Otrębski assumes then that Měžька is the
successor of the OP form *Mēgikā. The ending -ā
is found in such names as OP Jodeyko = Lith.
Juodeikà, etc. The root *mēg- is found in such
personal names as OP Megato and Megothe and the
place names Megothen and Migeyten. The root,
being common Baltic, is also known in Lith. Mėg-ỹs,
-io and is probably also to be found in the
Lithuanian verb mégti 'to like.' Otrębski,
76, says that we can reconstruct a *Mēg-ikā on the
basis of the names Meg-ato and Meg-othe if we
take into consideration the following series of
names: Bande, Bandot, Bandiko; Mine, Minate,
Mynothe, Mineko; Wayne, Waynothe, Wayniko, etc.

The name *Mēgikā was assimilated to the
Polish system on the analogy of noga 'foot' and
the diminutive nožька, nóžka. The name became
associated with native names in -měr(ъ),
particularly Kazi-měr(ъ) and Kazi-mir(ъ) and thus
we find both Měžька and Mižька and in further
adaptation to Polish usage we find Miž(ь)ko

(Mysko, Misko). Otrębski concludes that there
were many Old Prussian lexical borrowings in
Polish before the conquest of the Old Prussians by
the Teutonic knights.
10.065 Mulgeno. Jēgers, 1966, 122-124, discusses
Lith. smãgenês, smegenys, Latv. smadzenes,
smedzenis, smedzeņi 'brains' and OP mulgeno (EV -
74), usually corrected to *musgeno 'marrow.'
These words are usually connected with OCS mozgz
'brain,' moždanz (< *mozgēnz), Old High German
mar(a)g, mar(a)c, Sanskrit majján- 'marrow,' etc.
OCS mozgz would correspond with Lith. mãzgas,
Latv. mazgs which actually exist, but with the
meaning 'knot.' But since Lith. mazgaĩ can denote
'bunches of nerves, ganglia,' Jēgers asks if the
word could not have developed the meaning 'knot'
from an earlier meaning of 'knots of nerves,' etc.
Or perhaps the word *mazg- 'brain' was lost because
of homonymy with the word mazg- 'knot.' The -u-
of OP musgeno causes some difficulty according to
Endzelīns, 1943, 212, who proposed influence of
Polish mózg. Jēgers, 1966, 123, suggests a
comparison with Latv. muzgulis 'pack, knot,'
muzgulas 'clothing twisted together.'
    In 1969, 164, I suggested that the majority
opinion which corrected OP mulgeno to musgeno is
correct. I assumed then, as I do now, that the
orthographic -u- following the m- merely reflects
the labialization of the preceding consonant and
that the word should probably be phonemicized as
/mazgenā/. Then there is no problem to the usual
etymology which connects the word with Slavic
mozgz 'brains.'
10.066 Mukint. Vasmer, 1957, 352-353, compares
OP mukint 'to teach,' Lith. mokéti , Latv. mâcêt
'to know how to, to be able to' with Old Czech
makati 'to feel, to try,' mácěti 'to feel' and
Polish dial. makać 'to feel,' Upper Lusatian
makać 'to find, to touch, to uncover,' Lower
Lusatian makaś, -am 'to seek, to find.'
10.067 Mynsowe. Schmid, 1969, 127, suggests that
OP mynsowe (EV - 364) 'basin, bowl' is derived
with a suffix -owe from the word for 'meat,' cf.
OP menso (EV - 154, 374), GrG 15 meinso, IIIrd
catechism (Trautmann, 1910, 63, line 26) mensā

269

For an analogical formation one can compare Lith.
rankóvė 'sleeve' beside rankà 'hand, arm.' See 11.001.
10.068 Nadele. Kiparsky, 1968a, 247, agrees with
the generally accepted assumption that OP Nadele
(EV - 17) 'Sunday' comes from Proto-Polish
*nedělja (> Polish niedziela 'Sunday'). Rendering
of short e by a is to be expected; Proto-Polish
ě is rendered by e, which supposedly denoted a
long close [e] sound. The final -e can denote
either that the word is an e-stem or perhaps that
the German scribe heard a final schwa which he
wrote with e. Kiparsky's statement about the
final -e is quite convincing.
10.069 Narge. Otrębski, 1960b, 175, says that the
origin of the Lithuanian river name Nerìs is
quite clear, i.e., it contains the root found in
Lith. nérti 'to dive' and originally denoted
'depression, hollow, hole.' Other hydronyms with
the same root are well known in Lithuania, cf.,
e.g., Neretà, the right tributary of the Nemunėlis.
Old Prussian cognates are Narge, a river, Narigen,
a lake, Narus, a brook, etc. The river name Narew
is probably of Jatvingian origin.
10.070 Narus. Krahe, 1960, 122, compares the
river name Nárōn in Illyria with the Old Prussian
river name Narus, and such Lithuanian hydronyms
as Narasà and Narŏtis.
10.071 Neikaut. Toporov, 1960, suggests that
the meanings 'movement away from' and 'movement
to, towards' lies at the base of various verbal
stems formed from the root *ə₂en-/*ə₂n-. One such
stem is *nik-, cf. Slavic niknǫti 'to climb on,
to grow,' Lith. ap-nìkti 'to fall upon, to
attack,' į-nìkti 'to begin to do passionately,'
OP neikaut 'to enter into,' Latv. nàiks 'angry,
evil, quick, violent.'
10.072 Nerge. Ekblom, 1946/48, 151, proposes
that common Nordic *naering- and *naer[1] had the
meaning 'narrow waterway, sound.' We find Swedish
names beginning with the element När-, e.g.,
Närboås, Närsjöfjärden, etc., Njärven, a narrow
lake. Cf. also the English word narrows. Ekblom
suggests that the words *naering-, *naer[1] were
borrowed from Old Norse into Old Prussian during
the Viking period and then passed into German at

the time of the invasions of the Teutonic knights,
giving the attested forms Nerge, Nerige, Nering(e).
Ekblom, 1946/48, 155, notes that Lith. Nèrija with
ė as opposed to an OP *Nerijā with short e (cf.
the German place name Narmeln) seems to show an
adaptation to the long e of the German Nehrung.

Mažiulis, 1960, writes that the contemporary
Lithuanian name Nerìngà or more rarely Nerìjà is
unknown in early writings or in dialects of either
Latvian or Lithuanian and is completely unknown in
Old Prussian documents. The names Nerìngà and
Nerìjà are taken from documents of the Teutonic
order. Already in the first half of the 13th
century the form Neria appeared, but at first it
was applied only to the Frische Nehrung (Aistmarių
Neringa), i.e., the peninsula separating the gulf
of the Vistula from the Danzig bay. At a later
date probably the scribes of the order themselves
used the term to apply to the Curonian peninsula
(i.e., the strip of land separating the Curonian
gulf from the Baltic sea, known in Lithuanian as
the Kuršių Neringa). Mažiulis suspects, 1960, 313,
that the form Neria is from OP *Nerijā. Ekblom,
1946/48, objected that *Nerijā could not be
connected with Lith. nérti since from the semantic
point of view it would be hard to understand the
meaning 'to dive,' but Mažiulis, 1960, 313, points
out that Lith. nérti means not only 'untertauchen,
to dive in,' but also 'auftauchen, to emerge, to
come up.' The meaning of the name can easily be
understood to denote a strip of land which is in
the process of emerging from the water. According
to Mažiulis the forms Neringe (corresponding to
contemporary Lith. Nerìngà): Nerunge: Nerung are
found only in the documents of the Teutonic order
from the middle of the 14th century. These
parallel forms show the German suffix -ing- or
-ung- added to Nerige (=Nerie =Neria).
10.073 Noatis. Trubačev, 1958, 668-669, writes
that OP noatis (EV - 291) 'nettle,' Lith. notrė̃,
nõterė, Latv. nâtre, etc. is usually compared with
Polish nać 'leaves and stem of plants,' Slovene
nât, natî̃, both of which latter forms presuppose
a Slavic natь. But Trubačev thinks that it might
be better to compare Slavic natь with Lith. nókti

271

'to ripen.' OP noatis and the other Baltic
cognates should rather be connected with a Proto-
Germanic *natilōn, a derivative of *natōn. The
Proto-Germanic *natilōn furnishes Old High German
neʒʒila, Old Saxon netila, Swedish nätla, Norwegian
netla, English nettle, modern German Nessel. The
similarity of the Baltic and Germanic forms would
indicate a borrowing from Proto-Germanic, since
the t of the Baltic and Germanic forms would not
correspond if we were to assume a common proto-
form.
10.074 Patowelis. Ivanov, 1958b, 59-60, says
that the Tokharian A diminutive suffix -äly-
(e.g., lyk-äly- 'thin') is an exact cognate of
the Baltic -eli- found in Lithuanian -elis, -elė,
Latvian -elis, -ele and in Old Prussian nouns of
the type patowelis (EV - 179) 'step-father.'
10.075 Paustocaican. Sabaliauskas, 1968b, 159,
compares OP paustocaican (EV - 654) 'wild horse'
(pausto- 'wild,' caican 'horse') with Lith. kùika
'thin, poor mare,' Latv. kuîka 'bad horse,' Lith.
kaîkaras 'tall fellow; lazybones,' Latv. kaîkars
bad horse.' Sabaliauskas expresses considerable
doubt about Fraenkel's, 1955, 202, etymology which
connects the word with Latin caecus, Old Irish
caech 'blind,' Gothic haihs 'one-eyed.' Rather
the Baltic words are connected with the root found
in Lithuanian keîpti 'to become bad, weak, thin,'
kaîpti 'to disappear, to weaken; to faint.'
10.076 Paustocatto. According to Sabaliauskas,
1968b, 183, in Old Prussian the word for 'cat' is
mentioned only once in the compound paustocatto
(EV - 665) 'undomesticated cat,' but the name for
the cat is well attested in Old Prussian toponymy,
cf., Kath, Katelauke (< Kath plus laucks 'field'),
Kathemedien (< Kath plus median 'forest'),
Katpanye (< Kath plus pannean 'swamp').
10.077 Paymekopo. The Old Prussian place name
Paymekopo (1311) probably comes from Paymenkopo,
the first element of which is probably to be
connected with Lith. piemuõ, Gk. poimén 'shepherd'
and the second element of which is probably to be
connected with Lith. kãpas 'grave,' cf. OP
Auctacops, Auctukape: Lith. áukštas 'high, tall,'
and kãpas. For the vocalism of the Old Prussian

Cf. Finnish paimen 'shepherd.' (See Sabaliauskas, 1970, 21.)

10.078 Pecku. Lith. pēkus originally meant 'head of cattle, animal,' but it was used with the meaning 'herd of cattle' very frequently in the oldest writings. Now it is used with the meaning 'herd of animals' only in the dialect of Zietela, according to Sabaliauskas, 1970, 13. Examples from the IIIrd catechism show for OP pecku, however, the meaning 'herd of cattle': Preistan rūkans bhe kurpins Īst bhe pūton buttan bhe burwalkan Gannan bhe Malnijkans Laukan Pecku bhe wissans labbans 'In addition clothes and shoes, food and drink, house and yard, wife and children, field, cattle and all good things.'

10.079 Pelemaygis. Schwentner, 1952a, 152, compares OP pele-maygis (EV - 712) 'kestrel, Falco tinnunculus' with Lith. pelė, Latv. pele 'mouse' and Lith. mýgti 'to press, to pinch, to squeeze,' Latv. máigt 'to press,' maidzīt 'to press, to knead.' One can understand the word then as 'mouse-clamper, mouse-clencher,' a meaning which is similar to that of the Schleswig-Holstein duben-klemmer 'hawk, sparrow-hawk,' literally 'dove-clamper, dove-clencher.'

10.080 Pentnix. Kiparsky, 1968a, 248, says that if one accepts the correction of OP pentinx (EV - 22) to pentnix 'Friday,' then most likely the source is Proto-Polish *pętьnikъ which is related to Polish piątek < *pętъkъ just as Russian vtornik 'Tuesday' < Old Russian vьtorьnikъ is to Polish wtorek 'Tuesday' < *vъtorъkъ.

10.081 Perbanda. Jēgers, 1966, 128-129, notes that the root *bhen- 'to strike' is represented in Middle High German bane, ban, modern German Bahn, originally with the meaning '*something cut through a wood.' One could then trace the meaning 'portion of a field' for the Lith. bandà, Latv. banda back to a similar development. Originally the servant was given not a piece of arable land, but rather a bit of land which he had to clear and to which he had to establish access by clearing. Thus the meanings 'usefelness, money, profit' (Lith. bandà, Latv. banda, OP ni enbāndan 'not in vain') may have come from the meaning 'portion of land.'

The meaning 'to test, to try' (cf. Lith. bandýti, OP perbānda 'tempts') may have come from the concept of trying out a new weapon or an instrument by striking with it or waving it around.

Sabaliauskas, 1970, 7, says that in Lithuanian the most common name for a herd of animals is bandà. He continues further, 9, saying that, although we find no word corresponding to Lith. bandà in the Old Prussian texts, there are some place names and personal names which show that a cognate word could have existed in Old Prussian, cf., e.g., the place names Bandadis, Bandeynen, Bandeln, Banduken and the personal names Bandeyke, Bandiko, Banduke, Bandupe, Bandus. There is, however, another word which should be connected with the same root, i.e., OP nienbaenden which occurs in the IInd catechism in the commandment: Tou ni tur sten emnen twayse deywas nienbaenden westwey - Du solt den namen Gottes nicht unnützlich füren 'Thou shalt not take the name of (thy) God in vain.' Thus nienbaendan = German unnützlich which could be understood as meaning 'not useful, not for use.' For the semantic development one can compare Lith. naudà 'use, profit,' Latv. naûda 'money' beside Old Icelandic naut 'head of livestock,' Old English neat 'head of livestock, animal.'

Sabaliauskas, 1970, 10, connects Lith. bandà with the Indo-European root *bendh- 'to tie, to bind' and suggests that the etymological meaning would have been 'animals tied up in a pen.' Phonetically there is no problem, but the semantics introduces some doubt, because there is no historical documentation for such a way of keeping animals.

Sabaliauskas, 1970, 11, disputes Jēgers', 1966, equation, which includes Latv. beñde 'hangman, executioner,' beñdêt 'to murder, to kill,' also thought to be derived from the root *bhen- 'to strike.' According to Sabaliauskas Latv. beñde is most likely some kind of borrowing, and the semantic development in the direction: 'animal' > 'usefulness, utility' > 'land' is much more credible.

10.082 Percunis. Ivanov, 1958a, examines the
well known etymology of Lith. perkúnas, Slavic
*perunъ 'thunder god' which connects these words
with Celtic Hercynia, Gothic faírguni 'mountain'
< *perkʷunio-, Latin quercus 'oak.' Ivanov points
out, 101, that in the 16th and 17th centuries
Lithuanians were still worshipping the oak as the
sacred tree of the thunder god Perkūnas. One also
notes the Lithuanian superstition that lightning
never strikes the oak tree. Ivanov, 1958a, 106,
also mentions a quotation from a 1302 document of
the Galician prince Lev Danilovič in which the
borders of the holdings of a certain bishop were
defined as extending to Perunov dub 'Perun's oak.'

According to Ivanov, 1958a, 104, the suffix
*-uni- is represented in Gothic faírguni. An
exact correspondence to the suffix *-uni- in
Germanic *fergunja- is to be found not only in
Celtic Hercynia, but in a series of related words
in the Baltic languages with the same suffix.
The stem *perkunjā, to which Celtic Hercynia
goes back, corresponds to Lith. perkūnija 'storm
with thunder and lightning.' In addition we find
the toponym Perkūnija applied to a wooded area
(cf. also Hercynia in Hercynia silva). Ivanov
states further that the stem *perkūni from which
*perkunjā was formed was common to all the Baltic
languages and it is instructive that in the oldest
written document in any Baltic language, the
Elbing vocabulary (i.e., of course, the oldest
document known in 1958 - WRS) the stem is
represented as *perkuni-, viz., percunis (EV -
50) 'thunder.' The related forms pȩrkūnis,
pȩrkuonis, pȩrkàunis are found in Latvian
dialects. Inasmuch as the Lithuanian suffix -ūnė
may be traced back to *-ūn-ī one may see a reflection of the form *perkūnī in Lith. perkūnė
attested in 16th century Lithuanian texts.

Ivanov, 1958a, 108-109, also examines the connection between the god of thunder and the cult of the stone and the hill, cf. the Lithuanian name of the hill Perkūnkalnis, a hill with a large stone at the top. Ivanov, 109, compares this theme with that found in the cuneiform Hittite Song of Ullikummi in which perunaš 'a cliff' bears a son to the god Kumarbi. Ivanov concludes that it is possible to assume an ancient root *per- with a suffix *-un- and that it is not necessary to assume that Slavic lost the velar in an etymological stem *perk-.

The etymology is interesting and I would only object that OP percunis is rather weak evidence for the attempt to establish an *i-stem noun, since all the etymological *o-stem nouns are also render- ed with final -is in the Elbing vocabulary.

10.082a Plasmeno. Čop, 1971, 63, connects OP plasmeno (EV - 148) 'ball of the foot,' OCS plesna 'sole of the foot' (< *plet(ə)s-men-. *plet(ə)s-na) with the general Indo-European root for 'broad, flat' and suggests a further compari- son with Hittite palzahha- 'plinth, base.'

10.083 Playnis, plieynis. Trubačev, 1970, 546- 547, suggests that Lith. pliẽnas, Latv. pliens, OP playnis (EV - 521) 'steel' are most closely related to Lith. plénis (plénys), pléinė 'film of ashes on smoldering coals,' Latv. plēne 'thin flake of **ashes**,' OP plieynis (EV - 38) 'ash.' The entire family of words is derived from a root pl-/pel- with various extensions and which has meanings in the range of 'shell, covering, film, skin,' etc. As far as the realia are concerned, it can be noted that among the older traditional methods of making steel an important place was occupied by a gradual heating process and shaking off the scales from the cinder.

10.084 Pokūnst. Safarewicz, 1967, 249, proposes a form *kuntjō 'I preserve' which lies at the base of OP pokūnst 'to protect' and OCS sąkǫtati 'to calm,' Russian kutat' 'to muffle up in.'

10.085 Kiparsky, 1968a, 247, agrees with Milewski, 1947, 40, who suggests that Ponadele (EV - 18) 'Monday' is a direct borrowing from Polish po niedzieli 'after Sunday.' Kiparsky

would correct this to read rather a Proto-Polish
*po neděli. Kiparsky supposes that the German
scribes heard the final -i as [ə] which he
transcribed with e.
10.086 Powijstin. For OP powijstin (acc.)
'thing, matter,' Kiparsky, 1970b, 259-260, reconstructs a Proto-Baltic *po/avīd-tis. The Old
Prussian word is a parallel to such Slavic words
as Old Russian pověstь 'report,' Polish powieść
'novel,' Old Polish 'tale, report,' Czech pověst
'id.,' Serbo-Croatian pȍvest 'history,' Bulgarian
póvest 'story.' Kiparsky suggests that the
etymological meaning for the Old Prussian word
was similar to that of the Slavic word, but that
there was a change of meaning similar to that
observed, e.g., in Old Polish rzecz 'speech' >
modern Polish rzecz 'thing,' or Latin causa
'reason, cause' > French chose 'thing.' Kiparsky
compares also Finnish juttu 'story, anecdote,
business, thing' with Finnish jutella 'to speak,'
Estonian ütelda, Mordvinian joftams 'to say.'
The Old Prussian semantic shift could have been
influenced by Polish, cf. the use of Russian reč'
in the sense of 'thing, affair' in the West
Russian chancelory language in the 14th and 15th
centuries.
10.087 Powīrps. Sabaliauskas, 1966, 99, compares German Pawirpen, Powirpen 'free men who
hire themselves out from time to time' with OP
powīrps 'free' and Lith. pãvirpas but writes that
the German word could have come from either Old
Prussian or Lithuanian. In any case the
Lithuanian word was most likely taken from Old
Prussian.
10.088 Quaits. In 1969, 164-165, I proposed that
OP quaits 'will,' and related forms such as the
3rd pres. quoitā, quoitē 'wants' have a root which
is to be phonemicized as /kait-/ The Old Prussian
word is to be connected then with Lith. káitēti 'to
lack,   to be wanting' (Latv. kaitēt 'to be
harmful') and the semantic development is similar
to that observed in English in the several meanings of the word to want, i.e., from 'to be lacking, to be missing' to 'to desire, to wish.for.'
The further development of this root to quoi =

/kai/ as a modal particle is paralleled by the development of Slavic xotĕti, xъtĕti 'to want' into modern Bulgarian šte or Gk. thélō + na 'I wish that' into modern Gk. tha.

Likewise then the Old Prussian past passive participles enkaitītai, ankaitītai 'tempted' are cognate and to be phonemicized as /enkaitētai/. Also to be connected is GrG kayat thu, see also paragraph 4.207. 96

10.089 Rapeno. Sabaliauskas, 1968a, 95, proposes that OP rapeno (EV -435) 'young female horse, mare' is derived from *rape of Germanic origin, cf. German Rappe, Old High German rappe 'raven.' The word is also used in German with the figurative meaning of 'black horse.' There is also an Old Prussian suffix such as we see in the personal names Drutenne (cf. Lith. drūtas 'strong'), Jodenne (cf. Lith. júodas 'black'). Originally OP rapeno meant only 'black horse, the black one,' but later it was generalized to denote a horse or mare of any color. Or perhaps even the author of the Elbing vocabulary himself may have confused the meanings of 'young mare' and 'young black mare.'

10.090 Raugus, ructan-dadan. Jēgers, 1966, 142-143, connects Lith. ráugti, Latv. raûgt 'to sour' Lith. ráugas, Latv. raûgs 'yeast' with OP raugus (EV - 691) 'rennet.' Jēgers calls attention to the fact that Latv. savìlktiês denotes 'to run together, to draw together' and notes the Latvian expression: tik skābs, ka savęlk muti 'so sour that it draws the mouth together.' Jēgers compares also Lith. raûkas 'wrinkle,' raûkti 'to pucker,' Latv. ŗaûkt 'to contract,' ŗukt 'to shrivel up.' He is then led to ask if the meaning 'sour' does not derive from the observation that something sour draws the mouth together. Perhaps the same root is to be found in Hesychius hrougós·prósōpon 'face,' at the base of which lies the idea of a wrinkled face. Jēgers compares also the Greek expressions stúphō "I draw together,' kheílea stuphtheís 'having the lips drawn up by the taste,' intr. stúphein 'to be sour,' Latin coāgulum 'the curdled milk in the stomach of a sucking animal' and finally proposes that OP

278

ructan-dadan (EV - 690) 'sour milk' means '*run
together, drawn together milk,' i.e., 'coagulated
milk.'
10.091 Rickawie, rikijs. Jēgers, 1966, 67, disputes Endzelīns' notion that Latv. rìkuôt
surely only in the meaning. 'to harness a horse'
and perhaps in the meaning 'to busy oneself with'
is native Baltic and connected with Latv. rìks
'instrument.' In the other meanings 'to order,
to prepare, etc.' it is supposedly connected with
Lith. rykáuti 'to rule, to administer' and is not
to be separated from OP rickawie 'rules' which is
derived from the borrowed OP rikijs 'lord, master.'
But the concept 'to rule, to administer' can arise
from a meaning 'to put in order,' as Jēgers points
out.
10.092 Roaban. Fraenkel, 1959, 106, connects OP
roaban (EV - 467) 'variegated, striped' with Lith.
raĩbas, Latv. raibs 'id.' and further derives the
words from a root *rai- (< *roi-), *rei- found
also in Lith. raimas, rainas 'striped,' raĩbti,
reĩbti 'to be speckled, spotted,' ribéti, rìbti
'to glimmer,' ribà 'lighted line in a forest,
field, path, border.' These are in turn connected
with Lith. raĩstas, reĩstas 'swamp.' Lith.
raĩstas then has its meaning from the fact that
the swamp seems to the human eye to have many
various colors. Thus likewise Lith. balà, OCS
blato 'swamp' is connected with Lith. báltas, OCS
bělъ 'white' and Lith. pélkė 'swamp,' Latv. pelce
'puddle,' OP pelky (EV - 287) 'swampy meadow' are
to be connected with Lith. pìlkas 'grey.'
10.093 Sabatico. Kiparsky, 1968a, 248, writes
that if OP sabatico (EV - 23) 'Saturday' is not
taken directly from Latin sab(b)aticum, then the
word must go back to a Proto-Polish *sobotъka.
For the rendering of the suffix -ъka by -ico,
cf. ketwirtixe (ketwirtice, -ico?) 'Thursday.'
Elsewhere Proto-Polish -ъk- gives -uk-, cf. OP
somukis (EV - 537) 'lock,' etc. 97
10.094 Sackis. Van Windekens, 1960, 38, compares
OP sackis (EV - 598), Lith. sakaĩ, Latv. saki
'resin' with Tokharian A saku, B sekwe 'pus.'
10.095 Sarwis, sarxtes. Čop, 1956, 20-21, discusses the Hittite terms anda karija- 'to wrap,

to envelope,' šer karija 'to cover the top' and
establishes an Indo-European root *k'u̯er- 'to
cover.' He then compares the OP sarwis (EV -
418) 'weapon' and Lith. šárvas 'harness, armour,
cuirass, coat of mail' and OP sarxtes (EV - 425)
'sheath, scabbard.' Mažiulis, 1958, objects,
however, that OP sarwis as well as Lith. šárvas
are taken from Gothic sarwa as Būga, 1922, 64 (=
1959, 85) has shown. Mažiulis also objects to the
connection with sarxtes, which, he says, is from
the same root as Lith. sérg-ėti 'to watch, to
guard, to keep,' OP absergīsnan 'refuge, defense,'
butsargs 'householder.'

    Fraenkel, 1953, 30-31, connects Gk. kórus
'helmet' (cf. Gk. korússein 'to arm, to outfit')
with Lith. šarva, šárvas 'weapon' and OP sarwis.
Fraenkel disputes the etymology which derives the
words from Gothic sarwa 'weapon,' since, in his
opinion, the initial š- of the Lithuanian words
presupposes an Indo-European *k'-, an initial
sound which would correspond well to the initial
sound of Greek kórus.

10.096 Sawayte. For the etymology of OP sawayte
(EV - 16) 'week' Kiparsky, 1968a, 249, prefers the
explanation which identifies the element sa- as
denoting 'with' (such a prefix exists in Latvian
and Lithuanian, but is not found elsewhere in Old
Prussian) and the second element -wayte with OP
waitiāt 'to speak, to say.' The form corresponds
then exactly with Old Russian sъvětъ 'council,
gathering.' Presumably this denoted the day when
the individuals of the tribe (village) got together
for a meeting to decide what to do, cf. the
etymology of wissaseydis, para. 10.117. 98
10.097 Schutuan. Otkupščikov, 1971, 121, re-
iterates and supports the view that OP schutuan
(EV - 471) 'thread' can be connected directly with
the Russian dialect šitvo 'close-woven thread'
(častaja skvoznaja nit'). See also Trautmann,
1910, 422.
10.098 Scurdis. According to Jēgers, 1966, 40,
Lith. kùrti 'to heat,' Latv. kur̃t 'to start a
fire,' OP kūra 'created,' all go back to a root
which originally meant 'to cut .' One may also
connect OP scurdis (corrected from sturdis; EV -

324) 'device which sets the upper mill stone in motion,' Lith. skardýti 'to slaughter.'
10.099 Seggīt. Hamp, 1971, 44, notes that Jēgers, 1966, 75-76, has assumed for Latv. darît, Lith. darýti an etymological meaning of 'to clear, to make land arable,' cf. Latv. darījums 'a cleared meadow,' Lith. pradãrymas 'a recently cleared field.' Hamp suggests then that OP seggē, seggīt 'to do' can be compared with Lith. žãgaras 'branch, bushes, shrubbery,' žãgrė 'plough' and writes further that the Old Prussian verb originally meant 'to trim branches' and perhaps 'to clear land of trees and brush.' Hamp continues, 1971, 44-45, that this would point to a lost noun *žeg- meaning either 'branch' or 'bush.'

Hamp, 1974, rejects the connection of OP seggīt with Lith. sègti 'to fasten, to button up' on semantic grounds, and connections with the Indic root saj-, sañj- 'hang' on the basis of the fact that the Indic forms contain a nasal root and because we would see in the Indic forms an Indo-European etymological palatal rather than a pure velar. Hamp concludes, 89, "In summary we find the well defined Baltic set surrounding sègti; and an Indo-Iranian pair of uncertain relation or source *seg- and *seng- 'hang' and 'attach'. The relation of Slavic *seg- 'reach, grasp' is unclear. OIr. suainem 'rope, string' is morphologically complex and highly ambiguous."
10.100 Sētlauken. Blesse, 1957, 101, defines Latv. sẽta as 'yard; a peasant group, a definite peasant landholding; fence,' and notes, 103, the word sẽtlauki as meaning 'the fields of a sẽta.' He suggests then that the Old Prussian place name Sētlauken has a similar origin. The older explanation of Sētlauken as being comparable to Latv. sẽti lauki 'sown fields' has little meaning, since the characteristic of fields is to be sown all the time.
10.101 Seyr. On the basis of evidence from Greek, Hittite and Old Prussian, Ivanov, 1974, 199, establishes two fundamental forms for the Indo-European word for 'heart,' one of which *k'(e)r-(e)d-(i)- belonged to the active gender and the other of which *k'ēr belonged to the

281

inactive gender. Greek kardía, Hittite karateš-
teš 'your (sg.) insides,' OP sirsdau 'among,'
< *sird- + *d(a)u all give evidence of the first
reconstruction, whereas Greek kêr, OP seyr (EV -
124; which reflects a pronunciation *sēr in
Ivanov's opinion) and Hittite ki-ir which, in
Ivanov's opinion reflects a pronunciation *kēr,
all give evidence of the existence of the second
reconstruction. I am rather suspicious of the
reconstruction of a Proto-Indo-European form for
'heart' with an etymological long vowel plus -r,
see paragraph 6.703 and my articles 1973a and
1973b.

10.102 Sirgis. Sabaliauskas, 1968b, 153, notes
that in Lithuanian žìrgas denotes a 'fine beautiful
horse,' and OP sirgis (EV - 430) denotes 'stallion.'
Sabaliauskas says that it is unclear whether
Lithuanian or Old Prussian has retained the older
meaning, but that it should be pointed out that in
Lithuanian dialects (Dieveniškės, Trakai) the word
is used with the meaning 'stallion.' The word is
to be connected with Lith. žir̃gti, žer̃gti 'to
spread the legs wide apart,' žir̃gis 'decoration in
the form of a small horse on the roof,' žir̃gės,
žir̃giai 'two-branched tree for drying hide; poles
for drying clover or hay.' The primary meaning of
žìrgas was probably 'running fast,' cf. the Lithuanian interjection žìrgt to describe further movement. The Old Prussian word for horse is also well
represented in Old Prussian toponymy according to
Sabaliauskas, 1968b, 154, cf., e.g., Sirgelauwk
(< sirgis plus laucks 'field'), Sirgun, Sirgite,
Czirgelawken.

10.103 Skewre. Sabaliauskas, 1968b, 177, says
that the relationship between OP skewre (EV - 685)
'sow' and Lith. kiaùlė 'pig' is to be disputed
since the phonetic differences between the two
words is so great. The word may be reflected in
the Old Prussian place name Skeurekaym (< OP skewre
plus caymis 'village').

10.104 Soye. Hamp, 1956, 127, phonemicizes OP
soye (GrA - 49) and suge (EV - 49) as either
/sŭjē/ or /sūjē/ and in addition to the correspondence with Greek húein 'to rain' he compares
Albanian shi /ši/. Hamp writes, 128: "...we may

add to the well known correspondence OPruss.
lasasso, Lith. lašišà, Russ. losós', OHG. lahs,
TochB (= Kuchean = Westtocharisch) laks another
set binding Tocharian to Europe, and perhaps to
earlier Northern Europe: OPruss. /sūjē/: TochB
swese, su-/swās- 'rain'..., TochA swase, etc."
One wonders whether the Old Prussian phonemicization might not just as well be /sŭje/ or /sŭja/,
the final phoneme being merely the thematic vowel
known in Lithuanian as -a, but usually fronted to
-e after j- and palatalized consonants. See
Schmalstieg, 1959a and paragraph 5.001.

The hydronym Sъža, now the Sož (a left
tributary of the Dnepr), may correspond to OP suge
'rain' (if this name is to be compared with Old
High German sûgan, etc.). Toporov, 1959b, 62,
agrees with Hamp's proposal given in the preceding
paragraph. But if we accept the proposal of Hamp,
then the Old Prussian word can be compared with the
Russian hydronym Suja
10.105 Sunis, songos. Sabaliauskas, 1968b, 106-
107, disputes the various guesses concerning the
meaning of the orthography of songos (GrA - 42)
'dog' and proposes that the word is merely a
variant of sunis (EV - 703) 'dog' which would
correspond exactly to Latv. suns, Lith. šunis
'dog.' The word has also left clear traces in Old
Prussian toponymy where we find such names as
Sonne, Sonnaw, Sonnekaym, Suna, Sunegowe,
Sunecolowach, Sunike, Zunloszkeim. Perhaps the
word is also to be connected with the name of the
village Schönau not far from Danzig.
10.106 Swaigstan. Fraenkel, 1950b, 39, and
1952b, 145, wrote that OP swaigstan 'appearance,'
and erschwaigstinai 'enlightens' (with the past
act. prt. erschwaistiuns) are not to be connected
with Lith. žvaigždė 'star,' but rather with Lith.
šviẽsti 'to shine,' and Old Church Slavic světъ
'light,' Sanskrit śvétate 'is bright,' etc. The
g of the Old Prussian word is the result of the
insertion of a velar similar to that found in
Lith. žvaigždė, Latv. zvàigzne. OP swaigstan is
then to be connected with the name of the god
Suaikstix in all probability. Otrębski, 1950b,
275, suggests that Latv. zvaidrīt 'to shimmer, to

emit sparks' shows only a voiced variant of the
root *k'u̯eit-: *k'u̯oit- which we find in Lith.
šviẽsti 'to shine.' Beside the root *žvaid- we
find another root *žvaig-, represented in Latv.
zvaigala 'a cow with a star-shaped mark on the
forehead.'

10.107 Tickars. Jēgers, 1966, 101, examines the
etymological group represented by OP tickars
'right,' taykowuns 'made, created,' and teickut
'to create' and concludes that the fundamental
meaning of the latter word was originally 'to make
suitable, reliable.' The original idea behind
Lith. tìkras 'real, sure,' Latv. tikrs 'right,
good' and OP tickars was 'fit, useful, qualified.'

10.108 Tusnan. Čop, 1971, 44, connects OP tusnan
'quiet,' tussīse 'may he be silent,' Sanskrit
tū́ṣyati 'is calm, content,' Old Swedish thyster
'silent,' Lith. tausýtis 'to calm (of the wind)'
with Hittite tuḫuš(š)iya- 'to wait, to watch
quietly.'

10.109 Tuylis. Sabaliauskas, 1968b, 176, says
that OP tuylis (EV - 683; usually corrected to
cuylis) 'stud-boar' is ordinarily connected with
Lith. kuilỹs, Latv. kuĩlis 'id.' It is also known
in East Prussian German dialects and Sabaliauskas
quotes from Frischbier, 1882/38, Vol. I, 442, the
words Kuijel, Kujel 'id.' and kuijeln 'to fly
about, to run about.'

10.110 Twaxtan. I suggested, 1973b, 153, that
OP twaxtan (EV -553) 'bathing switch' was not to
be connected with Gothic þwahan, Old High German
dwahan 'to wash,' as it had been previously, cf.,
e.g., Trautmann, 1910, 453. The frequent confusion
of t and c found, e.g., in such words as turpelis
(EV - 509) 'shoemaker's last,' usually corrected to
curpelis and trupeyle (EV - 780) 'frog,' usually
corrected to crupeyle led me to suggest that the
reading twaxtan should be corrected to cwaxtan and
that the word should be phonemicized as /kvakstan/.
The second /k/ in /kvakstan/ is the typical Baltic
epenthetic velar between sibilant and dental, cf.,
e.g., OP klexto (EV - 333) 'sweeping rag' beside
Lith. klastỹklė 'feather duster.' Now the Slavic
word xvost is well attested in the sense of
'bathing switch.' I conclude then that OP twaxtan

or better cwaxtan is borrowed from Slavic /xvost/.
10.111 (*)Viting(a)s. Ekblom, 1957/58, 64, writes
that OP (*)viting(a)s represented in the German
transmission Witing, Weiting, Waiting, in Latin
Viting- 'member of a Dienstadels' is surely
borrowed from early Polish. The g of the word
shows that it must have come from a Slavic form
vitęgz.
10.112 Waidelotten. Sabaliauskas, 1966, 101,
lists German Waidelotten, Weidelotten in a group
of words which he calls Lithuanianisms in German.
He seems to give Lith. vaidilà 'Old Prussian pagan
priest' as the origin of the German word. But it
seems to me that both the Lithuanian and the German
words are borrowed from Old Prussian.
10.113 Waitiāmai. Safarewicz, 1967, 254, says
that OP waitiāmai 'we speak,' waitiāt 'to speak,'
Lith. dialect vaitenù 'I judge' have the same root
as Old Church Slavic věštajǫ, věštati 'to say, to
speak' but both the Slavic and the Baltic forms
give the impression of being independently created
on the basis of a common Indo-European root. See
also paragraphs 9.031, 10.096 and 10.114 below.
10.114 Wayte. Blesse, 1957, 117, says that
Latv. vaĩcât 'to ask' is derived from a Proto-
Baltic root *ṷait- found in OP wayte 'conversation,
utterance,' waitiāt 'to speak,' caryawoytis (EV -
416) 'military review,' Lith. vaitenù 'I judge,
suppose' and that all of these are to be compared
with the Slavic root větъ 'council, treaty' Russian
vitíja 'orator,' the Latvian place name Vĩtiņi,
the family name Vitiņš in the sense of 'advocate
for the people, chief.' According to Blesse, the
proto-form for Latv. vaĩcât could be *vaitināt,
*vaitīt, *vaitēt or even *vaitāt if one is to
judge by OP waitiāt which was possibly pronounced
as vaik'at.
    One may assume for the oldest Latvian a form
*vaits, *vaitis (cf. OP caryawoytis) with the
meaning 'conversation, negotiation, information'
and that from the forms *vaits and *vaitis the
forms *vaics and *vaicis may have been derived.
One notes a certain vacillation between t and c
elsewhere in Latvian, cf. uzruotīt: uzruocīt 'to
roll up.' (Blesse, 1957, 118.)

Blesse, 1957, 119, suggests that perhaps in
OP wayte the t was pronounced very much like a c,
cf. the Old Prussian personal name Aycze beside
Ayte. Blesse, 118, writes that the Latvian
family name Vaîts (also Vaiķis), Vaîtnieks is to
be connected with western Russian voit, Old
Russian voitz 'village magistrate.' He disputes
Gerullis' opinion, 1922, 192, that the Old Prussian
place names Waitegarben, Waitigarb, Woytegarben go
with Lith. vaîtas 'village magistrate.' According
to Blesse, we do not know whether there existed
a word similar to the Lithuanian word in Old
Prussian. If one were to connect these Old Prussian
place names with OP wayte 'utterance, conversation'
one would find a very appealing meaning for the
place names Waitegarben, etc., viz., 'the hill of
the conversation' or perhaps 'hill of the people's
meeting, where matters of government and social
life were discussed.'
10.115 Warne. Schwentner, 1958, 167, compares
Tokharian B wrauña, probably 'Prädigerkrahe, a kind
of crow' with Lith. várna, Latv. varna, OP warne,
Russian voróna, Czech vrána, Serbian vrâna, Old
Church Slavic vrana 'crow' and Lith. varnas, Czech
vran and Serbian vrân 'raven.'
    Schwentner, 1959, quotes Wolfgang Krause
to the effect that the Tokharian proper name
Wrauśke could be a diminutive of Tokharian B
wrauña 'raven,' which might perhaps place the
etymological connection with Lith. várna, Latv.
varna and OP warne in some doubt. Krause himself
admits that this etymological explanation of the
Tokharian personal name is only perhaps correct.
In favor of this possibility, however, is the well
known fact that personal names are frequently
derived from animal names, cf., e.g., OP Warnike
from warnis 'raven,' Polish Wronek, Czech
Havránek, Greek Kóraks 'raven.' Cf. also Fraenkel,
1955, 285, who quotes OP Warnekros (with repetition
of the r from original *Warnekos) from warne
'crow.'
10.116 Weders. Zaimov, 1960, 187, writes that the
Bulgarian word for 'snail,' veder is probably
connected with Old Church Slavic věděti 'to know'
and has the suffix -er, i.e., it denotes an

286

animal which is instructed, knows something. Much
less likely, in Zaimov's opinion, is the suggestion
of the connection with the concept 'water,' cf.
Slavic <u>vedro</u>, Sanskrit <u>udaram</u> 'stomach, womb,'
Lith. <u>vḗdaras</u> 'guts, viscera,' Latv. <u>vễdars</u>,
<u>vễders</u> 'stomach, belly,' OP <u>weders</u> as EV - 122
translated as 'belly,' as EV - 132 translated as
'stomach.' 99

10.117 <u>Wissaseydis</u>. Kiparsky, 1968a, 250-251,
notes that in all of Eastern Europe prior to the
introduction of the Semitic seven-day calendar
(which accompanied Christianization) there existed
an older calendar which depended completely on the
phases of the moon such that the 'moon day' (i. e.,
<u>Monday</u>) was always the first day of the new,
quarter, or full moon. Among non-Christian
peoples the old lunar week was retained into the
middle ages. Now an important affair such as a
military venture could only be undertaken on the
day after the full moon, i.e., Tuesday, for which
one may note the following names in various
languages of central Asia: Bashkir <u>otlangan</u> <u>kün</u>,
Chuvash <u>etlarñi</u> <u>gon</u>, Cheremis <u>kuškožmo</u>, Votjak
<u>pukśon</u> <u>nunal</u>, i.e., 'riding out day.' Every soldier
knows that for a military expedition on horseback
the horses and men must be well supplied.

Therefore Kiparsky, 1968a, 251-252, supports
the view of Mikkola, 1933, that OP <u>wissaseydis</u>
(EV - 19) 'Tuesday' means 'big breakfast, big
lunch (day),' the initial element <u>wiss-</u> to be
connected with Latv. <u>vaisla</u> 'propagation' and the
second element <u>-aseydis</u> to be connected with Latv.
<u>azaîds</u> 'breakfast, lunch.'

Knobloch, 1970, 270, would divide up the
word <u>wissaseydis</u> into the elements <u>wiss-</u> 'all'
and <u>-aseydis</u>, a form cognate with Latv. <u>azaîds</u>
'lunch, breakfast' and which would eventually
derive from an Indo-European *a<u>ĝh</u>-<u>oid(h)os</u> 'Zu-
speise.' The root <u>*oidh-</u> is also found in
Hesychius' <u>kak-ithḗs</u> 'poorly nourished' and in
Baltic and Slavic meant 'to eat.' The term *<u>vis-</u>
<u>azaidis</u> originally meant then '(day of the) big
meal.' Knobloch, 271, then says that this is to
be connected with the fact that among the Christians
in Poland the especially pious fasted not only on

287

those days required by the church, but also on Mondays, Wednesdays, Fridays and Saturdays. This left essentially only Tuesdays and Thursdays and the former was especially favored by the Baltic peoples for celebrations.

Knobloch, 1970, 271-272, objects to Kiparsky's etymology on the grounds that one would have to ask why with the meaning which Kiparsky assigns to 'moon-day' it would have been retained among the days of the week. Also one would have to show from the Bashkir, Chuvash and Votjak forms the name 'moon day' for the origin of this way of counting and its independence from the names of the week derived from the planets. Likewise Knobloch asks why one would delay until the afternoon of the expedition the big meal. Knobloch says further that there are no phonological nor semantic difficulties attendant on a derivation of the name from Old Polish. One should not forget that Adalbert of Prague had done missionary work among the Old Prussians already before the tenth century.

Pisani, 1973, proposes that in OP wissa-seydis the -ey- represents -ē- and that the root of the second element is sēd- 'to sit.' The initial element wissa- is the Baltic root for 'all.' Wissaseydis is to be understood then as 'the day when all sit,' i.e., 'the meeting day.' This has a parallel in German Dienstag, a loan translation of Martis dies, in which the initial element goes back to the name of the German war god Thingsus, the protector of the 'thing,' i.e., 'the people's parliament.' Perhaps then Tuesday was for the Germans and the Old Prussians a meeting day.

10.118 Wumpnis. Čop, 1971, 50, suggests that OP wumpnis (EV - 331) 'bake oven,' and umnode (EV - 330) 'bake house' may derive from an Indo-European *ump-no and therefore be connected with the Hittite r/n-stem ḫuppar 'cup, bowl, toureen,' Greek ipnós 'oven, kitchen' (which must have an etymological p according to Čop, 1971, 39, because Mycenean Greek shows the form i-po-no in which the p cannot reflect Indo-European *k^W), Old English ofen 'oven,' etc.

10.119 <u>Clumpis</u>. Milewski, 1947, 32, reconstructs
a Proto-Polish *k<u>ḷ</u>ạp, cf. Serbo-Croatian <u>klupa</u>,
Old Church Slavic <u>klạpь</u> 'bench,' as a source for
Old Prussian <u>clumpis</u> (EV - 216) 'chair.' Levin,
1974, 100, proposes a connection with Old Prussian
<u>klupstis</u> (EV - 140) 'knee,' Lith. <u>klùpti</u>, <u>klumpù</u>
'to kneel,' Russian <u>klypat'</u> 'to limp.'
10.120 <u>Kalso</u>. Levin, 1974, 101, suggests that a
derivation with an -s- suffix from the root *<u>kel</u>-
or *<u>kal</u>- found in OP <u>maluna-kelan</u> (EV - 321) 'mill
wheel,' Slavic <u>kolo</u> 'wheel' gives us OP <u>kalso</u>(EV - 345)
'bun.' The derivational procedure is also known
for Lith. <u>tamsà</u> 'darkness' from the verb <u>témti</u>
'to become dark.'
10.121 <u>Laitian</u>. For <u>laitian</u> 'sausage' (EV -
381) Levin, 1974, 102, suggests a correction to
*<u>ialitan</u> with <u>l</u> for <u>i</u>, <u>i</u> for <u>l</u>, <u>t</u> for <u>i</u> and <u>i</u> for
<u>t</u>, all of which are typical scribal errors in
EV. This would make even stronger the link with
Polish <u>jelito</u> 'sausage.' I think that Levin's
suggestion is excellent, although I am a little
surprised at the suggestion of so many scribal
errors in view of his professed faith in scribal
proficiency.
10.122 <u>Ploaste</u>. Levin, 1974, 103, suggests that
<u>ploaste</u> (EV - 491) 'sheet' is borrowed from Lith.
<u>plõštė</u> (contemporary meaning) 'shawl,' <u>plõščius</u>
(contemporary meaning) 'coat.'
10.123 <u>Saninsle</u>. Levin, 1974, 104, suggests that
<u>saninsle</u> (EV - 485) should be analyzed as <u>san</u>-
'together, with,' plus -<u>im</u>- (cf. OP <u>īmt</u> 'to take')
and a Baltic suffix *-<u>ksl-ē</u>: *<u>sanimkslē</u> could then
have passed to <u>saninsle</u> 'belt' (?).
10.124 <u>Dulsis</u>. Levin, 1974, 96, phonemicizes
<u>dulsis</u> (EV - 399) 'bung, spigot' as /dulzis/ and
derives it from Common Slavic *<u>dьlžь</u> 'opening in
a beehive,' East Slavic (Polesie) <u>dolž'</u> 'id.,'
Polish <u>dłużnik</u> 'board for shutting beehive.'
10.125 <u>Smunents</u>. Eckert, 1971, 73, notes that
Leskien, 1891, 585, had already seen the alternat-
ing -<u>ent</u>- in OP <u>smunents</u> 'man' and -<u>en</u>- in OP
<u>smunenisku</u> 'human' such that the word with -<u>ent</u>-
could be considered an original diminutive form
and thereby compared with Slavic -<u>ęt</u>-. Stang,
1966, 227, sees in OP *<u>smūnents</u> 'man' an

individualizing derivative of OP smūni 'person,'
cf. Lith. žmónės 'people,' which corresponds
historically with Slavic forms in -ęt-. In his
opinion these all got their diminutive meanings
in Slavic.

Eckert, 1971, 73, suggests then the following
steps in the historical development: (1) -(e)n-
stem [i.e., OP *smunen-] to (2) -t-enlargement
[i.e., OP *smunent-] to (3) i-stem [i.e., acc. sg.
smunentin, acc. pl. smunentins].
10.126 Brendekermnen. Eckert, 1971, 56, writes
that in the Old Prussian Enchiridion (IIIrd
catechism) the word brendekermnen 'pregnant' is
attested once. The initial element is to be
connected with OP pobrendints 'laden,'
pobrandisnan 'burden,' Lith. bręsti, Latv. briêst
'to ripen.' The second element (-kermnen) is
surely cognate with OP kermens 'body,' which
corresponds to Proto-Slavic *červo 'body, belly,
stomach, abdomen.' At least in South and East
Slavic we find meanings corresponding to those of
OP kermens and brendekermnen, cf. Russian čerěvo,
Ukrainian, Belorussian čerěvo, Slovene crevó
'body, belly,' and Old Church Slavic črěvo 'womb,'
from the latter of which we find Russian črevo
with derivatives of the type črevonositi 'to be
pregnant.' Cf. also the Russian dialect form
očerevet' 'to become pregnant.'

In Eckert's opinion, then, 1971, 57-58, OP
kermens is related to Proto-Slavic *červo from
*keru-o, just as Baltic kirmis 'worm, maggot,
snake,' Skt. kŕmi- 'worm, insect,' Old Irish cruim
'worm,' Proto-Slavic dial. *črm- (cf. Slovene čŕm
'anthrax,' Old Russian čerm'nī 'dark red, violet')
are to Proto-Slavic *črv-ь < *kiru-is (cf. Russian
červ' 'worm,' etc.) We find the same relationship
of the suffixes within Old Prussian itself, cf.,
e.g., the place names Kirmithen vs. Kirwiten, the
hydronyms OP Pilmen vs. Pilwin, Pilwen (cf. the
Lith. river name Pilvė). Probably, as Endzelīns,
1944, 68, has pointed out, the etymological suffix
of OP kermens is *-men-. Eckert, 1971, 59, also
calls attention to a somewhat similar explanation
in Nesselmann, 1873, 22.

Mažiulis, 1972b, 216, adds to the etymological

cognates Sanskrit carma 'skin,' but says that the
-kerm-nen (in brendekermnen) does not have the
meaning 'pregnant' as one of its semantic com-
ponents. The meaning of 'pregnant' or 'heavy'
comes from the element brende-. Thus the OP
expression sen brendekermnen denotes literally
'with a heavy (i.e., pregnant) body.'
10.127 Aubirgo. Mažiulis, 1975b, 83, notes that
usually OP aubirgo (EV - 347) 'cook' is divided
into a prefix au- and a root *birg-; the word is
then connected not only with OP birga-karkis
(EV - 358) 'large basting ladle,' Latvian birga
'coal-gas,' Lith. birg-alas (birg-e-las) 'bad
beer; bad soup,' but also with Latin ferctum
'sacrificial cake' from Latin *fergo 'I bake,'
etc., all assuming an Indo-European root *bherg-
'to bake, to cook' from Indo-European *bherg- 'to
move quickly, to boil, to cook.' One should agree,
according to Mažiulis, with such an etymology for
OP aubirgo, but with the following reservations.
One may doubt the reality of the reconstructed
Indo-Eruopean root *bherg- 'to bake, to cook' not
only because of the addition of the *-g-, but also
because the Indo-European root *bher(e)- here can
be of onomatopoetic origin, an independent development in the various Indo-European dialects. In
other words, one might speculate that one finds
a Baltic onomatopoetic root *birg- 'to buzz, to
hum, to bubble, to prattle, to boil, etc.'
Closest to retaining the original meaning would
be Lith. birg-alas (-elas, -ilas), i.e., 'a beer
such that when the barrel is opened it only fizzes,
but does not spurt forth.' From a Baltic root
*birg- with this meaning the derivation of Latv.
*birg- 'to emit steam' and OP *birg- 'to cook'
can easily be seen. An OP *birgan 'cooking'
supplied aubirgo and birgakarkis and perhaps the
place name Wose-birgo 'goat's bleating,' cf. Lith.
kárvė birzgia 'the cow moos.'
10.128 Birgakarkis. Mažiulis, 1975b, 84, agrees
with the usual division of birgakarkis (EV - 358)
'large basting ladle' into the elements birga- and
karkis. The initial element is discussed in the
preceding paragraph. Levin, 1974, 100, writes
that the second element -karkis is usually

compared with Polish korzkiew 'scoop, ladle,' cf.
Milewski, 1947, 32 and Trautmann, 1910, 312.
Endzelīns, 1943, 151, reads *karikis and connects
the word with Slavic korьcь 'ladle, spoon.'
Mažiulis, 1975b, 84, however, would correct the
reading of the Old Prussian word to *kartis, the
second graphemic -k- of -karkis being the result
of a confusion of OP palatalized t' and k', cf.
Lith. dialect šiĺk'is = šiĺt'is 'fire,' k'iltas =
standard Lith. tìltas 'bridge.' The closest
cognate of OP *kartis 'ladle' would be Lith. dial.
kar̃tis (io-stem) 'a measure for measuring grain.'
Mažiulis notes that Slavic korьcь has both the
meaning 'ladle, scoop' and the meaning 'measure
for measuring grain' and that Fraenkel, 1955, 225,
connects this Slavic word with Lith. dial. kar̃tis.
According to Mažiulis, 1975b, 84, Slavic korьcь
is to be connected with Slavic kor-a 'tree bark'
and Lith. kar-nà, kar-dà 'tree bark, bast,' kér-ti
to peel off, to drop off.' Thus OP birgakarkis is
to be corrected to *birgakartis and is to be defined as 'cooking spoon, kitchen spoon.' This
word has the same root as Baltic *ker-, *kir-
found in other OP words, e.g., (aclo-)cordo (see
paragraph 10.004) and kirno (EV - 637) 'shrub,
bush.'

10.129 Baytan. Mažiulis, 1975b, 85, writes that
OP baytan (EV - 346) which is glossed by German
zeeb does not denote 'a cake or kind of baked
goods,' as Trautmann, 1910, 310 and Endzelīns,
1943, 149, define it, but rather as Ziesemer,
1919/20, 144, and Marchand, 1970, 113, define
it, 'sieve.' The initial b- is to be replaced
by s- and the word is to be read as *saytan and
then obviously connected with Lith. síetas, Latv.
siêts, Polish and Russian sito 'sieve.' In
Mažiulis' opinion OP *saitan is to be derived from
West Baltic *seita(n) cf., e.g., OP braydis 'deer'
in which the -ay- can be derived from older *-ei-
according to Endzelīns, 1943, 153. Balto-Slavic
*seita (nom.-acc. sg. neut.) is derived with the
-ta- suffix from *sei- 'to sift,' cf. Lith.
sij-óti, Latv. sij-ât 'to sift.'

10.130. i͞urin, wurs. Bezlaj, in his article Problematika imen Vir in Skočidjevojka, forthcoming, compares OP i͞urin 'sea,' wurs (EV - 61) 'pond' with Slovene iríti se 'to foam, to cause waves to form.' A primary form iríti se and, in all probability, *irьjь could have come, by way of *jir- from an earlier *jyr-, which, in turn derived from Proto-Slavic *j͞ur-. Since Indo-European *j͞us 'you' gave Slavic vy, we also expect a form *vyrьjь from *j͞ur- and we do indeed find this in the Russian dialect form vyrь 'pool' (beside byrь). In Russian onomastics we find the hydronyms Vyrij, Vyrьja, Vyrьjanka, Vyra, etc. The doublet byrь does not appear in names and is therefore surely younger. One can also assume an original *vyrьjь for a series of Slovene forms such as viry (to be read virîj) in Trubar, contemporary dialect verîj (Poljane, Tolmin), berîj (Vrsno), vrîj, brêj (Goriška Brda), etc. Since in all of the South Slavic languages and also in Czech and Slovak the reflexes of Slavic *vyrьjь and *vir have merged and since they were partial synonyms, for all practical purposes it is impossible to distinguish the two stems. The name Vir is common in Slovene toponyms, but the appelative vir is used in the literary language only poetically in the sense 'fons' beside the common izvir 'source.' Only in the northern belt along the Drava do we find vir in the sense 'whirlpool, deeper place in the river.'

REFERENCES

Academy Dictionary = Lietuvių kalbos žodynas, Vol.
1 (2nd ed.), 1968; Vol. 2 (2nd ed.), 1969;
Vol. 3, 1956; Vol. 4, 1957; Vol. 5, 1959;
Vol. 6, 1962; Vol. 7, 1966; Vol. 8, 1970;
Vol. 9, 1973. Vilnius, Mintis.

Academy Grammar = Ulvydas, K. ed. in chief. 1965.
Lietuvių kalbos gramatika, Vol. 1. Vilnius,
Mintis.

Antoniewicz, J. 1958. The mysterious Sudovian
people. Archaeology 11.158-161.

-- 1965. The problem of the 'Prussian Street' in
Novgorod the Great. Acta Baltico-Slavica
2.7-25.

-- 1966. Baltic peoples in the light of
archaeology and toponymy. Acta Baltico-
Slavica 4.7-27.

Anttila, Raimo. 1974. Analogy.
(Kenraaliharjoituksia - Dress rehearsals).
Helsinki, University of Helsinki, Department
of General Linguistics.

Arumaa, Peeter. 1970. Zur Geschichte der baltischen
Genera. Donum Balticum, 22-29.

Augstkalns, A. 1930. Veclatviešu rakstu apskats.
Rīgas Latviešu biedrības Zinību komisijas Rakstu
krājums. 20.92-137. (Quoted from Ozols, 1965,
79 and 602.)

-- 1934. Mūsu valoda, viņas vēsture un
petītāji. Riga. (Quoted from Ozols, 1965,
78-79, 602.)

Balčikonis, J. 1954. Dabartinės lietuvių kalbos
žodynas. Vilnius, Valstybinė politinės
politinės ir mokslinės literatūros leidykla.

Baltic linguistics. 1970. Thomas F. Magner and
    William R. Schmalstieg, eds. University
    Park and London, The Pennsylvania State
    University Press.

Baltic literature and linguistics. 1973. Arvids
    Ziedonis, Jaan Puhvel, Rimvydas Šilbajoris
    and Mardi Valgemäe, eds. Columbus, Ohio
    State University, Association for the
    Advancement of Baltic Studies.

Balto-slavjanskij sbornik. (Dedicated to the
    memory of Jan Otrębski and Jonas Kazlauskas.)
    1972. V. N. Toporov, ed. Moscow, Nauka.

Bammesberger, Alfred. 1973. Abstraktbildungen in
    den baltischen Sprachen. Supplement to the
    Zeitschrift für vergleichende Sprachforschung,
    No. 22. Göttingen, Vandenhoeck and Ruprecht.

Benveniste, Emile. 1933. Le participe indo-européen
    en -mno-. Bulletin de la société de linguistique
    de Paris 34.5-31.

-- 1934. Questions de morphologie baltique.
    Studi Baltici 4.72-80.

Berneker. E. 1896. Die preussische Sprache.
    Strassburg, Karl J. Trübner.

Bezzenberger, Adalbert. 1874a. Ueber die A-Reihe
    der gotischen Sprache. Göttingen, Robert
    Peppmüller.

-- 1874b. Review of G. H. F. Nesselmann, Thesaurus
    linguae prussicae. Göttingische gelehrte
    Anzeigen, No. 39.1221-1250.

-- 1875. Litauische und lettische Drucke des 16.
    Jahrhunderts. Heft II. Göttingen, Robert
    Peppmüller.

-- 1878. Altpreussisches. Beiträge zur Kunde der
    indogermanischen Sprachen 2.135-141.

-- 1897. Review of Erich Berneker, Die preussische Sprache. Beiträge zur Kunde der indogermanischen Sprachen 23.283-321.

-- 1904. Zur textgeschichte des Elbinger vokabulars. Beiträge zur kunde der indogermanischen Sprachen 28.158-160.

-- 1907. Studien über die Sprache des preussischen Enchiridions. Zeitschrift für vergleichende Sprachforschung 41.65-127.

Bielfeldt, Hans Holm. 1970. Die baltischen Lehn- wörter und Reliktwörter im Deutschen. Donum Balticum, 44-56.

Blese, E. 1947. Latviešu literaturas vesture. Hanau, Gaismas Pils.

Blesse (Blese), Ernst. 1957. Lettische Etymologien Zeitschrift für vergleichende Sprachforschung 75.91-121.

Bloch, Bernard. 1948. A set of postulates for phonemic analysis. Language 24.3-46.

Braune, Wilhelm and Ernst A. Ebbinghaus. 1965. Althochdeutsches Lesebuch. 14th ed. Tübingen, Max Niemeyer.

Brechenmacher, J.K. 1957-63. Etymologisches Wörterbuch der deutschen Familiennamen. 2nd ed. Lief. 1-21. Glückburg.

Brückner, A. 1900. Ursitze der Slaven und Deutschen. Archiv für slavische Philologie 22.237-247.

Brugmann, Karl. 1904. Kurze vergleichende Grammatik der indogermanischen Sprachen. Strassburg, Karl J. Trübner.

Būga, K. 1908. Aistiški študijai. Part 1. St. Petersburg, Imperatoriškosjos mokslų akademijos spaustuvė = Buchdruckerei der kaiserlichen Akademie der Wissenschaften.

-- 1922. Kalba ir senovė. Kaunas, Švietimo Ministerijos leidinys. Reprinted in Rinktiniai raštai, Vol. 2.

-- 1924. Lietuvių kalbos žodynas. Kaunas, Švietimo Ministerija. Reprinted in Rinktiniai raštai, Vol. 3.

-- 1958. Rinktiniai raštai, Vol. 1. Z. Zinkevičius, ed. Vilnius, Valstybinė politinės ir mokslinės literatūros leidykla.

-- 1959. Rinktiniai raštai, Vol. 2. Z. Zinkevičius, ed. Vilnius, Valstybinė politinės ir mokslinės literatūros leidykla.

-- 1961. Rinktiniai raštai, Vol. 3. Z. Zinkevičius, ed. Vilnius, Valstybinė politinės ir mokslinės literatūros leidykla.

Burwell, Michael. 1970. The vocalic phonemes of the Old Prussian Elbing vocabulary. Baltic linguistics, 10-20.

Chaytor, H. J. 1945. From script to print. Cambridge, Heffer and Sons. (Quoted here from 1950 reprint.)

Čop, B. 1956. Notes d'étymologie et de grammaire hittites III. Slavistična revija. Linguistica. 9.19-40.

-- 1959/60. Etyma balto-slavica IV. Slavistična revija 12.170-193.

-- 1971. Indogermanica minora, I. Slovenska akademija znanosti in umetnosti. Razred za filološke in literarne vede. Ljubljana.

Curme, George O. 1952. A grammar of the German
language, 2nd ed., 7th printing. New York,
Frederick Ungar.

Donum Balticum. 1970. Velta Rūķe-Draviņa, ed.
Stockholm, Almqvist and Wiksell.

Donum Indogermanicum. Festgabe für Anton Scherer
zum 70 Geburtstag. 1971. Robert Schmitt-
Brandt, ed. Heidelberg, Carl Winter.

Duridanov, Ivan. 1969. Thrakisch-Dakische Studien.
Part 1. Die Thrakisch- und Dakisch-
Baltischen Sprachbeziehungen. Linguistique
balkanique, Vol. 13, No. 2. Sofia, Verlag
der bulgarischen Akademie der Wissenschaften.

Eckert, Rainer. 1959. K voprosu o sostave
gruppy imen suščestvitel'nyx s osnovoj na -ŭ
v praslavjanskom jazyke. Voprosy
slavjanskogo jazykoznanija 4.100-129.

-- 1963. Reste indoeuropäischer heteroklitischer
Nominalstämme im Slawischen und Baltischen.
Zeitschrift für Slawistik 8.878-892.

-- 1966. Liet. vãsara = Sl. vesná. Lietuvių
kalbotyros klausimai 8.143-154.

-- 1971. Baltistische Studien. (Sitzungsberichte
der sächsischen Akademie der Wissenschaften
zu Leipzig, Philologisch-historische Klasse,
Band 115, Heft 5.) Berlin, Akademie-Verlag.

-- 1974. Zu den nominalen i-Stämmen im
Altpreussischen. Zeitschrift für Slawistik
19.221-233.

Ekblom, R. 1946/48. Der ordensdeutsche
Ortsname Nerge 'Nehrung' ein nordgermanisches
Lehnwort? Språkvetenskapliga Sällskapets
Förhandlingar.

-- 1957/58. Nord. hvitingr als slavisches
Wanderwort. Språkvetenskapliga Sällskapets
Förhandlingar.

-- 1959. Balt. gudas und schw. gute
'Gotländer.' Rakstu krājums, 91-99.

Endzelīns, Jānis. 1935. Prūšu tekstu grafika.
Filologu biedrības raksti 15.86-103.

-- 1937. Baltische Streitfragen, 420-430.
Mélanges linguistiques offerts à M. Holger
Pedersen = Acta Jutlandica 9.1. Copenhagen,
Levin and Munksgaard.

-- 1943. Senprūšu valoda. Riga, Universitātes
apgāds. (With vocabulary.)

-- 1944. Altpreussische Grammatik. Riga, Latvju
grāmata. This is a German translation of
Senprūšu valoda = Endzelīns, 1943, but there
is no accompanying vocabulary.

-- 1948. Baltu valodu skaņas un formas. Riga,
Latvijas valsts izdevniecība.

-- 1951. Latviešu valodas gramatika. Riga,
Latvijas valsts izdevniecība.

-- 1956. Latvijas PSR vietvārdi. Part 1,
Fascicle 1. Riga, Latvijas PSR Zinātņu
akadēmijas izdevniecība.

-- (= Endzelynas, J.) 1957. Baltų kalbų garsai ir
formos. Vilnius, Valstybinė politinės ir
mokslinės literatūros leidykla. This is a
Lithuanian translation of Baltu valodu skaņas
un formas (= Endzelīns, 1948.)

-- 1970. Concerning the relationships of the
Prussian language with congeners. Baltic
linguistics, 53-60. This is an English
translation of Endzelīns, 1931. Par prūšu
valodas radniecības sakariem. Filologu
biedrības raksti 11.189-193.

-- 1971. Jānis Endzelīns' comparative phonology
    and morphology of the Baltic languages.
    The Hague and Paris, Mouton. An English
    translation of Endzelīns, 1948, see above.
    In addition to the translation by William R.
    Schmalstieg and B. Jēgers there are comments
    by Schmalstieg and Jēgers and a word index
    by Jēgers.

Falk, Knut-Olof. 1941a. Wody wigierskie i
    huciańskie. Studium toponomastyczne.
    Vol. 1. Uppsala, Almqvist and Wiksell.

-- 1941b. Wody wigierskie i huciańskie.
    Studium toponomastyczne. Źródła ręko-
    piśmienne. Vol. 2. Lund, Håkan Ohlsson
    and Uppsala, Almqvist and Wiksell.

-- 1966. Ze studiów nad hydronimią suwalską:
    Gnilik - Kelig. Acta Baltico-Slavica
    3.69-75.

Fleischer, W. 1968. Die deutschen Personennamen.
    Geschichte, Bildung und Bedeutung. 2nd ed.
    Berlin. Akademie-Verlag.

Fowkes, Robert A. 1957. Problems of Cymric
    etymology. Lingua Posnaniensis 6.90-111.

Fraenkel, Ernst. 1949. Lit. (j)éras 'lamm',
    lett. jẽrs, preuss. eristian usw.
    Indogermanische Forschungen 59.306-309.

-- 1950a. Baltisches und Slawisches. 3.
    Altpreussisches. b. Zu der unbeachteten
    Überlieferung des preussischen Vokabulars
    Simon Grunaus. Lingua Posnaniensis 2.120-
    122.

-- 1950b. Die baltischen Sprachen. Heidelberg,
    Carl Winter.

-- 1952a. Baltische Etymologien. 1. Lit. <u>arvas</u>
'frei', preuss. <u>arwis</u> 'wahr, gewiss': lit.
<u>ìrti</u> 'sich trennen, sich auflösen', <u>ardýti</u>
'trennen'. Zeitschrift für slavische
Philologie 21.138-154.

-- 1952b. Baltisches und Slawisches. I. Zur
Gutturalbehandlung im Baltischen und
Slavischen. Zeitschrift für vergleichende
Sprachforschung 70.129-146.

-- 1953. Zur griechischen Wortbildung.
Glotta 32.16-33.

-- 1955. Litauisches etymologisches Wörterbuch.
Heidelberg, Carl Winter; Göttingen,
Vandenhoeck and Ruprecht.

-- 1959. Etymologische Miscellen. 101-107.
Rakstu krājums.

Frischbier, H. 1882/83. Preussisches Wörterbuch.
Ost- und Westpreussische Provinzialismen in
alphabetischer Folge, I-II. Berlin.

Frisk, Hjalmar. 1970. Griechisches etymologisches
Wörterbuch. Vol. 2. Heidelberg, Carl Winter.

Gāters, A. 1954. Der baltische Name für Grummet.
Zeitschrift für vergleichende Sprachforschung.
71.113-117.

Gerullis, Georg. 1922. Die altpreussischen
Ortsnamen. Berlin, Leipzig.

Gimbutas, M. 1963. The Balts. New York,
Praeger.

Górnowicz, H. 1965. Rodowe nazwy miejscowe
Mazur i Warmii. Komunikaty Mazursko-
Warmińskie R. 1, 197-228.

-- 1974. Das altpreussische Suffix -īt- und das polnische Suffix -ic- in Ortsnamen des preussischen Pomesaniens. Zeitschrift für Slawistik 19.234-240.

Grinaveckis, V. 1965. Novoe v litovskoj dialektologii. Acta Baltico-Slavica 2.177-202.

-- 1972. Žem. jeĩnis ir muñsiai. Baltistica 8.73-77.

Hamp, Eric. 1956. Opruss. Soye 'rain.' Zeitschrift für vergleichende Sprachforschung 74.127-128.

-- 1971. Old Prussian seggē, seggīt. Baltistica 7.43-45.

-- 1972. Miscellanea. 263-271. Ètimologija 1970. Moscow, Nauka.

-- 1973. On Baltic, Luwian and Albanian participles in *-m-. Baltistica 9.45-50.

-- 1974. On false equations for OPruss. seggīt. Baltistica 10.87-89.

Hartknoch, Chr. 1679. Selectae dissertationes historicae de variis rebus Prussicis, Opera et studio Christophori Hartknoch, Anno MDCLXXIX. Reference from Mažiulis, 1966, 25.

Hermann, E. 1948. Ist Simon Grunaus Vaterunser lettisch? Nachrichten der Akademie der Wissenschaften in Göttingen, philologisch-historische Klasse. 1.19-29.

-- 1949. Eine unbeachtete Überlieferung des preussischen Vokabulars Simon Grunaus. Nachrichten der Akademie der Wissenschaften in Göttingen, philologisch-historische Klasse. 6.151-166.

Hill, Archibald. 1967. The current relevance of
    Bloch's 'Postulates.' Language 43.203-208.

Hockett, Charles. 1955. A manual of phonology.
    Indiana University publications in anthropology
    and linguistics, No. 11. Baltimore.

Holthausen, F. 1956. Etymologien. Indogermanische
    Forschungen 62.151-157.

Hrabec, St. 1958. Jeszcze raz o nazwie Mazowsze.
    Onomastica 4.225-246.

Ivanov, V.V. 1958a. K ětimologii baltijskogo i
    slavjanskogo boga groma. Voprosy
    slavjanskogo jazykoznanija 3.101-111.

-- 1958b. Toxarskaja parallel' k slavjanskim
    umen'šitel'nym formam. Slavjanskaja
    filologija. 2.58-63. Sovetskij komitet
    slavistov. IV meždunarodnyj s"ezd slavistov.
    Izdatel'stvo ANSSSR.

-- 1974. Iz ětimologičeskix nabljudenij nad
    baltijskoj leksikoj. Zeitschrift für
    Slawistik 19.190-200.

Ivanov, V.V. and V.N. Toporov. 1974. Baltijskaja
    mifologija. Zeitschrift für Slawistik
    19.144-157.

Jakulienė, A. 1969. Prūsų kalbos sangrąžiniai
    veiksmažodžiai. Baltistica 5.37-42.

Jansons, A. 1965. A. Donāta gramatikas tulkojums
    latviešu cilšu valodās 13 gs. Latvijas PSR
    Zinātņu akadēmijas vēstis 12.25-38.

Jēgers, B. 1958/61. Über die Verwandschaft von
    ai. panthās 'Weg.' Språkliga Bidrag 3.61-86.

-- 1966. Verkannte Bedeutungsverwandtschaften
baltischer Wörter. Göttingen: Vandenhoeck
and Ruprecht. Also published in Zeitschrift
für vergleichende Sprachforschung 80.6-162
and 291-307.

-- 1969. Einige baltische und slavische Verwandte
der Sippe von lit. dir̃ti. Studi Baltici
10.63-112.

-- 1970. Remarks on some Baltic names of tools of
the type Lithuanian kaltas 'chisel.'
Baltic linguistics, 81-86.

Kamiński, A. 1953. Jaćwież. Terytorium, ludność,
stosunki gospodarcze i społeczne. Łódź.

-- 1956. Materiały do bibliografii archeologicznej
Jaćwieży od I do XII w. Materiały starożytne
1.193-273. Warsaw.

-- 1963. Pogranicze polsko-rusko-jaćwieskie
między Biebrzą i Narwią. Rocznik Białostocki
4.7-41.

Karaliūnas, Simas. 1968. Kai kurie baltų ir
slavų kalbų seniausiųjų santykių klausimai.
Lietuvių kalbotyros klausimai 10.7-100.

Kazlauskas, Jonas. 1962. K razvitiju obšče-
baltijskoj sistemy glasnyx. Voprosy
jazykoznanija, No. 4.20-24.

-- 1965. Review of W. P. Schmid, Studien zum
baltischen und indogermanischen Verbum.
Baltistica 1.85-88.

-- 1967. Review of Acta Baltico-Slavica III.
Baltica in honorem Iohannis Otrębski.
Baltistica 3.237-243.

-- 1968. Lietuvių kalbos istorinė gramatika.
Vilnius, Mintis.

-- 1970. On the Balto-Slavic dative plural and dual. Baltic linguistics, 87-91. (Also published in a Lithuanian version in 1968 in Baltistica 4.179-183.)

Kiparsky, Valentin. 1949. L'emploi artificiel d'un préfixe étranger. Actes du sixième congrès international des linguistes. 501-504.

-- 1968a. Vorchristliches im altpreussischen Kalender. Baltistica 4.247-252.

-- 1968b. Das Schicksal eines altpreussischen Katechismus. Baltistica 4.105-107.

-- 1970a. Das Schicksal eines altpreussischen Katechismus II. Baltistica 6.219-226.

-- 1970b. Altpreussische Miszellen. Donum Balticum, 258-262.

Kluge, Friedrich. 1967. Etymologisches Wörterbuch der deutschen Sprache. 20th ed. bearbeitet von Walther Mitzka. Berlin, Walter de Gruyter.

Knobloch, Johann. 1970. Zu apr. Wissaseydis 'Dienstag.' Donum Balticum, 270-272.

Kortlandt, F.H.H. 1974. Old Prussian accentuation. Zeitschrift für vergleichende Sprachforschung 88.299-306.

Krahe, Hans. 1949/50. Alteuropäische Flussnamen. Beiträge zur Namenforschung 1.247-266.

-- 1955. Alteuropäische Flussnamen. K. Exkurs: Der Flussname Antia. Beiträge zur Namenforschung 6.

-- 1960. Beiträge zur illyrischen Wort- und Namenforschung. Indogermanische Forschungen 65.113-123.

-- 1964a. Idg. *enebh- in europäischen Flussnamen. Beiträge zur Namenforschung 15.10-16.

-- 1964b. Über einige Flussnamen-Komposita auf alteuropäischer Grundlage. Flussnamen aus baltischem Gebiet. Beiträge zur Namenforschung 15.2-10.

-- 1964c. Zwei elsässische Flussnamen. Beiträge zur Namenforschung 15.20-21.

-- 1965. Alte Gewässernamen zwischen Weichsel und Memel. Beiträge zur Namenforschung 16.1-8.

Krause, Wolfgang and Werner Thomas. 1960. Tocharisches Elementarbuch. Heidelberg, Carl Winter.

Kubicka, Weronika. 1967. Bibliografia języka staropruskiego (do 1965 r.). Acta Baltico-Slavica 5.257-296.

Kudzinowski, Czesław. 1964. Jaćwingowie w języku. Acta Baltico-Slavica 1.217-225.

Kulikauskas, Pranas. 1970. Panemunių dzūkai ir jotvingiai. In Panemunių dzūkai, Vyšniauskaitė, Angelė, ed. Pp. 12-32. Vilnius, Lietuvos TSR mokslų akademijos istorijos institutas.

Kurschat, Alexander. 1968ff. Litauisch-deutsches Wörterbuch = Thesaurus linguae lituanicae. Vols. 1-4. Göttingen, Vandenhoeck and Ruprecht.

Kuryłowicz, Jerzy. 1958. L'accentuation des langues indo-européennes. Wrocław, Kraków, PAN.

-- 1966. Bałtycka deklinacja na -ē-. Acta Baltico-Slavica 3.83-88.

Kuzavinis, K. 1964. Prūsų kalba. Vilnius, Vilniaus valstybinis pedagoginis institutas. Lietuvių kalbos katedra.

-- 1966. Etymologica. I. Baltų etnonimų kilmės klausimu. Baltistica 1.177-184.

-- 1968. Garbus - jotvingiškas žodis. Baltistica 4.65-67.

Labov, William, Malcah Yaeger and Richard Steiner. 1972. A quantitative study of sound change in progress. Vol. 1. Report on National Science Foundation Contract NSF-GS-3287. Philadelphia, U.S. Regional Survey, 204 N. 35th St.

Lasch, Agathe. 1914. Mittelniederdeutsche Grammatik. Halle a. S., Max Niemeyer.

Leclercq, Jean. 1961. The love of learning and the desire for God. Translated by Catharine Misrahi. New York, Fordham University Press. (English translation of L'Amour des lettres et le désir de Dieu, Les éditions du Cerf, Paris.)

Leskien, A. 1876. Die Declination im Slavisch- litauischen und Germanischen. Reprinted in Leipzig by the Zentral-Antiquariat der deutschen demokratischen Republik (1963).

-- 1891. Die Bildung der Nomina im Litauischen. (Abhandl. d. K. S. Gesellsch. d. Wissensch. XXVIII.) Leipzig.

Levin, Jules F. 1972. Slavic borrowings in the Elbing vocabulary and their implication for Prussian phonology. General Linguistics 12.149-158.

-- 1973. -Jā stems and -ē stems in the Elbing vocabulary. Baltic literature and linguistics, 189-196.

-- 1974. The Slavic element in the Old Prussian
    Elbing vocabulary. (University of California
    publications in linguistics, No. 77).
    Berkeley, Los Angeles and London, University
    of California Press.

-- 1975a. Toward a graphology of Old Prussian
    monuments: the Enchiridion. Paper presented
    at the Third All-Union Conference on Baltic
    Linguistics, Vilnius, Sept. 26-28, 1975.

-- 1975b. Dynamic linguistics and Baltic
    historical phonology. General Linguistics
    15.144-158.

Lithuanian Academy Dictionary - See Academy
    Dictionary.

Lituanistikos darbai = Lithuanian Studies,
    Vincas Maciūnas, ed. 1973. New York,
    Franciscan Fathers Press, 910 Willoughby
    Ave., Brooklyn, N.Y. 11221.

Łowmiański, Henryk. 1966. Pogranicze słowiańsko-
    jaćwieskie. Acta Baltico-Slavica 3.89-98.

Marchand, James. 1970. Some remarks on the German
    side of the Elbing vocabulary. Baltic
    linguistics, 108-117.

Marstrander, Carl J. 1945. En germansk religiøs
    terminus i gammelprøysisk. Norsk Tidsskrift
    for Sprogvidenskap 13.344-352.

Martinet, André. 1939. Equilibre et instabilité
    des systèmes phonologiques. Proceedings of
    the Third International Congress of Phonetic
    Sciences, 30-34. Ghent.

-- 1955. Le couple senex-senatus et le 'suffixe'
    -k-. Bulletin de la société de linguistique
    de Paris. 51.42-56.

Marvan, Jiří. 1973. Deciphering the Old
    Prussian 'message.' Baltic literature and
    linguistics, 181-187.

Mažiulis, Vytautas. 1958. Kalbos smulkmenos.
    Kalbotyra 1.223-224.

-- 1960. Dėl Neringos vardo. Lietuvių kalbotyros
    klausimai 3.301-315.

-- 1963a. Zametki po prusskomu vokalizmu. Voprosy
    teorii i istorii jazyka: Sbornik v čest'
    professora B.A. Larina. 191-197. Leningrad,
    Izdatel'stvo Leningradskogo universiteta.

-- 1963b. K baltijskoj paralleli slavjanskogo
    *moĩdъ 'molodoj.' Kalbotyra 7.215-216.

-- 1964a. Zametki po prusskoj ètimologii (1-2).
    Problemy indoevropejskogo jazykoznanija.
    Moscow.

-- 1964b. Zum baltisch-slawischen *tū/*tŭ 'Du.'
    Zeitschrift für Slawistik 9.256-257.

-- 1965. Remarques sur le vocalisme du vieux
    prussien. Acta Baltico-Slavica 2.53-59.

-- 1966a. Prūsų kalbos paminklai. Mintis,
    Vilnius.

-- 1966b. Dėl prūsų etimologijų. Kalbotyra
    14.101-106.

-- 1966c. Zum baltischen o-stämmigen genitivus
    singularis. Acta Baltico-Slavica 3.107-112.

-- 1966d. K balto-slavjanskoj forme dativa (mn.
    i dv. č.). Baltistica 2.43-53.

-- 1968. Zum preussischen bzw. baltischen
    Instrumental Singular. Baltistica 4.23-29.

-- 1970. Baltų ir kitų indoeuropiečių kalbų santykiai: Deklinacija. Vilnius, Mintis.

-- 1971. Review of Baltic linguistics (Magner, Thomas F. and William R. Schmalstieg, eds.). Baltistica 7.101-106.

-- 1972a. Iš baltų veiksmažodžio fleksijos istorijos. Baltistica, Priedas (= Supplement) 1.95-100.

-- 1972b. Review of Rainer Eckert, Baltistische Studien. Baltistica 8.215-217.

-- 1974. Altpreussische Etymologien. Zeitschrift für Slawistik 19.212-220.

-- 1975a. Seniausias baltų rašto paminklas. Baltistica 11.125-131.

-- 1975b. Prūsų etimologijos. Baltistica 11.83-85.

McCluskey, Stephen C., William R. Schmalstieg and Valdis Zeps. 1975. The Basel epigram: a new minor text in Old Prussian. General Linguistics 15.159-165.

Mikalauskaitė, E. 1938. Priešreformacinių laikų prūsiško Tėve Mūsų nuotrupa. Archivum Philologicum (Kaunas) 7.102-106.

Mikkola, J.J. 1933. Zur Erklärung einiger baltischen Wörter. Studi Baltici 3.131-133.

Milewski, Tadeusz. 1947. Stosunki językowe polsko-pruskie. Slavia Occidentalis 18.21-84.

-- 1966. Przyczynki do akcentologii bałto-słowiańskiej. Acta Baltico-Slavica 3.113-126.

Naert, Pierre. 1961. La situation linguistique de l'aïnou. Aïnou et indoeuropéen 2. Nouvelles étymologies. Orbis 10.394-410.

Nagy, Gregory. 1970. Greek dialects and the
transformation of an Indo-European process.
Cambridge, Mass., Harvard University Press.

Nalepa, Jerzy. 1961/65. Wigry, nazwa największego
jeziora Jaćwieży. Språkliga Bidrag. 4.17-25.

-- 1964. Jaćwięgowie, Nazwa i lokalizacja.
Białostockie towarzystwo naukowe: Kompleksowa
Ekspedycja Jaćwięska = Prace Białostockiego
towarzystwa naukowego 2.

-- 1966a. Przyczynek do znajomości toponomastyki
i mowy Jaćwięgów. Acta Baltico-Slavica
3.127-133.

-- 1966b. Połeksznie (Pollexiani) - plemię
jaćwięskie u północno-wschodnich granic
Polski. Rocznik Białostocki 7(1968).
7-34 pp. plus map.

-- 1969. Znaczenie jaćwięskiej nazwy Sejny.
Slavia Orientalis 18.189-190.

-- 1971a. Próba nowej etymologii nazwy Galindia
czyli Golędź. Opuscula slavica I =
Slaviska och baltiska studier 9.93-115.
Slaviska institutionen vid Lunds universitet.

-- 1971b. Jaćwięska terrula Cresmen. Opuscula
slavica I = Slaviska och baltiska studier
9.117-126. Slaviska institutionen vid Lunds
universitet.

-- 1971c. Skandynawia a staropruska Skanda i
Skandawa. Opuscula slavica I = Slaviska
och baltiska studier 9.145-150. Slaviska
institutionen vid Lunds universitet.

Nepokupnyj, A. P. 1971. Z movnoji spadščyny
jatvjahiv. Movoznavstvo 5, No. 6.18-25.

-- 1972. K sostavu i geografii litovskix i belo-
russko-slavjanskix sootvetstvij (parallelej)
prusskim prefiksal'nym obrazovanijam.
Baltistica 8.11-18.

-- 1973a. Prusskaja ětimologija v trudax Ja.
Endzelina i leksika primorskix govorov
baltijskix i bližajšix k prusskomu arealu
dialektov vostočnoslavjanskix jazykov.
Latvijas PSR zinātņu akadēmijas vēstis 2
(307).76-83.

-- 1973b. Litovskaja i prusskaja antroponimija v
issledovanijax i materialax po nemeckim
familijam. Baltistica 9.83-87.

-- 1973c. Prusskie slavizmy i leksika kašubskix
i varminsko-mazurskix govorov pol'skogo
jazyka. Baltistica 9.171-182.

-- 1974a. Pol'sk. pedy 'koromyslo' - relikt
prusskoj leksiki. Baltistica 10.151-156.

-- 1974b. Lingvogeografičeskie svjazi litovskix
i belorusskix form nazvanij g. Djatlovo i
ego okrestnostej. 144-154. Balto-
slavjanskie issledovanija, T. Sudnik, ed.
Moscow, Nauka.

Nesselmann, G.H.F. 1845. Die Sprache der alten
Preussen an ihren Überresten erläutert.
Berlin, G. Reimer.

-- 1851. Wörterbuch der Littauischen Sprache.
Königsberg. Verlag der Gebrüder Bornträger.

-- 1873. Thesaurus linguae prussicae.
Berlin, Harrwitz and Gossmann.

Niedermann, M., A. Senn and Fr. Brender. 1932.
Wörterbuch der litauischen Schriftsprache.
Vol. 1. Heidelberg, Carl Winter.

Otkupščikov, Ju. V. 1971. Iz istorii balto-
slavjanskix leksičeskix otnošenij.
Baltistica 7.119-128.

Otrębski, Jan. 1948. Uwagi o nazwach miejscowości,
ustalonych na Pomorzu Mazowieckim. Slavia
Occidentalis 19.342-360.

-- 1950a. Miscellanées onomastiques. 4. L'origine
du nom Mieszko. Lingua Posnaniensis 2.74-79.

-- 1950b. Review of Ernst Fraenkel, Die baltischen
Sprachen. Lingua Posnaniensis 2.274-277.

-- 1955. Über die Herkunft des Preussennamens.
Lingua Posnaniensis 5.76-78.

-- 1958a. Zagadnenie Galindów. 37-41. Studia
Historica w 35-lecie pracy naukowej H.
Łowmiańskiego. Warsaw, PWN.

-- 1958b. Gramatyka języka litewskiego. Vol. 1.
Warsaw, PWN.

-- 1960a. 'Vistula.' Lingua Posnaniensis
8.254-261.

-- 1960b. Beiträge zur baltisch-slawischen
Namenkunde. Beiträge zur Namenforschung
11.172-178.

-- 1961. Jazyk jatvjagov. Voprosy slavjanskogo
jazykoznanija. 5.3-8.

-- 1962. Beiträge zur baltisch-slawischen
Namenkunde. Beiträge zur Namenforschung
13.148-149.

-- 1963a. Das Jatwingerproblem. Die Sprache
9.157-167.

-- 1963b. Dainavà - nazvanie odnogo iz
jatvjažskix plemen. Voprosy slavjanskogo
jazykoznanija 7.3-6.

-- 1963c. Baltisch-Slawische Miszellen. Lingua Posnaniensis 9.115-121.

-- 1963d. Namen von zwei Jatwingerstämme. Slawische Namenforschung 29.204-209.

-- 1964. Udział Jaćwingów w ukształtowaniu się języka polskiego. Acta Baltico-Slavica 1.207-216.

-- 1965. Die baltische Philologie und ihre Bedeutung für die indogermanische Sprachwissenschaft. Zeitschrift für vergleichende Sprachforschung 79.69-88.

Ozols, Arturs. 1965. Veclatviešu rakstu valoda. Riga, Liesma.

Paul, Hermann. 1956. Deutsches Wörterbuch. 5th ed. Bearbeitet von Alfred Schirmer. Halle (Saale), Max Niemeyer Verlag.

Pisani, V. 1954. Griech. glóssa. Indogermanische Forschungen 61.141-146.

-- 1965. Il paganesimo balto-slavo. Storia delle religioni, G. Castellani, ed. Vol. 2.807-857. Torino, Unione tipografico-editrice torinese.

-- 1973. Baltoslavica. Baltistica 9.51-52.

Pop, Sever. 1950. La dialectologie. Vol. 1. Dialectologie Romane. Publications universitaires de Louvain. Recueil de travaux d'histoire et de philologie, 3e série, Fascicule 38.

Powierski, J. 1965a. Najdawniejsze nazwy etniczne z terenu Prus i niektórych obszarów sąsiednich. Komunikaty Mazursko-Warmińskie 88.161-183.

-- 1965b. Kształtowanie się granicy pomorsko-
    pruskiej w okresie od XII do początku XIV w.
    Zapiski historyczne 30, No 2.7-33; No 3.7-27.

-- 1967. Review of J. Nalepa, Jaćwięgowie, Nazwa
    i lokalizacja. Acta Baltico-Slavica 5.355-
    358.

Prinz, Jurgen. 1968. Die Slavisierung baltischer
    und Baltisierung slavischer Ortsnamen im
    Gebiet des ehemaligen Gouvernements Suvalki.
    Wiesbaden, Otto Harrassowitz.

Puhvel, Jaan. 1973. The Baltic pantheon.
    Baltic literature and linguistics 99-108.

Rakstu krājums veltījums akadēmiķim profesoram
    dr. Jānim Endzelīnam. 1959. E. Sokols, K.
    Graudiņš et al., eds. Riga, Latvijas PSR
    Zinātņu akadēmijas izdevniecība.

Robinson, David F. 1972. The Göttingen
    (ex-Königsberg) collection of Old Lithuanian
    and Old Prussian books. General Linguistics
    12.145-148.

Rosenkranz, B. 1957. Zur Überlieferungsgeschichte
    des preussischen Vokabulars Simon Grunaus.
    113-117. Mnēmēs kharin. Gedenkschrift Paul
    Kretschmer, Vol. 2, Vienna.

Rudnicki M. 1957/58. Nazwiska wielkopolskie typu
    Jany Brychcy. Sprawozdania Poznańskiego
    towarzystwa przyjaciół nauk. 20.22-24.

-- 1961. Prasłowiańszczyzna Lechicka-Polska.
    Vol. 2. Wspólnota słowiańska. Wspólnota
    Lechicka-Polska. Poznań. Poznańskie
    towarzystwo przyjaciół nauk. Wydział
    filologiczno-filozoficzny. Prace komisji
    filologicznej. Vol. 19, Fascicule 2.

Rūķe-Draviņa, Velta. 1955. Die Benennung des Wacholders im Baltischen. Orbis 4.390-409.

-- 1955/58. Tendenser vid de substantiviska stammarnas utveckling i baltiskan. Språkliga Bidrag 4.81-96.

Sabaliauskas, Algirdas. 1957. Dėl žirnio pavadinimo kilmės. Literatūra ir kalba 2.346-355.

-- 1958. Baltų kalbų žemės ūkio augalų pavadinimų kilmės klausimu. Literatūra ir kalba 3.454-461.

-- 1960. O proisxoždenii nazvanija maka v baltijskix jazykax. Kratkie Soobščenija Instituta Slavjanovedenija 28.70-73.

-- 1966. Lietuvių kalbos leksikos raida. Lietuvių kalbotyros klausimai 8.5-142.

-- 1967. Žodžiai atgyja. Vilnius, Mintis.

-- 1968a. Dėl pr. rapeno 'jauna kumelė' kilmės. Baltistica 4.95.

-- 1968b. Baltų kalbų naminių gyvulių pavadinimai: jų kilmė ir santykis su atitinkamais slavų kalbų pavadinimais. Lietuvių kalbotyros klausimai 10.101-190.

-- 1970. Iš baltų kalbų gyvulininkystės terminologijos istorijos. Lietuvių kalbotyros klausimai 12.7-81.

-- 1973. Review of R. Eckert, Baltistische Studien. Lietuvių kalbotyros klausimai 14.243-245.

-- 1974. Zur Herkunft von litauisch palvė. Zeitschrift für Slawistik 19.210-211.

Safarewicz, Jan. 1961. Ze słownictwa bałto-
słowiańskiego. Slavia Antiqua 8.11-25.
Also published in Safarewicz, 1967,
see below.

-- 1967. Studia językoznawcze. Warsaw,
PWN.

Savukynas, B. 1963. Dėl M. Rudnickio Galindos,
Priegliaus ir Suduvos etimologinių aiškinimų.
Review of M. Rudnicki, 1961. Lietuvių
kalbotyros klausimai 6.320-325.

-- 1966. K probleme zapadnobaltijskogo substrata
v jugozapadnoj Litve. Baltistica 1.165-176.

Schall, Hermann. 1963. Die baltisch-slavische
Sprachgemeinschaft zwischen Elbe und Weichsel.
Atti e memorie del VII Congresso intern. di
scienze onomastiche, 2. Florence.

-- 1964. Baltische Dialekte im Namengut Nordwest-
slawiens. Zeitschrift für vergleichende
Sprachforschung 79.123-167.

-- 1966a. Kurisch-selische Elemente im Nordwest-
slawischen. Proceedings of the Eighth
International Congress of Onomastic Sciences.
451-462. The Hague, Mouton. (= Janua
linguarum, series major, Vol. 17, D. P. Blok,
ed.)

-- 1966b. Baltische Gewässernamen im Flusssystem
'Obere Havel' (Südost-Mecklenburg).
Baltistica 2.7-42.

-- 1970. Preussische Namen längs der Weichsel.
Donum Balticum, 448-464.

Schmalstieg, William R. 1959. The alternation
e/a in Old Prussian: a phonemic interpretation.
Annali, Istituto universitario orientale di
Napoli 1.191-195.

-- 1960. Baltic ei and depalatalization. Lingua 9.258-266.

-- 1961. Primitive East Baltic *-uo-, *-ie- and the 2nd sg. ending. Lingua 10.369-374.

-- 1964. The phonemes of the Old Prussian Enchiridion. Word 20.211-221.

-- 1968a. Labialization in Old Prussian. Studies in Slavic linguistics and poetics in honor of Boris O. Unbegaun. 189-193. R. Magidoff, G. Sheve: et al., eds. New York, New York University Press.

-- 1968b. Review of Chr. S. Stang, Vergleichende Grammatik der baltischen Sprachen. Language 44.388-398.

-- 1969. Four Old Prussian etymologies. Baltistica 5.163-166.

-- 1970. The Old Prussian verb. Baltic linguistics, 127-156.

-- 1970a. Review of Gregory Nagy, Greek dialects and the transformation of an Indo-European process. General Linguistics 10.195-199.

-- 1971a. A new look at the Old Prussian pronoun. Baltistica 7.129-138.

-- 1971b. Old Prussian kērdan. Baltistica 7.47-48.

-- 1971c. Die Entwicklung der ā-Deklination im Slavischen. Zeitschrift für slavische Philologie 36.130-146.

-- 1972a. Denominative verbs with the suffix -j-. La linguistique 8.123-136.

-- 1972b. Baltų ir slavų kalbų vokalizmo sistemų raidos chronologija. Baltistica, Priedas (= Supplement) 1.159-164.

-- 1972c. Old Prussian comparatives in -ais-.
    Baltistica 8.7-10.

-- 1973a. New thoughts on Indo-European phonology.
    Zeitschrift für vergleichende Sprachforschung
    87.99-157.

-- 1973b. Several studies on Old Prussian.
    Lituanistikos darbai 3.153-170.

-- 1974. An Old Prussian Grammar: the phonology
    and morphology of the three catechisms.
    University Park and London, The Pennsylvania
    State University Press.

-- 1976. Speculations on the Indo-European active
    and middle voices. Zeitschrift für
    vergleichende Sprachforschung

Schmid, Wolfgang P. 1958. Altpreussisch lasto
    'Bett.' Indogermanische Forschungen 63.220-
    227

-- 1958b. Baltisch kurtas und andere Tier-
    bezeichnungen. 129-137. Sybaris, Fest-
    Schrift Hans Krahe. Wiesbaden.

-- 1962. Zu Simon Grunaus Vaterunser. Indogermanische
    Forschungen 67.261-273.

-- 1963. Studien zum baltischen und indogermanischen
    Verbum. Wiesbaden. Otto Harrassowitz.

-- 1964. Baltische Beiträge IV. Zum altpreussischen
    Flexionstyp endyrītwei 'ansehen.' Indogermanische
    Forschungen 69.125-129.

-- 1967. Baltische Sprachen und Völker. 14-20.
    Reallexikon der Germanischen Altertumskunde.
    Beck, Heinrich, Herbert Jahnkuhn et al., eds.
    Berlin, New York, Walter de Gruyter.

-- 1968. Baltische Beiträge VI. Zu altpreussisch
    asmai 'ich bin.' Indogermanische Forschungen
    73.355-361.

-- 1969. Zur Geschichte des Formans *-āu̯on-/-ău̯o-/
-ā. Indogermanische Forschungen 74.126-138.

Schmitt-Brandt, Robert. 1971. Die Herausbildung der
slavischen Sprachgemeinschaft. Donum
Indogermanicum. 224-243.

Schmittlein, Raymond. 1948. Études sur la
nationalité des Aestii. I. Toponymie
lituanienne. Bade.

Schulze, W. 1908. Pán und Pūṣán. Zeitschrift für
vergleichende Sprachforschung 42.81, 374.

Schwentner, E. 1952a. Altpreussisch pelemaygis.
Zeitschrift für vergleichende Sprachforschung
70.152.

-- 1952b. Lit. kikilis 'Buchfink, Hänfling.'
Zeitschrift für vergleichende Sprachforschung
70.152.

-- 1955. Altpreussisch keutaris 'Ringeltaube.'
Zeitschrift für vergleichende Sprachforschung
73.113-114.

-- 1958. Tocharische Tiernamen. 2. Toch. B. Wrauña
'Krähe.' Indogermanische Forschungen 63.165-
168.

-- 1959. Tocharisch B Wrauśke. Beiträge zur
Namenforschung 10.173.

Sedov, V.V. 1964. Kurgany jatvjagov. Sovetskaja
arxeologija. No. 4. 36-51.

-- 1968. Jatvjažskie drevnosti v Litve. Lietuvos
TSR MA Darbai, Ser. A. 1(26).177-185.

Senn, Alfred, A. Salys, et al. 1932ff. Wörterbuch
der litauischen Schriftsprache. Vols. 1-4.
Heidelberg, Carl Winter.

Shopay, Olga C. 1970. Old Prussian adverbs in -n.
Baltic linguistics, 157-163. (Reprinted from

The Slavic and East European Journal, 1967,
11.296-301.)

Sjöberg, A. 1969. Ob odnoj drevneprusskoj
    poslovice. Scando-Slavica 15.275-276.

Skardžius, Pranas. 1932. Lietuvių latvių žodyno
    kalbos dalykai. Archivum Philologicum
    (Kaunas) 3.47-54.

Šlaski, Kazimierz. 1967. Review of Jan Powierski,
    1965b. Acta Baltico-Slavica 5.358-360.

-- 1969. Problem zajęcia Ziemi Chełmińskiej
    przez Prusów. Acta Baltico-Slavica 6.213-
    218.

-- 1970. Przyczyny polityczne zaboru Ziemi
    Chełmińskiej przez Prusów w XIII wieku.
    Acta Baltico-Slavica 7.23-30.

Sommer, Ferdinand. 1914. Die indogermanischen
    iā und io-Stämme im Baltischen. Leipzig.
    Abhandlungen der philologisch-historischen
    Klasse der königl. sächsischen Gesellschaft
    der Wissenschaften, Vol.30, No. 4. B.G.
    Teubner.

Specht, F. 1928. Zu den altpreussischen Verbal-
    formen auf -ai, -ei, -sai, -sei.
    Zeitschrift für vergleichende Sprachforschung
    55.161-184.

-- 1954. Zur Bildung des Infinitivs im Baltischen.
    Indogermanische Forschungen 61.249-255.

Stang, Christian S. 1930. Altpreussisch quai,
    quei, quendau. Norsk Tidsskrift for
    Sprogvidenskap 4.146-155. Also printed in
    Stang, 1970, 121-129.

-- 1942. Das slavische und baltische Verbum.
    Oslo, Jacob Dybwad.

321

-- 1957. Eine preussisch-slavische (oder baltisch-slavische) Sonderbildung. Scando-Slavica 3.236-239. Reprinted in Stang, 1970, 69-72.

-- 1961. Zum baltisch-slavischen Verbum. International Journal of Slavic Linguistics and Poetics 4.67-74. Reprinted in Stang, 1970, 73-80.

-- 1962. Die athematischen Verba im Baltischen. Scando-Slavica 8.161-170. Reprinted in Stang, 1970, 196-205.

-- 1966. Vergleichende Grammatik der baltischen Sprachen. Oslo, Bergen, Tromsö, Universitetsforlaget.

-- 1970. Opuscula linguistica. Oslo, Bergen, Tromsö, Universitetsforlaget.

-- 1971. Lexikalische Sonderübereinstimmungen zwischen dem Slavischen, Baltischen und Germanischen. Oslo, Bergen, Tromsø,[sic], Universitetsforlaget.

Steponavičienė, I. 1974. Dėl lietuviškų vietovardžių prūsinimo kryžiuočių ordino raštuose. Baltistica 10.163-168.

Szemerényi, Oswald. 1970. The Indo-European name of the "heart". Donum Balticum, 515-533.

-- 1973. Marked-unmarked and a problem of Latin diachrony. Transactions of the philological society. 55-74.

Tautavičius, A. 1966. Lietuvių ir jotvingių genčių gyventų plotų ribų klausimu. Lietuvos TSR MA Darbai, Ser. A. 2(21).161-180.

-- 1968. Dopolnitel'nye zamečanija po voprosu o granicax meždu jatvjažskimi i litovskimi plemenami. Lietuvos TSR MA Darbai, Ser. A 1(26).187-190.

Thumb, A. and R. Hauschild. 1958. Handbuch des
Sanskrit. Vol. 1, Part 1. 1959. Vol. 1,
Part 2. Heidelberg, Carl Winter.

Thurneysser, Leonhard. 1583. Maelişāh kai
Hermeneia Das ist ein Onomasticum und
Interpretatio oder aussführliche Erklerung
Leonharten Thurneyssers zum Thurn,
Churfürstischs Brandenburgischs bestalten
Leibs Medici. Uber Etliche frembde und (bey
vield hochgelarten, die der Lateinischen und
Griechischen Sprach erfahren) unbekannte
Nomina, Verba, Prouerbia, Dicta, Sylben,
Caracter und sonst Reden. Berlin, Nicolaus
Voltzen.

Toporov, V.N. 1958. Zametki po prusskoj
ètimologii. 1. Pruss. arrien. 2. Pruss.
dēigiskan. 3. Pruss. etnistis. 4. Pruss.
etskīuns. Voprosy slavjanskogo jazykoznanija
3.112-119.

-- 1959a. Dve zametki iz oblasti baltijskoj
toponimii. Rakstu krājums, 251-266.

-- 1959b. O baltijskix sledax v toponimike
russkix territorij. Lietuvių kalbotyros
klausimai 2.55-63.

-- 1960. Indoevropejskij koren' *∂_2en/*∂_2n v
baltijskom i slavjanskom. Lingua Posnaniensis
8.194-211.

-- 1961a. K voprosu ob èvoljucii slavjanskogo i
baltijskogo glagola. Voprosy slavjanskogo
jazykoznanija 5.35-70.

-- 1961b. Lokativ v slavjanskix jazykax. Moscow,
Izdatel'stvo ANSSSR.

-- 1962. O nekotoryx arxaizmax v sisteme
baltijskogo glagola. International Journal
of Slavic Linguistics and Poetics 5.31-57.

-- 1963a. Issledovanija po baltijskoj ětimologii
(1957-1961). Ětimologija. 250-261. Moscow,
Izdatel'stvo ANSSSR.

-- 1963b. Zametki po indoevropejskoj ětimologii.
3. Eśče raz o xettskom ųaųarkima. 189-190.
Ětimologija. Moscow, Izdatel'stvo ANSSSR.

-- 1966a. O baltijskom ělemente v gidronimii
verxnego Dnepra. 285-297. Studia linguistica
slavica baltica Canuto-Olavo Falk sexagenario
a collegis amicis discipulis oblata.
(= Slaviska och baltiska studier, 8.
Slaviska institutionen vid Lunds universitet.)

-- 1966b. Ob odnoj 'jatvjažskoj' mifologeme v
svjazi so slavjanskoj parallel'ju. Acta
Baltico-Slavica 3.143-149.

-- 1966c. K voprosu o toponimičeskix sootvetstvijax
na baltijskix territorijax i k zapadu ot
Visly. Baltistica 1.103-111.

-- 1966d. O baltijskix ělementax v gidronimii i
toponimii k zapadu ot Visly. Slavica
Pragensia 8.255-263.

-- 1970. K balto-skandinavskim mifologičeskim
svjazjam. Donum Balticum, 534-543.

-- 1972. Zametki po baltijskoj mifologii.
Balto-slavjanskij sbornik, 289-314.

-- 1974. Ob indoevropejskix sootvetstvijax odnomu
baltijskomu mifologičeskomu imeni Balt.
Puš(k)ait-: dr.-ind. Pūṣán, dr.-greč. Pán.
3-48. Balto-slavjanskie issledovanija,
Tamara Sudnik, ed. Moscow, Nauka.

Toporov, V.N. and O.N. Trubačev. 1961.
Baltijskaja gidronimija verxnego Podneprov'ja.
Lietuvių kalbotyros klausimai 4.195-217.

Trautmann, Reinhold. 1909. Apreuss. Kaaubri.
Zeitschrift für vergleichende Sprachforschung
42.369.

-- 1910. Die altpreussischen Sprachdenkmäler.
Göttingen, Vandenhoeck and Ruprecht.

-- 1925. Die altpreussischen Personennamen.
Göttingen, Vandenhoeck and Ruprecht.

Trubačev, O.N. 1958. Slawische Etymologien.
Zeitschrift für Slawistik 3.668-681.

-- 1965. Zametki po ètimologii i onomastike:
na materiale balto-germanskix otnošenij.
16-24. Pytannja onomastyky. Materialy
II Respublikans'koji narady z pitan'
onomastyky. Kiev. Instytut movoznavstva
im. O.O. Potebni. Akademija nauk ukrajins'koji
RSR.

-- 1970. Ètimologičeskie zametki. Donum
Balticum, 544-547.

Trubetzkoy, N.S. 1939. Grundzüge der Phonologie.
Travaux du cercle linguistique de Prague 7,
Prague.

Ulpis, A., ed. 1969. Lietuvos TSR bibliografija.
Vol. 1. 1547-1861. Vilnius, Mintis.

Vaillant, André. 1947a. Vieux-slave otŭvě 'il
répondit.' Revue des études slaves 23.152-
155.

-- 1947b. Lituanien be-, slave bě. Revue des
études slaves 23.151-152.

-- 1958. Grammaire comparée des langues slaves.
Vol. 2, Part 2. Lyon and Paris, Éditions
IAC.

-- 1962a. Slave žĭnje-, žęti 'moissoner.' Revue
des études slaves 41.59-60.

-- 1962b. Vieux-prussien -winūt, polonais winować.
Acta universitatis Carolinae. Philologica.
3.449-452.

-- 1968a. Vieux-prussien enkopts 'enterré.'
Baltistica 4.253.

Van Wijk, N. 1918. Altpreussische Studien. The
Hague, Martinus Nijhoff.

Van Windekens, A.J. 1960. Études d'étymologie
et de grammaire comparée. Lingua Posnaniensis
8.30-43.

-- 1962. Nouvelles études sur l'étymologie et le
vocabulaire de l'aïnou. Orbis 11.234-242.

Vanagas, Aleksandras. 1968. K voprosu o
dialektnoj differenciacii baltov, obitavšix
na territorii Litvy (po dannym gidronimiki).
Lietuvos TSR MA Darbai, Ser. A. 1(26). 143-155.

-- 1970. Panemuniṳ dzūkṳ toponimijos svarbesnieji
bruožai. 33-48. Panemuniṳ dzūkai. Vilnius,
Lietuvos TSR MA Istorijos institutas.

Vasmer, Max. 1957. Baltisch-slavische Wort-
gleichungen, 351-353. Ezikovedski
izsledvanija v čest na akad. Stefan Mladenov.
Sofija. Bьlgarskata akademija na naukite.

Vilkuna, K. 1957/58. Zur ältesten Geschichte der
Woche. Volk-Liv 21/22.197-215.

Vitkauskas, V. 1966. Apie kai kuriṳ žemaitiškṳ
žodžiṳ vartojimą. Lietuviṳ kalbos leksikos
raida = Lietuviṳ kalbotyros klausimai 8.155-
168.

Witkowski, Teodolius. 1970. Baltische Ortsnamen
westlich der Oder? Donum Balticum, 562-573.

Wer ist wer? Das Deutsche Who's Who. XVI.
Ausgabe von Degeners wer ist's?. I.
Bundesrepublik Deutschland, West-Berlin.

Wolff, Adam. 1966. W sprawie nazwy Jaćwięgów.
Acta Baltico-Slavica 3.187-190.

Zabrocki, L. 1939/47. Czas teraźniejszy w
dialekcie pruskim Sambii. Slavia Occidentalis
18.305-380. Rés. 540-542.

-- 1948. Kilka uwag o nazwach pomorskich. Kilka
nazw pruskich. Slavia Occidentalis 19.398-402.

-- 1961. Transpozycje strukturalne prusko-polsko-
niemieckie w zakresie nazw topograficznych
Pomorza Mazowieckiego. 201-231. Pierwsza
Międzynarodowa Slawistyczna Konferencja
Onomastyczna. Wrocław.

Zaimov, J. 1960. Die bulgarischen Namen der
Schnecke. Etymologische Untersuchung.
Zeitschrift für Slawistik 5.187.

Zdancewicz. T. 1963. Gwary powiatu sejneńskiego
na tle procesów osadniczych. Materiały do
dziejów ziemi sejneńskiej. Białystok.

Ziesemer, W. 1919/20. Zum deutschen Text des
Elbinger Vocabulars. Beiträge zur Geschichte
der deutschen Sprache und Literatur 44.138-146.

Zinkevičius, Zigmas. 1966. Lietuvių
dialektologija. Vilnius, Mintis.

-- 1972. Dėl žem. jeĩnis. Baltistica 8.163-166.

Žulys, V. 1966. Keleto retų žodžių istorija.
Baltistica 1.151-160.

FOOTNOTES

1) On the basis of hydronyms, Schmid, 1967, 14-15,
establishes an original Baltic area which runs in
the south from the mouth of the Persante in
Pomerania east to Kiev and Kursk and then turns
north passing slightly east of Moscow and then
somewhat north, but not quite reaching Jaroslavl'
and then west to the mouth of the Venta in Latvia.
About one-sixth of this area is now Baltic. The
Baltic hydronymy developed from the Indo-European/
Old European hydronomy and within this area we
encounter such Aistian (or Baltic) names.
According to Schmid this shows that Baltic developed
from an original centum language which was overcome
by a wave of satemization from the south-east and
therefore was separated from the Western Indo-
European languages.

2) The transcription of Arabic Brus as B^urus is
perhaps preferable since classical Arabic initial
consonant clusters of the type /br-/ were, of
course, impossible and some vowel had to be inserted
in the pronunciation, but in the writing only in a
vocalized text. Vocalized Burus = بُرُوسُ ; unvocalized بروس

3) Sabaliauskas points out (oral communication)
that there is a place named Sasnavà not far from
the city of Kapsukas (formerly Mariampolė).

4) One can draw a parallel between Lith. skaláuti
'to wash' and Old Prussian Skalva on the one hand
and Lith. praũsti 'to wash' and Old Prussian Prūsa
on the other hand.

5) At the end of the 18th century one of the lakes
near Trakai was known as Galvys or Galvis according
to Mažiulis (oral communication).

6) The form jatvjagy would seem to be only an
accusative or instrumental plural of jatvjagъ.

7) It should be kept in mind that Szeszupa is the
Polish rendering of Lith. Šešupė.

8) But Mažiulis suggests (oral communication) that
the initial h- in these words may be the result of
White Russian influence.

9) Mažiulis objects (oral communication) that
perhaps Lith. Garbus underwent metatony, cf. Lith.
láimė 'luck, fortune' vs. laĩmùs 'fruitful.'

328

Another possibility is that perhaps the Old Prussian
word had an acute intonation.
10) Mažiulis notes (oral communication) that the
location of <u>Laksde</u> in Lithuania is unknown.
11) Still Mažiulis says (oral communication) that
the <u>x</u> of <u>Polexia</u> can be read as <u>ś</u> or <u>š</u>.
12) Būga, 1961, 144 (= 1924, 83) says that
<u>Drohyczyn</u>, the capital of the <u>Pollexiani</u>, which the
Russians call <u>Dorogičinъ</u> is probably originally a
Slavic place name, cf. Polish <u>drogi</u>, Russian
<u>dorogoj</u> (= Latvian <u>dargs</u> 'dear'). In Būga's
opinion the basic proto-Slavic form would have
been *<u>Dargūkīnas</u> or *<u>Dargūkeinas</u>.
        Otrębski, 1961, 6, however, says that the
original form of the name was *<u>Darg-ūt-īnas</u> and
only changed into *<u>Darg-ūk-īnas</u> as a result of the
confusion of the palatal consonants <u>t'</u>, <u>d'</u>: <u>k'</u>, <u>g'</u>.
*<u>Darg-ūt-īnas</u> is to be interpreted as the name of
a place belonging to a certain *<u>Darg-ūt'</u>. Words with
the suffix -<u>ūtis</u> with a diminutive meaning are well
known in the Lithuanian language. In the former
territory of the Jatvingians, however, this suffix
is known in place names, e.g., <u>Bogūtis</u>, the name of
a lake near Seirijai. According to Otrębski, the
root <u>darg-</u> is known in the Baltic languages, but
rarely. In any case Otrębski mentions the Old
Prussian personal name <u>Dargel</u>. For some reason
Otrębski does not mention Latvian <u>dargs</u> 'dear.'
13) Mažiulis is of the opinion (oral communication)
that the <u>ē</u> of Sambian (Samland) dialect became <u>ī</u>
except in word-final position.
14) Būga, 1961, 127, (= 1924, 74) had connected the
Old Prussian <u>sups</u>, <u>subban</u> with the Slavic (Polish)
<u>swoboda</u>.
15) It should be pointed out here that Lithuanian
dialects also have imperative forms without -<u>k</u>.
Such forms are certainly derived from old optatives
in which the final *-<u>s</u> was lost as a result of an
assimilation with the reflexive particle.
Zinkevičius, 1966, 371, gives the forms for the
second singular as follows:

(į)a-stem	nèš'(ì)	nešiẽs 'carry'
i-stem	mylỹ	myliẽs 'love'
a-stem	rãšai	rãšais 'write'

16) Mažiulis (oral communication) suggests that
insuwis is remodeled according to a form similar
to Lith. liežùvis 'tongue.'
17) As I have noted in my 1974 work, 73-74 and
328, I would rather agree with Trautmann, 1909,
369, who says that the word would correspond with
a Lith. kaubrẽ. Apparently Trautmann merely guessed
at the possible existence of such a Lithuanian word,
but such a word is attested in the Academy Dictionary,
Vol. 5, p. 417.
18) One could also compare Old Prussian sausan with
Dacian Sausa.
19) Levin, 1974, 68, points out that rather than
Lith. vogõnè, the nearest Lithuanian cognate to
Old Prussian wogonis is vogõnas.
20) Levin, 1974, 101, counters Milewski's thesis
that glawo is evidence of the high prestige of
Polish with the statement that in those cases where
we find stylistic differentiation, the meaning
'head' is usually the lower meaning, cf., e.g.,
German Haupt 'leader, chief,' Kopf 'head,' Latin
caput 'head' (French chef), Latin testum 'pot'
(French tête 'head'), Russian golova 'head,'
glava 'chapter.'
21) Levin, 1974, 73, objects that the semantic
differentiation does not necessarily represent the
'degrading' of kelmis 'hat.' Likewise Levin objects
that the noun salmis does not seem to be a borrowing
from the period after the establishment of a strong
Slavic state bordering on Pomesania. If, as
Milewski suggests elsewhere, salmis was borrowed
from a Pomoranian dialect without metathesis, it
does not seem likely that the word would have had
the prestige that Polish supposedly had in Pomesania
before the conquest. The word may represent a pre-
metathesis Slavic *šelmъ, or perhaps an East Slavic
*šelmъ borrowed through Lith. šalmas. Levin quotes
Gimbutas, 1963, 167, who says that Russian helmets
have been found in the graves of Prussian feudal
lords from the 10th to the 12th centuries A.D.
22) Levin, 1974, 61, notes that Vilkuna, 1957/58,
has described the ancient European method of
keeping track of the days. This consisted of
inserting a peg in a seven-hole vertical calendar.
The top hole represented, of course, Sunday and

the middle hole represented Wednesday, so the Old
Prussian name does not necessarily represent a
calque from the German at all, but may well have
been created as a native word in Old Prussian to
denote 'Wednesday.'
23) Sabaliauskas finds that the meaning of palleyde
and Lith. paláidas, paléisti are perhaps too
different to allow one to establish an etymological
connection.
24) Mažiulis (oral communication) suggests a
possible correction of Warbo to Sargo (cf. gotte
for butte 'house').
25) Mažiulis objects (oral communication) that
elsewhere we never find the diphthong /au/ written
as a. On the other hand I might counter that this
could be a simple misprint, viz., the omission of
the letter u by the printer. Prof. Jules Levin has
pointed out to me (oral communication) that the
Old Prussian word for 'on' is no (or na), not
not *ant, which is posited merely on the basis of
Lith. añt 'on.'
26) Sabaliauskas suggests (oral communication)
that labonache may be a distorted form of lūbeniks
'priest' and that perhaps the translation should
read something like: "To your health, sir! You are
not a priest father if you want to drink and don't
want to pay money."
27) Mažiulis follows Būga, 1961, 133 (= 1924, LXXVII)
who says that pōs-kail(i)s would be the same as
Lith. pa sveikas 'a little bit more healthy, hello'
and similar to the expressions kakarýkuo pa
kakarýkuo, vis tą-patį gíed 'cockadoodle and (more)
cockadoodle, he keeps singing the same thing.'
According to Būga, on this model the Samogitians
would say: sveĩkas pà sveĩkas geria vyrai 'to one's
health (and even more) to one's health drink the
men.' The Sudovians would have pronounced such a
sentence as kailəs pōs kailəs.
28) But perhaps the forms pogeitty and puietti at
least are not imperatives. The first form occurs
in the Ist catechism (Trautmann, 1910, 7, line 30):
steweydan segeitty kodesnimma yous pogeitty pray
maian menisnan - Sōlches thut so offt jhrs trinckt
zu meinem gedechtnis. The second form occurs in the
IInd catechism (Trautmann, 1910, 13, line 31):

331

Stewidan segeyti kudesnammi joes puietti prey
mayian minisnan - Solches thut so offt jhrs
trincket zu meinem gedechtnis 'Do this as often as
you (shall) drink to my memory.' As a 2nd pl.
indicative form I would suggest a phonemicization
/pujete/ or /pājete/ (or, if there exists a phoneme
/ō/, /pōjete/). I would not be certain then of
the exact correspondence between these forms and
the form poyte of the Basel epigram.
29) Perhaps the *ny- is unnecessary and the epigram
refers to some student custom according to which the
person who didn't drink was required to pay money.
One could imagine a drinking game such that a person
who had finally reached his limit of drinking was
forced to pay for the drinks of others. Or perhaps
one might combine the suggestion of Sabaliauskas
(see footnote 26) with this latter suggestion and
interpret the sentence to read: "To your health,
sir! You aren't a priest father! (i.e., you don't
have to observe the rules of propriety). If you
want, drink; if you don't want to (or won't) drink,
then pay money." This would also explain the
apparent imperative forms of poyte and doyte.
30) Prof. Oswald Szemerényi has suggested to me
(oral communication) that the suffering of the
young man is occasioned not by having drunk too
much, but rather by the lack of alcoholic
refreshment, i.e., he needs a drink very badly.
31) Mažiulis suggests (oral communication) that
the graphemic sequence ei may stand for phonetic
[ií] and that the graphemic sequence ou may stand
for phonetic [uʮ], sounds similar to those found in
Samogitian Lithuanian dialects.
32) Mažiulis suggests (oral communication) that the
final -i of quai is not a particle but the result
of an analogical development according to (st-)ai.
33) Mažiulis objects (oral communication) that
there is no -i after the -u- in the following
examples: aucktimmiskū, deinenisku, laimisku,
perarwisku and asmu. Now many writing systems
sometimes use the same graphemes to denote several
different phonemes and sometimes use different
graphemes to denote the same phoneme. This was
certainly the case for the use of the Latin alphabet in Middle Low German, see Lasch, 1914, passim.

Therefore I suggest that in the case of
aucktimmisikai and asmai the final -ai merely
denotes a long vowel /ā/. In the case of
deinenisku, laimisku and perarwisku I assume a
stress somewhere other than on the final syllable
and that the final -i just wasn't noted by the
scribe. In view of the considerable usage of ů
to denote /ua/ in older Latvian and Lithuanian
texts, there would hardly seem to be anything surprising to find u denoting /uā/. The scribe was
obviously influenced by the labialization of the
preceding consonant.
34) Although the catechisms were indeed printed
texts it is appropriate to quote here Chaytor,
1945, 1, who wrote: "When we take up a printed
edition of a medieval text, provided with an introduction, a critical apparatus of variant readings,
notes and glossary, we bring unconsciously to its
perusal those prejudices and prepossessions which
years of association with printed matter have made
habitual. We are liable to forget that we are
dealing with the literature of an age when ortho-
graphical standards varied and grammatical accuracy
was not highly esteemed, when language was fluid
and was not necessarily regarded as a mark of
nationality..."
35) Mažiulis suggests (oral communication) as
better examples Lith. dial. mergas '(of the) girl'
(gen. sg.) where the -ā- is found (instead of -o-)
on analogy with the -a from the nominative singular.
Similarly vagāt for standard Lith. vagóti 'to make
furrows' beside dial. vagója = standard Lith. vagója
(3rd pres.). Likewise one finds dãs 'will give' =
standard Lith. duõs (3rd fut.) presumably on the
analogy of some unstressed form.
36) Mažiulis (oral communication) finds both the
contamination theory and the suggestion of Slavic
influence doubtful.
37) Burwell's ā₂ would have derived under unclear
conditions from an old short a.
38) Mažiulis (oral communication) objects that the
examples which I have given do not have reference
to the writing of *ā. The a in the 'mixed diphthongs' -ar- is, admittedly, a completely different
matter. Writings with -o- and -u- are probably

somehow connected with the well-known fact that
Germanic *-ō- was diphthongized to Old High German
-uo- and then finally monophthongized to Modern
German -u-.
39) Mažiulis objects (oral communication) that in
13th to 15th century texts the old *ā is written
only with the letter o, never with a. On the other
hand, apparently even the Proto-Baltic short *a is
rendered by o at times in the Elbing vocabulary,
cf. wobse [EV - 789] beside Lith. vapsà 'wasp.'
40) This was my view as I presented it in several
articles. I am more inclined now to accept Levin's
1975b view on the development of the Lithuanian
vocalic system. Previously I had assumed it was
necessary to connect the development of Indo-
European *ō to East Baltic uo in Latvian and
Lithuanian. I assume now a separate development in
the two languages, as does Mažiulis now (oral
communication). Mažiulis has also pointed out to
me that it is easier to explain Samogitian ọu as
deriving directly from *ō rather than from *uo.
41) The reason for this assumption is that there
seems to be no reason to propose that Latvian ā was
ever anything else but ā. Likewise the passage of
Proto-Baltic *ā to Lithuanian ō seems to be a
relatively recent phenomenon as we can see from the
rendering of Proto-Baltic *ā by a in Mosvidius
(Mažvydas).
42) One could perhaps imagine a lengthening of
Proto-Baltic short /e, a/ in stressed open syllables.
One might point out that OP ladis [EV - 56] 'ice'
may show a lengthened stressed vowel in the initial
syllable, since we do not find doubling of the
consonant -d-. On the other hand perhaps in
OP passalis [EV - 57] 'frost' the initial syllable
may have been short since we do find the doubling
of the -s-. The position of stress in this word
remains, of course, problematical.
43) Mažiulis points out (oral communication),
however, that perhaps this is not a good example,
because we also find Lith. grambolė.
44) Mažiulis reminds me again (oral communication)
of the possibility that the -a- in galwas-dellīks
is short. I think that in all probability Mažiulis
is correct in this assumption because we seem to

have clear evidence of the loss of short vowels in the final syllables, cf. deiws as opposed to deiwas (one time) as the nominative singular.

45) Mažiulis (oral communication) says that the words bordus and golis show the -o- in fundamentally different positions. In bordus the o is in a closed syllable and functions as the initial element of a 'mixed diphthong,' whereas in golis the o is in an open syllable.

46) Mažiulis (oral communication) suggests that the graphemic -ae- in Staey and Pallapsaey reflects /ā/. I tend to think that they might well reflect what the German scribe may have heard as /ā/, but I would not like to posit a long diphthong */āi/ which would be unknown elsewhere in Baltic or Slavic.

47) Mažiulis (oral communication) thinks that the genitive plural ending could well be -un. I agree that this is quite possible and concur with Mažiulis' opinion. An ending -un would fit very well with the evidence of the other Baltic languages.

48) Mažiulis (oral communication) points out that the confusion of i and e is all in the direction of e not i.

49) Mažiulis objects (oral communication) that the Lithuanian and Old Prussian parallels are not relevant because we have to do with a different system in the two instances.

50) Mažiulis (oral communication) considers it unlikely that the etymological accusative plural forms would have differed in Old Prussian and Lithuanian.

51) It might be pointed out that the usual stress of this word is láiškas, not laĩškas. This latter form, however, corresponds with the OP Lāiskas. For a full discussion see my 1974 work, footnote 13, 310-315.

52) According to Jules Levin (oral communication) this is a function of the feature system which allows for only two degrees of vocalic height. Those vowels which are -High +Low must be distinguished in some way or other and the easiest way to distinguish them in feature analysis is to consider rounding a concomitant feature of the -Long -High vocalic segments.

53) But perhaps this should be viewed as a disagreement on notational rather than substantive grounds.

54) The comments here are not directed against any particular individual as such, but rather against certain prevailing attitudes.

55) The shift in the position of the etymologically long and short low vowels could be explained by Labov's principle that peripheral vowels tend to rise and non-peripheral vowels tend to fall.

56) If Levin is right that a German scribe would have written <u>la</u> for palatalized <u>l</u> plus <u>e</u>, then perhaps <u>ladis</u> [EV - 56] 'ice' is a good example of this, cf. Lith. lẽdas 'id.'

57) According to Levin (oral communication) true phonemic palatalization exists only in languages like Russian which contrast a plain consonant with a consonant plus yod ($\underline{C}$ + $\underline{j}$) vs. a true palatalized consonant. Thus Levin says that even a surface structure palatalized consonant could be construed as an underlying consonant plus yod. There may have been phonetically palatalized consonants in Old Prussian, but the phonetic palatalization may not have been phonemically relevant.

58) The Academy Dictionary, Vol. 5, p. 738, lists the fifth meaning of pẽdẽ as <u>sandalas</u>.

59) Mažiulis points out (oral communication) that the German knights did not know either Lithuanian or Old Prussian.

60) Even within the IIIrd catechism we find one occurrence of <u>pogirschnan</u> and one occurrence of <u>pogirsnan</u> 'praise,' see Trautmann, 1910, 403. Likewise we find <u>pirschdau</u> 'before, in front of' most commonly, but also one occurrence of <u>pirsdan</u> (the latter to be corrected to <u>pirsdau</u> according to Trautmann, 1910, 399). We also encounter <u>usts</u> 'sixth' in the IInd catechism vs. <u>wuschts</u> in the Ist catechism and <u>uschtai</u> in the IIIrd catechism. Thus it would seem that for the translators of the catechisms at least there was no contrast between /s/ and /š/ after /r/ and /u/.

61) As mentioned in footnote 44, I believe that Mažiulis is right in seeing in <u>galwas-dellīks</u> a final short -<u>as</u>. Thus it would seem unlikely that word-final *-<u>ās</u> existed in Old Prussian.

Therefore the expectation that *-ās would turn up
as *-us or *-os would be quite vain. Historically,
of course, *-ās does seem to be represented by -as
in galwas-dellīks.
62) Endzelīns, 1943, 58, suggested that the -u was
from Indo-European *-ōi just like Gk. -ǭ and Lith.
-ui. I would suggest rather an etymological *-ō
here. Perhaps the -u denoted /-ua/. On the other
hand the -u may have stood for /(u)ai/ and the
scribe may just not have heard the final -i. Or
perhaps the final -i was just dropped in certain
types of speech. Other examples of the vacillation
between the writings -ai and -u are also found,
see 5.200, but chiefly following labial and velar
consonants.
63) This explanation, according to Endzelīns,
1943, 59, goes back to Berneker, 1896, 196 and
Brugmann, but Endzelīns objects, 1943, 60, that
the Old Prussians did not learn their paradigms
from grammars, in which the accusative case follows
immediately the dative case.
64) A. Girdenis (per litteras) suggests the
comparison of the forms in -ai with such a form as
Lith. tój = tóji, the nom. sg. fem. definite form
of tàs 'this, that.'
65) But the form menschon in Mažiulis' opinion
(oral communication) actually reflects a gen. pl.
pl. ending -un.
66) Mažiulis suggests, 1970, 311, that the
ending in the form perpettas 'slanderously'
(literally per- 'over,' -pettas 'the shoulders')
may be connected with the Sanskrit nom.-acc. pl.
(sen-)ās 'armies,' Gothic (gib-)os 'gifts,' Lith.
(ger-)ōs-(ias) 'the good,' = Latv. (maz-)ãs 'the
small' < *-ās-. Endzelīns, 1943, 64, quotes
Berneker, 1896, 195 and Bezzenberger, 1907, 81, for
a similar view, but Endzelīns also suggests that
perhaps the -as should be corrected to -ãs = -ans.
67) The genitive singular form of amsis could
possibly be phonemicized as /amzis/ if the noun
belongs to what Mažiulis, 1970, 264, terms a i₂-
stem class noun, i.e., an old non-apophonic
neuter gender. Of course, both amsis and nierties
could be etymological *ē-stem nouns, in which case
the gen. sg. ending would probably have been -es

< *-ēs.

68) Sabaliauskas (oral communication) would rather connect Slavic *pьs-ъ with Russian pestryj 'variegated.'

69) One may also compare the Lithuanian Samogitian dialect form lyjantie 'raining.'

70) Perhaps the -y of smoy merely denotes the length of the preceding vowel. One might suggest a possible phonemicization */zmō/ or */zmā/.

71) Mažiulis, 1970, 269-270, suggests that as a result of the loss of the *-u- in the nom. sg. soun-s 'son' the noun passed into the *o-stem category. This explains then the appearance of such *o-stem accusative singular forms as sounan, saunan, saunan. Mažiulis has also pointed out to me the existence of the Lith. *o-stem form pẽkas 'cattle.' (Oral communication.)

72) There is, of course, some dialect evidence for a Lithuanian *o-stem dative singular in *-ai < *-oi, in what Mažiulis, 1970, 134, calls non-paradigmatic case forms, usually adverbialized forms, cf., e.g., (lìg pačiám vãkar-)ie 'until evening.'

73) According to Jules Levin (oral communication) the statement to the effect that the spelling a for short [ae͡] does not occur, is, of course, limited to word-final position. An obvious example showing a for short [ae͡] is OP nadele (EV - 17) 'Sunday.'

74) Trautmann, 1910, 88, 353, transcribes this word as caryawoytis, not karyawoytis as does Levin. The word is hard to make out in Mažiulis, 1966a, 67.

75) Sabaliauskas, 1973, 244, writes that Eckert, who has been studying problems of the Indo-European heteroclitic declension particularly in the Baltic and Slavic languages, is inclined to find more examples in Latvian than in Lithuanian. Nevertheless, some of Eckert's examples seem suspicious to Sabaliauskas. For example, in addition to Lith. sáule, Latv. saũle, OP saule, Eckert also gives Latv. sàuls 'sun.' But this latter form comes eventually from a description of a Latvian dialect by L. Latkovsks (American version of the name Latkovskis) in which one of the most characteristic features is the passage of *ē-stem nouns into the i-stem category, cf., e.g., standard Latv. upe 'river,' which is rendered by dialect ups.

338

Thus one may suspect that Latv. sàuls is a modern
dialect feature rather than an ancient Indo-
European form.
76) There is the possibility that in closed
syllables the initial vowel of such Proto-Baltic
sequences as *-arC, *-alC, *-erC, *-elC was
lengthened and perhaps diphthongized, so that a
form *garmē > *garmē > goarme written as gorme.
77) Endzelīns, 1943, 75, says that in the IInd
catechism we find stes two times where e is either
from the 'bright' a or else from the other cases
in which we find the stem vowel -e-. But if the
-e- could be from the 'bright' a in two cases why
couldn't it be such in every case?
78) Mažiulis, 1970, 170-176, suggests that there
could well have been a pronominal stem nom. pl.
masc. *-ei giving Slavic ti 'these, those.' Other
evidence for this ending comes from Lith. tiẽ
'these, those,' Old Latin (SERV-)EI 'slaves,' etc.
Slavic forms such as (vlьc-)i 'wolves' which show
the second palatalization of the velar may come
from contaminations of *(vlьc-)ě with *(vlьč-)i,
in which the ending of the first form derives from
*-oi and the ending of the second form derives from
*-ei. Mažiulis' idea seems quite acceptable to me.
79) Bezzenberger, 1907, 109, suggested that *dis
became -ts and is represented in such forms as
astits 'is,' etc. It might be pointed out also
that the form din is used with prepositions too,
e.g., preidin 'to him' (Trautmann, 1910, 71),
kirsa din 'over him' (Trautmann, 1910, 57). Of
course, what develops in a verbal form may be
generalized to prepositional phrases also.
80) One may note the remarkable parallelism
between the Tokharian B genitive dual form
tainaisǚñ and the OP gen. pl. tenneison, tenneison,
tanassen, tanaessen, forms which I have phonemicized
as /tanasan/ or /tanaisan/, 1974, 125. See also
Krause-Thomas, 1960, 164.
81) Mažiulis (oral communication) suggests that
the phonemicization of schins could be /šins/.
There would be evidence for such a phonemicization
since we find, e.g., a Lithuanian nom. sg. masc.
form šìs 'this.' One can compare also the fact
that for the i-stem nouns we find the nominative

singular in -is beside an accusative plural in -is
< *-ins. In addition he suggests that perhaps the
gen. sg. fem. schisses could be phonemicized with
a short second vowel, viz., /šisǎs/. If this *a̅-
stem gen. sg. form is interpreted as being derived
from */šis+ja̅s/, then one might assume a
phonemicization /šišǎs/.
82) Zinkevičius, 1972, 163, notes that for the
southern Samogitian dialect forms of the third
person definite pronoun we find the acc. sg. fem.
jeñje (= standard Lith. ją̃ją) and the inst. sg.
fem. jénje (= standard Lith. ją́ją) in which the
*-n- has not disappeared before the spirant -j-.
Variants of these forms in which the *-n- and the
*-j- have been metathesized are acc. sg. fem. jeĩne
< jeĩnę and the inst. sg. fem. jéine respectively.
These variants have served as a model for the
creation of the nom. sg. masc. jeĩnis 'he,' nom.
sg. fem. jeĩnė 'she.' Thus in Zinkevičius'
opinion apparently the Lithuanian dialect forms
have nothing to do with OP ains, etc.
83) Mažiulis, 1964b, suggests that both East and
West Baltic retain traces of the Indo-European
doublets *tu̅ and *tŭ for the nominative singular of
the 2nd person pronoun. In standard Lithuanian tù
derives from *tu̅ whereas Samogitian tọ̀ derives from
*tŭ. Old Prussian tou derives from the form *tu̅
whereas tu derives from *tŭ. Probably the relationship between Baltic *tu̅ and *tŭ corresponds to the
tonic versus the atonic use of the personal pronoun,
cf. also Old High German du̅:du, etc. Possibly there
also had existed in Slavic a form *tŭ beside *tu̅ >
attested ty. The form *tŭ would have merged with
tь 'that' < *tos.
84) The word kermeneniskan occurs as a noun in the
following expression (Trautmann, 1910, 35, line 32):
ka̅igi stwi ast steisi pickullas stessei Swi̅tas bhe
nou̅son kermeneniskan qua̅its - Als da ist des
Teuffels der Welt und unsers fleisches wille - since thi
is the will of the devil, the world and our flesh.'
Trautmann, 1910, 356, labels this a feminine
accusative singular noun. It would indeed seem to
be accusative singular in form, but it is unclear to
me why it has to be labeled feminine. Perhaps
because it is apparently an abstract noun derived

from an adjective. The syntax of the construction
would seem to require a genitive case here, but the
form seems to be clearly an accusative, unless,
perhaps, one understands this as a genitive plural.
I would assume that this form, although used as a
noun, is originally an adjective.
85) See Mažiulis, 1970, 83, who also suggests
that the Balto-Slavic neuter singular form was in
*-o and as such is a greater archaism than OP
(assar-)an 'lake' (EV - 60) = Greek (dōr-)on 'gift.'
86) Mažiulis (oral communication) has suggested to
me that such a form as mile could actually be an
etymological preterit used as a present tense. I
am rather impressed by this thought, since we cannot,
of course, be certain that Abel Will really knew
the difference between the present and the preterit
tenses. See also paragraph 8.301.
87) The form asmau (which occurs once according to
Trautmann, 1910, 29, 304) is possibly a misprint
for *asmua, a form parallel with asmu, but one in
which the -a is expressed in the orthography,
whereas elsewhere the -u- itself may be sufficient
to express what the Germans heard as the diphthong
/ua/. (Cf. also gallu 'head' beside galwas-delliks
'chief article.') The symbol ų was used in earlier
Latvian and Lithuanian texts to denote /ua/, so it
would seem probable that it might have had the same
function in Old Prussian. One might object that in
Latvian and Lithuanian there is a small o written
above the u, whereas in Old Prussian this small o
is lacking. On the other hand, although we know
that Hans Weinreich had a small e to put above
various vowels, we do not know whether he had an o
or not. At least we never find one in the texts of
the catechisms. Perhaps Weinreich received a manuscript with the small o written above the u, but he
merely chose to disregard it. My own impression
from years of reading proof is that printers seem
to take delight in omitting diacritics, or at least
in using the wrong diacritic if there is a possibility
of confusion.
88) I am inclined to agree with Bezzenberger who
wrote, 1874a, 42, that the orthographic sequences
-tai, -tei, -ti all stand for -te.

89) B. Jēgers suggests (per litteras) that the
second element of Aclocordo reminds one of Middle
High German korde 'rope, string.' Although the
word is a borrowing from French it might be
interesting to investigate whether the word was
used in the Baltic area in the early centuries of
this millenium.
90) močùtę should probably be corrected to močiùtę.
91) See also para. 3.303, but Mažiulis (oral
communication) considers the word to be a native
Baltic word. I myself don't see how it could be
derived from a form *bhrendis, as Duridanov, 1969,
21, suggests, if the word is a native Baltic word.
92) Both Sabaliauskas (oral communication) and
B. Jēgers (per litteras) have suggested to me that
a dog such as the curtis was most probably
imported.
93) Jēgers (per litteras) recalls his own explanation (1969, 87) according to which Latvian druvêtiês
'to be alarmed, to be frightened,' and more
especially sadruvêt 'to threaten, to frighten; to
take offence, to worry oneself' are to be compared.
Jēgers objects to Marstrander's explanation since
the word trûwen is never used as a Christian term
as Marstrander, 347, himself points out. Why should
the Old Prussians have taken the word trûwen and
changed its meaning rather than take the common
and long attested glöuben, etc.?
94) Levin, 1974, 102-103, proposes a very similar
etymology, adding Lith. lóžė 'bowing of grain under
the weight of the ears,' ložìntis 'to wager,'
Latv. ležna, leža 'lazybones.'
95) Fraenkel, 1955, 432, would also connect Lith.
meĩsti 'to pray,' etc. See also Jēgers,
Commentationes Balticae 4, 1956/57, 29-39.
96) Jēgers suggests (per litteras) that maybe one
should compare rather Lith. kaĩsti 'to heat' (root
kait-) with an etymological meaning 'to burn,'
hence 'to want eagerly,' cf. the English expression
burning desire and Latvian degt 'to burn' in the
sense 'to be seized by a burning passion, desire.'
97) Levin, 1974, 60, suggests, however, that the
word ketwirtire really does attest to an Old Prussian
suffix *(i)re. Additional words with this suffix
may be paustre (EV - 624) 'wilderness,' sixdre

(EV - 737) 'yellowhammer (bird),' cf. sixdo (EV - word 26) 'sand,' passupres (EV -225) 'wood rack on a kitchen wall' (see suppis [EV - 327] 'millpond dam'). The form ketwirtire could then be original and need not be corrected to ketwirtixe, ketwirtice, ketwirtico or the like.

98) Sabaliauskas, 1966, 112-113, writes that OP Possissawaite 'Wednesday,' formed on the model of German Mittwoch, appeared in some East Prussian Lithuanian dialects. (But see footnote 22.) As a result of a misunderstanding of the word pussewaite, in Nesselmann's 1851 dictionary there appeared the name of the week, waite. Apparently Nesselmann, having gotten from the area of Labguva the word Pussewaite 'Wednesday,' incorrectly divided it into the two parts Pusse- and -waite. Later Nesselmann, 1873, 138, noted that this word should be dropped from his 1851 Lithuanian dictionary. See 3.507.

99) Jēgers (per litteras) disputes Zaimov's connection of weders with Slavic věděti and asks: 'What does the snail know?' The snail is rather an animal which crawls on its belly or has a large belly and this is the origin of the Bulgarian word veder.

Abbreviations

Bulg. - Bulgarian
EV - Elbing vocabulary
fn. - footnote
Ger. - German
Gk. - Greek
GrA - Königsberg university library copy of Simon
    Grunau's vocabulary
GrC - Königsberg government archives copy of Simon
    Grunau's vocabulary
GrF - University of Helsinki copy of Simon Grunau's
    vocabulary
GrG - Göttingen university library copy of Simon
    Grunau's vocabulary
GrH - Hartknoch's copy of Simon Grunau's vocabulary
Latv. - Latvian
Lith. - Lithuanian
MHG - Middle High German
OCS - Old Church Slavic
OHG - Old High German
OP - Old Prussian
S.Cr. - Serbo-Croatian
Skt. - Sanskrit

Word Index

For most of the languages in the word index
the alphabetical order observed is that of the
Latin alphabet as used for standard American English
The exceptions are as follows: 1) for Greek the
alphabetical order of the Greek alphabet is used;
2) for Estonian, Finnish, Latvian, Lithuanian and
the Slavic languages, the alphabetical order is
that of the standard dictionaries; 2) for Serbo-
Croatian the order of the Croatian Latin alphabet
is observed. The numbers following each word refer
to the paragraphs, not to the pages.

Albanian

drā, drǝ-ni - 10.028
*kēsk', kohë, korɛ -
   10.051

shi - 10.104
zjarm - 8.500

Anglo-Saxon
(see Old English)

Arabic

Brus, Burus - 1.007,
   fn. 2
B^{u}rūs - 1.005, fn. 2

Jintiar, Jintiaz -
   2.010

Armenian

akaws - 11.105
aĭk'at - 10.056
gaṙn - 10.033
lezu - 10.042

ôj, auj - 6.971
oroǰ - 10.033
sirt - 6.703
siseṙn - 10.048

Avestan

gafya - 2.106
hizvā - 10.042
kū - 5.101
mana - 7.802
pasu- - 5.610

raōxšna- - 6.910
sraōniš - 6.971
vâ - 7.809
yār- - 10.033
yūš - 7.806
yūžǝm - 7.806

Baltic

-ait- - 6.981
*Ant-iv-ing-as - 2.010
*artla[n] - 10.004
*at-volas, *at-volis -
   10.010
bal-, bel-, bil-, -
   2.112
*bē - 10.018
*bhrendis - fn. 91
*birg- - 10.127
*darg-, *Dargūtĭnas -
   2.803, fn. 12
*der- - 10.026
*dī- - 10.027
dul-b, dul-g, dul-k,
   dul-v - 2.103
*'dvar-as - 6.965
*ei- - 10.017
-eit- - 6.981
*ekētē - 11.105
*ež - 7.800
*gǎl- - 1.193

-gala, *Gala,
   *Galindā, Galindo
   - 1.190
gem- - 4.205
*gerbh- - 10.039
*gī- -10.038
*Jāta, *Jātuva,
   *Jātuvingai - 2.006
*Jāt-vā - 2.007
Jotva - 2.008
*jūsōn - 7.807
kait - fn. 96
*karikis, *ker-,
   *kir- - 10.128
kirmis - 10.126
krēs-, kres- - 2.807
*leǧh- - 10.055
*leipā - 2.100
*Lei-t[u]va - 2.007
*Lukas - 2.501
*mai - 11.002
*maigti - 11.006

*maldas - 10.063
med- - 2.801
*Nebēst- - 2.015
*nóšōn - 7.807
*ǒlisǒ - 10.002
*Pa-luk-s-ija - 2.502
pel-, pl- - 10.083
*Perkūn- - 9.120
*perkūni, *perkūnī,
  *perkūniā - 10.082
*p°/avīd-tis - 10.086
*Prūsa - 1.008
*qer-, *qerd- - 10.049
*'rag-as - 6.965
*sai - 11.002
Saud-, Sud-, Sūd- 2.002
*seitan - 10.129

*skēi, *skī- - 10.036
sūd- - 2.002, 2.004
*Sūdava - 2.003
*šeinas - 2.810
*tai - 11.002
*tā-u, *tī, *tāv-ė -
  2.812
*tū - 7.801
*uait- - 10.114
*⌣udā - 2.016
*u̯ōsón - 7.807
*valgiaitē - 11.005
*vas, **vōs - 7.809
*Vel- - 9.120
*vina- - 7.700
*žeg- - 10.099
žvaid-, žvaig- -
  10.106

Bashkir
otlangan kün - 10.117

Belorussian
abmahac' - 9.010
artaj - 9.032
bryzgul' - 9.032
burvalak - 9.032
vahán - 3.401
vajcjać - 9.031
vjazy - 9.032
l'ado - 1.191, 10.060
l'adzina - 1.191

nautda, nikać - 9.032
pasojta, pasta - 9.032
peramoha - 9.010
čerëvo - 10.126
Jatvez' - 9.200
Jatfa - 2.208
Jac'viž - 2.601

Breton
lann - 1.191, 10.060   oguet - 11.105

Bulgarian
veder - 10.116, fn. 99   povest - 10.086
kruša - 3.502   šte - 10.088
kuk, kuker, kukir -   jasto - 6.974
  10.021
leda, ledina - 1.191

Celtic
Hercynia - 10.082   *nǒvis - 6.971
Landes - 1.191   ocet - 11.105
                   (Cornish)

Cheremis & Chuvash
kuškožmo - 10.117   etlarńi gon - 10.117
  (Cheremis)   (Chuvash)

Czech

Havránek - 10.115
lada, lado - 1.191
máčeti, makati -
   10.066 (Old Czech)
nese - 8.112
obora - 10.001

pověst - 10.086
řitězně - 3.412
tina - 2.812
udáti se - 10.012
ujec - 3.200
vran, vrána - 10.115

Dacian

Bálauson, Burtinus -
   3.305
Bersovia - 3.301
Boutae, Boúttis -
   3.302
Drasdea - 3.305

Galtis - 3.305
Hresidína - 3.305
Sausa - 3.305, fn. 18
Scaugdae, Skabēs -
   3.305
Tautomedes - 3.305

Danish

hyben - 3.203

Dutch

slinderen - 10.057

English

Aistian - 1.000, 1.002,
   1.003, 1.005
bed - 10.036
burning - fn. 96
class, clean, clear -
   5.620
dead - 10.036
desire - fn. 96
Frisian - 1.008
from - 10.036
he - 6.040, 10.036
her, him - 6.040
hip - 10.043
Ilfing - 1.003
Jatvingian - 2.006,
   2.009, 2.408
loam - 10.059
Mazovian - 2.005

narrows - 10.072
nettle - 10.073
Prussian - 1.005, 1.009
read - 9.400
rose - 10.036
she - 6.040
stone - 5.325
Sudovian - 2.001,
   2.005, 2.006
thaw - 2.812
their, there - 9.400
us - 6.040
Vaidelota - 4.222
want - 10.088
warm - 8.500
we - 6.040
window - 10.003

kadakas - 10.044
ütelda - 10.086

Estonian

äes - 11.105

ankerias - 5.917
jutella, juttu -
   10.086
kala - 3.203
katajas - 10.044

Finnish

lohi - 5.317
paimen - 10.077
vuota - 5.317
äes - 11.105

kūto - 10.050
Kicher - 10.048
Kindlein - 6.802
kindt - 4.204
klette - 5.600
kniendt - 6.706
kommen - 3.506, 4.702
Kopf - fn. 20
krantz - 4.703
Krebisdorff - 4.700
Kuijel, kuijeln -
    10.109
kujel - 3.602, 10.109
Kulmerland - 1.111
Kummet - 5.605
Kurp - 10.054
kurtze - 8.062
Labiau - 2.811
Laksde - 2.302
lange - 4.700
lasset, lieber - 8.062
Laufft - 4.704
leffel - 5.600
Leiblich - 7.910
leid - 4.717
leimet - 4.204
leitseyl - 10.004
Lescowiz, Lesewicz - 6.980
lieber - 8.062
liebes - 4.702
liegen - 3.506
liess - 6.709
malcz - 11.008
man - 4.202
margéll, marjéll -
    3.602
maul - 4.601, 10.008
mehr - 4.711
mehret, mich - 8.510
mein - 4.702
meinem - fn. 28
Menschen - 6.709
mir - 8.062
mit - 6.709, 9.141
Mittwoch - 3.507, fn. 98

Most - 4.204
Nachmahd - 10.101
namen - 10.081
Narmeln, Neria, Nerije,
    Nerung, Nerunge -
    10.072
neeren - 8.510
Nehrung - 1.008,
    10.072
Nemlich - 7.910
Nessel - 10.073
nicht - 4.601, 4.711,
    6.802, 10.008,
    10.081
nim - 11.005
nit - 4.207
Nolde, nolden - 4.204
o - 4.702
Ochsen - 4.601, 10.008
oder - 6.706
offt - fn. 28
Oppen - 5.314
palleyde - 3.600,
    fn. 23
palwe - 3.602, 9.060
parlenke, porrepil -
    3.600
pawirpen, powirpen -
    3.601, 10.087
pēde - 9.050
pinsch, pintsch -
    3.602
potter, puttir -
    4.204
Preussen, Prûzzen -
    1.005
Pusch - 10.041
Puschkaytus - 9.141
Rad - 6.300, 8.040
Rappe - 10.089
rockke - 4.217
ros - 5.600
Sahm - 9.040
Sajna, Sajno -
    2.810

Saluitz - 6.980
sambt - 9.141
Samland - 4.702, 9.040
sauffen - 4.704
Schaaken - 5.313
Schein - 9.300
Schlaff - 6.709
schlaffen - 11.006
Schlitten, Socken,
　söller, Sonnabend,
　Stieftochter,
　Stoppel, Stube -
　5.605
Schönau - 10.105
Schroter, stechmess' -
　5.600
sebengest'ne,
　stopassche - 4.100
seid, sich - 8.510
sein - 3.506
seinen, Sohn - 6.802
setzen - 4.703
sie - 4.703, 9.141
slusim, sorgalio,
　sunde, sweike -
　3.600
so, Solches, Sōlches -
　fn. 28
solt - 4.601, 10.008,
　10.081
Sonnenstuhl - 4.700
stehendt - 6.706
stelle - 8.062
stos, Sudawen - 4.702
Sudauen - 2.408, 9.141
Sudauischer Winkel -
　1.300
Sudlant, Sudowerland -
　2.408
Talk(e) - 3.601
Tapiau - 2.811
tauen, Tawe, Tawelle -
　2.812
teig, teigig, teigicht -
　10.025

Teuffel - 4.704
Teuffels - fn. 84
Thingsus - 10.118
thut, trincket,
　trinckt - fn. 28
tieffen - 6.709
treber - 11.008
treiber - 4.702
Treuge - 4.203
trinck - 4.217, 11.005
trincke, tuch - 4.703
Trincken - 11.005
Uggehnen - 5.314
uñ - 8.510
und - 6.706, 6.802,
　9.101, fn. 84
Unnd - 6.802
unnützlich - 10.081
unser - 4.701, 4.703,
　6.706
unsers - fn. 84
Vater - 6.706, 6.802
VAter - 4.701
verbinden - 4.601,
　10.008
verheisen - 6.802
vnd - 4.704
vnglaubigen - 9.141
vorvues - 5.700
Vrische Mer - 1.008
Vuerstant - 2.105
Wagentreiber - 4.702
waidelotte - 3.508,
　3.600
Waidelotten, Weidelot-
　ten - 10.112
Waiting, Weiting -
　10.111
Warp - 10.015
weise - 8.062
Weisse, Wesze, Wimat -
　4.204
weissen - 4.703
Weissenberg - 4.700
Welt - 6.802, fn. 84

wende, will – 8.510
wenig, weniger – 6.802
werben – 4.208
Wie – 9.141
wille – fn. 84
wils – 4.206
wiltu – 4.207, 6.706
Wind – 7.700
wird – 8.013
witing – 3.600, 10.111
Wo – 4.207

Woche, Wochen – 3.506
Wolken – 5.605
Wonditten, Workeim,
   Wormditt, Wotter-
   keim – 5.314
wort – 6.709
Zarm, Zerm – 3.601
zeeb – 10.129
zu – 4.703, 4.704,
   8.062, fn. 28

Germanic

*fergunja – 10.082
*freska, *Frūsa,
  *Frūsja – 1.008
Ing(u)aevones – 1.008
*mōder – 5.801
*natilōn, *natōn –
  10.073

*rape – 10.089
*trūwēn, *trūwō- –
  10.029, fn. 93
*þauan – 2.812
Wit-land – 1.008
*xelmaz – 3.403,
  3.405

Gothic

ahva – 10.005
aistan – 1.004
broþar – 5.801, 6.702
dagis – 6.014
dalaþ – 11.003
du – 10.029
fadar – 6.702
faíhu – 5.610, 6.600
faírguni – 10.082
fōn – 6.910
fraslindan – 10.057
funins – 6.910
gastins – 6.505
gibos – fn. 66
guda – 10.029
guma – 6.983
haihs – 10.075
jaind – 11.003
jer – 10.033
jus – 7.806
land – 1.191, 10.060

mais – 6.801
nauþs – 3.203
nawis – 6.971
niunda – 3.005
-ozan – 6.802
rimis – 10.020
samaþ – 11.003
sarwa – 10.095
stains – 5.325
trauan – 10.029
tuggo – 10.042
þis – 6.014
þizai, þizos –
  7.010
þwahan – 3.203, 10.110
waírilos – 3.203
wars – 11.004
wulf-is – 6.014

Greek

Abalus – 1.001
aíkloi – 10.016
haímata – 3.004

’ákmōn – 6.701
alphḗ – 10.006
aulōn – 10.014

akhlús - 10.005
Galíndai - 1.000
didáskōn - 10.018
dídosai - 8.107
dōron - fn. 85
egố - 7.800
élaphon - 3.303
ériphos - 10.033
ễn - 10.018
ēréma - 10.020
tha, thélō - 10.088
thermós - 8.500
iota - 1.001
ipnós, i-po-no
  (Mycenean) - 10.118
kak-ithḗs - 10.117
kapnós - 10.043
káptō - 10.030
kardía - 10.101
kễr - 6.703, 10.101
klónis - 6.971
Kóraks - 10.115
kórus, korússein -
  10.095
koruphḗ - 2.301
kúrnoi - 10.022
lúseia, lúseias,
  lúseie - 8.061
meno- - 8.500
na - 10.088
né(F)os - 6.940
nóthoi - 10.022

'ógmos, ǒksina -
  11.105
'ónoma - 4.220
Osioi, Ostiatoi,
  Ostoi - 1.001
ǒphnís - 6.910
Pán - 9.121, 9.140,
  9.145
páter - 6.702
patḗr - 6.701
pékein, pékos - 5.610
peúkē - 5.406
poimḗn - 10.077
pólins - 6.505
pósis - 3.006, 6.910
prósōpon - 10.090
pũar - 9.140
pónō - 5.300
hrougós - 10.090
soudinoí - 1.000
stúphein, stuphtheís,
  stúphō - 10.090
tau - 1.001
húein - 10.104
phéromai - 8.100
phérousa - 10.042
phrā́ter - 5.801
kheílea - 10.090
khõrai - 6.340
hṓra- 10.033

Hittite

a-da-an-za - 11.009
akkala - 11.105
alkišta(n)- - 10.058
anda kariⱼa- - 10.095
eku- - 10.005
halkueššar, halkuešnaš -
  10.006
hallu-, halluwanu -
  10.014
huppar - 10.118

hurtaiš - 6.400
ish-as - 6.014
karates-teš, *ker, ki-ir
  10.101
palzaḫḫa- - 10.082a
perunaš - 10.082
šer kariⱼa - 10.095
tuḫuš(š)iya- - 10.108
ⱡaⱡarkima - 10.037
zaḫhaiš - 6.400

Icelandic

gap - 2.106
hlaun - 6.971

Nárōn - 10.070

adæg - 11.105
  (Ossetian)

korpa - 2.301
suddi - 2.004

Illyrian

Iranian

*kur-na - 10.022
panu - 6.910

Jatvingian

Berzniki - 2.810
bílsas - 2.111, 2.112
Cresmen - 2.808
Deimě, Deimenà -
  2.811
dùlgas - 2.102, 2.111,
  2.112

is - 2.204
kirsna- - 3.200
seina - 2.809
Sejna, Sejny - 2.810
Skomand - 2.805, 2.808
Tainas - 2.812
*-udā - 2.404
Zelwa - 2.810

Kurdish

kotir - 10.050

Latin

Ador - 4.217
anguis - 6.971
aquā - 10.005
Ars - 4.401
Ausca - 9.104
Barthia - 1.140, 1.190,
  1.194
Borussi, Borussia -
  1.005
Borusus - 3.503
Borvssorum - 9.141
Bruzi - 1.005, 1.007
caecus - 10.075
caput - fn. 20
causa - 10.086
cicer - 10.048
clibanus - 4.700
clūnis - 6.971
coāgulum - 10.090
coeli - 9.101
coelis - 4.701
Colmensis - 1.110, 1.111
cor - 6.703
Crasima - 2.808
Crasimam, Crasime -

  2.804
credere - 10.029
Cresmen - 2.804, 2.805,
  2.806, 2.807, 2.808
Curlandia - 4.400
Dadosesani - 3.409
Dainowe - 2.408
De - 9.141
dea - 9.104
denowe - 2.600
deum - 9.101
dingua - 10.042
egō - 7.800
equae - 6.340
es - 4.701
est - 9.104
et - 9.101, 9.141
ferctum - 10.127
*fergo - 10.127
fīō - 11.106
foideratei - 6.061
formus - 5.400
fracēre, fracēs,
  fracesco - 10.028
frater - 6.702

forum - 4.700
Galindia - 1.190
Getae - 3.302
Getai, Getta,
    Gettarum, Getwese -
    2.008
glēsum - 3.508
grūs - 1.006
Hestis - 1.002
homō - 6.701, 6.983
Idolatria - 9.141
in - 4.701
Jatwesen - 2.600
Jentuesones, Jentuosi -
    2.010
lapideus - 4.700
Lethonia - 4.400
līmus - 10.059
Lubovia - 1.110
lūna - 6.910
maior, minor - 4.401
Martis dies - 10.117
Nadrovia - 1.170
Nadrovius - 9.040
Nattangia - 1.140
    1.158, 1.194
nēmo - 6.983
noster - 4.701
novus - 6.940
occa - 11.105
palus, pratum - 4.700
pater - 4.701, 6.701-2
pecu - 6.600
pecus - 5.610
Percunas - 4.222
Pogesani - 1.130
Pogesania - 1.122,
    1.130, 1.140
Polexia - 2.500, 2.502,
    fn. 11
Pollexiani - 2.012,
    2.408, 2.500, fn. 12
Pomesania - 1.120, 1.121
pons - 4.700
potis - 6.910

Potus - 4.217
Pruciam, Prucorum,
    Pruschia, pruteni,
    prutheni, Pruze,
    Pruzis, Pruzorum,
    Pruzos, Pruzze,
    pruzzi, Pruzziae,
    Pruzzorum - 1.005
Prussus - 9.040
Prutia - 4.400
Pruzi - 1.007
quercus - 10.082
qui - 4.701
qvei - 6.061
radiorum - 9.104
rupēs, rupis - 6.400
sab(b)aticum - 10.093
sacrificiis - 9.141
salve - 4.710
Sambia - 1.160
Sambria - 4.400
Samius - 9.040
sanctificetur - 4.701
Saturnus - 9.101
Scalovia - 1.180
Secale - 4.217
sedēre - 8.401
sēmen - 6.704, 6.910
servei - 6.061, fn. 78
silva - 2.002, 10.082
Sol - 9.102
solis - 9.104
Sudeta silva - 2.002
Sudi, Sudow-enses,
    Sudow-ienses, Sudow-
    ite, Sūduva - 2.001
Sudovia - 1.181
Sudowie - 2.804, 2.808
terra Sudorum - 2.001,
    2.408
terrae - 9.101
terrula Cresmen -
    2.804, 2.808
testum - fn. 20
trium - 4.700

355

356

358

rāt - 10.011
rauda, raudas - 2.404
raûgs, raûgt, raûkt,
 rukt - 10.090
rìks, rìkuôt - 10.091
sadruvêt - fn. 93
saki - 10.094
saũle - 6.910, fn. 75
sàuls - fn. 75
sàuss, strazds - 3.305
sa-vāri - 10.001
savęlk, savìlktiês -
 10.090
sawu, Schwanna,
 Siszen - 9.302
Semmes - 4.218, 4.219,
 4.226
sešas - 3.506
sešiniece, sešņiece -
 3.506
sęta, sěti, sětlaũki -
 10.100
sev - 3.006
siêts, sijât - 10.129
symmes - 4.218, 4.226
sir̂senis, sir̂sins -
 6.910
skâbs - 3.305, 10.090
skaluot - 4.224
smadzenes, smedzenis,
 smedzeņi - 10.065
sud-eksis - 2.002
suns - 10.105
svalbadi - 4.226
svētīts, svets - 4.223
sviêsts - 10.007
swalbadi - 4.218
šwehts - 4.219
Sweytz - 4.218, 4.219,
 4.223
šķiets - 10.036
-t - 3.007
tā - 4.225
taɑe - 4.218, 4.225,
 4.226

tam, tev - 3.006
tãrpa, těrpa, tèrpt -
 10.031
tavs, Thews, tows - 4.223
taws, tehws - 4.219
tev -3.006
tęvainis, tęvs - 4.601
Thewes - 4.218, 4.219,
 4.223, 4.225
Thol, Tholpes - 4.218
thowe, Tolpes - 4.226
thowes - 4.218, 4.219,
 4.223, 4.226
thu - 4.218, 4.226
tik - 10.090
tikrs - 10.107
trešs - 3.005
tur - 4.206
ûdens - 2.016, 6.910
un - 4.223
unde - 4.218, 4.223,
 4.226
uodzis - 6.971
uoguot, -uot - 4.224
uôsis - 5.301, 5.701
uosta, uosts - 3.201
uõte, uotiņa, uotīte,
 uõts - 2.011
upe, ups - 6.976, fn. 75
uzruocīt, uzruotīt -
 10.114
vãciẽtis - 6.981
vaĩcât, *vaics, *vaicis,
 Vaiķis, *vaitāt,
 *vaitēt, *vaitinât,
 *vaitis, *vaitīt,
 Vaĩtnieks, Vaĩts,
 Vītiņi, Vitiņš -
 10.114
vaidelis - 3.508
vaisla - 10.117
vāls - 10.010
(v)alstība - 4.226
vārds, virs, Vnde -
 4.223

359

vārna - 10.115
vārsti, vārstīt -
  10.037
vãrti - 6.950
vêdars, vêders - 10.116
vētra - 3.201
viŋa - 7.701
viŋš - 7.700, 7.701
visa - 4.223, 4.226
wãrdtcz, wedde,
  wursson - 4.223
walstibe - 4.225
wardes - 4.218, 4.219,
  4.220, 4.223, 4.225,
  4.226

wards, wisse - 4.219
wede - 4.218, 4.219
wysse, worsumi - 4.226
Worsunij - 4.218,
  4.223
wusse - 4.218, 4.219,
  4.223, 4.226
zâle - 5.300
zeme - 5.918
zināt - 9.300
zuose - 6.972
zvaidrīt, zvaigala -
  10.106
zvàigzne - 9.300, 10.106
zweytzgisch - 4.226

Lithuanian

ãčiū - 2.305
Agiõnė, Ãgumas, ãklas,
  aklà, aĩmės - 10.005
áičvaras, áitas,
  áit(i)varas - 10.017
aĩgara, aĩgaras -
  10.016
aisčiai, Aisetã,
  Aisetaĩ, Aĩsetas,
  Aistà, Aistija -
  1.004
aĩt - 5.707
akà, ãkas, akéčios,
  aketė̃, akéti, akìs -
  11.105
ãkys - 6.709
aklãvirvė - 10.004
akmo - 3.503
akmuõ - 6.014
algà - 10.006
algõs - 5.401, 5.805,
  6.310
alìksnis, alksnà,
  Aĩksnas, aĩksnis -
  10.002
Alytùs - 2.702
alùs - 3.500, 6.600
anas - 4.711
angìs, ántis - 6.971

añt - 4.601, 6.709,
  fn. 25
añtrą - 4.704
ap-, ãparos, apì-varos,
  apý-varos, apý-voras,
  ãpvaros - 10.001
apgalė, ap-kéikti,
  atveřpti - 9.010
apnìkti - 10.071
ar - 9.300
ardýti, arvas - 10.009
ãria - 4.601, 6.709
árklas, arklãvirvė -
  10.004
árti, artójas - 2.113
aš - 7.800
ašvà - 5.001
Ašvijà - 5.931
atólas - 10.010
atskíesti - 10.036
atúoda(u)giai,
  atúodogiai - 10.024
áugti - 4.204
auksakalỹs, auksìnis -
  3.501
áukštas - 2.113, 10.077
aũlas, aulỹs - 10.014
-auninkas, -auti -
  4.224

360

dérgti - 10.028
deřkti - 9.300
dẽst, ḍesti - 5.707
dét, déti - 5.702
deviñtas - 3.005
diena - 10.018
diẽvas - 3.001, 4.501,
  9.101
Diẽvo rýkště - 9.110
dimstis - 6.978
dìrba - 6.961
dirbãs - 11.106
dyréti, dýrojo, dýroti -
  8.402
diřti - 10.026
dodi - 4.223
dóna, dōnininkai -
  5.702
dosnùs - 5.303
Drabùžis - 5.935
dragės - 3.501, 6.903
draũdžia - 8.053
Drava, Drujà, Drúoja -
  1.171
drūtas - 10.089
Dubýsa - 5.932
duktẽ - 6.702, 6.703
dùkter, dùkter' - 6.702
dukterès, dukteřs -
  6.703, 6.709
Dul̃-b-is, dū̃liava,
  dul̃-k-as, dùl-k-ti,
  Dul̃-k-upis, Dùl-pis,
  Dùl-upis, Dul-v-as,
  dul-v-éti - 2.103
Dùlgas - 2.102, 2.103,
  2.112
dùlkės - 2.305
dūnininkai - 7.701
dúoja - 2.114
dúokel' - 8.066
dúomi - 4.206
duomies - 8.101
dúona - 3.200, 5.702
dúonos - 4.501, 4.503

duõs - 4.501, 4.502
  fn. 35
dúoti - 2.114, 5.303
dùrys - 9.020
ẽdis - 6.200, 6.974
ẽglė - 2.305, 5.001,
  6.401, 6.976, 10.004
eglìs, eglìšakė -
  6.976
ẽgu - 4.713
eiglùs, eiklùs, einùs¡
  eĩtena, éit(i)varas, -
  10.017
eĩkel', esle - 8.066
eykete - 4.202, 8.063
eĩki, eĩkite - 8.063
eĩnam(e) - 8.110, 8.202
eĩnat(e) - 8.110
Eĩšìškės - 5.934
eĩt - 5.800, 8.110
eĩti - 5.707
ekėčios, eketẽ, ekéti -
  11.105
élnė - 5.001, 6.401
éngti (eñgti) - 10.013
er - 9.300
éras - 6.930, 10.033
erẽlis - 6.910
ésti - 3.002
eš̌ - 7.800
ežẽ - 6.401
ež(e)gỹs - 2.104
ẽžeras - 2.302, 5.001
Ežerỹnas - 5.935
Ẽžerūna, Ẽžeruona -
  5.937
Gáil-iekas, Gáil-intas -
  2.702
gãlas - 1.193, 5.400
galéti - 1.190, 11.004
galià, Galindai, gelmẽ,
  gilùs - 1.193
Galinčius, Galìnda, Galìndas,
  Galindis, Galindžius,
  Galìniai, galìnis

362

365

6.708, 6.983
žmuõi - 6.708
žõdis, žõgis - 2.108
žõdžio - 6.400
žolė̃ - 5.300, 10.055

gadà'g - 10.044

arwes - 4.203
eppil - 4.203

kruša - 3.502

bréndon - 3.303

blo - 5.605
commot - 5.605
driuua, drôst, drûên,
  drûwe, drûwen -
  10.029
gidriuui - 10.029
gromot - 5.605
hemel, hoer - 5.605
jor - 5.605

ban, bane - 10.081
blâ - 5.605
daz - 6.802
eg(e)de - 11.105
glöuben - fn. 93
kint - 6.802
korde - fn. 89

este - 1.004, 11.301
Henning - 9.400
hövetman - 5.324
inster - 5.324

llan - 1.191

joftams - 10.086

žvaigžde� - 9.300,
  10.106
žvaĩgžde̢ - 5.800
žvãkė, žvakigalis -
  6.976
žvėris - 5.803

Livonian
  kadà'g - 10.044

Low German
  sudde, suddeln -
  2.004

Lower Sorbian
  makaś, -am - 10.066

Messapian

Middle German
  sacken, schene, slete,
  sonnobent, stiftacht',
  stobe, stuppel,
  suller - 5.605
  vorch - 5.605
  vulbem - 4.100
  vussale - 5.605
  wimpro, wulken - 5.605

Middle High German
  schine - 5.605
  trūwen - 10.029, fn. 93
  vrîliche - 10.009
  wēnege - 6.802
  wimmât, wimmet - 4.204
  wintbrâ - 5.605

Middle Low German
  jair - 6.300, 8.040
  Maideborgh, Maidheburch,
  Mayborgeschen,
  Meideborch - 11.005
  raid - 6.300, 8.040
  trūwen - 10.029, fn. 93

Middle Welsh
  lleth, llyth - 10.056

Mordvinian

hjūpa - 3.203, 10.043   njupa - 3.203
netla - 10.073

Old Church Slavic

azъ - 7.800

blato - 10.092

bo - 10.018

bě - 10.018

bělъ - 10.902

vezǫsti - 10.042

veliši - 8. 107

viděti, viždъ - 8.012

vrana - 10.115

vъtorъ - 11.108

vъtrь - 3.200

vědě - 8.012, 8.100

věděti - 8.012,
   10.116

věmь - 8.012

větrъ - 3.201

věštati - 9.030,
   10.113

věštajǫ - 10.113

gvozdъ - 10.041

grъbъ - 2.301

gǫgnivъ - 10.020

da - 8.040

damь - 8.100, 11.002

dajǫ - 2.114

dvorě - 9.020

děliti - 10.027

žena - 3.200

žeravlь - 1.006

živeši - 8.107

žito - 3.200

istъ - 1.004

klǫpь - 10.119

krъvi - 3.004

luna - 3.200

mene - 7.802

mladъ - 10.063

moždanъ - 10.065

mozgъ - 3.200, 10.065

mъstъ - 4.204

me - 7.803

novъ, nyně - 6.940

plesna - 10.082a

pьšenica - 3.200

ravьnъ - 3.200

ralo - 10.004

rosa - 3.305

rǫcě - 6.340

svobodь - 3.006, 7.600

světъ - 10.106

slovese - 5.917

sobь - 7.600

sta - 8.040, 8.403

suxъ - 3.305

sъkǫtati - 10.084

syrъ - 2.002

sěděti - 8.401

sětь - 6.950

sę - 7.803

tebě - 4.208

ti - 4.206 (enclitic
   dat. sg.)

ti - 7.011 (nom. pl.
   of tъ)

timěno - 2.812

timěnьje, tina - 2.812

tretьjь - 3.005

tьlo, tьlo - 9.106

tьstь - 3.200

těxъ - 7.011

tę - 7.803

ulica - 10.014

umirajǫ - 10.018

umyti - 3.200

učę - 10.018

cělъ - 3.200

česo - 6.011, 6.014,
   7.010

črьnъ - 3.200

jelьxa - 10.002

jazva - 3.200

językъ - 3.200, 10.042

Old English

bēatan - 10.034
Crist - 10.029
dagas, dóm-æs - 6.014
ealu - 6.600
East-land, East-lande -
  1.003
eg(e)de - 11.105
Est-mere, Êst-um -
  1.003
furh - 2.106
guma - 6.983

moder - 5.801

Ilfing - 1.003
lām - 10.059
land - 1.191
neat - 10.081
ofen - 10.118
on - 10.029
stān - 5.325
truwian - 10.029
þawian - 2.812
warian - 11.004
wislemuda - 1.003

Old Frisian

Old High German

alu - 6.600
an - 10.029
ancho - 10.007
bōz(z)an - 10.034
dewen, douwen - 2.812
du, dū - fn. 83
dwahan - 10.110
ecken, egen, egida -
  11.105
got - 10.029
hiufo - 10.043
hornaz, hornūz - 6.910
lahs - 10.104
land - 1.191
leim, leimo - 10.059

mar(a)c, mar(a)g -
  10.065
nezzila - 10.073
rappe - 10.089
ruod - 10.011
sûgan - 10.104
taha(la) - 3.203
trûenne - 10.029
trū(w)ēn - 3.203
waganso - 6.910
warm - 5.400
wecki - 6.910
wels - 3.203
ze - 10.029

Old Icelandic
(see Old Norse)

Old Irish

beri - 8.302
brathir - 6.702
caech - 10.075
cruim - 10.126
don - 6.983
dú - 6.983

duine - 6.983
land - 1.191, 10.060
lann - 1.191
suainem - 10.099
tenge - 10.042

Old Norse

á - 10.029
auga - 10.003
bauta - 10.034
dregg - 3.501
Fjǫrgyn - 9.110

gap - 2.106
godagas - 6.011
goð - 10.029
hlaun - 6.971
hvalr - 3.203

land – 10.060
leira – 3.203
naut – 10.081
*nær ⁱ – 10.072
*næring – 10.072
rōmr – 10.011
tal – 10.039
telja – 10.039
trúa – 10.029

þess – 6.011
þeyja – 2.812
þjalfi, þor – 9.110
varr – 11.004
víkingr – 3.600
vindauga, vindr –
    10.003
vǫrr – 3.203

Old Prussian

abasus – 5.900
Abglopte, abgloyte,
    Abklopte – 4.703
aboros – 10.001
absergīsnan – 10.095
Abskande – 10.001
accodis – 10.003
ackewijstin – 6.051
ackins – 6.504, 6.505,
    6.974
ackis – 6.504, 6.709,
    10.003, 11.105
aclo – 10.005
aclocordo – 10.004,
    10.128, fn. 89
adder – 6.706, 6.801,
    6.802
addle – 2.305, 5.001,
    6.401, 10.004
æsse – 4.223, 5.403
æst –5.403
*ag-, aglo, *aglu –
    10.005
*aigulō – 10.016
ainan – 6.040, 6.709,
    8.062
ains – 4.704, 7.701,
    fn. 82
*aita – 10.017
aketes – 6.430, 11.105
*aklā – 10.005
*aklakardā – 10.004
aklo – 10.005
/akutis/ – 10.003
*algā – 10.005

ālgas – 5.401, 5.805,
    6.310, 10.006
*algo – 10.005
*aliks-nas – 4.712
Aliskande, al(i)skands –
    10.002
*alisk-ans – 4.712
alkīnisquai, *alkīnis-
    quan – 5.100, 6.320
alne – 5.001, 6.401
Alskande – 10.002
alu – 6.600
amsis – 6.501, fn. 67
an- – 6.606
-ana- – 4.712
anctan, ancte – 4.204,
    10.007
andangon – 4.701
andangonsv̄n – 4.701,
    6.606
angis – 6.971
angle – 4.204, 10.016
angurgis – 5.502,
    5.914, 5.915, 5.917
*āngus – 10.013
ankaitītai – 10.088
ansalgis – 5.502
Anse – 2.011
Ansnicz, Ansnit –
    4.700
ansonis – 6.910
antars – 11.108
antis – 6.971
antres – 4.704
ape – 6.976

dats, dāts - 5.303
dātwei - 4.717, 5.303, 5.305
-dau - 7.900
dauris - 9.020, 9.021
Dawes - 4.208
debbes - 4.220, 4.223
debica - 6.100, 6.977
deicktan, deickton, deicton - 6.950
dēigiskan - 10.025
deineniskai - 5.200
deinenisku - 5.200, fn. 33
deinennin, deininan - 4.223
*deiv-ai - 6.015
*deiv-an - 6.015, 6.331
*deiv-ans - 6.015
Deivs - 9.107, 9.108, 9.109
deiw- - 9.400
deiwa - 6.052
deiwan - 6.030, 6.602
deiwas - 3.001, 6.010, 6.011, 6.012, 6.014, 6.210, 6.602, 6.964, fn. 44
deiwe - 6.052
deiws - 3.001, 6.210, 6.605, 6.709, 6.802, fn. 44
*deiw-u - 6.605
delbas - 4.218, 4.219, 4.223, 4.225, 4.226
dellijks - 6.977
dengan - 6.709
dengenennis, dengniskas 7.300
dereis - 8.060, 10.026
dessempts - 5.703
dessimpts - 3.600, 5.703
dessimts - 9.350, 9.352

Deves - 4.501, 4.502
dewes - 4.502, 11.004
deywas - 10.081
deywis - 3.001
dijgi - 6.802
dijlapagaptin - 6.975
dīlas, dīlnikans - 10.027
din - 7.200, fn. 79
Dinge - 3.305
dīnkaumai - 8.204
dīnkaut - 8.540
dīnkauti - 8.055
dīnkauts - 8.303
*dis - fn. 79
Diviriks - 9.110
doacke - 3.203
doalgis - 5.301, 5.323, 6.971
Dobyse - 5.932
dodi - 4.218, 4.219, 4.223, 4.226
does - 4.501, 4.502
dompne - 10.023
*dōt - 4.717
doyte - 4.600, 4.601, 4.710, 4.717, fn. 29
Drabose - 5.935
dragios - 3.501, 5.503, 6.903, 10.028, 11.008
Drasda - 3.305
draudieiti - 8.053, 8.060
*dravis - 1.170
drawine - 6.600
driāudai - 5.406, 8.040
Drosten - 3.305
-*dru - 6.600
Drutenne - 10.089
druwi - 10.029
Druwien - 6.706
druwis - 10.029
druwīt - 1.170, 3.203, 10.029
duaris - 9.020

378

duckis - 3.602
duckti - 6.700, 6.702
Dulgen, Dul-kam,
  Dulo-kaym - 2.103
dulsis - 10.124
dumpbis - 5.924
dusi - 5.923
dusin - 6.974
dūsin - 6.420
dwaris - 9.020
dyrsos - 4.202
Dywone-lauken - 5.313
eb-immai - 10.001
ebsentliuns - 3.003
ebsgnā - 8.040
ebsignāsi - 8.108
edeitte - 8.053, 8.060
Eg - 4.600, 4.601,
  4.710, 4.713, 4.717
*eigulō - 10.016
Eikschisken, Eiksisch-
  ken - 5.934
-ēimai - 8.010
eines, eins - 4.704
ēisei - 8.010
ēit - 5.800, 8.010,
  8.107, 8.110
-el- - 4.712
emmens - 4.220, 6.700,
  6.707
emnen - 6.707, 10.081
emnes - 4.223
empijreisku - 6.320
en - 5.001, 6.020,
  6.050, 6.051, 6.709
enbāndan - 10.081
endangon - 4.223
endeirā - 8.402,
  10.026
endeirīt - 10.026
endirīs - 8.060, 8.403
endirisna - 6.708
endyrītwei - 8.402,
  10.026
engels - 8.064

engraudīsnas - 6.802
enis - 4.704
/enkaitētai/,
  enkaitītai - 10.088
enkopts - 10.030
enterpen, enterpon -
  10.031
enwāngiskan - 7.910
ep- - 5.001
epkieckan - 9.010,
  10.032
ep-war(r)īsnan - 9.010,
  9.350
er- - 9.300, 9.301,
  9.302
erains, erderkts -
  9.300
Eren - 10.033
eristian - 6.930,
  10.033
erkīnina, erlaikūt,
  erlāngi, ermīrit,
  ernaunīsan,
  ernaunīsnan,
  ernertiuns,
  erpilninaiti - 9.300
erschwāigstinai -
  9.300, 10.106
erschwāistiuns - 10.105
ersinnat, ertreppa -
  9.300
es - 4.218, 4.220,
  4.223, 4.226, 7.800
Esenen - 5.935
*esmă, *esmā, *esmai -
  8.104
*esmau, *esmō, *esmū -
  8.106
esse - 4.223 (preposi-
  tion), 4.701 (verb)
essei - 4.223, 5.403,
  8.010
est - 4.220
estei - 5.403, 8.010
et- - 5.001, 10.035

etbaudints - 10.034
-ete, -ethe - 4.703
et-lāikusin - 8.510
*etnija - 10.035
etnīstin - 6.602
etnīstis - 6.501,
  6.602, 6.802, 6.975,
  10.035
*etnīt - 10.035
etskīans - 10.036
etskīmai - 8.011
etskīsai - 8.011,
  10.036
etskīuns, etskyuns -
  10.036
etwerpeis, etwērpimai -
  4.223
etwerpsennin - 6.974
etwerpsnā - 5.802
etwerreis - 10.037
etwiērpt - 5.802, 9.010
et-winūt - 8.540
eykete - 4.202, 8.063
eyswo - 3.200
*gabula - 3.305
gaide - 4.204
Gaila, Gailgarben -
  4.700
gaitke - 4.503
galbimai - 11.004
Galinden, Galindien -
  1.192
gallan - 5.400
gallintwey - 1.193
gallu - 5.324, fn. 87
gallū - 5.324, 5.803,
  6.300
Galten-garb, Galtgarbe -
  3.305
galwas-dellīks - 5.324,
  6.310, fn. 44, fn. 61,
  fn. 87
galwo - 3.405, 5.700,
  6.300
Galynde - 1.192

gannai - 6.340, 6.709
Gannan - 10.078
gāntsan - 6.802
Garbas, Garbaś - 2.301
Garbeninken, Garbenyken -
  2.301
garbis - 2.301, 10.033
Garbow - 2.301
gardas, Gardo(a)eten -
  9.103
garian - 5.911, 5.913
garkity - 5.923
gayde - 4.204
gaylis - 2.702
Gaytko - 4.503
geauris - 5.501, 5.503,
  5.504, 5.505
gegalis - 3.507
gēide - 5.504
geigete - 4.703, 4.704
geitien - 4.223
geitin - 4.223, 8.303
geitka - 4.501, 4.503
geitke - 4.503
geits - 3.200, 10.038
gēiwan - 5.002
geiwans - 8.030
geiwin - 6.920
gelatynan - 10.055
gelbineis, /gelbinējas/,
  /gelbinējis/ - 10.040
gema, gemia, gemmons,
  *gena - 4.205
gen-ai, *gen-an,
  gen-ans - 6.015
-genis, genix - 10.017
genna - 4.205, 6.300
gennai - 6.340, 6.709
gennāmans - 6.360
gennan - 6.602
gennans - 6.370
gennas - 6.602
genno - 3.200, 4.205
gerbais, gerbaisa -
  11.005

gerbaiti - 9.400,
    11.005
gerbeis - 11.005
gerbt - 9.400, 11.005
gērbt - 10.039
gerdaus - 8.055
Gerten - 4.700
gerwe - 6.401
gewineis - 10.040
Geygey, Geygeythe -
    4.704, 11.107
Geylegarben - 4.700
geytko - 4.503
geytye - 5.503, 10.002
geytys - 10.002
geywien - 6.420, 6.920,
    6.974
giēidi - 5.504
gignis - 4.703
gijwans - 8.030
gijwin - 6.420, 6.920,
    6.974
gijwis - 6.410, 6.920
gillin - 6.709
gingis, gińis - 4.703
ginnewīngiskan - 7.910
gīrbin - 10.039
gischer - 4.218, 4.220
*gīva, *gīvasei, giwa -
    8.107
giwammai - 8.030, 9.351
gīwan - 5.002
giwāntei - 6.706
gīwasi - 8.030, 8.107,
    8.110
giwassi - 6.040, 8.030,
    8.107, 8.110
giwei - 6.402, 6.920
giwemmai - 9.351
glawo - 3.405, 5.700,
    fn. 20
glēsum - 3.508
gleuptene - 5.501
gnabsem - 4.204
gnigethe - 4.703

golimban - 5.311
golis - 5.400, fn. 45
gorme - 5.400, 6.920,
    fn. 76
*Gorovīten, Gorowyten,
    Gorowythen - 6.981
gosen - 4.202
gotte - 4.204, fn. 24
goven - 4.202
grabis - 2.301
gramboale - 5.301,
    5.323
grandico - 6.977
*grandis - 6.971
Graschyn - 5.935
graudis - 6.971
greanste - 6.973
grecon, grekun -
    6.070
Gresen - 5.935
grīkai - 6.060
grīkan - 6.070
grīkans - 6.801
grikaut - 8.062
grīku - 6.020
Grindos - 5.313
griquan - 5.100, 6.070
*gudān- - 10.041
gudde - 1.130, 10.041
*gud(de_wobalne -
    10.041
gunnimai - 10.038
gunsix - 6.977
guntwei - 10.038
gygynethe - 4.703
gyntos - 4.202
haltnyka - 4.204
hest - 5.403
ho - 4.702
höfftmannin - 5.324
hoho, hu - 4.702
*ialitan - 10.121
iau - 4.711
iaukint - 5.500
-ico - 10.093

īdai - 6.974
idaiti - 8.051, 8.060
īdeiti - 8.053
īdin - 3.002, 6.974
īdis - 6.200, 6.974
iest - 4.202
*ik - 4.713, 4.714
*īk - 4.713
-ik(a)s, -iko - 6.977
ilga, Ilgene - 2.102
Ilgenpelke - 4.700
ilgi - 2.102
ilgimi - 6.040
Ilgoue - 2.102
imai- - 8.066
imma - 6.040, 8.111,
  8.303
immais - 8.051
īmt - 10.123
-ind- - 1.192
īnsan - 8.062
instixs - 6.977
instran - 5.324
insuwis - 3.200, 6.200,
  10.042, fn. 16
ioūmans - 6.080, 7.808,
  11.201
ioumas - 6.080
ioūmas - 6.080, 11.201
ioūs - 7.806
iousan - 6.070
ioūsan - 5.302, 6.070
iouson - 5.405, 6.070,
  7.807, 8.062
iquoitu - 4.207,
  4.601, 6.706, 4.713
ir - 4.223
Iragarbis - 10.033
is - 2.204
isarwiskas - 10.009
Isslene - 5.931
isspresennien - 7.910
isspressennen - 8.062
īst - 10.078
īstai - 6.020, 6.974

-īt- - 6.980
iūrin - 3.304, 10.130
iuse - 3.502
Iwogarge - 4.700
iz-īra - 4.220
*jau - 4.711
*jaunas - 6.940
jiz-jīr(a) - 4.220
Jodenne - 10.089
Jodeyko - 10.064
joes - fn. 28
*jūs, *jusōn - 7.807
ka·- 7.400
*kā - 5.101
kaāubri - 3.203, 10.043
kackint - 8.520
kad(d)en - 5.402, 9.351
kadegis - 10.044
kai - 6.802
*kai - 7.400
/kai/ - (phonemiciza-
  tion of) quoi 'wants,
  will', - 8.203,
  10.088
kāigi - fn. 84
Kailes - 4.703, 4.704
Kailess - 4.703
kails - 4.601, 4.703,
  4.705
kailūstiskun - 3.200,
  4.705
kailəs - fn. 27
kāima-luke - 5.800,
  5.804
kaimīnan - 5.801
/kait-/ - 10.088
/kaitá/ - 4.601, 8.011,
  8.203
/kaiŕe tu/ - 4.207
/kaitēt/ - 8.203
kaithu - 4.207
kakīnt - 8.520
Kalcz, Kalioth - 10.045
kalis - 3.203, 10.045
kalpus - 10.046

lieda - 4.204
līgan - 3.406
līmauts - 8.303
lindan - 1.191, 10.060
linga-saytan - 9.032
līse - 10.061
lituckekers - 10.048
loase - 10.055
Lockeneyn - 2.802
lonix - 6.977
Loyne - 4.218, 4.219,
 4.223
lūbeniks - 9.400,
 fn. 26
lubnigs - 9.400
ludini, *ludinis -
 10.062
ludis - 3.405
Lulegarbis - 2.301
lunkan - 6.100
lyda - 4.204
madlan - 6.331, 6.709
madlas - 6.340, 6.709
madlikan - 6.930
maian - fn. 28
maiggun - 6.709, 6.920
*maigū - 6.920
maim - 6.040
māim - 5.708, 6.040,
 8.064
mais - 7.820
Maise - 4.204
maitātunsin - 8.510
Maiters - 4.210
maldai - 6.061, 8.060,
 10.063
maldaisei, maldaisimans,
 maldaisins - 6.802
Malde, Maldenne -
 10.063
maldian - 5.503,
 10.063
malnijkai - 6.021
Malnijkans - 10.078
malnijkikamans - 6.802

malnijkiku - 3.004,
 6.021, 6.060
malnīku - 6.020
maltnicka - 4.204
malunakelan - 3.503,
 6.904, 10.120
malunastabis - 3.503
malunis - 3.503, 6.904,
 6.978
mangos, mangoson -
 4.210
mans - 4.220, 7.809,
 8.510
Mantegarbs - 2.301
Marcopole - 9.106
Markopole - 9.107
mas - 7.804
massais - 6.802
mattei - 6.974
mause - 4.703
mayian - fn. 28
mayse - 4.204, 4.218,
 4.219, 4.223, 4.226
Maysegaln - 5.931
maysta - 3.409
maytter - 4.210
/mazgenā/ - 10.065
meddo - 6.601
Mede - 3.305
Medeniken, Medenouwe -
 2.801
median - 1.120, 2.801,
 5.503, 5.911, 10.076
medies - 6.200, 6.904
Medinen - 2.801
medione - 5.503
Medis - 3.305
Megato, *Mēgikā,
 Megothe, Megothen -
 10.064
meicte - 11.006
meida - 4.204
Meinse - 4.202, 11.001
meinso - 10.067, 11.001
melato - 5.911, 5.913

menisnan - fn. 28
mennei - 7.802, 8.062
mensā - 5.300, 5.803,
　6.300, 6.310, 8.040,
　10.067
mensai - 6.300, 8.040
menschon - 6.350,
　fn. 65
menses - 5.401, 6.310
menso - 5.300, 6.300,
　10.067
merga - 4.202
mērgan - 5.200, 5.804,
　6.310, 6.330
*mērgas - 6.310
mergo - 3.602
mergu - 5.804, 6.300
*mer̃guan, mer̃gu̯as -
　6.310
mergūmans - 5.804,
　6.360
*mergũs - 6.310
merguss - 4.202
mergwan - 5.100, 5.200,
　6.310
*mergwas - 6.310
mes - 4.220, 7.804,
　7.809
mestan - 3.409, 5.900
mettan - 5.911
Mey - 4.702
Meysegaln - 5.931
mien - 7.803, 8.510
Migeyten - 10.064
mijlis - 8.403
mijls - 8.062
mile - 4.702
milē - 8.030, fn. 86
miles - 4.702
Minate, Mine, Mineko -
　10.064
minisnan - 6.911, fn. 28
mistran, mistrastippi -
　4.220
moazo - 5.301, 5.700,

5.701
Moi - 4.702
moicte - 11.006
moska, mosla -
　4.204
mothe - 5.300, 6.700,
　6.702
moy - 4.702, 9.121
mues - 4.702
muisieson - 6.801
mukin- - 9.400
mukint - 10.066
mulgeno - 10.065
munis - 4.218, 4.219,
　4.220, 4.226
musgeno - 3.200,
　10.065
mūti - 5.801, 6.700,
　6.702, 6.707
mutien - 6.420
mūtien - 6.420, 6.707,
　6.974
mūtin - 5.300, 6.420,
　6.707, 6.974
myasta - 3.409
myle - 4.702, 9.121
mynkus - 4.202
Mynothe - 10.064
mynsis - 3.410
mynsowe - 10.067
mystlastibbi,
　mystlastippi - 4.220,
　4.226
na - 1.170, 4.223
　5.302,
　fn. 25
nackt - 4.202
nadele - 5.900, 10.068,
　fn. 73
Nadravō - 1.170
Nadrowia - 9.040
nadruvi̯as, na-druvis,
　nadruwīsnan - 1.170
-nag - 4.220
naktin - 6.974

389

polīnka - 5.200, 8.030, 8.520
Polkuiten - 6.982
Pollexiani - 2.500, fn. 12
pomatre - 5.601
ponadele - 5.900, 10.085
Popalwen - 9.060
poprestemmai - 8.030
poquelbton - 6.706
Porden - 3.305
pōs - fn. 27
pōs-kail(i)s - fn. 27
poskails - 4.704
poskayles - 4.704, 4.705
Poss - 4.704
possissawaite - 3.507, 6.976, fn. 98
postai - 8.040
postāsei - 8.108
postippin - 4.220
postkayles - 4.704
posty - 9.032
*pōt - 4.715
potaukinnons - 6.802
*pōton - 5.706
Potrimppo - 9.130
Potrimps - 9.103, 9.109, 9.144
*pōtvei - 4.715
poūis - 6.200
poūt, poutwei - 4.715
powaisennis - 6.210
powiērptei - 8.056, 8.062
powijstin - 10.086
powīrps - 3.504, 10.087
poyte - 4.600, 4.601, 4.710, 4.714, 4.715, 4.717, fn. 28, fn. 29
prabitscun, prabusquan, prābutskan - 5.200
prahes - 4.218, 4.219, 4.223

prakāisnan - 5.800
Prastian - 2.105
pray - fn. 28
pre - 4.220
prei - 6.020, 6.040, 6.709, 8.062
prei- - 4.220
Prēi - 10.078
preibillīsnai - 6.709
prēidin - fn. 79
preigērbt - 9.010
prēi-pīrstans - 5.802
prey - fn. 28
Prio - 6.903
prosnan -5.703
prowela - 8.301
proweladin - 7.200, 8.040
prūs- - 1.007
Prūsa - fn. 4
Prūsas - 1.007
prūsiskai, prūsiskan - 1.005, 1.007
prusnan - 5.703
puckolle - 4.704
pugeitty - 4.717
puietti - 4.717, fn. 28
puieyti - 4.717
Purde, Purden - 3.305
Puschkaytus - 9.141
pusne - 3.507
puszkailes - 4.704
Puškaits - 9.106, 9.107, 9.108, 9.121, 9.140, 9.141, 9.142, 9.143, 9.144, 9.145
pūton - 5.300, 5.706, 10.078
pyienkts - 5.502, 5.920
quai - 5.101, 7.400, fn. 32
quaits - 10.088
quāits - 4.223, fn. 84
*quan, quei, quendau - 5.101
quoi - 7.400 (pronoun)

quoi - 4.713, 4.714,
8.011, 8.203, 8.510,
10.088 (verb)
*quoi-ă,*quoi-ei,
*quoi-o - 8.203
quoitā - 8.011, 10.088
quoitāmai - 8.011
quoitē - 4.601, 4.714,
8.011, 10.088
quoitēti - 8.011
quoitijlaiti - 8.066
quoitīlaisi - 8.066,
8.107
quoitu - 4.714
Randoin - 10.022
rānkan, rānkān - 5.802
*rañk-ān - 6.331
rānkans - 5.802, 6.331,
6.370, 9.352
rapeno - 10.089
ratinsis - 3.410, 5.900
raugus - 10.090
Rause, Rawse, Rawsze -
5.932
reddisku - 6.060
rekis - 4.601
rekyse - 4.600, 4.601,
4.710, 11.200
Resdynen, Resedynen -
3.305
reykeis - 4.601
rickawie - 10.091
rickie - 4.222
rickis - 4.601
Rickoyto - 9.130
rikeis, /rikēj[a]s/ -
4.601
rikijs - 4.601, 6.200,
10.091
rīkīs - 4.601, 4.710
rikisnan - 3.412
roaban - 5.301, 10.092
Rokelawken - 4.700
ructan-dadan - 10.090
Ruggis - 4.217

Rugkelayke - 4.700
rūkans - 10.078
Rumbow - 3.305
russis - 5.600
rykyes - 4.601
sa- - 10.096
sabatico - 10.093
sackis - 10.094
sacramenten - 5.402
*saitan - 10.129
saligan - 5.502, 5.913,
10.055
sālin - 5.300
salmis - 3.403, 3.405,
fn. 21
salowis - 3.200
Salseniken - 5.931
salta - 6.100
Saltone - 5.932
salūban - 3.507
Salūbin - 6.040
same, samyen - 5.911,
5.918
san, saninsle - 10.123
sansy - 6.972
Sargo - fn. 24
sarwis, sarxtes -
10.095
sasins - 1.110
Sassene - 5.931
Sassenpile - 1.110
sātuinei - 8.110
Saud-en, Saud-iten -
2.002
saule - 6.910, fn. 75
saunan, saūnan - 6.709,
fn. 71
saūnas - 6.015, 6.709
sausan - fn. 18
Sause - 3.305
Sawarycke - 2.902
sawayte - 3.507, 10.096
Sawlawken - 5.931
Sawliskresil - 4.700
saydit - 4.202

*saytan - 6.950, 10.129
scaydy - 6.901
scaytan - 10.036
schai - 7.500, 11.003
schan, schans - 7.500
Schawden - 5.934
schen, schian,
  schiēise - 7.500
schiēison - 6.070,
  7.500
schien - 7.500, 10.008
schiens, schin - 7.500
schins - 7.500, fn. 81
schis - 7.500
schisman - 6.051, 7.500
schismu - 6.020, 7.500
schissai - 7.500
schisses - 7.500, fn. 81
schlaītiskai - 6.320
Schokym - 5.313
schostro - 3.409, 4.202
schumeno - 5.502, 5.506
schutuan - 5.502, 5.506,
  10.097
schuwikis - 5.502,
  5.506
schwante - 4.702
Schwente - 9.121
Scoken - 5.313
scrutele - 5.600
scurdis - 10.098
Sczeszuwa - 5.932
*sē - 6.703
sebbei - 3.006, 7.802
sēd- - 10.117
segē - 8.107
segeitty, segeyti -
  fn. 28
seggē - 8.030, 10.099
seggēsei - 8.107
seggīt - 9.350, 10.099
seggītei - 8.054
seina - 2.809
seiti - 8.510
Sele - 5.932

Semegallen - 5.935
semen - 6.700, 6.704,
  6.910
semmē - 5.002, 5.805,
  5.911, 6.401, 9.350,
  9.352
semmes - 4.218, 4.219,
  4.226
semmey - 5.918, 6.410
sem(m)ien - 6.420
semmiey - 6.410
sen - 6.023, 6.040,
  6.060, 6.331, 6.709,
  6.801, 7.310, 8.064,
  10.126
senditans - 6.331
sengidaut - 9.010
sēnku - 6.040
Sessow - 5.932
Setin - 5.931
sētlauken - 10.100
seydis - 3.200
Seymen - 5.935
seyr - 6.700, 6.703,
  10.101
-si - 7.803
sīdans, sīdons - 5.002
sien - 7.500 (demonstra-
  tive pronoun)
sien - 7.803, 8.510,
  10.012 (reflexive
  pronoun)
signai - 8.040
sijran - 6.703, 6.709
silkas - 3.401
Sillyn - 5.935
-sin - 7.803, 8.510
sīran - 6.703, 6.709
sirans, sīras - 6.703,
  6.709
Sirgelauwk, sirgis,
  Sirgite, Sirgun -
  10.102
sirmen - 3.601
sirsdau - 7.900, 10.101

sirsilis - 6.910
sīru - 6.020, 6.023,
  6.703
Sirwinte - 5.931
sis - 7.500
sixdo, sixdre - fn. 97
Skabeike, Skabeyke -
  3.305
Skalva - 9.040, fn. 4
Skalweit - 9.040
Skawdegede - 3.305
Skellānts - 9.350
Skeurekaym - 10.103
skewre - 5.501, 5.503,
  5.504, 10.103
skīstai - 6.021
Skomand - 2.805
Skrunden - 5.931
slaunis - 6.971
smonenawis - 6.708
smoy - 3.405, 6.700,
  6.708, fn. 70
smūnenisku - 6.060,
  10.125
smunentien - 6.708
smunentin - 6.707,
  6.708, 6.709, 10.125
smunentinan, smunenti-
  nans - 6.708, 6.709
smunentins - 6.708,
  10.125
smunentiuaus - 6.708,
  6.709
smunents - 6.708,
  10.125
smūnets - 6.708
smūni - 6.708, 6.983,
  10.125
soalis - 5.300, 5.301
Soke - 5.313
som-pisinis - 3.200
somukis - 10.093
Sones - 4.210
songos, Sonnaw, Sonne,
  Sonnekaym - 10.105

Sorpalwe - 9.060
sounan - 6.709
soūnan - 6.605, 6.709,
  fn. 71
soūnas - 6.015, 6.602,
  6.709
soūnon - 5.800, 5.801,
  6.802
sounons - 6.015, 6.602
soūns - 5.800, 5.801,
  6.601, fn. 71
Soye - 4.202, 10.104
Sparke - 3.305
spartisku - 6.320
sta - 4.222, 6.100,
  6.706
Stab-ynden - 1.192
Stabynotilte - 4.700
Staey - 5.401, fn. 46
stai - 6.300, fn. 32
stakamecczer - 5.600
Stakelisken - 5.931
stallēti - 6.051
stan - 4.601, 6.706,
  6.709, 8.303, 10.008,
  10.078
stānintei, stāninti -
  6.706
stas - 7.000, 7.011
stawīdsmu - 6.801
staytan - 10.036
ste - 6.040
*stē - 5.101
steimans - 6.802
stēimans - 6.023,
  6.802
stēise, steisei - 7.010
stēisi - 7.010, fn. 84
Steismu - 6.020
stēismu - 6.802
steison - 6.070, 6.708
stēison - 5.405, 6.070
sten - 5.401, 10.081
*sten, *stendau - 5.101
stes - 7.011, fn. 77

stesmn - 6.020

stesmu - 3.006, 4.601,
6.012, 6.020, 6.023,
6.331, 6.603, 6.709,
10.008

stesse - 6.011, 6.012,
6.014, 7.010, 11.202

stessei - 6.010, 7.010
fn. 84

stess(e)mu, stesses -
11.202

steweydan, Stewidan -
fn. 28

sticlo - 5.923

Stiessewite, Stresse-
wite - 6.982

Strewe - 5.931

strigeno - 3.200

stu - 6.040

sturdis - 10.098

stwen - 5.101, 10.008

stwendau - 5.101

stwi - 5.101, 6.709,
fn. 84

Suaikstix - 10.106

subban - fn. 14

subbsmu - 9.400

subs - 3.006, 7.600,
9.400

subsai - 9.400

Sūduva - 2.002

suge - 10.005, 10.104

sui̯ristio - 3.408

/sŭje, sŭja, sŭjē/ -
10.104

Suna - 10.105

*sunas - 6.709

sūndan - 3.406, 3.600

Sunecolowach, Sunegowe,
Sunike - 10.105

sunis - 5.933, 10.105

sunos - 6.015, 6.602,
6.709

*sūn-u - 6.605

sunun - 6.602, 6.605

*sūnus - 6.602

supana - 3.405

suppis - fn. 97

sups - 7.600, 9.400,
fn. 14

supsas, supsei, supsmu -
9.400

supūni - 3.404, 3.405

sutristio - 3.408,
6.903

Svaixtix - 9.102,
9.109

swaian - 6.603, 6.802

swāigstan - 5.800,
9.300, 10.106

swais - 7.820

swente, swenthe -
4.702

swentz - 4.220

sweriapis - 5.921

swetan - 3.409

sweytz - 4.218, 4.219,
4.220, 4.223

swintan - 6.070

swintints - 4.223

Swintoppe - 5.931

Swintove - 5.937

swints - 4.220, 4.223,
8.064

swīrins - 5.803

swītan - 3.409, 6.802

Swītas - fn. 84

swyntins - 4.701

Symyliskin - 5.931

syndens - 5.401

Syse - 5.932

Sysmare - 5.935

Szalltona - 5.932

Szwaybrotto - 9.130

Szyse - 5.932

-t - 3.007

Tainas - 2.812

tallokinikis - 3.601

tanæssen - 5.401,
7.300, fn. 80

tanassen - 7.300,
  fn. 80
tannā - 7.300, 7.310,
  9.351
tannans - 7.300
tans - 8.303
tāns - 7.300, 7.310
Tapelawke, Taplawken -
  4.700
tarkue - 3.403
*tas - 7.000, 8.111
tauto - 3.305
tauwyschies,
  tauwyschis - 6.210
tawa - 6.706, 11.007
tāwa - 4.223, 6.052,
  11.007
tawas - 4.220
tawe - 11.007
tāwe - 6.052, 11.007
tawischas, tawischis -
  6.210
Tāws - 6.802
taykowuns - 10.107
tebbe - 7.802
tebbei - 3.006, 4.206,
  7.802
teickut - 10.107
*teīkais - 8.062
teīks - 8.056, 8.062
*teīks(i) - 8.062
teinu - 6.802
teisis - 6.410
Teljavel' - 9.110
tenna - 7.300, 7.310
tennā - 7.300, 7.310,
  9.351
tennan - 7.300, 7.310
tennans - 7.300
tennei - 6.061, 7.300,
  7.310
tennēi, tennēimans -
  7.300
tenneison, tennēison -
  7.300, fn. 80

tennen, ten(n)esmu,
  tennessei - 7.300
testamentan,
  testamenten,
  testaments - 6.100
*tēvelis, *tēvis -
  4.712
Thawe - 4.701, 11.007
Thawthe - 3.305
thetis - 4.220
thewelyse - 4.600,
  4.601, 4.710, 4.712,
  11.200
Thewes - 4.218, 4.219,
  4.220, 4.223, 4.225
thewis - 4.220, 4.601,
  4.712
thi - 4.208, 11.004
tho - 4.711
Thobesze - 5.932
thoi - 4.206, 11.002
thoneauw - 4.600,
  4.601, 4.710, 4.711
thor - 4.202, 4.206,
  11.002
thowe - 4.220
thowes - 4.218, 4.219,
  4.220, 4.223, 4.226
thu - 4.202, 4.207,
  4.218, 4.220, 4.226,
  4.701, 10.088,
  11.002, 11.003
thuer(i) - 4.202, 11.002
tickars - 10.002,
  10.107
tickers - 4.202
tien - 4.208, 7.803,
  8.510
tikrōmiskan - 5.302
tin - 4.208, 6.040,
  7.803
tirt(i)s - 3.005
tisties - 3.200, 3.412,
  6.904
tīt - 6.802

tlāku - 4.601, 10.008
Tlokunpelk - 5.620
to - 4.714
Tollauken - 4.700
tollin, tols - 5.404
-ton - 6.605
tou̱ - 7.801, 10.081
tou̅ - 7.801, fn. 83
tou̅lan - 5.800
Towe - 4.701
Trankoiten, *Trankoĭten,
  Trankoten - 6.981
trencke - 4.702
trēnien - 8.062
Treonkaymynweysigis -
  4.700
tresde - 3.305
Trimps - 9.107, 9.108,
  9.109
trupeyle - 10.110
-ts - 8.112, 8.303,
  fn. 79
tu - 4.601, 4.711,
  4.713, 4.714, 4.717,
  7.801, 10.008, fn. 83
tū - 7.801
tuckoris - 3.407,
  5.923
tula- - 9.106
Tulekoĭte, Tulekoyte -
  6.981
tūlninai - 8.110
tūlninaiti - 8.510
-tun - 3.007, 6.605
tur - 4.206, 10.081
turei - 4.601, 8.110,
  10.008
turīt - 4.206, 8.013
turpelis - 10.110
turri - 4.206, 8.013,
  8.111
tusnan, tussīse -
  10.108
tuylis - 3.602, 10.109

twais - 4.220, 4.223,
  7.820,
  8.064
twaxtan - 3.203, 10.110
twayse - 10.081
-twei - 3.007, 4.601,
  6.604
ucka - 6.802, 9.101
uckce- - 9.101
*udā - 2.404
Ugeyne - 5.314
Umne - 4.700
umnode - 10.118
Umpna - 4.700
undan, unds - 6.910,
  9.400
*u̯ōsōn - 7.807
-upe - 1.200
Uppin - 5.314
uraisin, uraisins,
  uremmans - 6.802
urminan - 5.400
urs - 5.315, 6.802
uschtai - fn. 60
uschts - 3.506
usts - 3.506, fn. 60
Vaidelota - 4.222
*varbāt(un) - 11.004
varp- - 10.015
*vas - 7.809
verp- - 10.015
vese - 4.702
/vid-ā/ /vid-ē/ -
  8.040
virp- - 10.015
(*)viting(a)s - 10.111
*vōs - 7.809
Vuoreine, Vuoronnye -
  5.314
wackis - 6.920
Wagipelki - 4.700,
  6.976
wagnis - 6.910
waideler - 3.600

waidelotte - 3.508,
3.600
waidimai, waiditi -
8.010
waidolotten - 9.130
waikai - 6.060
waikammans - 6.080,
9.351
waisei - 8.010
waisnan - 6.911
waispattin - 6.910
Waiswilgen - 5.937
Waitegarben - 10.114
waitiāmai - 10.113
waitiāt - 9.030,
10.096, 10.113,
10.114
Waitigarb - 10.114
*wait-sn-ā - 6.911
waldūnen - 5.402
waldwico - 3.403, 3.408
walnennint - 8.510
wans - 7.809, 8.510
war, wara - 4.208
Warbo - 4.208, fn. 24,
11.004
wardes - 4.218, 4.219,
4.220, 4.223
wargan - 4.223
wargien - 5.502, 5.911,
5.913
Warkaym, Warmediten,
Warmen - 5.314
warne - 6.976, 6.979,
10.115
*Warnekos, Warnekros -
10.115
Warnikaym - 6.976,
6.979
Warnike, warnis -
10.115
warrien - 6.420
warsus - 3.203
wartinna - 8.510
warto - 4.208, 6.950,
9.021

warton - 4.208
Waygi-kaymen,
Waygis-pelkis,
Waykis-pelkis -
6.976
Wayne, Wayniko,
Waynothe - 10.064
Wayswille - 5.937
wayte - 10.096, 10.114
wedais - 8.060
weddē - 8.111, 9.350,
9.352
weddē-din - 8.040
weddeis - 3.007, 4.223,
8.060
wede - 4.219
weders - 10.116, fn. 99
wedeys - 8.053
weijsewingi - 8.510
Weis-pelke - 2.106
weloblundis - 5.924
Werennye - 5.314
werpsnā - 6.911
Wersaka, Wersszaka -
5.932
Werstian - 2.105
Werszaka - 5.932
wertei - 6.061, 8.060
westwey - 10.081
wetro - 3.201
Weyssen - 2.106
Weywirse - 5.935
widdai - 8.040
widdewū - 9.352
widdewūmans - 6.360,
9.352
wijr-ai - 6.060
wijrikan - 6.930
*winawū - 8.540
winna - 7.700
winnen - 5.402, 7.700
winnis - 6.971
wins - 7.700
winsus - 9.032
-winūt - 8.540

wīrans - 5.801
wirdai - 6.020, 6.709
wirdan - 6.331
wirdemmans - 9.351
wirds - 4.220
wirps - 10.015
wīrst, *wīrsta - 8.013
wīrstai - 8.013, 8.115
wīrstmai - 8.013
wisge - 4.202
wissa - 6.100
wissai - 6.050, 6.060
wissamans - 6.331
wissan - 4.223
wissans - 6.050, 6.709,
   10.078
wissas - 6.709, 6.802
wissaseydis - 10.096,
   10.117
witing - 3.600
Witowudi - 9.130
woasis - 5.301, 5.701
woble - 6.976, 6.979
Woblicayn - 6.976
Woblikaym - 6.976,
   6.979
Wobsdis - 5.313
wobse - 4.712, 10.001,
   fn. 39
Wogenis - 5.314
wogonis - 3.401, fn. 19
wolgeit - 11.005
wolti - 6.401, 6.972
Wondithen, Woppe,
   Worelauke, Worennie,
   Worennye, Worenyge -
   5.314
Worit - 5.315
Workaym, Worlavken,
   Wormedith, Wormen -
   5.314
worm-yan - 1.140, 5.301,
   5.400, 5.918
Worsunij - 4.218, 4.223
Worwayn - 5.314

Wose-birgo - 10.127
wosee - 5.300, 6.976,
   6.979
Wosenbirgo - 5.313
wosigrabis - 6.976,
   6.979
Wosispile - 4.700,
   5.313
Wossicz - 6.981
Woterkeim - 5.314
Woysewite - 6.982
Woytegarben - 10.114
Wrenie - 5.314
wubri - 6.901
wumbaris - 3.410, 5.924
wumpnis - 10.118
wundan - 6.910
Wundithen - 5.314
wupyan - 5.918
Wurkaym, Wurlauken,
   Wurlauks, Wurmdit -
   5.314
wurs - 10.130
Wurschayto - 9.130
Wurwaynen - 5.314
wuschts - 3.506, fn. 60
Wuschycz - 6.981
Wusewithen - 6.982
Wusitcz - 6.981
wusse - 4.218, 4.219,
   4.223
wutris - 3.200
Wutterkaym - 5.314
wyssens - 5.401
ymays - 11.005
yous - fn. 28
Zele - 5.932
Zereens - 5.935
Zeymen - 5.935
zuit - 3.408
Zunloszkeim - 10.105

Old Saxon

hiopo - 3.203, 10.043

land - 1.191, 10.060

humuns - 6.983

kwlg, kwlk - 10.022

kabūtar, kapūtar,
kautar, kebūter -
10.050

aću - 2.305

bałbotać, bambiza -
2.305

Berzniki - 2.810

Bialla - 4.700

Białystok - 2.016

bierze, bježe, b^veže -
2.207

bob - 3.200

bołbotać, boźi -
2.305

bryzgać - 1.007

byle - 8.066

bźeže - 2.207

cieść - 3.412

Cytowiany - 2.812

Czarna Hańcza - 2.011

chart - 3.411

daję -2.114

dąb - 5.924

dążyć - 2.201

de Trankwitz - 6.981

Derazina - 2.803

dłoto - 3.200

długi - 2.102

dłużnik - 10.124

drogi - fn. 12

Drohiczyn - 2.803

Drohyczyn - fn. 12

drożdże - 3.501

dulki - 2.305

dusza - 5.923

duży - 2.201

netila - 10.073

Oscan

mais - 6.801

Pehlevi

Persian

kurrah - 10.022

Polish

Dziadoszan - 3.409

dziękować - 8.540

Ełk - 2.501, 2.502

Garbas, Garbaś - 2.301

gąz - 2.201

Gdańsk(o) - 10.041

Gieląd, Gielądzkie
Jezioro - 1.193

Go-, Go-pło - 1.191

gorczyca - 5.923

Gorowychen - 6.981

gowen - 4.202

gozd - 10.041

guz, guzik - 2.201

gwozd - 10.041

-īc-, -ice, -icy -
6.980

iegla - 2.305

iest - 4.202

Jatwa - 2.208

jelito - 10.121

jesień - 3.200

-jucha - 2.807

kadyk - 10.044

Karczewicy - 6.980

karczma - 3.411

karw - 3.200, 10.023

kąkol - 5.924

*kłąp - 10.119

konopia - 6.903

korzkiew - 9.070, 10.128

*kremen-jucha - 2.807

krusza - 3.502

krzemień - 2.807
Krzemieniucha - 2.806,
2.807, 2.808
Krzemienna Gura,
Krzemionka - 2.806
Krzyżewo - 2.805
kurp - 10.054
Landa - 1.191
las - 2.500
Laskowice, Lasowice -
6.980
Ląd, Lądzin - 1.191
Lejpuny - 2.109
-lek- - 2.502
Lenda, *Lęchъ, *Lęd-,
Lęd-chъ - 1.191
Lipowiec - 2.100
Londzin - 1.191
ludzie - 3.405
*Łajpuny - 2.109
łani - 6.977
*Łejpuny - 2.109
Łék - 2.501
Łoknica - 2.802
łuna - 3.200
makać - 10.066
maź, mazać, mazia,
Mazowsze, *maz(ur) -
2.005
*m'ęż - 3.410
miasto - 2.207, 3.409
Miedzianka - 2.801
miąż(sz) - 3.410
Mieszko - 10.064
Mir, Mirowicy - 6.980
Misko - 10.064
mjasto, mniasto -
2.207
mogę, mogymy, możemy -
8.114
mózg - 10.065
Mysko - 10.064
na - 2.209
nać - 10.073
Narew - 10.069

niasto - 2.207
Niebieszczany - 2.015
niedziela - 10.068
niedzieli - 10.085
niesie - 8.112
niewinowaty - 8.540
noga - 10.064
nogach, nogak - 2.209
nóżka - 10.064
obora - 10.001
olsza - 10.002
-owice,-owicy - 6.980
pedy - 9.050
*pętъkъ, pętъnikъ -
10.080
Pierschowicze,
Pierzchovice - 6.981
piątek - 10.080
piwo, pjivo - 2.207
pło - 1.191
po - 2.500, 2.502
*po neděli,
po niedzieli - 10.085
Podlasie, Podlesie -
2.503
*po-gedzanie,
*pogudiane,
*po-gъdzane - 1.130
pojaćwiński - 2.201
*Po-lek-ś-e - 2.502
Polesianie - 2.500
Polesie - 2.500, 2.503
Polexia - 2.500, 2.501,
2.502
Polkewicz, Polkewyce -
6.982
Pollexiani - 2.408,
2.500
Połabie, *Połeksie,
*Połeksze - 2.502
*Połkowicy - 6.982
*po-miedzanie - 1.120
Pomorze - 2.502
powieść - 10.086
Powisle - 2.502

400

Ṛtvẹgy - 2.010 (Old
  Russian

Sanskrit

ādīrghas - 10.020	majján- - 10.065
ahám - 7.800	mā́m - 7.803
ālōhitas - 10.020	māṃsám - 5.803
anakti - 10.007	-mā́na- - 8.500
ānīlas - 10.020	mātā́ - 5.801, 6.701
añjas - 10.007	nāma - 6.704
asthāt - 8.403	náva- - 6.940
áśvā - 5.001	nīlas - 10.020
Ashvins - 9.144	nūnám - 6.940
āti-ḥ - 6.971	okah - 5.500
bhárase - 8.107	párś-āna - 2.106
bhītís - 10.019	paśú - 5.610
bhrā́tā́ - 5.801	páti - 3.006, 6.910
carma - 10.126	pitā́, pítar - 6.702
chinátti - 10.036	púruṣa-ḥ - 1.006,
dádhi, dadhnás -	1.008
6.910	púruṣa-ḥ - 1.006
dalíh - 6.977	Pūsán- - 9.121, 9.140,
devī́ - 6.972	9.141, 9.143, 9.144,
dīrghas - 10.020	9.145
dravā́ḥ, drávati -	pūsaryá, puṣnā́ti -
1.171	9.140
dviṣé - 8.100	púṣpa - 9.121
eta- - 10.017	púṣyati - 9.121, 9.140
garda-bhá - 7.600,	rā́jā - 6.701, 6.702
11.106	rā́jan - 6.702
gharmáḥ - 5.400, 8.500	rasā́ - 3.305
granthí-ḥ - 6.971	rā́sa-bha - 7.600,
hamsī - 6.972	11.106
hāp(h)ikā - 2.106	roditi - 8.012
jíhvā́ - 10.042	rōhitas - 10.020
jīvasi - 8.107	Rudra - 9.143
kākambīra - 9.141	sa-bha - 7.600, 11.106
kapóta- - 10.050	saj-, sañj- - 10.099
krinánti - 10.038	senās - fn. 66
(Vedic)	sūnúh - 5.801
*krinā́ti - 10.038	svásā́, svásar - 6.702
krīnāti - 10.038	śróni-ḥ - 6.971
(Vedic)	śvétate - 10.106
krītáḥ - 10.038	tas - 11.202
kŕmi - 10.126	tasmai - 3.006, 11.202
kú, kutra - 5.101	tas-ya - 6.014, 11.202

tava - 4.220
te - 4.206
tr̥tīya- - 3.005
tubhyam - 4.206
túṣyati - 10.108
tvā́m - 7.803
udaram - 10.116
úraṇah - 10.033

brȁt - 5.801
gvozd - 10.041
jagugnivъ - 10.020
jèsēn - 5.001
klupa - 10.119
krȕška - 3.502
lȅdina - 1.191

bol-jī̆š̆ - 6.802
*bě̆ - 11.106
*bě̆l-es- - 2.111
valъ - 10.010
vasъ - 7.807
vedi - 3.007
vedro - 10.116
vidati - 8.040
vinova-, vinuje- -
   8.540
*vir - 10.130
vitęgъ - 10.111
vlъci - 6.061, fn. 78
*vlъcě̆, vlъči - fn. 78
*vold- - 3.403
*vŭ̆-, *vŭ̆n-, *vuntar-,
   *vuntor- - 11.108
vy - 7.809, 10.030
*vyrъjъ - 10.130
vě̆dě̆ti - fn. 99
vě̆tъ - 10.114
*gă̆l- - 3.305
*Galindis - 1.190
*gvozdъ - 10.041
*gin- - 10.038
*govędo, -gola - 1.190
*Go-lęd-inъ, *Golędъ -
   1.191

vah - 7.809
váhantī - 10.042
vidhávā - 9.352
vīráh - 5.801
vr̥kī́ - 6.972
vr̥sa-bhá - 7.600,
   11.106
Yama - 9.144

Serbo-Croatian

mȁti - 5.801
mlâd - 10.063
nese - 8.112
òbor - 10.001
pȍvest - 10.086
vrân, vrȁna - 10.115
zîd - 3.200

Slavic

*Dargūkeinas, *Dargū-
   kīnas, *Dargūt',
   *Dargūtīnas - fn. 12
*dilgo - 2.102
dobri - 6.061
*dolb-to - 3.200
*dulgo - 2.102
-dъ - 7.900
*dъlgъ - 2.102
*dъlžъ̆ - 10.124
*dъlgъ - 2.102
žito, žęti - 10.038
iz - 2.204
imę - 6.700
kaditi - 10.044
Kazi-mir(ъ),
   Kazi-měr̆(ъ) -
   10.064
kolo - 10.120
kopati - 10.030
kora - 10.128
Korytnica - 2.011
korъcъ - 10.128
kositi - 10.051
*kremenъ, kresmen -
   2.807
*krčbma - 3.411
*krъstъjan- - 5.900

405

lanь - 6.977
*-le - 8.066
lešti - 10.055
ljudinь - 10.062
lęgǫ - 10.055
maslo - 10.007
melniczas - 3.503
Mižьka, Miž(ь)ko - 10.064
moždanь, *mozgenь, mozgъ - 10.065
mojь - 7.820
*moldъ - 10.063
*měg-, *Mēgikā, Měžьka, Měžьko, -měr(ь) - 10.064
měriti - 9.300
*město - 3.409, 5.900
na - 7.900
*navь - 6.971
nadъ 7.900
nasъ - 7.807
natь - 10.073
*nedělja - 5.900, 10.068
niknǫti - 10.071
nitь - 10.035
*nožьka - 10.064
oko, okъno - 10.003
*ordlo - 10.004
*Pa-lǔk-s-ijo - 2.502
*per, *perdъ - 7.900
*perunь - 10.082
po, podъ - 7.900
*Po-lьk-s-ьje - 2.502
*pous-, *pus-, pux- - 9.121
*pьsu - 6.600, fn. 68
s- - 2.016
svojь - 7.820
sixъ - 7.500
*slovos - 5.917
slyšati - 5.611
-stok - 2.016

*stьklo - 5.923
sъ - 2.204
Sъža - 10.104
*syrisko - 3.408
*sěnokosъ - 10.051
*sęg- - 10.099
*tajati, *tajǫ - 2.812
tvojь - 7.820
ti - 6.061, fn. 78
*timen-, tina - 2.812
tok- - 2.016
tъ - fn. 83
*tъkařь - 3.407, 5.923
ty - fn. 83
*tъstь - 3.412
udobь - 6.977
usta - 3.201
učiti - 5.500
xvost - 10.110
xotěti - 10.088
*xъrtъ - 10.022
xъtěti - 10.088
časъ - 10.051
*červo - 10.126
čislo - 10.039
*črv- - 10.126
*črm- - 10.126
čьso, čьsomu - 11.202
čьstь, čьtǫ - 10.039
*šelmь - 3.403, fn. 21
šołmь - 3.405
*jьgьla - 10.016
*(j)ěda, *(j)ědь, *(j)ěsto - 6.974
*jūr- - 10.130
juxa - 3.502
Jat(ь)vez', Jat(ь)vežь- 2.601
*Jet-ьv-ęg-ъ - 2.010
*ǫžь, ǫtь - 6.971

406

Slovene

berîj, brêj - 10.130
črevó, čŕm - 10.126
iríti se, izvir -
  10.130
klékati - 10.052
nât, natî - 10.073

ôl - 6.600
pivo - 6.600
verîj, vir, virîj,
  viry, vrîj -
  10.130

Spanish

Galindo - 1.000

Swedish

gotlänning - 10.041
gute - 10.041
hiūpon - 3.203
linda - 1.191

Njärven, Där-, Närboăs
  Närsjöfjärden - 10.072
nätla - 10.073
súdda - 2.004
thyster - 10.108 (Old
  Swedish)

Thracian

Brentopara - 3.303
Díggion - 3.305
Iuras - 3.304
Kabúlē, Kersēs,
  Kersi-baulos - 3.305

Purdae - 3.305
Rumbo-dona - 3.305
Sparkē - 3.305

Tokharian

kantwa, kantwo, käntu -
  10.042
lake - 10.055
laks - 10.104
lipa, lipetär,
  līpitär(-ne) - 8.403
lyk-äly - 10.074
lyukā-me - 8.403

-mām - 8.500
saku, sekwe - 10.094
su-/swās-, swase,
  swese - 10.104
tainaisäñ - fn. 80
wrauña, Wrauśke -
  10.115
yok- - 10.005

Ukrainian

vajtjati - 9.031
v'jazy - 9.032
nykaty - 9.032

peremoha - 9.010
čerěvo - 10.126
jarka - 10.033

Umbrian

erietu - 10.033

homonus - 6.983

Upper Lusatian
(Sorbian)

kruśva - 3.502
makać - 10.066

wobora - 10.001

Veps

ägeh, äges - 11.105
ägesta//da - 11.105

kadag - 10.044
šorpad - 11.105

Addenda et Corrigenda

11.000 Although Schall, 1964, 156, writes
kraujawirps (see 10.015), Trautmann, 1910, 90 and
362, transcribes the word as Crauyawirps. In
Mažiulis, 1966a, 70, the initial letter also
appears to me to be a C-.

11.001 Although Schmid quotes Hermann, 1949, 151,
who reads the word as Meinso, it should be pointed
out that Mažiulis, 1966a, 250, reads this word as
Meinse. See 10.067.

11.002 In his 1975 article, Einige Bemerkungen
zur Göttinger Version von Simon Grunaus alt-
preussischem Vokabular, Scando-Slavica 21.119-125,
Stang discusses this vocabulary. He agrees, 120,
with Mažiulis, 1966a, 251, that one should read
GrG 89 as Ny thueri thu rather than ny thuer thu
as does Hermann, 1949, 152. Stang suggests that the
form thueri is indeed a 3rd person form and that
the root vowel is long. Stang draws a parallel
with the Lithuanian by-form turéti 'to have,'
which exists along with the standard Lithuanian
turéti 'to have' with a short root vowel.

     Stang also agrees with Mažiulis, 1966a, 251,
that one should read GrG 90 as Dam thoi rather than
Dam thor as Hermann, 1949, 152, would have it.
The 1st sg. form dam would seem to correspond
exactly to Old Church Slavic damь according to
Stang, 121. He suggests than that OP dam retains
the trace of the etymological athematic 1st sg.
ending *-mi, a suggestion which seems to me to be
quite reasonable. The reading thoi 'to you'
would be a dative singular 2nd person pronoun.
Stang notes, 121, that the Lithuanian enclitics
mi, ti, si may go back respectively to *mie, *tie,
*sie and then to Proto-Baltic *mai, *tai, *sai.

11.003 In GrG 94 kayat thu 'Wo wiltu hin'
Stang, 1975, 122-123, suggests an analysis in
which the initial element kay- denotes 'where,' cf.
OP schai 'here,' and the second element -at has a
dental formant perhaps of the same origin as that
found in adverbs of place in the Germanic languages,
cf. Gothic samaþ 'to the same place,' dalaþ
'below,' jaind 'thither,' etc. The element -a-
may have been detached from stems ending in -a-,
but see 4.207. The form /kai/ in my opinion is

just a fossilized form of the verb 'to want.'
11.004 GrG 95 is Warbo thi Dewes - Behut dich
Gott 'May God protect you.' Stang, 1975, 123,
proposes that warbo is the present form of a verb
*varbāt(un) 'to protect' and should be connected
with Gothic wars 'careful,' Old Norse varr
'attentive, careful,' Anglo-Saxon warian 'to
watch over, to guard over.' The OP word would
show an enlargement in -b(h)-. Perhaps we see
this same enlargement in OP galbimai 'we help,'
Lith. gélbėti 'to help' if these two words are to
be connected also with Lith. galéti 'to be able.'
11.005 Stang notes that GrG 28 gerbeis - Beichten
'to confess,' 35 Pogeis - Trincken 'to drink,'
38 plateis - Bezalen 'to pay,' 36 wolgeit - Essen
'to eat' are, like Old Prussian imperatives in
general, old optatives. Stang adds that it is
difficult to say why the verbal forms in Grunau are
so often in the imperative. I would say that this
is no problem at all. The Germans were accustomed
to using the imperative with the Old Prussian serfs.
The inferior position of the Old Prussian with
regard to the German master must always be kept
in mind. There is no surprise that the German
would have learned that the imperative mood was the
most effective way of getting action from the
Old Prussians.

In any case, as Stang points out, 1975, 124,
in the catechisms the imperative ends for the most
part in -ais, -aiti or -eis, -eiti. According to
Stang the former forms go back to *-ois, *-āis and
the latter go back to *-i̯ois and *-ēis (analogical
remodelings from optative stems in *-i̯ē-). GrA
92 ymays - nim 'take' and GrA 14 pogeys - trinck
'drink,' GrG 35 pogeis - Trincken 'drink' are then
regular. Stang says, 124, that GrG 28 gerbeis
'confess' could be a i̯e/o-verb, although one should
compare GrA 53 gerbaisa (with an unclear final -a)
and the imperatives gerbais, gerbaiti from gerbt
'to speak' in the Enchiridion. Stang says, 125,
that if GrG 36 wolgeit does indeed derive from
*valgi̯aitē, one must accept an i-present and an
infinitive in -īt (< *-īti or < *-ēti). Stang
adds, however, that it is conceivable that the
-eit in wolgeit is a mistake for -ait. I would

think it quite likely that the German scribe did not distinguish well between the diphthongs /ei/ and /ai/ in Old Prussian and could easily have confused them. Or, of course, there is the possibility that he could render Old Prussian /ai/ by either orthographic ei or ai. The phonemic significance of the graphemic sequences ei(y), ai(y) doesn't seem to be that well established. According to Lasch, 1914, 84, we find in early Middle Low German texts ai, e.g., the name Maideborgh (1250), Maidheburch (1294), later Meideborch, but in younger texts again, ay (Mayborgeschen). As Chaytor (see fn. 34) says, we attack the medieval texts with the prejudices of spelling consistency of contemporary times.

11.006 Stang, 1975, 125, reports that whereas GrA 59 meicte - schlaffen 'to sleep' is rendered with an -e- in the initial syllable, Mažiulis, 1966a, 250, reads GrG 34 as moicte rather than meicte as would Hermann, 1949, 151. Stang suggests that a form moicte may reflect Baltic *maigti and therefore be a form with a-vocalism (i.e., o-grade) as in many other athematic (originally perfect-present) verbs. This seems to me to be a very reasonable assumption. Stang adds, however, that because of the difficulty in distinguishing o and e in the text, he does not dare to rely on the reading moicte.

11.007 If Trautmann, 1910, 447, is correct, then Stang's statistics in paragraph 6.052 are slightly off. The form *tāwe does not exist at all. The form tawe is attested three times; the form thawe is attested four times; tāwa is attested two times; tawa is attested four times.

11.008 A better English translation for dragios in paragraph 6.903 would be '(brewer's) yeast.' The word dragios (EV - 386) is preceded by EV 383 piwis - bier 'beer,' EV 384 piwamaltan - malcz 'malt,' EV 385 piwemtis - treber 'grains (for brewing).'

11.009 In regard to Jēgers' theory as expounded in paragraph 6.950 I would assume that the oldest layer of Indo-European did not have diathesis, so it is unnecessary to regard the participle in -t- as a passive participle. Some of its meanings

411

may be active meanings. One may note, for example,
that the Indo-European participle in *-ont- is
ordinarily an active participle, but that in
Hittite it can function as a passive participle
with transitive verbs, e.g., a-da-an-za 'eaten'
as given by E. Sturtevant, A comparative grammar of
the Hittite language, 1951, New Haven and London,
Yale University Press, p. 78.
11.010. In connection with 5.911 it may be
remarked that if OP pleske (EV - 253) 'harness'
is cognate with Lith. plèškė 'id.' the example is
not appropriate because presumably we would have
OP /ē/ not short /e/, i.e., I would imagine a
phonemicization /plēskē/.
11.011 In reference to 2.100 and elsewhere one
might recall the well known fact that place names
tend to preserve older phonological forms of words,
i.e., they do not undergo phonological changes as
fast as do other words in a given language. Most
specialists in onomastics operate, unfortunately,
with the neogrammarian rule concerning the un-
exceptionability of sound laws. This rule has been
under attack in recent years. Pragmatic research
has shown that sound change takes place first in
some morphemes and then later in other morphemes.
Place names seem to be among the last in which
sound change takes place. Thus the preservation
of the Baltic diphthong *ei in a place name is not
an iron-clad guarantee that the name is not
Lithuanian or Latvian. Theoretically at least the
ei in such place names could merely be an East
Baltic diphthong which had failed to undergo the
monophthongization to *$\bar{e}_2$ and then the passage to
ię.
11.100 Too late for inclusion in this work I
received a copy of the authoritative book,
Prusskij jazyk: slovar' (A - D), Moscow, Nauka
(1975) by the brilliant Soviet linguist, V.N.
Toporov. The volume under discussion is planned
as the first in a series of four volumes devoted
to the Old Prussian language. The first three
volumes will be an etymological dictionary and the
fourth volume is planned as a summary of all the
investigations in comparative historical grammar
and lexicology of the Old Prussian language.

The fundamental part of this work is lexical
purely as a result of the fact that most of the
material available to scholarship in this area is
lexicon. According to Toporov (p. 1) the word,
its semantics and the realia which stand behind the
word are the most reliable link in the chain in
our knowledge about the Old Prussian 'Wörter und
Sachen.' Old Prussian phonetics abounds in un-
clarities which are rooted in the inability of the
orthographic system to reflect Old Prussian speech.
In addition we are confronted by the confusion of
dialect features in the speech of the informant and
the scribe. Lacunae in Old Prussian morphology
are especially great. Incomplete and incorrect
paradigms result from: (1) the fact that extant
texts do not contain grammatical structures which
would require the use of many grammemes, (2) the
fact that the scribe frequently was limited by his
inability to understand grammatical features unknown in German and (3) the fact that the Old
Prussian language itself was deteriorating rapidly.
The syntax is obscured by the fact that the extant
texts represent a slavish translation from German
for the most part.
11.101 Our knowledge of the lexicon is more
secure also as a result of the fact that for the
major texts in Old Prussian there are German
equivalents available for the vocabulary items.
All of the foregoing considerations lead one to
the conclusion that the first desideratum is an
etymological dictionary of Old Prussian.

This dictionary, however, is not limited to
the inclusion of well known cognates from Baltic,
Slavic, Germanic, etc., but places Old Prussian in
a broader perspective by introducing items from
Anatolian, Tokharian, Middle Iranian, Dardic,
Illyrian and Thracian. In addition the dictionary
contains not only lexical material, but also
contains reconstructions having to do with the
cultural and spiritual life of the Old Prussians.

Toporov writes (p. 7), that the dictionary
is to contain the entire apellative lexicon of
Old Prussian (including even the names encountered
in the Old Prussian texts). That includes whatever is attested in the texts and the dictionaries,

whatever is reconstructed on the basis of Old
Prussian toponymic, hydronymic and onomastic
data, and borrowings encountered in East Prussian
German dialects, Polish and Cassubian dialects, in
Old Lithuanian texts (foremost among which is
Bretkūnas) and in documents of the German knights.
11.102 Although in many cases certain pieces of
information are lacking, each dictionary entry in
its theoretically maximal form could contain the
following items: (1) definition of the word with
the quotation of the German equivalent (if it
exists); (2) designation of the place in the texts
where the word is encountered and the corresponding
contexts; (3) indication of the grammatical form
(in verbs the class according to Schmalstieg's system
of classification); (4) information relating to the
interpretation of the writing of the word and, in
particular, conjectures of various sorts; (5) information on the composition of the word; (6)
etymological parallels in the various Indo-
European languages, the parallels given (where-
ever possible) in hierarchical order with a designation both of the nearest analogies and
supplementary background if this is useful in
defining the place of the word in its context and
evolutionary tendencies; (7) the semantic motivation
of the proposed etymology and typological parallels
if possible; (8) information on the corresponding
'realia'; (9) Old Prussian data of toponymic and
onomastic character; (10) areal characteristics of
the word; (11) references to earlier works
(particularly those published after Trautmann,
1910); (12) possible transcriptions, phonemic,
broad phonetic, narrow phonetic, mixed (with
variant interpretations).
11.103 Toporov notes (p. 10) that V. Mažiulis'
guiding principle is a very scrupulous and careful
adherence to the texts, whereas my own work is
characterized by my suggestions of a myriad of
variants bordering on arbitrariness. On the other
hand he says that the latter approach is useful
against the background of a stronger tradition
distinguished by the desire for such a high degree
of precision that the system of rules,
exceptions and limitations was turned into the

search for an absolute which deprived many of the
achieved results of the sanction of probability and
greatly narrowed the possibilities of further
investigations in the hope of the discovery of
some ideal system of correspondences. Toporov opts
for a middle ground between the stronger tradition
of absolute reliance on the spelling and the
broader perspective which I have proposed. He
sees in the two approaches a useful competition of
ideas which may lead to improved results.

11.104 The plan of these volumes is excellent
and the treatment is exhaustive. Undoubtedly this
will be the most complete book on Old Prussian
since the publication of Die altpreussischen
Sprachdenkmäler by Trautmann in 1910. It is
fortunate for Balticists that Toporov has undertaken this task, since his breadth of learning
is truly phenomenal, ranging from contemporary
English and Russian literature to the classical
languages, Tokharian, Indic, etc. It would be
difficult to find a scholar of similar range in
the West who would be able to do what Toporov has
begun.

11.105 But I would proceed now to the examination
of individual items. To give an idea of the
exhaustiveness of the study I shall quote from the
entry aketes (p. 67). Toporov defines the word
as 'harrow,' notes that it is word 255 in the
Elbing vocabulary where the German translation is
Egde. It is a nom. pl. fem. which has exact
parallels in East Baltic, viz., Lith. akéčios,
ekéčios 'harrow' (cf. also Lith. akéti, eketi 'to
harrow'), Latv. ecēšas, ecēkšas, ecēša 'harrow'
(cf. also ecēt 'to harrow'). One's attention is
attracted to the fact that in the Baltic languages
this word is almost always a pluralia tantum.
This shows the harrow to be made up of a series
of parts, either teeth (wedges), in which case
the word is the successor of the Indo-European
root *ak'-, *ok'- in various languages, or,
alternatively that the harrow has a number of
holes (Russ. očki 'eyelets') into which the teeth
are fastened (cf. Old Prussian ackis, Lith. akìs,
Latv. acs 'eye,' etc.). This latter characteristic
of the harrow as a motive for the etymology of

the corresponding words has been emphasized by
Specht, who has pointed out the similarity of the
Ligurian cave paintings of the multi-eyed harrows
of the Bronze Age and the archaic harrows used
until recently in Lithuania. According to another
proposal a connection is reconstructed between
Indo-European *ok'etā (with two series of four
teeth) and Indo-European *ok'tōu- 'eight,' the
dual of *ok'-t-. Worthy of attention also is the
fact that in the Slavic languages there is no name
for a harrow which would correspond to the Baltic
words. Another essential characteristic is that
parallels to the Baltic word are found almost
exclusively in western Indo-European languages,
cf. OHG egida, MHG eg(e)de, German Egge, Anglo-
Saxon eg(e)de, OHG egen, ecken, German eggen
(Proto-Germanic *agjan). It is characteristic
that, as in the Baltic languages, there are both
a noun 'harrow' and a verb 'to harrow.' Other
parallels include Welsh ocet, oged, Cornish ocet,
Breton oguet, Latin occa (apparently from *otikā
<*ok'ita), ancient Greek oksina (with a definition
from Hesychius who describes it as 'a certain
agricultural instrument with iron pegs and drawn
by oxen'), Toporov continues by saying that
Homeric Gk. ógmos, Hittite akkala, Armenian akaws
'furrow' are not cognate. From eastern Indo-
European languages one can compare Ossetian adāeg
'furrow' (< *agāed, i.e., with a metathesis of
the same type as that encountered in Latin). It
is characteristic that this word went into the
Finno-Ugric languages from Baltic, cf. Finnish,
Estonian äes, i.e., Baltic *eketē > Proto-Finnic
*äkete > *äketi > *äkesi > *ä,es > *äes. Especially
indicative are data from Veps: ägeh, äges
'harrow,' ägeh šorpad 'the teeth of the harrow,'
ägesta//da. The Baltic words require a series of
supplementary explanations. The relationship
between the Lithuanian noun akéčios and the verb
akéti explains (1) the long ē (> Lith. ė) in the
noun as a result of the influence of the verbal
form and (2) allows one to separate out the
element -et- as a suffix. The initial a- in a
series of East Baltic forms changed to e- before
a following front vowel (Lith. ekéčios, Latv.

ecesas). The initial a- in OP aketes can in
principle show the preservation of the old form
(*ok'et-> *aket-) just like the East Baltic forms
with a-. Baltic k instead of Indo-European *k'
is sometimes explained by the fact that here
there was a geminate kk or else an aspirate kh.
Perhaps it would be less risky to see in the
Baltic words, just as in Ossetian adáeg, the
result of the penetration of a western Indo-
European technical term into the languages in
question. This latter suggestion would be in
accord with the extreme western position of
Baltic and Ossetian languages. In further
development the Baltic words could enter a new net
of dependencies, cf. OP aketes, Lith. akēčios,
vs. Lith. aketé, eketé, aka, akas 'hole in the
ice.' In order to save space I have specifically
omitted the literature cited by Toporov in this
entry, but I count some 27 references. Such
admirable thoroughness suggests that Toporov's
dictionary is a suitable companion piece to the
outstanding Litauisches etymologisches Wörterbuch
by Ernst Fraenkel. Toporov's dictionary is,
however, much more modern in its approach.
11.106 Similarly to most Indo-Europeanists,
Toporov, 209-210, establishes proto-forms of the
verb 'to be' such as *bh/u/iiō (> Latv. biju,
Lat. fīō, etc.) and *bhuē-t (> Proto-Slavic *bē).
I assume, however, that the earliest etymologically
reconstructable form of the verb 'to be' was
*bhe/o, merely two phonemes, an initial consonant
and an ablauting vowel, see Schmalstieg, 1973a,
107. This older form of the root is noted as the
second element of some Sanskrit compounds, cf.,
e.g., vrsa-bhá 'bull,' garda-bhá, rasa-bha 'ass,'
sa-bha 'assembly.' It may also be found in the
Lithuanian prefix be-(dirbãs) '(still) working.'
Those cases where we would reconstruct Indo-
European *bhē derive from an earlier *bhoy-; those
cases where we would reconstruct *bhī derive from
an earlier *bhey-; those cases where we would
reconstruct *bhū derive from an earlier *bhew-.
All of this was by way of a monophthongization
which took place within Indo-European, see my
1973a work, 101-102. As I have written before,

I assume that the Indo-European forms were created
by accretions to minimorphemes rather than
deletions from maximorphemes. Thus in those forms
where we do not find the sequence *bhu- I assume
that the *-u- never existed. Thus both Slavic
bě and OP bēi bei derive from *bhē < *bhoy-.
11.107 Toporov (p. 206) discusses the form
begeyte found in Meletius (see para. 4.704). The
word is found in sequence with Geygey and
Geygeythe as noted. According to Toporov one
may, of course, see in Geygeythe a remodeling of
Beygeythe, cf. Beigeite beygeyte, but then it
would be unclear why only the first of the two
words was remodeled. Along with this one could
construct other hypotheses, e.g., an interpretation
in connection with the similar Russian words gej,
gejte 'hey, hey.' In this case Geygeythe
begaythe could mean 'Hey, off with you.' I
might suggest that if Old Prussian was indeed a
dying language, we might see here the influence
of German gehen 'to go' here. Thus Geygeythe
could derive from German geh, geh with an Old
Prussian ending *-te in the second part.
11.108 Under the entry antars 'other; second'
Toporov (p. 94) rightly connects OCS vьtorь,
although there have been objections to this
etymology. I assume that the Proto-Slavic
tautosyllabic sequence *an developed in the
following manner: *anC > *unC > (initial position)
*vŭnC (see Schmalstieg, 1971c). Once the form
*vŭnC had been developed the Slavic word *vŭntor-
(or *vŭntar-) came to appear as a compound with
a prefix *vŭn- and a root *-tor- (*-tar-). But
typically *vŭn- was the prevocalic form of the
prefix and *vū- was the preconsonantal form.
Therefore *vū- replaced *vŭn-.
11.109 It would require a second book merely to
discuss all the interesting and valuable thoughts
Toporov has assembled here. I have made only
casual comments here. Again I would say that
Toporov is to be congratulated on producing an
absolutely brilliant and encyclopedic work which
will be valuable not only as an etymological
dictionary of Old Prussian, but also as an
etymological dictionary of Baltic and Indo-European.

11.200 In reference to 4.710 A. Girdenis relates
(per litteras) that in a part of western Samogitia
(Low Lithuania) after -s and other final consonants
an optional shwa-type vowel is added at times, e.
g., vãksə, tûoksə. The too frequent use of this
vowel by some speakers is ridiculed as a speech
defect. Girdenis suggests then that this might
explain the final -e of rekyse and thewelyse who
might be the object of humorous censure for wanting
to drink at somebody else's expense.
11.201 In reference to 5.704, 6.080 and 7.808 I
should like to draw attention to A. Girdenis'
suggestion (per litteras) that there may have been
nasal vowels in Old Prussian. According to Girdenis
after nasal consonants there may have been no
clear contrast between a and ạ. In clear, careful
speech there was nasalization of the vowel, but
in rapid speech such nasalization was less clear.
Thus, either noūmas or noūmans may reflect the
etymological situation. If noūmas is original,
then the nasalization may have arisen in the vowel
following the nasal consonant. The same relationship holds for ioūmas and ioūmans respectively.
11.202 In reference to 7.010 and 7.011 I should
like to call the reader's attention to the
suggestion of A. Girdenis and A. Rosinas (per
litteras) that a gen. sg. fem. stesses may be
from *stas-ịās and thereby represent a definite
pronoun form similar to that of the Lith. gen.
sg. fem. tõsios '(of) that.' Frequently the
nom. sg. masc. is used as a stem on which other
case forms are created. A gen. sg. masc. form such
as stesse may derive then from *stas-ịā, a dat.
sg. masc. stess(e)mu may derive from *stas-ịamu,
etc. For the gen. sg. masc. such a hypothesis
would also reconfirm the reconstruction of the *o-
stem gen. sg. ending as *-ā, see 4.601. In
addition one might ask to what extent the nom.
sg. may have functioned as a stem for the case
endings in the pronouns of other Indo-European
languages. One might suppose that the nom. sg.
masc. tas in Sanskrit functioned as a stem for the
gen. sg. masc. tas-ya and the dat. sg. masc. tasmai. Perhaps also a nom. sg. masc. stem *kʷis >
was used for the Slavic gen. sg. masc. *kʷis-os

419

čьso, dat. sg. masc. *k^{W}is-am-am > čьsomu.

11.300 In reference to 5.317 one might note that
Finnish evidence for a Proto-Baltic *o̲ is not on
very firm ground. In the proceedings of the
Congressus tertius internationalis Fenno-ugristarum,
Tallinnae habitus, 17.-23. VIII 1970, Pars I, Acta
linguistica, pp. 130-132, Nullo Minissi shows that
the assumption of a Proto-Baltic *o̲ is unnecessary
to explain the Finnish evidence. According to
Minissi, 132, "The early Aryan vocalic system and
that of early Baltic have as a common characteristic
the absence of a back half-open labialized vowel
as an independent phoneme; on the contrary German,
Finno-Ugric and Finnic possess such a phoneme.
Hence the variants of Aryan /a̲/ and Baltic /a̲/
that, by context, underwent a velarized articulation,
in Finno-Ugric and in Finnic had to be assumed as
articulatory variants of /o̲/ and therefore were
rendered by this phoneme and replaced by the
customary realization of it."

11.301 In reference to 1.004 I have only been
able to find Westphalian est^e 'Räucherboden.'

ADDITIONAL PUBLICATIONS OF INTEREST TO LINGUISTS
AND BALTICISTS.   THE PENNSYLVANIA STATE
UNIVERSITY PRESS, 215 Wagner Bldg., University
Park, Pa. 16802.

Baltic Linguistics. 1970. A collection of articles
on Baltic linguistics by such scholars as
Henning Andersen, Warren Cowgill, L.
Dambriunas, A. Klimas, Calvert Watkins et al.
Edited by Thomas F. Magner and William R.
Schmalstieg. Price: $12.50. (177 pp.)

An Old Prussian Grammar: The Phonology and
Morphology of the Three Catechisms. 1974.
William R. Schmalstieg. The first grammar of
Old Prussian ever published in English.
Price: $13.50. (x + 358 pp.)

General Linguistics, a quarterly journal devoted to
all aspects of linguistics, descriptive,
historical, psycholinguistics, etc.
Edited by William R. Schmalstieg and Philip
Baldi. Subscription rates: $12.50 in the
United States; $13.50 in Canada and Latin
America; $14.50 elsewhere in the world.

The publications listed below are available from
The Department of Slavic Languages, N-438
Burrowes Bldg. University Park, Pa. 16802.

Readings in Old Prussian. 1965. Selections from
the Old Prussian catechisms with accompanying
German text and English translation.
Compiled by William R. Schmalstieg. Price:
$1.00. (iii + 21 pp.)

Lithuanian-English Glossary of Linguistic
Terminology. 1971. English glosses and some
definitions taken from older and modern
Lithuanian linguistic works. Compiled by
William R. Schmalstieg and A. Klimas. Price:
$3.50. (v + 115 pp.)